Betty Crocker®

Very Best
HOME
COOKING

301 SEASONAL **COMFORT FOOD** RECIPES
FOR EVERY MEAL OF THE DAY

RODALE.

Internet addresses and telephone numbers given in this book were accurate at the time it went to press.

© 2014 by General Mills, Minneapolis, Minnesota

Interior and Cover Photography © General Mills Photography Studios and Image Library

Printed in the United States of America
Rodale Inc. makes every effort to use acid-free ♾, recycled paper ♻.

Front Cover Recipe Photos (clockwise from top):
Tall, Dark and Stout Chocolate Layer Cake, page 390; Gorgonzola Twice-Baked Potatoes with Bacon, page 76;
Asparagus and Goat Cheese Quiche, page 166; and Cheesecake Pancakes, page 213

Back Cover Recipe Photos (clockwise from top): Apricot-Stuffed French Toast, page 2;
Asparagus Soup with Brie Bruschetta, page 130; Grilled Ribs with Cherry Cola Barbecue Sauce, page 244;
and Chocolate Bourbon Pumpkin Cheesecake, page 392

Book design by Joanna Williams

Library of Congress Cataloging-in-Publication Data is on file with the publisher.

ISBN 978-1-62336-382-6

2 4 6 8 10 9 7 5 3 1   direct mail hardcover

We inspire and enable people to improve their lives and the world around them.
For more of our products, visit rodalestore.com or call 800-848-4735.

Dear Friends,

Bringing loved ones together for delicious family meals is one of the greatest joys home cooks share. But you don't need a holiday or special occasion to make special moments happen: When you rely on recipes from *Betty Crocker Very Best Home Cooking*, you can trust that any meal together is sure to be memorable. This exclusive collection of foolproof dishes—tested and perfected by the Betty Crocker Kitchens—puts a wide range of family-pleasing comfort foods right at your fingertips.

With more than 300 step-by-step recipes organized by season, it's easy to use the freshest ingredients and the best cooking methods throughout the year. For example, craving hearty dishes to satisfy cold-weather appetites? Start your day with the Overnight Tex-Mex Egg Bake that requires you do little more than turn on the oven in the morning. Later, try the Creamy Turkey Wild Rice Soup or the Slow Cooker New Hoppin' John.

Does a lighter dish feel in order? Choose from dozens of refreshing salads, sides and grilled dishes, like the Corn and Black Bean Salad with Tortilla Wedges or Grilled Seafood Packs with Lemon-Chive Butter. Like all the recipes in this collection, both are undeniably delicious any time of year, but their flavors truly shine as the centerpiece for a perfect spring or summer gathering.

Of course, beyond the easy-to-follow recipes and lush color photography, Betty Crocker cookbooks are also filled with good ideas and tips for success. This edition is no exception. Perhaps you need a new recipe for something portable to take to a picnic, potluck or the occasional tailgate party, or maybe you're just looking for a way to put a fresh twist on your regular holiday fare—you'll find more than 20 specialized menus and planning ideas here, from a traditional Christmas Dinner to Terrific Tailgate Eats. (Hint: If you've been curious to deep-fry a turkey, make sure you check out the detailed instructions on page 357.)

Whatever the occasion, here you will find plenty of recipes that make entertaining easy—but don't forget to plan for dessert! From bite-size treats like Praline Mini Cakes to tried-and-true classics like Luscious Lemon Meringue Pie, the very best meals end with signature sweets from the Betty Crocker collection, and for every season there are many tempting options available.

Warmly,

Contents

Winter

Apricot-Stuffed French Toast

Enjoy a tasty breakfast—apricot-stuffed French toast!

PREP TIME: 55 MINUTES • **TOTAL TIME:** 1 HOUR 10 MINUTES • **MAKES 6 SERVINGS**

1 loaf (8 ounces) or $1/2$ loaf (1-pound size) day-old French bread

1 package (3 ounces) cream cheese, softened

3 tablespoons apricot preserves

$1/4$ teaspoon grated lemon peel

3 eggs

$3/4$ cup half-and-half or milk

2 tablespoons granulated sugar

1 teaspoon vanilla

$1/8$ teaspoon salt

$1/8$ teaspoon ground nutmeg, if desired

2 tablespoons butter, melted
Powdered sugar, if desired

1. Spray 13 x 9-inch pan with cooking spray.

2. Cut bread crosswise into twelve 1-inch slices. Cut a horizontal slit in the side of each bread slice, cutting to—but not through—the other edge.

3. In medium bowl, beat cream cheese, preserves and lemon peel with electric mixer on medium speed about 1 minute or until well mixed. Spread about 2 teaspoons of the cream cheese mixture inside the slit in each bread slice. Place stuffed bread slices in pan.

4. In medium bowl, beat eggs, half-and-half, granulated sugar, vanilla, salt and nutmeg if desired with fork or wire whisk until well mixed. Pour egg mixture over bread slices in pan, and turn slices carefully to coat. Cover and refrigerate at least 30 minutes but no longer than 24 hours.

5. Heat oven to 425°F. Uncover French toast and drizzle with melted butter. Bake 20 to 25 minutes or until golden brown. Sprinkle with powdered sugar if desired.

BETTY'S SUCCESS TIP

You might be surprised to learn that the most flavorful part of a lemon is the part you normally throw away: the peel. The yellow part of the lemon peel (called the rind or the zest) contains lemon oil, a powerful concentrate of citrus. Including the zest of the lemon in your cooking adds a refreshing flavor without the acidity of lemon juice. Care must be taken when removing the zest to not remove the bitter white pith that lies just underneath. Although you can use a box grater, the best tool is called a microplane grater (similar to an old-fashioned wood rasp). It grates the zest evenly but avoids scraping the underlying pith.

1 SERVING: Calories 310; Total Fat 16g (Saturated Fat 8g); Sodium 380mg; Total Carbohydrate 32g (Dietary Fiber 1g); Protein 9g; **Exchanges:** 1 Starch; 1 Other Carbohydrate; 1 High-Fat Meat; $1^1/2$ Fat; **Carbohydrate Choices:** 2

Banana-Chocolate Chip Gran-Oatmeal

Oatmeal goes from dull to delicious when you break up a few granola bars, add some milk and toppings and microwave. Quick, easy, awesome!

PREP TIME: 5 MINUTES • **TOTAL TIME:** 5 MINUTES • **MAKES 1 SERVING**

2   **Nature Valley® oats 'n honey crunchy granola bars**
1/3   **cup low-fat milk**

2   **tablespoons semisweet chocolate chips**
2/3   **fresh banana, sliced**

1. In microwavable bowl, place granola bars; top with milk. Microwave on Medium for 25 to 30 seconds or until milk is warm.

2. Using spoon, break bars in milk into granola pieces. Top with chocolate chips and banana slices.

1 SERVING: Calories 420; Total Fat 14g (Saturated Fat 5g); Sodium 200mg; Total Carbohydrate 64g (Dietary Fiber 5g); Protein 8g; **Exchanges:** 2 1/2 Starch; 2 Other Carbohydrate; 2 1/2 Fat; **Carbohydrate Choices:** 4

Easy-on-the-Budget Jolly Holiday Brunch

Looking for ways to host holiday brunch without leaving a hole in your pocket? Look no further than these popular easy recipes to get you started. Your guests will be impressed, and your wallet will still have some extra cash in it when you hit those end-of-the-year sales!

FOILED PLACE SETTINGS

- Make designer holiday place mats and place cards using heavy foil gift wrap. For place mats, cut gift wrap into 18 x 12-inch pieces. If desired, use a little glue to attach doilies to the center, or decorate with glitter paint or stickers.
- For place cards, cut gift wrap into 4 x 2-inch pieces, and fold in half so they stand up. On one side, glue a piece of plain paper and add each guest's name, then attach a sparkling snowflake made from paper or a purchased ornament.
- Roll silverware in napkins, and tie with metallic ribbon or foil-wrapped wire.

BUTTER 'EM UP

- Cut thin slices of butter into pretty holiday shapes using tiny cookie cutters in star, tree and bell shapes. Or place softened butter in holiday ice-cube molds.
- Freeze, then pop out the shapes and refrigerate or freeze in a single layer.
- Look for these holiday cutters and molds at kitchen and home stores.

GREAT GARNISHES

- A few sprigs of fresh rosemary or frozen cranberries are lovely dusted with powdered sugar to look snowy.
- Or cut shapes from slices of bell pepper with those little holiday cookie cutters to garnish quiche.

MEALTIME MAKEOVER

- There's no need to buy holiday dishes or glassware to set a festive table. Just decorate what you already own. Tie holiday ribbons with jingle bells or a keepsake ornament around napkins to make napkin rings.
- Decorate the base of stemmed water or wine glasses with ribbons or metallic cord.

MENU

Cranberry-Orange Slush Cocktails **49**

Iced Pumpkin Chex® Mix **33**

Overnight Tex-Mex Egg Bake **7**

Apple, Cheese and Toasted Walnut Salad **82**

French Breakfast Puffs **14**

Muffin Glory Cake **18**

Maple-Nut Streusel Coffee Cake **17**

New Year's Day Breakfast Casserole

Start New Year's Day with this cheesy sausage casserole—perfect for breakfast.

PREP TIME: 20 MINUTES • **TOTAL TIME:** 10 HOURS 15 MINUTES • **MAKES 8 SERVINGS**

10 ounces ciabatta bread, cut into 1-inch cubes (6 cups)
2 cups milk
8 eggs
1 tablespoon chopped fresh oregano leaves
1 pound bulk spicy pork sausage

1 large onion, chopped (1 cup)
1 red bell pepper, chopped
2 cups shredded sharp Cheddar cheese (8 ounces)
Additional chopped fresh oregano leaves

1. On 17 x 12-inch half-sheet pan, place bread cubes. Let stand uncovered 8 hours to dry.

2. In large bowl, mix milk, eggs and 1 tablespoon oregano. Add bread to egg mixture, stirring to coat. Cover; refrigerate 1 hour.

3. Heat oven to 350°F. Lightly grease 13 x 9-inch (3-quart) glass baking dish with cooking spray. In 12-inch skillet, cook sausage, onion and bell pepper 8 minutes, stirring frequently, until sausage is no longer pink. Drain.

4. Add sausage mixture and 1 cup of the cheese to bread mixture, stirring well. Pour into baking dish; sprinkle with remaining 1 cup cheese.

5. Bake 40 to 45 minutes or until center is set and cheese is bubbly. Let stand 10 minutes. Sprinkle with additional oregano.

1 SERVING: Calories 436; Total Fat 27g (Saturated Fat 13g); Sodium 907mg; Total Carbohydrate 23g (Dietary Fiber 1g); Protein 26g; **Exchanges:** 1 Starch; 1/2 Vegetable; 2 High-Fat Meat; 1 Fat; **Carbohydrate Choices:** 1 1/2

Overnight Tex-Mex Egg Bake

Spice up your breakfast menus by serving an egg casserole featuring spicy sausage, green chiles and salsa.

PREP TIME: 20 MINUTES • **TOTAL TIME:** 9 HOURS 25 MINUTES • **MAKES 10 SERVINGS**

- 12 ounces bulk spicy pork sausage
- 5 cups frozen southern-style hashbrown potatoes (from 32-ounce bag)
- 1 can (4.5 ounces) Old El Paso® chopped green chiles, undrained
- 3 cups shredded Colby-Monterey Jack cheese (12 ounces)

- 6 eggs
- 1½ cups milk
- ¼ teaspoon salt
- 1 cup Old El Paso® Thick 'n Chunky salsa

1. Spray 13 x 9-inch glass baking dish with cooking spray. In 10-inch skillet, cook sausage over medium heat 8 to 10 minutes, stirring occasionally, until no longer pink. Drain on paper towels.

2. Spread frozen potatoes in baking dish. Sprinkle with sausage, green chiles and 1½ cups of the cheese. In medium bowl, beat eggs, milk and salt with fork or wire whisk until well blended. Pour over potato mixture. Sprinkle with remaining 1½ cups cheese. Cover and refrigerate at least 8 hours but no longer than 12 hours.

3. Heat oven to 350°F. Bake uncovered 50 to 60 minutes or until knife inserted near center comes out clean. Let stand 10 minutes. Cut into squares. Serve with salsa.

BETTY'S SUCCESS TIPS

- If you can't find a 12-ounce package of pork sausage, you can use a 16-ounce package.
- No need to wait! You can bake this dish right away if you like.
- Warm corn bread with honey butter and a fruit salad of orange, grapefruit and mango pieces give your brunch a southwestern flair.
- Cubed hashbrown potatoes are called "southern-style," and shredded potatoes are called "country-style." Either one can be used in casseroles like this.

1 SERVING: Calories 350; Total Fat 20g (Saturated Fat 10g); Sodium 1,120mg; Total Carbohydrate 25g (Dietary Fiber 3g); Protein 19g; **Exchanges:** 1½ Starch; 2 High-Fat Meat; 1 Fat; **Carbohydrate Choices:** 1½

Breakfast Panini

Grilled sandwiches filled with ham, veggies and cheese ready in 10 minutes—a hearty Italian breakfast recipe.

PREP TIME: 10 MINUTES • **TOTAL TIME:** 10 MINUTES • **MAKES 2 PANINI**

2 eggs
1/2 teaspoon salt-free seasoning blend
2 tablespoons chopped fresh chives
2 whole wheat thin bagels
2 slices tomato

2 thin slices onion
4 ultra-thin slices reduced-sodium deli cooked ham
2 thin slices reduced-fat Cheddar cheese

1. Spray 8-inch skillet with cooking spray; heat skillet over medium heat. In medium bowl, beat eggs, seasoning and chives with fork or whisk until well mixed. Pour into skillet. As eggs begin to set at bottom and side, gently lift cooked portions with spatula so that thin, uncooked portion can flow to bottom. Avoid constant stirring. Cook 3 to 4 minutes or until eggs are thickened throughout but still moist and creamy; remove from heat.

2. Meanwhile, heat closed contact grill or panini maker 5 minutes.

3. For each panini, divide cooked eggs evenly between bottom halves of bagels. Top each with 1 slice tomato and onion, 2 ham slices, 1 cheese slice and top half of bagel. Transfer filled panini to heated grill. Close cover, pressing down lightly. Cook 2 to 3 minutes or until browned and cheese is melted. Serve immediately.

BETTY'S SUCCESS TIP

For a little variety, change the fillings by using turkey instead of ham and Swiss cheese instead of the Cheddar.

1 PANINI: Calories 26; Total Fat 7g (Saturated Fat 2^1/$_2$g); Sodium 410mg; Total Carbohydrate 32g (Dietary Fiber 2g); Protein 15g; **Exchanges:** 2 Starch; 1/2 Very Lean Meat; **Carbohydrate Choices:** 2

Bacon-and-Egg Braid

Crescent dough sheets provide a simple addition to this flavorful braid made with bacon and eggs—perfect for a warm breakfast.

PREP TIME: 20 MINUTES • **TOTAL TIME:** 45 MINUTES • **MAKES 6 SERVINGS**

5 slices bacon	1/4 teaspoon salt
1 medium onion, finely chopped (1/2 cup)	1/4 teaspoon freshly ground pepper
6 eggs	1 can (8 ounces) crescent refrigerated seamless dough sheet
1/4 cup mayonnaise	3/4 cup shredded sharp Cheddar cheese (3 ounces)
1/4 teaspoon red pepper sauce, if desired	

1. Heat oven to 375°F. In 10-inch skillet, cook bacon until crisp; drain on paper towels. Reserve 1 tablespoon drippings in skillet. Cook onion in bacon drippings over medium heat 2 minutes or until tender.

2. In medium bowl, beat eggs, mayonnaise, pepper sauce, salt and pepper with whisk until well blended. Add egg mixture to skillet; cook 4 minutes, stirring occasionally, until set.

3. On ungreased cookie sheet, unroll dough and press into 12 x 9-inch rectangle. Spoon eggs down center of dough to within 1 1/2 inches of each short side. Place bacon over eggs; sprinkle with cheese.

4. With sharp knife, make cuts 1 1/2 inches apart on long sides of dough to within 1/4 inch of filling. Bring ends over filling, then alternately cross strips over filling.

5. Bake 22 to 24 minutes or until golden brown and no longer doughy. Cut crosswise into slices. Serve warm.

1 SERVING: Calories 403; Total Fat 27g (Saturated Fat 10g); Sodium 775mg; Total Carbohydrate 17g (Dietary Fiber 0g); Protein 15g; **Exchanges:** 1 Starch; 1 High-Fat Meat; 3 Fat; **Carbohydrate Choices:** 1

Apple, Bacon and Cheddar Bread Pudding

Bacon, Cheddar and apples make a great combo for brunch, lunch or even supper.

PREP TIME: 25 MINUTES • **TOTAL TIME:** 3 HOURS 20 MINUTES • **MAKES 12 SERVINGS**

3 tablespoons butter or margarine	2½ cups milk
3 medium Granny Smith apples, peeled and coarsely chopped (3 cups)	1 teaspoon ground mustard
3 tablespoons packed brown sugar	2 teaspoons Worcestershire sauce
4 cups cubed firm bread	¼ teaspoon salt
1 pound bacon, cooked and chopped	⅛ teaspoon pepper
2 cups shredded sharp Cheddar cheese (8 ounces)	5 eggs

1. Grease 2-quart casserole. In 10-inch skillet, melt butter over medium heat. Cook apples in butter 2 to 3 minutes, stirring occasionally, until crisp-tender. Stir in brown sugar; reduce heat to low. Cook 5 to 6 minutes, stirring occasionally, until apples are tender.

2. Layer half each of the bread, bacon, apples and cheese in casserole. Repeat with remaining bread, bacon, apples and cheese.

3. Mix all remaining ingredients; pour over cheese. Cover tightly and refrigerate at least 2 hours but no longer than 24 hours.

4. Heat oven to 350°F. Bake uncovered 40 to 45 minutes or until knife inserted in center comes out clean. Let stand 10 minutes before serving.

BETTY'S SUCCESS TIPS

- There's no need to remove the crusts from the bread.
- Layer 2 medium green onions, thinly sliced, with the bread, bacon, apples and cheese.

1 SERVING: Calories 275, Total Fat 18g (Saturated Fat 9g); Sodium 475mg; Total Carbohydrate 17g (Dietary Fiber 1g); Protein 13g; **Exchanges:** 1 Starch; 3 Fat; **Carbohydrate Choices:** 1

Apple Crisp Pancakes

Apple crisp and pancakes rolled into one. Diced apples add chunky goodness to the Bisquick® batter and then before flipping, the pancakes get topped with a brown sugar-oatmeal streusel.

PREP TIME: 15 MINUTES • **TOTAL TIME:** 25 MINUTES • **MAKES 13 SERVINGS**

Streusel Topping

- 1/4 cup plus 2 tablespoons packed brown sugar
- 1/4 cup Gold Medal® all-purpose flour
- 1/4 cup old-fashioned or quick-cooking oats
- 2 tablespoons plus 2 teaspoons cold butter

Toppings, If Desired

- Powdered sugar
- Real maple syrup
- Sweetened whipped cream

Pancakes

- 2 cups Original Bisquick® mix
- 1/2 teaspoon ground cinnamon
- 1/4 teaspoon ground nutmeg
- 1 cup peeled, diced (1/4-inch) Granny Smith apple
- 1 cup milk
- 2 eggs

1. In medium bowl, mix brown sugar, flour, and oats. Cut in butter using pastry blender or fork until mixture is crumbly. Set aside.

2. In large bowl, stir all pancake ingredients until well blended. Heat nonstick griddle to 350°F or 12-inch skillet over medium-high heat. (To test griddle, sprinkle with a few drops of water. If bubbles jump around, heat is just right.) Brush lightly with vegetable oil or spray with cooking spray before heating to help prevent streusel from sticking to griddle.

3. For each pancake, pour 1/4 cupful batter onto hot griddle. Sprinkle each pancake evenly with scant 2 tablespoons streusel mixture. Cook 2 to 3 minutes or until bubbly on top and dry around edges. Turn; cook other side until light golden brown around edges, about 1 minute to 1 minute 30 seconds. Scrape off griddle between batches of pancakes if necessary.

4. To serve, serve pancakes streusel side up and top as desired using any of the toppings listed.

1 SERVING: Calories 167; Total Fat 6g (Saturated Fat 2g); Sodium 265mg; Total Carbohydrate 24g (Dietary Fiber 1g); Protein 4g; **Exchanges:** 1 Starch; 1 Fat; **Carbohydrate Choices:** 1 1/2

Bananas Foster French Toast

French toast gets a tasty twist with the addition of bananas, rum extract and pecans. The use of cinnamon bread is ideal!

PREP TIME: 20 MINUTES • **TOTAL TIME:** 9 HOURS 10 MINUTES • **MAKES 8 SERVINGS**

8 slices cinnamon bread, cut into $^1/_2$-inch cubes (about 8 cups)	1 teaspoon rum extract
8 eggs	6 ripe bananas, cut into $^1/_2$-inch slices
1 cup milk	1 cup chopped pecans
2$^1/_2$ cups real maple syrup	

1. Spray bottom of 13 x 9-inch (3-quart) baking dish with cooking spray. Arrange bread cubes in baking dish. In large bowl, beat eggs, milk and $^1/_2$ cup of the maple syrup with wire whisk. Pour over bread in baking dish. Cover and refrigerate 8 hours or overnight.

2. Heat oven to 350°F. Uncover; bake 35 to 40 minutes or until golden brown along edges. Let stand 7 to 10 minutes before serving.

3. Meanwhile, in medium microwavable bowl, microwave remaining 2 cups maple syrup uncovered on High 1 to 2 minutes, stirring every 30 seconds, until warm. Stir in rum extract.

4. Sprinkle banana slices and pecans evenly over bread; drizzle with 1 cup of the warmed syrup mixture. Serve immediately with remaining syrup.

BETTY'S SUCCESS TIPS

- Serve with crisp bacon or sausage.
- Rum extract can be found in the baking section of your local grocery store.

1 SERVING: Calories 620; Total Fat 17g (Saturated Fat 3g); Sodium 260mg; Total Carbohydrate 105g (Dietary Fiber 4g), Protein 11g; **Exchanges:** 2 Starch; 1 Fruit; 4 Other Carbohydrate; $^1/_2$ High-Fat Meat; 2$^1/_2$ Fat; **Carbohydrate Choices:** 7

Danish Apple-Almond Cake

Whip up a homemade coffee cake and have it in the oven in minutes.

PREP TIME: 20 MINUTES • **TOTAL TIME:** 2 HOURS • **MAKES 8 SERVINGS**

½ cup butter or margarine, softened
½ cup granulated sugar
3 eggs
1 teaspoon almond extract
1½ cups Original Bisquick® mix

3 medium baking apples, peeled, cut into eighths
1 teaspoon powdered sugar
¼ cup sliced almonds, toasted, if desired

1. Heat oven to 325°F. Spray bottom of 9-inch springform pan with cooking spray.

2. In large bowl, beat butter and granulated sugar with electric mixer on high speed 1 minute. Add eggs and almond extract; beat on medium speed about 10 seconds. Add Bisquick mix; beat on medium speed about 30 seconds or until combined.

3. Spread batter in bottom of pan. Press apple pieces, cut sides down, into batter. Bake 1 hour to 1 hour 10 minutes or until apples are tender and cake is golden brown.

4. Cool 30 minutes at room temperature. Remove side of pan. Sift or sprinkle powdered sugar over top of cake; sprinkle with almonds. Serve warm.

BETTY'S SUCCESS TIPS

- To toast almonds, bake in an ungreased shallow pan at 350°F for 6 to 10 minutes, stirring occasionally, until fragrant and light brown.
- Serve with coffee topped with an indulgent topping of whipped cream and a sprinkle of nutmeg.

1 SERVING: Calories 320; Total Fat 18g (Saturated Fat 9g); Sodium 420mg; Total Carbohydrate 33g (Dietary Fiber 1g); Protein 5g; **Exchanges:** 1½ Starch; ½ Other Carbohydrate; 3½ Fat; **Carbohydrate Choices:** 2

French Breakfast Puffs

Get ready for "oohs" and "aahs" when you serve these heavenly rolls. Coated with cinnamon and sugar, these quick-fix breakfast puffs are a favorite in Betty's Kitchens.

PREP TIME: 10 MINUTES • **TOTAL TIME:** 35 MINUTES • **MAKES 15 PUFFS**

$1/3$ cup shortening	$1/4$ teaspoon ground nutmeg
$1/2$ cup sugar	$1/2$ cup milk
1 egg	$1/2$ cup sugar
$1^1/2$ cups Gold Medal® all-purpose flour	1 teaspoon ground cinnamon
$1^1/2$ teaspoons baking powder	$1/2$ cup butter or margarine, melted
$1/2$ teaspoon salt	

1. Heat oven to 350°F. Grease 15 medium muffin cups, $2^1/2$ x $1^1/4$ inches.

2. Mix shortening, $1/2$ cup sugar and the egg thoroughly in large bowl. Stir in flour, baking powder, salt and nutmeg alternately with milk. Divide batter evenly among muffin cups.

3. Bake 20 to 25 minutes or until golden brown.

4. Mix $1/2$ cup sugar and the cinnamon. Roll hot muffins immediately in melted butter, then in sugar-cinnamon mixture. Serve hot.

BETTY'S SUCCESS TIPS

- Toss 2 tablespoons finely chopped nuts into the cinnamon-sugar mixture for Nutty French Breakfast Puffs.
- Or make Baked Mini Donut Holes. Prepare the recipe as directed, except divide the dough among 24 greased mini muffin cups, 2 x $3/4$ inch, and bake 11 to 13 minutes.
- Make more cinnamon-sugar mixture than you'll need, and store the rest to use later. Try it sprinkled on buttered toast or stirred into cooked rice.

1 PUFF: Calories 200; Total Fat 11g (Saturated Fat 5g); Sodium 180mg; Total Carbohydrate 23g (Dietary Fiber 0g); Protein 2g; **Exchanges:** 1 Starch; $1/2$ Fruit; 2 Fat; **Carbohydrate Choices:** $1^1/2$

Maple-Nut Streusel Coffee Cake

Mmm! Treat yourself to a quick homemade coffee cake that's loaded with a crunchy nutty topping and lots of maple flavor.

PREP TIME: 20 MINUTES • **TOTAL TIME:** 1 HOUR 20 MINUTES • **MAKES 9 SERVINGS**

Streusel

- 1/2 cup packed brown sugar
- 1/4 cup Gold Medal® all-purpose flour
- 1/4 cup chopped pecans
- 3 tablespoons butter or margarine, melted

Coffee Cake

- 1 1/2 cups Gold Medal® all-purpose flour
- 3/4 cup packed brown sugar
- 1/2 cup chopped pecans
- 1/2 cup vegetable oil
- 1/4 cup milk
- 1 teaspoon baking powder
- 1 teaspoon maple extract
- 1/2 teaspoon baking soda
- 1/2 teaspoon salt
- 2 eggs, beaten
- 1 container (8 ounces) sour cream

1. Heat oven to 350°F. Spray bottom only of 8-inch square pan with cooking spray. In small bowl, mix all streusel ingredients with fork until crumbly; set aside.

2. In large bowl, mix all coffee cake ingredients with spoon just until flour is moistened. Spread half of the batter in pan. Sprinkle with half of the streusel. Drop remaining batter by spoonfuls over streusel; carefully spread over streusel. Sprinkle with remaining streusel.

3. Bake 35 to 45 minutes or until toothpick inserted in center comes out clean. Cool 15 minutes. Serve warm.

BETTY'S SUCCESS TIP

You can use 1/2 cup fat-free egg product for the fresh eggs.

1 SERVING: Calories 490; Total Fat 29g (Saturated Fat 8g); Sodium 320mg; Total Carbohydrate 51g (Dietary Fiber 1g); Protein 6g; **Exchanges:** 1 1/2 Starch; 2 Other Carbohydrate; 5 1/2 Fat; **Carbohydrate Choices:** 3 1/2

Muffin Glory Cake

Mmm! Warm coffee cake with a sweet drizzled glaze. Apples, carrots and pineapple make glorious additions to an easy muffin mix recipe.

PREP TIME: 15 MINUTES • **TOTAL TIME:** 1 HOUR 15 MINUTES • **MAKES 9 SERVINGS**

- 1 box Betty Crocker® cinnamon streusel muffin mix
- 1/2 cup chopped peeled apple
- 1/2 cup shredded carrot
- 1/2 cup chopped walnuts
- 1/2 cup flaked coconut
- 1/4 cup vegetable oil
- 2 eggs
- 1 can (8 ounces) crushed pineapple in juice, undrained
- 1/2 cup powdered sugar
- 1 to 2 teaspoons water

1. Heat oven to 400°F. Grease bottom only of 8-inch square pan with shortening or cooking spray. In medium bowl, stir together Muffin Mix, apple, carrot, walnuts and coconut. In small bowl, stir together oil, eggs and pineapple; stir into muffin mixture. Spread in pan. Sprinkle with Streusel (from Muffin Mix).

2. Bake 38 to 42 minutes or until toothpick inserted in center comes out clean. Cool 15 minutes.

3. In small bowl, mix powdered sugar and enough of the 1 to 2 teaspoons water until smooth and thin enough to drizzle. Drizzle over warm cake.

BETTY'S SUCCESS TIP

Serve this treat for brunch with an egg bake and fresh fruit.

1 SERVING: Calories 390; Total Fat 18g (Saturated Fat 4¹/₂g); Sodium 320mg; Total Carbohydrate 52g (Dietary Fiber 2g); Protein 5g; **Exchanges:** 1¹/₂ Starch; 2 Other Carbohydrate; 3¹/₂ Fat; **Carbohydrate Choices:** 3¹/₂

Beer Battered Grilled Cheese Sandwiches

Melty cheese, smoky bacon and beer-battered bread make this grilled cheese the ultimate comfort food.

PREP TIME: 20 MINUTES • **TOTAL TIME:** 25 MINUTES • **MAKES 2 SANDWICHES**

6 slices hickory-smoked bacon	³/₄ cup pale ale beer
4 slices rustic white bread	¹/₄ cup Gold Medal® all-purpose flour
2 slices provolone cheese (³/₄ ounce each)	¹/₄ teaspoon chipotle chili powder
2 slices Cheddar cheese (³/₄ ounce each)	1 tablespoon butter
1 egg	

1. In 12-inch nonstick skillet, cook bacon until crisp; drain on paper towels.

2. On 2 of the bread slices, place 1 slice provolone cheese, 3 slices bacon and 1 slice Cheddar cheese. Top with remaining bread slices.

3. Heat griddle or skillet over medium-high heat or to 375°F. In shallow bowl, beat egg, beer, flour and chili powder with fork until smooth. Dip each sandwich into batter, giving it a few seconds on each side to absorb the batter; drain excess batter back into bowl.

4. Melt butter on hot griddle. Place sandwiches on griddle. Cook 3 to 4 minutes on each side until golden brown.

BETTY'S SUCCESS TIP

If you need to serve a crowd, this recipe can be doubled or tripled. Prepare all of the sandwiches first and then dip in the beer batter and cook them all at once on a griddle.

1 SANDWICH: Calories 570; Total Fat 33g (Saturated Fat 16g); Sodium 1,220mg; Total Carbohydrate 40g (Dietary Fiber 2g); Protein 28g; **Exchanges:** 2¹/₂ Starch; 3 High-Fat Meat; 1¹/₂ Fat; **Carbohydrate Choices:** 2¹/₂

Pesto, Kale and Sweet Potato Pizza

Pressing flaxseed, sesame seed and pepitas into the dough adds hearty crunch to this flavorful pizza.

PREP TIME: 25 MINUTES • **TOTAL TIME:** 45 MINUTES • **MAKES 6 SERVINGS**

1 can (11 ounces) refrigerated thin pizza crust
2 tablespoons sesame seed
2 tablespoons flaxseed
6 tablespoons pepitas (pumpkin seeds)
1 cup diced peeled sweet potato
2 tablespoons olive oil

1 teaspoon ground cumin
1/2 teaspoon chili powder
1/2 teaspoon salt
4 cups kale, stems removed, chopped
1/2 cup basil pesto
8 ounces fresh mozzarella cheese, thinly sliced

1. Heat oven to 400°F for dark or nonstick pan, 425°F for all other pans. Spray 15 x 10-inch pan with sides with cooking spray. Unroll dough in pan; starting at center, press dough into 15 x 10-inch rectangle. Sprinkle evenly with sesame seed, flaxseed and 4 tablespoons of the pepitas. Gently press seeds into dough.

2. Toss sweet potato, 1 tablespoon of the olive oil, the cumin, chili powder and 1/4 teaspoon of the salt. Place in ungreased large roasting pan. Place pizza crust and sweet potatoes in oven; bake about 8 minutes or until crust is light brown and sweet potatoes are softened.

3. In medium bowl, mix kale, remaining 1 tablespoon olive oil and remaining 1/4 teaspoon salt. Massage 2 to 3 minutes or until kale is softened.

4. Spread pesto on partially baked crust. Top with half of the mozzarella cheese. Top with kale and sweet potatoes, followed by remaining mozzarella cheese.

5. Bake 8 to 10 minutes or until crust is crisp and cheese is melted. Sprinkle with remaining 2 tablespoons pepitas. Cut into strips to serve.

1 SERVING: Calories 560; Total Fat 36g (Saturated Fat 11g); Sodium 880mg; Total Carbohydrate 38g (Dietary Fiber 5g); Protein 19g; **Exchanges:** 1 Starch; 1/2 Other Carbohydrate; 1 Milk; 1/2 Vegetable; 1 High-Fat Meat; 4 Fat; **Carbohydrate Choices:** 2 1/2

Apple-Cheese Melts

Enjoy this cheesy apple sandwich—warm and ready in 10 minutes.

PREP TIME: 5 MINUTES • **TOTAL TIME:** 10 MINUTES • **MAKES 2 SANDWICHES**

2 slices French or Italian bread, each 1 inch thick
2 tablespoons applesauce
1 medium apple, cored and cut into rings

2 ounces fat-free Cheddar cheese, sliced
2 ounces Gorgonzola cheese, crumbled

Set oven control to broil. Place bread on ungreased cookie sheet. Broil with tops about 4 inches from heat until golden brown; turn. Spread applesauce on bread slices. Place half of apple rings on each bread slice. Top with cheeses. Broil just until cheese begins to melt.

1 SANDWICH: Calories 288; Total Fat 9g (Saturated Fat 4g); Sodium 779mg; Total Carbohydrate 35g (Dietary Fiber 4g); Protein 19g; **Exchanges:** 1 Starch; 1 Fruit; 1 Lean Meat; **Carbohydrate Choices:** 2

Onion, Cheese and Almond Focaccia

Enjoy this Italian flatbread recipe baked using Italian pizza crust, onions, cheese and almonds—ready in just 25 minutes!

PREP TIME: 5 MINUTES • **TOTAL TIME:** 25 MINUTES • **MAKES 16 SERVINGS**

1 package (14 ounces) prebaked original Italian pizza crust (12 inch)

⅓ cup honey mustard

2 tablespoons butter or margarine

1 cup chopped onions

2 cups shredded smoked Cheddar or Gouda cheese (8 ounces)

½ cup sliced almonds

1. Heat oven to 375°F. Place pizza crust on ungreased cookie sheet. Spread with mustard.

2. In 10-inch skillet, melt butter over medium-high heat. Cook onions in butter, stirring occasionally, until tender.

3. Spoon onions evenly onto pizza crust. Sprinkle with cheese and almonds. Bake 15 to 20 minutes or until cheese is melted. Cut into 16 wedges.

1 WEDGE: Calories 190; Total Fat 12g (Saturated Fat 4g); Sodium 290mg; Total Carbohydrate 14g (Dietary Fiber 1g); Protein 8g; **Exchanges:** 1 Starch; **Carbohydrate Choices:** 1

Easy Cheese and Bacon Quiche

A press-in-the-pan Bisquick® crust? Serving quiche has just become extra easy.

PREP TIME: 15 MINUTES • **TOTAL TIME:** 55 MINUTES • **MAKES 8 SERVINGS**

1¼ cups Original Bisquick® mix
¼ cup butter or margarine, softened
2 tablespoons boiling water
1 package (6 ounces) sliced Canadian bacon, chopped
1 cup shredded Swiss cheese (4 ounces)

4 medium green onions, thinly sliced (¼ cup)
1½ cups half-and-half
3 eggs
½ teaspoon salt
¼ teaspoon ground red pepper (cayenne)

1. Heat oven to 400°F. Grease bottom and side of 9-inch pie plate with shortening. Stir Bisquick and butter until blended. Add boiling water; stir vigorously until soft dough forms. Press dough in bottom and up side of pie plate, forming edge on rim of plate.

2. Sprinkle bacon, cheese and onions over crust. In medium bowl, beat half-and-half, eggs, salt and red pepper with spoon until blended. Pour into crust.

3. Bake 35 to 40 minutes or until edge is golden brown and center is set.

BETTY'S SUCCESS TIPS

- Chop the Canadian bacon, shred the cheese and slice the onions the day before; store separately in refrigerator.
- Beat the half-and-half mixture; store covered in refrigerator.

1 SERVING: Calories 300; Total Fat 21g (Saturated Fat 11g); Sodium 790mg; Total Carbohydrate 15g (Dietary Fiber 0g); Protein 13g; **Exchanges:** 1 Starch; 1½ High-Fat Meat; 1½ Fat; **Carbohydrate Choices:** 1

Spicy Ham 'n Greens Quiche

Enjoy this cheesy quiche that's made with ham, collard greens and Original Bisquick® mix—a delicious dinner!

PREP TIME: 20 MINUTES • **TOTAL TIME:** 1 HOUR 5 MINUTES • **MAKES 6 SERVINGS**

1½ teaspoons olive oil	1 cup milk
1 cup chopped cooked ham	2 eggs
½ bag (16-ounce size) frozen chopped collard greens, thawed, drained	½ cup Original Bisquick® mix
1 medium onion, chopped (½ cup)	¼ teaspoon salt
1½ cups shredded pepper Jack cheese (6 ounces)	

1. Heat oven to 400°F. Lightly spray 9-inch glass pie plate with cooking spray. In 10-inch skillet, heat oil over medium-high heat. Cook ham in oil 5 minutes, stirring occasionally, until browned. Stir in greens and onion. Cook 5 minutes longer until onion is tender and liquid is evaporated. Spoon half of the mixture into pie plate. Sprinkle with ¾ cup of the cheese. Repeat layers.

2. In medium bowl, stir milk, eggs, Bisquick mix and salt with fork or whisk until smooth. Pour over greens and cheese.

3. Bake 25 to 35 minutes or until knife inserted in center comes out clean. Let stand 10 minutes before serving.

1 SERVING: Calories 244; Total Fat 15g (Saturated Fat 7g); Sodium 658mg; Total Carbohydrate 14g (Dietary Fiber 2g); Protein 15g; **Exchanges:** ½ Starch; 1 Vegetable; 1 High-Fat Meat; **Carbohydrate Choices:** 1

Smoked Turkey Waldorf Salad

Add smoked turkey to this classic apple-celery-walnut combination to transform it into a satisfying main dish salad—ready in just 10 minutes!

PREP TIME: 10 MINUTES • **TOTAL TIME:** 10 MINUTES • **MAKES 4 SERVINGS**

2 medium red apples, chopped

$1/2$ cup chopped celery

$1/2$ pound smoked turkey, cubed ($1^{1}/_{2}$ cups)

$1/3$ cup reduced-calorie mayonnaise or salad dressing

4 cups torn Bibb or Boston lettuce

$1/4$ cup chopped walnuts, toasted, if desired

1. In medium bowl, combine apples, celery, turkey and mayonnaise; mix well.

2. Arrange lettuce on individual plates. Spoon apple mixture onto lettuce. Sprinkle with walnuts.

BETTY'S SUCCESS TIPS

- Use escarole or leaf lettuce in place of the Bibb lettuce.
- To toast walnuts, spread on a cookie sheet and bake at 350°F for 5 to 7 minutes or until golden brown, stirring occasionally.
- To add a bit of a tang to this salad, add 1 tablespoon lemon juice and $1/2$ teaspoon grated lemon peel.
- Garnish the salad with lemon wedges or long curls of lemon zest (peel). Cut long strips of lemon zest from the lemon with a lemon zester or a sharp paring knife.

1 SERVING: Calories 230; Total Fat 13g (Saturated Fat 2g); Sodium 690mg; Total Carbohydrate 15g (Dietary Fiber 3g); Protein 12g; **Exchanges:** $1/2$ Starch; $1/2$ Fruit; 1 Other Carbohydrate; 2 Very Lean Meat; 2 Fat; **Carbohydrate Choices:** 1

Creamy Turkey Wild Rice Soup

Looking for a creamy dinner using Progresso™ Recipe Starters™ mushroom cooking sauce? Then try this turkey and wild rice soup that's ready in just 20 minutes.

PREP TIME: 5 MINUTES • **TOTAL TIME:** 20 MINUTES • **MAKES 6 SERVINGS**

1 cup diced carrots
1 large onion, chopped (1 cup)
2 cans (18 ounces each) Progresso™ Recipe Starters™ creamy Portabella mushroom cooking sauce
2 cups cubed cooked turkey
1½ cups cooked wild rice
½ teaspoon dried thyme leaves

Garnish, if desired
Chopped fresh parsley

1. In 4-quart saucepan, heat 1 cup water, carrots, onion, ½ teaspoon salt and ¼ teaspoon pepper to boiling. Reduce heat; cover and cook 4 to 6 minutes or until carrots are tender.

2. Stir in all remaining ingredients except parsley; heat to boiling. Reduce heat to low; simmer 10 minutes to blend flavors, stirring occasionally. Sprinkle with parsley.

BETTY'S SUCCESS TIPS

- Add ½ cup diced cooked ham with the turkey.
- Quick-cooking wild rice is faster to prepare than regular wild rice and is equally delicious. Or look for cans of cooked wild rice.

1 SERVING: Calories 260; Total Fat 13g (Saturated Fat 3½g), Sodium 620mg; Total Carbohydrate 21g (Dietary Fiber 2g); Protein 15g; **Exchanges:** 1½ Starch; 1 Fat; **Carbohydrate Choices:** 1½

Curried Squash Soup

Creamy and rich with a hint of curry, homemade organic squash soup is ready in 30 minutes!

PREP TIME: 30 MINUTES • **TOTAL TIME:** 30 MINUTES • **MAKES 5 SERVINGS**

1 tablespoon olive oil or butter
1 medium onion, chopped ($^1/_2$ cup)
1 clove garlic, finely chopped
1$^3/_4$ cups Progresso® reduced-sodium chicken broth (from 32-ounce carton) or 1 can (14 ounces) vegetable broth
$^1/_4$ cup apple juice

2 boxes (10 ounces each) Cascadian Farm® frozen organic winter squash, thawed
2 teaspoons curry powder
$^1/_2$ teaspoon coarse salt (kosher or sea salt)
$^1/_4$ cup half-and-half

1. In 4-quart saucepan, heat oil over medium heat. Cook onion and garlic in oil 3 to 5 minutes, stirring frequently, until tender.

2. Stir in broth, apple juice, squash, curry powder and salt. Heat to boiling, stirring occasionally. Simmer uncovered 5 minutes, stirring occasionally.

3. Stir in half-and-half. Cook 3 to 5 minutes, stirring occasionally, until hot (do not boil).

BETTY'S SUCCESS TIP

This soup can be made up to 24 hours in advance. Just heat in the microwave or in a saucepan until hot (you'll want to avoid boiling the soup).

1 SERVING: Calories 110; Total Fat 4g (Saturated Fat 1$^1/_2$g); Sodium 430mg; Total Carbohydrate 14g (Dietary Fiber 2g); Protein 3g; **Exchanges:** $^1/_2$ Other Carbohydrate; 1 Vegetable; 1 Fat; **Carbohydrate Choices:** 1

Squash and Lentil Bisque

A rich blend of true fall favorites—squash, apples, onions and lentils—is topped with broiled cheese bread. This bisque is "souper"!

PREP TIME: 20 MINUTES • **TOTAL TIME:** 1 HOUR 15 MINUTES • **MAKES 6 SERVINGS**

2   medium butternut or acorn squash, cooked and chopped
2   medium green apples, chopped (2 cups)
1   medium red onion, chopped
1/2   cup unsweetened applesauce
1   cup apple juice
1/4   teaspoon ground nutmeg
1/8   teaspoon ground red pepper (cayenne)

1   can (14 ounces) vegetable broth
1/2   cup dried lentils (4 ounces), sorted and rinsed
3/4   cup shredded reduced-fat mozzarella cheese (3 ounces)
6   slices French bread, 1/4 inch thick
    Additional chopped red onion, if desired

1. Heat squash, apples, onion, applesauce, apple juice, nutmeg, red pepper and 1 cup of the broth to boiling in 3-quart saucepan, stirring occasionally; reduce heat. Cover and simmer 20 minutes.

2. Place squash mixture in blender or food processor. Cover and blend on medium speed until smooth; return mixture to saucepan. Stir in lentils and remaining broth. Heat to boiling; reduce heat. Cover and simmer 25 to 30 minutes, stirring occasionally, until lentils are tender.

3. Set oven control to broil. Sprinkle cheese on bread slices. Place on rack in broiler pan. Broil bread with tops 3 inches from heat about 2 minutes or until cheese is bubbly. Top each serving of soup with slice of cheese bread and chopped onion.

BETTY'S SUCCESS TIP

Create a sensation by serving this soup in edible squash bowls. Cut butternut or acorn squash in half, and remove seeds and fibers. Cook the squash halves before filling with soup.

1 SERVING: Calories 215; Total Fat 3g (Saturated Fat 2g); Sodium 420mg; Total Carbohydrate 47g (Dietary Fiber 11g); Protein 11g; **Exchanges:** 1 Starch; 2 Fruit; 1 Very Lean Meat; **Carbohydrate Choices:** 3

Sweet Potato Soup

Looking for a hearty dinner? Then check out this tasty soup made with sweet potatoes that is ready in an hour.

PREP TIME: 15 MINUTES • **TOTAL TIME:** 60 MINUTES • **MAKES 4 SERVINGS**

2 large dark-orange sweet potatoes (1½ pounds)
1 cup chicken broth
¼ cup orange juice
¼ teaspoon salt

¼ teaspoon ground nutmeg
1 cup milk
¼ cup chopped pecans
Additional ground nutmeg, if desired

1. Heat enough water to cover sweet potatoes to boiling in 2-quart saucepan. Add sweet potatoes. Cover and heat to boiling; reduce heat. Simmer 30 to 35 minutes or until potatoes are tender when pierced with a fork; drain. When potatoes are cool enough to handle, slip off skins; discard skins.

2. Place potatoes in blender or food processor. Add ½ cup of the broth. Cover and blend on medium speed until smooth.

3. Return blended mixture to saucepan. Stir in remaining broth, the orange juice, salt and ¼ teaspoon nutmeg. Cook over medium-high heat, stirring constantly, until hot. Stir in milk. Cook, stirring frequently, until hot. Sprinkle with pecans and additional nutmeg.

BETTY'S SUCCESS TIP

You may omit step 1 by using a 23-ounce can of sweet potatoes in place of the fresh sweet potatoes. Be sure to add the juices from the can with the potatoes to make the soup more flavorful.

1 SERVING: Calories 195; Total Fat 7g (Saturated Fat 1g); Sodium 440mg; Total Carbohydrate 27g (Dietary Fiber 3g); Protein 6g; **Exchanges:** 1 Vegetable; 1 Fat; **Carbohydrate Choices:** 2

30-Minute Beer Cheese Soup

Love beer cheese soup? Here's a version you can make in just 30 minutes!

PREP TIME: 30 MINUTES • **TOTAL TIME:** 30 MINUTES • **MAKES 5 SERVINGS**

½ cup butter or margarine	⅛ teaspoon ground red pepper (cayenne)
¾ cup finely chopped carrots	3 cups Progresso® chicken broth (from 32-ounce carton)
½ cup finely chopped celery	1 cup whipping cream
¼ cup finely chopped onion	4 cups shredded sharp Cheddar cheese (16 ounces)
1 cup quick-mixing flour	1 can (12 ounces) beer
½ teaspoon paprika	
⅛ teaspoon black pepper	

1. In 4-quart Dutch oven, melt butter over medium heat. Add carrots, celery and onion; cook about 10 minutes, stirring occasionally, until celery and onions are transparent.

2. Stir in flour, paprika, black pepper and ground red pepper. Add broth; heat to boiling over medium heat. Boil and stir 1 minute.

3. Reduce heat; stir in whipping cream and cheese. Heat until cheese is melted, stirring occasionally. Stir in beer. If desired, serve with popcorn.

BETTY'S SUCCESS TIP

Popped popcorn is the classic garnish for beer cheese soup.

1 SERVING: Calories 790; Total Fat 64g (Saturated Fat 40g); Sodium 1,240mg; Total Carbohydrate 26g (Dietary Fiber 1g); Protein 28g; **Exchanges:** 1½ Starch; 3½ High-Fat Meat; 7 Fat; **Carbohydrate Choices:** 2

Iced Pumpkin Chex® Mix

Brown sugar, pumpkin and pumpkin pie spice mix up in a microwave-easy munchy mix that's ready in just 15 minutes

PREP TIME: 15 MINUTES • **TOTAL TIME:** 15 MINUTES • **MAKES 14 SERVINGS**

2 cups Cinnamon Chex® cereal
2 cups Wheat Chex® cereal
2 cups Honey Nut Chex® cereal
$1/2$ cup pumpkin seeds
$1/4$ cup brown sugar
$1/4$ cup canned pumpkin
1 tablespoon pumpkin pie spice
$1/4$ cup butter or margarine
2 teaspoons vanilla

Cream Cheese Icing

1 square (1 ounce) premium white chocolate
1 ounce cream cheese, softened

1. In large microwavable bowl, mix cereals and pumpkin seeds. Line cookie sheet with waxed paper or foil. In small bowl, mix brown sugar, pumpkin and pumpkin pie spice; set aside.

2. In 2-cup microwavable measuring cup, microwave butter on High about 30 seconds or until melted. Add pumpkin mixture; microwave about 30 seconds or until hot. Stir in vanilla.

3. Pour pumpkin-butter mixture over cereal and seeds, stirring until evenly coated. Microwave uncovered on High 5 minutes or until mixture begins to brown, stirring every minute. Spread on waxed paper to cool.

4. While mix is cooling, microwave white chocolate on High 30 seconds or until melted; stir in softened cream cheese. Drizzle over top of mix; refrigerate 5 minutes or until set.

5. Place in festive Ziploc® Brand containers and bags to share with family and friends!

1 SERVING: Calories 180; Total Fat 7g (Saturated Fat $3^{1}/_{2}$g); Sodium 190mg; Total Carbohydrate 24g (Dietary Fiber 1g); Protein 3g; **Exchanges:** 1 Starch; $1/2$ Other Carbohydrate; $1^{1}/_{2}$ Fat; **Carbohydrate Choices:** $1^{1}/_{2}$

Mini Rosemary-Garlic Focaccias

Olive oil and rosemary are the classic ingredients you'll find in easy-to-make Bisquick® mix focaccia.

PREP TIME: 15 MINUTES • **TOTAL TIME:** 25 MINUTES • **MAKES 24 BISCUITS**

2¼ cups Original Bisquick® mix
⅔ cup milk
2 teaspoons olive or vegetable oil

½ teaspoon dried rosemary leaves, crushed
½ teaspoon garlic powder

1. Heat oven to 450°F. In medium bowl, mix Bisquick mix and milk until soft dough forms; beat 30 seconds. If dough is too sticky, gradually mix in enough Bisquick mix (up to ¼ cup) to make dough easy to handle.

2. Place dough on surface generously dusted with Bisquick mix; gently roll in Bisquick mix to coat. Shape into a ball; knead 10 times. Roll ¼ inch thick. Cut with 2-inch cutter dipped in Bisquick mix. On ungreased cookie sheet, place dough rounds about 2 inches apart. Brush with oil. Sprinkle with rosemary and garlic powder.

3. Bake 8 to 10 minutes or until golden brown. Serve warm.

BETTY'S SUCCESS TIPS

- Serve these miniature focaccia biscuits with any Italian meal.
- Shiny aluminum cookie sheets of good quality produce the best biscuits. If the cookie sheet is brown, black or darkened from a buildup of fat, the bottoms of the biscuits will be darker in color. Reducing the oven temperature to 400°F may help.
- Place the cookie sheet on the center oven rack. That way, the biscuits will brown evenly on both the tops and bottoms.

1 BISCUIT: Calories 50; Total Fat 2g (Saturated Fat ½g); Sodium 140mg; Total Carbohydrate 8g (Dietary Fiber 0g); Protein 1g; **Exchanges:** ½ Starch; ½ Fat; **Carbohydrate Choices:** ½

Slow Cooker Shortcut Cranberry Barbecue Meatballs

Cranberry-orange sauce adds a twist to these fix-and-forget appetizer meatballs everyone will love!

PREP TIME: 10 MINUTES • **TOTAL TIME:** 3 HOURS 10 MINUTES • **MAKES 24 SERVINGS**

- 1 cup barbecue sauce
- 1/2 cup (from 9.2-ounce jar) cranberry-orange sauce
- 1/2 teaspoon ground mustard
- 1/2 teaspoon ground ginger
- 1/2 teaspoon salt
- 2 packages (16 ounces each) frozen meatballs, thawed
- 2 tablespoons chopped fresh parsley

1. Mix all ingredients except meatballs and parsley in 2- to 2 1/2-quart slow cooker until well blended. Add cold meatballs.

2. Cover and cook on low heat setting 2 to 3 hours or until thoroughly heated. Stir in parsley.

3. Serve meatballs with cocktail forks or toothpicks. Meatballs will hold on low heat setting up to 2 hours; stir occasionally.

BETTY'S SUCCESS TIPS

- You can substitute frozen cranberry-orange sauce for the shelf-stable type. Just thaw before using.
- These meatballs are great to bring to a gathering. Just place them in the slow cooker and plug them in when you get to your destination. You're ready to go without using the host's precious oven space!

1 SERVING: Calories 130; Total Fat 6g (Saturated Fat 2g); Sodium 370mg; Total Carbohydrate 10g (Dietary Fiber 0g); Protein 8g; **Exchanges:** 1 Fruit; **Carbohydrate Choices:** 1

Cheesy Reuben Appetizer

If you're a Reuben sandwich fan, you'll love these easy-to-make appetizers.

PREP TIME: 10 MINUTES • **TOTAL TIME:** 25 MINUTES • **MAKES 20 SERVINGS**

1 package (8 ounces) cream cheese, softened
1½ cups shredded Swiss cheese (6 ounces)
½ cup Thousand Island dressing
4 ounces deli sliced corned beef, chopped

½ cup well-drained sauerkraut
Pretzel crackers, if desired
Cocktail rye bread slices, if desired
Chopped fresh chives, if desired
Sliced radishes, if desired

1. Heat oven to 400°F.

2. Mix cream cheese, 1 cup of the Swiss cheese, the dressing and corned beef. Spread in pie plate, 9 x 1¼ inches, or quiche dish, 9 x 1½ inches. Top with sauerkraut and remaining ½ cup Swiss cheese. (Cover and refrigerate up to 24 hours, if desired.)

3. Bake about 15 minutes or until bubbly around edge. Serve hot with pretzel crackers or cocktail bread. Garnish with chives and radishes.

BETTY'S SUCCESS TIPS

- Create Cheesy Rachel Appetizer by using 4 ounces deli sliced turkey, chopped, instead of the corned beef.
- To soften cream cheese, simply let it come to room temperature.

1 SERVING: Calories 220; Total Fat 10g (Saturated Fat 5g); Sodium 220mg; Total Carbohydrate 1g (Dietary Fiber 0g); Protein 4g; **Exchanges:** 2 Fat; **Carbohydrate Choices:** 0

Apricot-Glazed Coconut-Chicken Bites

Bisquick® mix provides a simple addition to a bite-size chicken appetizer that's ready in 50 minutes.

PREP TIME: 15 MINUTES • **TOTAL TIME:** 50 MINUTES • **MAKES 36 SERVINGS**

1/4 cup butter or margarine, melted
1/2 cup sweetened condensed milk
2 tablespoons Dijon mustard
1 1/2 cups Original Bisquick® mix
2/3 cup flaked coconut
1/2 teaspoon salt
1/2 teaspoon paprika

1 pound boneless skinless chicken breasts, cut into 1-inch pieces
1/2 cup apricot spreadable fruit
2 tablespoons honey
2 tablespoons Dijon mustard
1 tablespoon white vinegar
Hot mustard, if desired

1. Heat oven to 425°F. Spread 2 tablespoons of the melted butter in a 15 x 10 x 1-inch baking pan.

2. Mix sweetened condensed milk and 2 tablespoons Dijon mustard. Mix Bisquick, coconut, salt and paprika. Dip chicken into milk mixture, then coat with Bisquick mixture. Place coated chicken in pan. Drizzle remaining butter over chicken. Bake uncovered 20 minutes.

3. Meanwhile, in small bowl, stir together spreadable fruit, honey, 2 tablespoons Dijon mustard and the vinegar. Turn chicken; brush with apricot mixture. Bake 10 to 15 minutes longer or until chicken is no longer pink in center and glaze is bubbly. Serve with hot mustard.

BETTY'S SUCCESS TIP

Simplify cleanup by lining the pan with aluminum foil before spreading butter in the pan.

1 SERVING: Calories 90; Total Fat 4g (Saturated Fat 2g); Sodium 160mg; Total Carbohydrate 10g (Dietary Fiber 0g); Protein 3g; **Exchanges:** 1 Starch; 1/2 Fat; **Carbohydrate Choices:** 1/2

Maple Chicken Drummies

Maple syrup is the surprise that makes these chicken drummies finger-lickin' good!

PREP TIME: 15 MINUTES • **TOTAL TIME:** 1 HOUR 10 MINUTES • **MAKES 20 SERVINGS**

$^1/_4$ cup real maple syrup or honey

$^1/_4$ cup chili sauce

2 tablespoons chopped fresh chives

1 tablespoon soy sauce

$^1/_2$ teaspoon ground mustard

$^1/_4$ teaspoon ground red pepper (cayenne), if desired

2 pounds (about 20) chicken drummettes

1. Heat oven to 375°F. Mix all ingredients except chicken. Place chicken in ungreased jelly roll pan, $15^1/_2$ x $10^1/_2$ x 1 inch. Pour syrup mixture over chicken; turn chicken to coat.

2. Bake uncovered 45 to 55 minutes, turning once and brushing with sauce after 30 minutes, until juice of chicken is no longer pink when centers of thickest pieces are cut. Serve chicken with sauce.

BETTY'S SUCCESS TIP

Marinate the drummettes in the maple syrup mixture in the refrigerator for up to 1 hour for extra flavor, using a re-sealable plastic food-storage bag for ease. Bake as directed. Serve the drummettes with blue cheese dressing or chili sauce.

1 SERVING: Calories 60; Total Fat 2g (Saturated Fat 1g); Sodium 100mg; Total Carbohydrate 4g (Dietary Fiber 0g); Protein 6g; **Exchanges:** 1 Lean Meat; **Carbohydrate Choices:** 0

Fig and Blue Cheese Appetizer Tarts

Crescent rolls make easy work of these party appetizers filled with a delicious fig-orange mixture.

PREP TIME: 30 MINUTES • **TOTAL TIME:** 60 MINUTES • **MAKES 16 TARTS**

3 ounces $\frac{1}{3}$-less-fat cream cheese (Neufchâtel; from 8-ounce package), softened

$\frac{2}{3}$ cup crumbled blue cheese (3 ounces)

$\frac{1}{4}$ cup Smucker's® Sweet Orange Marmalade

2 tablespoons balsamic vinegar

16 dried Mission figs, coarsely chopped (1 cup)

1 can (12 ounces) big crescent rolls

$\frac{1}{2}$ cup Fisher® Chef's Naturals® Chopped Pecans

1. Heat oven to 350°F. In small bowl, mix cream cheese and blue cheese with fork until well blended; set aside.

2. In 1-quart saucepan, stir marmalade and vinegar over low heat until mixed; stir in figs. Cook over low heat 5 to 7 minutes, stirring occasionally, until figs are softened. Remove from heat.

3. Remove crescent dough from package, but do not unroll. Cut roll of dough into 16 slices. On 2 ungreased cookie sheets, place slices 2 inches apart. Press center of each slice to make indentation, $1\frac{1}{2}$ inches in diameter.

4. Place 1 heaping teaspoon cheese mixture into each well. Top cheese with about 1 tablespoon fig mixture and $1\frac{1}{2}$ teaspoons pecans.

5. Bake 15 to 19 minutes or until golden brown. Remove from cookie sheets to cooling rack; cool 10 minutes. Serve warm.

1 TART: Calories 170; Total Fat 8g (Saturated Fat $3\frac{1}{2}$g); Sodium 270mg; Total Carbohydrate 20g (Dietary Fiber 1g); Protein 3g; **Exchanges:** $\frac{1}{2}$ Starch; 1 Other Carbohydrate; $1\frac{1}{2}$ Fat; **Carbohydrate Choices:** 1

Crostini with Caramelized Onion Jam

Serve your family this crostini that's topped with caramelized onion and cream cheese—a wonderful appetizer.

PREP TIME: 20 MINUTES • **TOTAL TIME:** 1 HOUR 15 MINUTES • **MAKES 24 SERVINGS**

2 tablespoons olive or vegetable oil
2 medium sweet onions, thinly sliced (about 2 cups)
2 teaspoons garlic, finely chopped
1 teaspoon kosher (coarse) salt
2 tablespoons packed brown sugar
$1/4$ cup red wine vinegar
$1/2$ cup chicken or vegetable broth

24 slices ($1/4$ inch thick) baguette French bread
Cooking spray
$1/4$ cup cream cheese or chèvre (goat) cheese, softened (2 ounces)
1 teaspoon chopped fresh thyme or oregano leaves

1. In 2-quart saucepan, heat oil over medium-high heat. Stir in onions and garlic; cook uncovered 10 minutes, stirring every 3 to 4 minutes.

2. Add salt, brown sugar, vinegar and broth. Heat to boiling; reduce heat. Cover and simmer 30 minutes.

3. Remove cover, increase heat to medium-high. Cook 2 to 5 minutes, stirring frequently, until most of the liquid is reduced and the mixture is the consistency of jam. Remove from heat; set aside.

4. Heat oven to 325°F. Place bread slices on ungreased cookie sheet; spray lightly with cooking spray. Bake 6 to 9 minutes or until crispy.

5. Place 1 teaspoon caramelized onions on each bread slice; top with 1 rounded teaspoon cream cheese. Sprinkle with herbs.

1 SERVING: Calories 45; Total Fat 2g (Saturated Fat $1/2$g); Sodium 120mg; Total Carbohydrate 6g (Dietary Fiber 0g); Protein 1g; **Exchanges:** $1/2$ Starch; $1/2$ Fat; **Carbohydrate Choices:** $1/2$

Gorgonzola- and Hazelnut-Stuffed Mushrooms

Rich and spicy Gorgonzola pairs well with earthy mushrooms in a timeless hot appetizer. Hazelnuts provide a pleasant crunch.

PREP TIME: 30 MINUTES • **TOTAL TIME:** 50 MINUTES • **MAKES 8 SERVINGS**

1 pound fresh whole mushrooms
$^1/_3$ cup crumbled Gorgonzola cheese
$^1/_4$ cup Progresso® Italian-style bread crumbs
$^1/_4$ cup chopped hazelnuts (filberts)

$^1/_4$ cup finely chopped red bell pepper
4 medium green onions, chopped ($^1/_4$ cup)
$^1/_2$ teaspoon salt

1. Heat oven to 350°F. Remove stems from mushroom caps; reserve caps. Finely chop enough stems to measure about $^1/_2$ cup. Discard remaining stems.

2. Mix chopped mushroom stems and remaining ingredients in small bowl until well blended. Spoon into mushroom caps, mounding slightly. Place in ungreased jelly roll pan, $15^1/_2$ x $10^1/_2$ x 1 inch.

3. Bake 15 to 20 minutes or until thoroughly heated. Serve warm.

BETTY'S SUCCESS TIPS

- Walnuts or pistachios can be used instead of the hazelnuts.
- Arrange the warm mushrooms on a serving platter, and add whole hazelnuts and oregano sprigs for a festive flair.
- Italian Gorgonzola is rich and creamy with a mild yet slightly pungent flavor and aroma. If you can't find Gorgonzola, use blue cheese instead.

1 SERVING (about 4 mushrooms): Calories 67; Total Fat 4g (Saturated Fat 1g); Sodium 271mg; Total Carbohydrate 1g (Dietary Fiber 1g); Protein 4g; **Exchanges:** $^1/_2$ Vegetable; $^1/_2$ Fat; **Carbohydrate Choices:** 0

Gorgonzola and Toasted Walnut Spread

The fabulous flavor of toasted walnuts infuses every bite of this rich and creamy spread. Have it ready in 10 minutes!

PREP TIME: 10 MINUTES • TOTAL TIME: 10 MINUTES • MAKES 16 SERVINGS

1 cup crumbled Gorgonzola cheese	$^1/_2$ cup chopped walnuts, toasted
1 package (8 ounces) cream cheese, softened	1 tablespoon chopped fresh parsley
3 tablespoons half-and-half	French bread slices
$^1/_4$ teaspoon freshly ground pepper	Apple and pear slices

1. Reserve 1 tablespoon of the Gorgonzola cheese for garnish. In food processor, place cream cheese, remaining Gorgonzola cheese, half-and-half and pepper. Cover and process just until blended.

2. Reserve 1 tablespoon of the walnuts for garnish. Stir remaining walnuts into cheese mixture. Spoon into shallow serving bowl. Sprinkle with reserved Gorgonzola cheese, walnuts and the parsley. Serve with bread slices and apple and pear slices.

BETTY'S SUCCESS TIPS

- Here's a delicious spread you can make up to 3 days ahead of time. Store covered in the refrigerator.
- To toast walnuts, bake uncovered in an ungreased shallow pan at 350°F for about 10 minutes, stirring occasionally, until golden brown.

1 SERVING: Calories 105; Total Fat 10g (Saturated Fat 5g); Sodium 160mg; Total Carbohydrate 1g (Dietary Fiber 0g); Protein 4g; **Exchanges:** 2 Fat; **Carbohydrate Choices:** 0

Apricot Baked Brie

Apricot preserves add a burst of fruitiness that complements the creamy texture of Brie.

PREP TIME: 20 MINUTES • **TOTAL TIME:** 45 MINUTES • **MAKES 12 SERVINGS**

$\frac{1}{3}$ cup apricot preserves

$\frac{1}{4}$ cup chopped pecans

2 tablespoons finely chopped red onion

1 sheet puff pastry (from 17.3-ounce package), thawed

1 round (8 ounces) Brie cheese, cut horizontally in half

1 tablespoon whipping (heavy) cream or half-and-half

1. Heat oven to 400°F. Line cookie sheet with foil or cooking parchment paper; lightly spray foil or paper with cooking spray. In small bowl, mix preserves, pecans and onion; set aside.

2. On lightly floured surface, roll pastry into 10 x 14-inch rectangle. Using the round of cheese as a pattern, cut a pastry circle 3 to 4 inches larger than the cheese. Set aside excess pastry.

3. Spread half of the preserves mixture in center of pastry circle, leaving 3-inch edge. Place 1 cheese round (in rind) on preserves. Spoon remaining preserves over cheese. Top with remaining cheese round.

4. Gently fold edges of pastry up and over cheese to cover, folding and pinching edges to seal. Place seam side down on cookie sheet. Cut out decorative pieces from excess pastry. Brush pastry with whipping cream; place pastry cutouts on top.

5. Bake 20 to 25 minutes or until golden brown. Serve warm.

BETTY'S SUCCESS TIPS

- Sourdough bread slices, crispy crackers or apple and pear slices go well with this dressed-up cheese appetizer.
- Assemble the Brie the day before, cover tightly and refrigerate. Just before serving, bake as directed.

1 SERVING: Calories 170; Total Fat 11g (Saturated Fat 4$\frac{1}{2}$g); Sodium 105mg; Total Carbohydrate 15g (Dietary Fiber 0g); Protein 4g; **Exchanges:** 1 Starch; 2 Fat; **Carbohydrate Choices:** 1

Hot Crab Dip

A mixture of creamy cheeses, sweet crabmeat, pungent spices and toasted almonds, this crab dip can't be beat.

PREP TIME: 15 MINUTES • **TOTAL TIME:** 35 MINUTES • **MAKES 20 SERVINGS**

1 package (8 ounces) cream cheese, softened

$1/4$ cup grated Parmesan cheese

4 medium green onions, thinly sliced ($1/4$ cup)

$1/4$ cup mayonnaise or salad dressing

$1/4$ cup dry white wine or apple juice

2 teaspoons sugar

1 teaspoon ground mustard

1 clove garlic, finely chopped

1 can (6 ounces) crabmeat, drained, cartilage removed and flaked

$1/3$ cup sliced almonds, toasted, if desired
Crackers for serving

1. Heat oven to 375°F. Mix all ingredients except crabmeat and almonds in medium bowl until well blended. Stir in crabmeat.

2. Spread crabmeat mixture in ungreased pie plate, 9 x $1^1/4$ inches, or shallow 1-quart casserole. Sprinkle with almonds.

3. Bake uncovered 15 to 20 minutes or until hot and bubbly. Serve with crackers.

BETTY'S SUCCESS TIPS

- Prepare this favorite from the '50s, and spread it in a casserole dish up to 4 hours ahead. Cover and refrigerate; bake as directed.
- For holiday parties, sprinkle extra sliced green onions in a wreath shape, and make a bow with pimiento.

1 SERVING: Calories 95; Total Fat 8g (Saturated Fat 3g); Sodium 95mg; Total Carbohydrate 2g (Dietary Fiber 0g); Protein 4g; **Exchanges:** $1/2$ High-Fat Meat; 1 Fat; **Carbohydrate Choices:** 0

Asian Fondue

Progresso® chicken broth provides a simple addition to this quick appetizer. Cook chicken, beef and vegetables in an Asian-inspired fondue mixture—a tasty snack.

PREP TIME: 15 MINUTES • **TOTAL TIME:** 15 MINUTES • **MAKES 8 SERVINGS**

1 pound boneless skinless chicken breasts, cut into $1/4$-inch strips	$5^1/4$ cups Progresso® chicken broth (from two 32-ounce cartons)
1 pound boneless beef top sirloin steak, cut into $1/4$-inch strips	2 tablespoons soy sauce
1 medium zucchini, cut into $1/2$-inch slices	2 or 3 thin slices gingerroot
1 medium red bell pepper, cut into 1-inch cubes	2 cloves garlic, thinly sliced
$1/2$ pound snow pea pods, strings removed, cut crosswise in half	$3/4$ cup peanut sauce
	$1/2$ cup sweet-and-sour sauce

1. On serving plate, arrange chicken, beef, zucchini, bell pepper and pea pods.

2. In 2-quart saucepan, mix broth, soy sauce, gingerroot and garlic. Heat to boiling. Pour into fondue pot; keep warm over heat. (Or follow manufacturer's directions to heat in fondue pot.)

3. Spear chicken, beef and vegetables on fondue forks and cook in broth mixture until chicken is no longer pink in center, beef is desired doneness and vegetables are crisp-tender. Let small pieces of food remain in broth. Serve chicken, beef and vegetables with peanut sauce and sweet-and-sour sauce.

BETTY'S SUCCESS TIP

When done with the fondue, add 1 to 2 cups shredded Chinese (napa) cabbage to remaining broth mixture. Heat to boiling; boil 1 to 2 minutes. Serve in small bowls.

1 SERVING: Calories 280; Total Fat 10g (Saturated Fat 2$1/2$g); Sodium 950mg; Total Carbohydrate 14g (Dietary Fiber 2g); Protein 33g; **Exchanges:** $1/2$ Other Carbohydrate; 1 Vegetable; 4 Lean Meat; **Carbohydrate Choices:** 1

Cheese Fondue with Roasted Vegetable Dippers

Serve this flavorful three-cheese dip with bread and a variety of vegetables—an elegant appetizer.

PREP TIME: 30 MINUTES • **TOTAL TIME:** 30 MINUTES • **MAKES 12 SERVINGS**

Dippers

- 2 cups fresh cauliflower florets
- 1 medium green bell pepper, cut into 1½-inch pieces
- 1 medium red bell pepper, cut into 1½-inch pieces
- 1 medium yellow summer squash, cut into ½-inch slices
- 1 package (8 ounces) fresh whole mushrooms
- 2 cups French bread cubes
- 1 tablespoon olive oil

Fondue

- 4 ounces Havarti cheese, shredded (1 cup)
- 1 cup shredded sharp Cheddar cheese (4 ounces)
- 1 cup shredded American cheese (4 ounces)
- 2 tablespoons all-purpose flour
- 1 cup dry white wine
- ¼ teaspoon garlic powder

1. Heat oven to 450°F. In large bowl, toss dippers with oil to coat evenly; arrange in ungreased 15 x 10 x 1-inch pan. Bake 15 to 20 minutes or until vegetables are crisp-tender and bread cubes are toasted.

2. In medium bowl, toss cheeses and flour to mix. Place wine in 2-quart saucepan; cook over medium heat about 1 minute or until very hot. DO NOT BOIL. Add cheese mixture ½ cup at a time, stirring each time until melted. Cook until very warm. Pour into fondue pot. Stir in garlic powder. Keep warm over medium-low heat.

3. To serve, skewer roasted vegetables and bread cubes with fondue forks to be dipped into warm cheese.

BETTY'S SUCCESS TIPS

- In French, the word *fondue* means "melted." In gastronomy, a fondue is a recipe cooked and served in a heated pot right at the dinner table. Cheese fondue and chocolate fondue are popular in the United States. In vogue in the 1970s, fondue is making a comeback, particularly for relaxed entertaining.
- Havarti is a pale and creamy Danish cheese marked with small holes. Its mild, slightly tangy flavor makes Havarti a popular sandwich cheese. Sprinkle chopped fresh chives over the cheese mixture in the fondue pot.
- Garnish the platter of roasted vegetables and bread with long strands of chives or sprigs of another fresh herb.

1 SERVING: Calories 170; Total Fat 11g (Saturated Fat 6g); Sodium 320mg; Total Carbohydrate 8g (Dietary Fiber 1g); Protein 8g; **Exchanges:** ½ Starch; 1 Vegetable; ½ High-Fat Meat; 1½ Fat; **Carbohydrate Choices:** ½

Cheesy Beer Fondue

Serve warm fondue that's made with beer and Progresso™ Recipe Starters™ cheese sauce—a tasty appetizer ready in 10 minutes.

PREP TIME: 10 MINUTES • **TOTAL TIME:** 10 MINUTES • **MAKES 18 SERVINGS**

1   can (18 ounces) Progresso™ Recipe Starters™ creamy three cheese cooking sauce
$^{1}/_{2}$ teaspoon ground mustard
$1^{1}/_{2}$ cups shredded Cheddar cheese (6 ounces)

$^{1}/_{3}$ cup beer or nonalcoholic beer
     French or sourdough bread, cut into chunks, or pretzel rods, if desired

Garnishes, if desired
Chopped fresh chives or parsley

1. In 2-quart saucepan, heat cooking sauce and ground mustard to boiling, stirring occasionally. Remove from heat; stir in cheese until melted. Stir in beer until well blended.

2. Pour cheese mixture into electric or ceramic fondue pot over low heat. Sprinkle with chives. Using fondue forks or wooden skewers, dip bread pieces or pretzels into warm cheese mixture.

BETTY'S SUCCESS TIPS

- No fondue pot? Spray 1- to 2-quart slow cooker with cooking spray. Spoon dip into slow cooker to keep warm; do not cover. Dip will hold on Low heat setting up to 2 hours.
- Stir in $^{3}/_{4}$ cup Green Giant® Valley Fresh Steamers® frozen broccoli cuts, cooked, drained, chopped, and 2 tablespoons diced red bell pepper or diced pimiento, drained, with cheese in step 1. Continue as directed.

1 SERVING: Calories 45; Total Fat 3$^{1}/_{2}$g (Saturated Fat 2); Sodium 135mg; Total Carbohydrate 1g (Dietary Fiber 0g); Protein 2g; **Exchanges:** $^{1}/_{2}$ High-Fat Meat; **Carbohydrate Choices:** 0

Cranberry-Orange Slush Cocktails

A refreshing alternative to rich holiday eggnog. Have it on hand for drop-in guests!

PREP TIME: 10 MINUTES • **TOTAL TIME:** 8 HOURS 10 MINUTES • **MAKES 30 SERVINGS**

1 can (12 ounces) frozen orange juice concentrate, thawed

1 can (12 ounces) frozen cranberry juice concentrate, thawed

2 cups brandy

1 bottle (32 ounces) cranberry juice cocktail

2 bottles (1 liter each) lemon-lime soda pop or sparkling water

1. Mix all ingredients except soda pop in nonmetal container. Divide among pint containers. Cover and freeze at least 8 hours until slushy.

2. For each serving, mix equal amounts of slush mixture and soda pop in glass.

BETTY'S SUCCESS TIPS

- Float a few cranberry-filled ice cubes in each glass of this fruity slush. To make cubes, place a couple of cranberries in each compartment of an ice-cube tray. Fill with a mixture of equal parts cranberry juice cocktail and water. Once frozen, use these "cranberry cubes" to freshen up this slush or other fruit-flavored drinks.

- The slush freezes most quickly in 1-pint containers and can be used directly from the freezer. You can freeze it in one large container for punch, but it will take 1 or 2 days to freeze until slushy.

1 SERVING: Calories 140; Total Fat 1g (Saturated Fat 0g); Sodium 10mg; Total Carbohydrate 26g (Dietary Fiber 0g); Protein 0g; **Exchanges:** 2 Fruit; $1/2$ Fat; **Carbohydrate Choices:** 2

Beef Tenderloin with Herb-Dijon Crust

Get ready for the oohs and aahs when you put this spectacular roast (with super-easy herb crust) on the table.

PREP TIME: 15 MINUTES • **TOTAL TIME:** 1 HOUR 15 MINUTES • **MAKES 8 SERVINGS**

$1/4$ cup chopped fresh parsley	2 pounds beef tenderloin, trimmed
$1/4$ cup chopped fresh basil leaves	$3/4$ teaspoon salt
$1/4$ cup chopped fresh thyme leaves	$1/4$ teaspoon freshly ground black pepper
$1/4$ cup chopped fresh oregano leaves	3 tablespoons Dijon mustard
3 cloves garlic, finely chopped	

1. Heat oven to 400°F. In small bowl, mix parsley, basil, thyme, oregano and garlic; set aside.

2. Spray bottom of roasting pan with cooking spray. Place beef in pan; sprinkle with salt and pepper. Spread mustard evenly over beef; pat parsley mixture over mustard. Insert ovenproof meat thermometer so tip is in center of thickest part of beef.

3. Bake uncovered 35 to 45 minutes or until thermometer reads at least 140°F (for medium-rare doneness).

4. Place beef on cutting board. Cover loosely with foil; let stand 15 minutes or until thermometer reads 145°F. (Temperature will continue to rise about 5°F, and beef will be easier to carve.) Cut beef into $1/2$-inch-thick slices.

BETTY'S SUCCESS TIPS

- For medium doneness, bake 45 to 50 minutes or until thermometer reads at least 150°F. Cover; let stand 15 minutes or until thermometer reads 160°F.
- Do some taste-testing of various brands of Dijon mustard. Not only do they vary in color, from bright yellow to brownish yellow, but their flavors vary as well.

1 SERVING: Calories 180; Total Fat 8g (Saturated Fat 3g); Sodium 400mg; Total Carbohydrate 2g (Dietary Fiber 0g); Protein 25g; **Exchanges:** $3^1/2$ Lean Meat; **Carbohydrate Choices:** 0

Roast Goose with Apple Stuffing

Enjoy the flavors of autumn in this hearty, fragrant roast.

PREP TIME: 1 HOUR 30 MINUTES • **TOTAL TIME:** 5 HOURS 10 MINUTES • **MAKES 8 SERVINGS**

1 whole goose, 8 to 10 pounds, thawed if frozen
2 cups water
1 small onion, sliced
3/4 teaspoon salt
6 cups soft bread crumbs (9 slices)
1/4 cup butter or margarine, melted
1 1/2 teaspoons chopped fresh sage leaves or 1/2 teaspoon dried sage leaves

3/4 teaspoon chopped fresh thyme leaves or 1/4 teaspoon dried thyme leaves
1/2 teaspoon salt
1/4 teaspoon pepper
3 medium tart apples, chopped (3 cups)
2 medium celery stalks (with leaves), chopped (1 cup)
1 medium onion, chopped (1/2 cup)
1/4 cup Gold Medal® all-purpose flour

1. Remove excess fat from goose.

2. Heat giblets, water, sliced onion and 3/4 teaspoon salt to boiling in 1-quart saucepan; reduce heat. Cover and simmer about 1 hour or until giblets are tender. Strain broth; cover and refrigerate. Remove meat from neck and finely chop with giblets. Toss giblets and remaining ingredients except the flour in large bowl.

3. Heat oven to 350°F. Fill wishbone area of goose with stuffing first. Fasten neck skin to back with skewer. Fold wings across back with tips touching. Fill body cavity lightly. (Do not pack—stuffing will expand while cooking.) Fasten opening with skewers, and lace with string. Pierce skin all over with fork.

4. Place goose, breast side up, on rack in shallow roasting pan. Insert meat thermometer so tip is in thickest part of inside thigh muscle and does not touch bone.

5. Roast uncovered 3 to 3 1/2 hours (if necessary, place tent of aluminum foil loosely over goose during last hour to prevent excessive browning), removing excess fat from pan occasionally, until thermometer reads 180°F and juice of goose is no longer pink when center of thigh is cut. The center of the stuffing should be 165°F. Place goose on heated platter. Let stand 15 minutes for easier carving.

6. Pour drippings from pan into bowl; skim off fat. Return 1/4 cup drippings to pan (discard remaining drippings). Stir in flour. Cook over medium heat, stirring constantly, until smooth and bubbly; remove from heat.

7. Add enough water to reserved broth, if necessary, to measure 2 cups. Stir into flour mixture. Heat to boiling, stirring constantly. Boil and stir 1 minute. Serve goose with apple stuffing and gravy.

BETTY'S SUCCESS TIPS

- The rich flavor of goose is often balanced with tart fruit, such as the apples used in this recipe.
- Shave a little time off the preparation by omitting step 2 (do not cook giblets, and do not add to stuffing ingredients). And use 2 cups chicken broth in step 7.

1 SERVING: Calories 84; Total Fat 55g (Saturated Fat 16g); Sodium 1,000mg; Total Carbohydrate 27g (Dietary Fiber 3g); Protein 59g; **Exchanges:** 1 Starch; 1 Fruit; 8 High-Fat Meat; 2 Fat; **Carbohydrate Choices:** 2

Thai Red Curry Coconut Chicken

A great quick weeknight meal to prepare during the busy holiday season!

PREP TIME: 20 MINUTES • **TOTAL TIME:** 25 MINUTES • **MAKES 4 SERVINGS**

1 container (6 ounces) Liberté®
   Méditerranée coconut yogurt
¼ cup chicken broth
2 tablespoons Thai red curry paste
1 teaspoon finely chopped gingerroot
2 cloves garlic, finely chopped
1 tablespoon olive oil
1 pound boneless skinless chicken
   breasts, cut into bite-size chunks

1 tablespoon creamy peanut butter
1 cup sugar snap pea pods
1 red bell pepper, diced (1 cup)
   Salt and pepper, if desired
2 cups cooked rice
   Chopped fresh cilantro, if desired
   Lime wedges, if desired

1. In medium bowl, mix yogurt, chicken broth, curry paste, gingerroot and garlic until well blended. Set aside.

2. In 12-inch nonstick skillet, heat oil over medium-high heat. Add chicken; cook 3 to 4 minutes or until chicken is no longer pink in center. Add peanut butter; cook 1 to 2 minutes or until chicken is well coated.

3. Reduce heat to medium; stir in pea pods and bell pepper. Simmer 3 to 5 minutes, stirring occasionally, until vegetables are crisp-tender. Stir in yogurt mixture; cook 1 to 2 minutes longer or until thoroughly heated. Season with salt and pepper.

4. Serve over rice. Sprinkle with cilantro, and serve with lime wedges.

BETTY'S SUCCESS TIP

Try with brown or jasmine rice.

1 SERVING: Calories 390; Total Fat 13g (Saturated Fat 4½g); Sodium 240mg; Total Carbohydrate 37g (Dietary Fiber 2g); Protein 32g; **Exchanges:** 2½ Starch; 3½ Lean Meat; **Carbohydrate Choices:** 2½

Family New Year's Eve Fondue Party

Here's a dip-and-dunk evening that is loads of fun and simply good eating! Host this party when young kids are part of the festivities and a formal sit-down dinner just doesn't work. Discover the fun of fondue entertaining—one of winter's little pleasures.

A TOAST TO THE NEW YEAR

- A nonalcoholic version of our Cranberry-Orange Slush Cocktails (page 49) or sparkling apple cider in stemmed glasses makes toasting in the New Year extra-festive for one and all! Kids feel really special when they can drink from stemmed glasses, too.
- Afraid of breaking your good crystal? You can pick up plastic stemmed glasses at party or import stores.

FLASHLIGHT DANCING WORKS OUT THE WIGGLES

- Are you ready to rock and roll? Between the cheese fondue and dessert, pass out flashlights to all the family members. Then turn on some music with a good beat, and turn out the lights.
- Dancing and blinking the flashlights to the music is midnight madness for any age! Just be sure to move furniture and lamps to the side of the room so you can avoid any crashes.

SAFETY FIRST

If there are young children in your family, here are some tips to make sure any fondue evening is both fun and safe for all:

- Use slow cookers that stay cool on the outside (borrow some from the neighbors if necessary) instead of fondue pots.
- Place them on the table just before serving, and keep electric cords out of the reach of children. Remove the pots as soon as the meal is over.
- Or if you prefer, skip the slow cooker idea. Instead, ladle the hot fondue from a pot on the counter into small bowls or custard cups.
- And have a care when using long-handled forks and cocktail picks around little ones!

MENU

Crunchy Kale Salad with Yogurt Vinaigrette **79**

Crusty French bread

Cheese Fondue with Roasted Vegetable Dippers **47**

Dark Chocolate Raspberry Fondue **99**

Pesto-Glazed Salmon Fillet

Impress dinner guests with this Italian-inspired baked salmon recipe. It's easy, too, with just three ingredients and 5 minutes of prep time. Enjoy!

PREP TIME: 5 MINUTES • **TOTAL TIME:** 45 MINUTES • **MAKES 8 SERVINGS**

> 2 **pounds salmon fillet**
> $1/_3$ **cup mayonnaise or salad dressing**
> $1/_3$ **cup basil pesto**

1. Heat oven to 375°F. Spray 13 x 9-inch glass baking dish with cooking spray. Place salmon fillet, skin side down, in dish. In small bowl, stir together mayonnaise and pesto; spread over salmon.

2. Bake uncovered 30 to 35 minutes or until salmon flakes easily with fork. Let stand 5 minutes. Place on serving platter. Cut into serving pieces.

BETTY'S SUCCESS TIPS

- You'll find prepared pesto, a blend of basil, garlic, olive oil and Parmesan cheese, with the fresh pasta in the refrigerated section of your supermarket.
- Continue the Italian theme of this dish with a homemade or bagged Caesar salad and Gorgonzola Twice-Baked Potatoes with Bacon (page 76).
- Place the salmon on a serving platter, and garnish with lemon wedges, fresh basil leaves and red currants for a pretty, festive touch.

1 SERVING: Calories 280; Total Fat 20g (Saturated Fat $3^1/_2$g); Sodium 190mg; Total Carbohydrate 0g (Dietary Fiber 0g); Protein 24g; **Exchanges:** $3^1/_2$ Lean Meat; 2 Fat; **Carbohydrate Choices:** 0

Winter Root and Sausage Casserole

Come home to this herbed root vegetables and smoked sausage casserole that's slow cooked for a filling dinner!

PREP TIME: 20 MINUTES • **TOTAL TIME:** 9 HOURS 20 MINUTES • **MAKES 6 SERVINGS**

1 large baking potato, cut into
  $1/2$-inch cubes
1 large dark-orange sweet potato,
  peeled, cut into $1/2$-inch cubes
2 medium carrots, sliced
1 medium parsnip, sliced
1 medium onion, chopped
1 pound smoked sausage, sliced

1 (14.5-ounce) can ready-to-serve
  chicken broth
1 (14.5-ounce) can chunky tomatoes
  with garlic and Italian herbs, undrained
2 teaspoons sugar
$1/2$ teaspoon dried thyme leaves
$1/4$ teaspoon pepper
$1/4$ cup chopped fresh parsley

1. In $3^1/2$- to 4-quart slow cooker, combine all ingredients except parsley; mix well.

2. Cover; cook on Low setting for 7 to 9 hours.

3. Just before serving, stir in parsley.

BETTY'S SUCCESS TIPS

- There are two varieties of sweet potatoes. One type has pale yellow flesh with a crumbly dry texture similar to that of a white potato. The other type has darker orange flesh that is sweet and moist. For the prettiest color and richest flavor, use an orange-fleshed sweet potato.
- To make a vegetarian casserole, omit the sausage and use vegetable broth in place of the chicken broth.
- For a chill-chasing menu, serve this casserole with warm biscuits and honey, plus mugs of hot orange-spice tea.

1 SERVING: Calories 430; Total Fat 25g (Saturated Fat 9g); Sodium 1,520mg; Total Carbohydrate 29g (Dietary Fiber 4g); Protein 21g; **Exchanges:** 2 Starch; 2 Other Carbohydrate; 2 High-Fat Meat; $1^1/2$ Fat; **Carbohydrate Choices:** 2

Shepherd's Pie Skillet

Rely on this English classic for a complete meal of meat, potatoes and veggies, all in one dish. It's super easy with Hamburger Helper® and Betty Crocker® potatoes.

PREP TIME: 25 MINUTES • **TOTAL TIME:** 30 MINUTES • **MAKES 6 SERVINGS**

1 pound lean (at least 80%) ground beef
Hot water and milk called for on Hamburger Helper box
1 box Hamburger Helper® Salisbury
1½ cups Green Giant® frozen mixed vegetables, thawed

Betty Crocker® Potato Buds® mashed potatoes (dry) for 6 servings
Water, milk and butter called for on mashed potatoes box for 6 servings
¼ cup shredded Cheddar cheese (1 ounce)
Chopped fresh parsley

1. In 10-inch skillet, cook beef over medium-high heat 5 to 7 minutes, stirring frequently, until brown; drain. Stir in hot water, milk, sauce mix and uncooked pasta (from Hamburger Helper box) and thawed vegetables. Heat to boiling, stirring occasionally.

2. Reduce heat; cover and simmer about 10 minutes, stirring occasionally, until pasta and vegetables are tender. Remove from heat.

3. Meanwhile, make potatoes as directed on box for 6 servings. Spoon and gently spread mashed potatoes over pasta mixture. Sprinkle with cheese. Cover; let stand about 5 minutes or until cheese is melted. Sprinkle with parsley.

BETTY'S SUCCESS TIP

Love garlic mashed potatoes? Stir in some finely chopped fresh garlic to your liking.

1 SERVING: Calories 440; Total Fat 19g (Saturated Fat 10g); Sodium 790mg; Total Carbohydrate 47g (Dietary Fiber 2g); Protein 21g; **Exchanges:** 3 Starch; 2 Lean Meat; 2 Fat; **Carbohydrate Choices:** 3

African Squash and Chickpea Stew

Enjoy this hearty stew for dinner, made using squash and chickpeas—perfect for African cuisine.

PREP TIME: 30 MINUTES • **TOTAL TIME:** 45 MINUTES • **MAKES 4 SERVINGS**

4 teaspoons olive oil
2 large onions, chopped (2 cups)
1 teaspoon ground coriander
1½ teaspoons ground cumin
½ teaspoon ground cinnamon
½ teaspoon ground turmeric
¼ teaspoon salt
¼ teaspoon ground red pepper (cayenne)
2 cups butternut squash, peeled, seeded, cut into 1-inch cubes

2 cups vegetable broth
1 can (14.5 ounces) low-sodium diced tomatoes, undrained
1 can (15 ounces) chickpeas (garbanzo beans), drained, rinsed
1½ cups thinly sliced okra
½ cup chopped fresh cilantro leaves
⅓ cup raw unsalted hulled pumpkin seeds (pepitas), toasted

1. In 5-quart Dutch oven or saucepan, heat 3 teaspoons of the oil over medium heat. Add onions to oil; cook 10 minutes, stirring occasionally, until golden brown. Add all spices; stir until onions are well coated. Cook about 3 minutes, stirring frequently, until glazed and deep golden brown. Stir in squash; coat well with seasoned mixture. Stir in broth, tomatoes and chickpeas. Heat soup to boiling; reduce heat. Cover and simmer about 15 minutes or until squash is tender.

2. Meanwhile, in 8-inch skillet, heat remaining 1 teaspoon oil over medium-high heat; add okra to oil. Cook 3 to 5 minutes, stirring frequently, until tender and edges are golden brown; stir into stew.

3. Divide stew evenly among 4 bowls. For each serving, top stew with 2 tablespoons chopped cilantro and generous 1 tablespoon pumpkin seeds.

BETTY'S SUCCESS TIPS

- To toast pumpkin seeds, in 8-inch skillet, heat pumpkin seeds over medium heat 3 to 5 minutes, stirring occasionally, until seeds are light brown. (Watch carefully; they can burn quickly.)
- Okra is a common vegetable found in African cuisine; available in grocery stores year-round, it's a great thickener. For the best texture and flavor, sauté it as we do in this recipe before adding to the stew. Choose fresh okra that is dry and firm.

1 SERVING: Calories 390; Total Fat 13g (Saturated Fat 2g); Sodium 650mg; Total Carbohydrate 54g (Dietary Fiber 12g); Protein 15g; **Exchanges:** 2 Starch; ½ Other Carbohydrate; 3½ Vegetable; 2½ Fat; **Carbohydrate Choices:** 3½

Brown Rice-Stuffed Butternut Squash

Bake this delicious rice-, sausage- and veggie-stuffed butternut squash to make a hearty dinner for four.

PREP TIME: 30 MINUTES • **TOTAL TIME:** 1 HOUR 10 MINUTES • **MAKES 4 SERVINGS**

- 2 small butternut squash (about 2 pounds each)
- 4 teaspoons olive oil
- 1/4 teaspoon salt
- 1/2 teaspoon freshly ground pepper
- 1/3 cup brown basmati rice
- 1 1/4 cups reduced-sodium chicken broth
- 1 fresh thyme sprig
- 1 bay leaf
- 2 links (3 ounces each) sweet Italian turkey sausage, casings removed
- 1 small onion, chopped (1/3 cup)
- 1 cup sliced crimini mushrooms
- 1 cup fresh baby spinach leaves
- 1 teaspoon chopped fresh or 1/4 teaspoon dried sage leaves

1. Heat oven to 375°F. Cut each squash lengthwise in half; remove seeds and fibers. Drizzle cut sides with 3 teaspoons olive oil; sprinkle with salt and pepper. On cookie sheet, place squash, cut-sides down. Bake 35 to 40 minutes until squash is tender at thickest portion when pierced with fork. When cool enough to handle, cut off long ends of squash to within 1/2 inch of cavities (peel and refrigerate ends for another purpose).

2. Meanwhile, in 1-quart saucepan, heat remaining 1 teaspoon oil over medium heat. Add rice to oil, stirring well to coat. Stir in chicken broth, thyme and bay leaf. Heat to boiling; reduce heat. Cover and simmer 30 to 35 minutes until all liquid is absorbed and rice is tender. Remove from heat; discard thyme sprig and bay leaf.

3. In 10-inch nonstick skillet, cook sausage and onion over medium-high heat 8 to 10 minutes, stirring frequently, until sausage is thoroughly cooked. Add mushrooms. Cook 4 minutes or until mushrooms are tender. Stir in cooked rice, spinach and sage; cook about 3 minutes or until spinach is wilted and mixture is hot. Divide sausage-rice mixture between squash halves, pressing down on filling so it forms a slight mound over cavity.

BETTY'S SUCCESS TIP

Depending on the size squash you start with for this recipe, you'll have about 4 1/2 cups cubed or 3 cups mashed squash left over. Freeze leftover cooked squash in freezer containers or resealable freezer plastic bags for up to 1 year.

1 SERVING: Calories 350; Total Fat 10g (Saturated Fat 2g); Sodium 670mg; Total Carbohydrate 50g (Dietary Fiber 5g); Protein 14g; **Exchanges:** 2 Starch; 4 Vegetable; 2 Fat; **Carbohydrate Choices:** 3

Green Chile Chicken Lasagna

You don't need to boil oven ready lasagna noodles, which cuts prep time. The mild enchilada sauce pairs well with chicken.

PREP TIME: 25 MINUTES • **TOTAL TIME:** 1 HOUR 35 MINUTES • **MAKES 10 SERVINGS**

1 container (15 ounces) ricotta cheese	2 cans (4 ounces each) Old El Paso® chopped green chiles
1 egg	1 package (8 ounces) oven ready lasagna (12 noodles)
1 cup grated Parmesan cheese	
2 cups chopped cooked chicken	4 cups shredded mozzarella cheese (16 ounces)
2 cans (10 ounces each) Old El Paso® green enchilada sauce	

1. Heat oven to 350°F. In medium bowl, mix ricotta cheese, egg and $1/2$ cup of the Parmesan cheese; set aside. In another medium bowl, mix chicken, enchilada sauce and green chiles.

2. In ungreased 13 x 9-inch (3-quart) baking dish, spread 1 cup of the chicken mixture. Top with 3 uncooked lasagna noodles; press gently into chicken mixture. Spread with $2/3$ cup of the ricotta mixture. Sprinkle with 1 cup of the mozzarella cheese. Repeat layers 3 times. Sprinkle with remaining $1/2$ cup Parmesan cheese. Cover with foil.

3. Bake 45 minutes. Remove foil; bake 10 to 15 minutes longer or until lasagna is tender, cheese is bubbly and edges are lightly browned. Let stand 10 minutes before serving.

BETTY'S SUCCESS TIPS

- The lasagna noodles won't cover the entire baking dish; they expand as they absorb liquid and cook, so when the dish is done, the lasagna will fill the pan. Look for oven ready lasagna with the rest of the dry pasta in the grocery store.
- Green enchilada sauce is milder than red enchilada sauce. Red enchilada sauce can be substituted, but the flavor will be spicier.
- Lasagna can be made the night before, refrigerated and baked the next day. Add a few minutes of bake time.

1 SERVING: Calories 420; Total Fat 20g (Saturated Fat 11g); Sodium 880mg; Total Carbohydrate 28g (Dietary Fiber 1g); Protein 33g; **Exchanges:** $1^1/_2$ Starch; $1/_2$ Other Carbohydrate; 4 Lean Meat; 1 Fat; **Carbohydrate Choices:** 2

Slow Cooker New Hoppin' John

A no-fuss version of Hoppin' John features just six ingredients and convenient slow cooker preparation.

PREP TIME: 10 MINUTES • **TOTAL TIME:** 8 HOURS 20 MINUTES • **MAKES 4 SERVINGS**

- 2 smoked pork hocks (about 1¼ pounds)
- 1¾ cups Progresso® reduced sodium chicken broth (from 32-ounce carton)
- 1 tablespoon dried chopped onion
- 2 cans (15.8 ounces each) black-eyed peas, drained, rinsed

- ½ pound smoked sausage, cut in half lengthwise, then cut crosswise into 1-inch pieces
- ½ cup uncooked instant rice

1. Spray 3½- to 4-quart slow cooker with cooking spray. Place pork hocks in cooker. Add 1 cup of the broth (refrigerate remaining broth). Top pork with onion, peas and sausage.

2. Cover; cook on Low heat setting 8 to 10 hours.

3. Remove pork from cooker; place on cutting board. Pull meat from bones, using 2 forks; discard bones, skin and fat. Return pork to cooker. Add remaining broth and the rice. Increase heat setting to High. Cover; cook 10 minutes or until rice is tender.

BETTY'S SUCCESS TIPS

- Planning on leftovers? The rice will continue to soak up the juices, making this more of a casserole the next day. The flavor is still nice, but add a little water before reheating if you prefer a soup.
- Have plenty of red pepper sauce and corn bread on hand to go with this southern treat.
- Have this stew on New Year's Day. Legend has it, eating black-eyed peas on New Year's Day ensures prosperity in the coming year.

1 SERVING: Calories 510; Total Fat 20g (Saturated Fat 8g); Sodium 1,290mg; Total Carbohydrate 52g (Dietary Fiber 8g); Protein 29g; **Exchanges:** 3 Starch; 0 Fruit; ½ Other Carbohydrate; ½ Fat; **Carbohydrate Choices:** 3½

A Winter Progressive Dinner Party

Enjoy a scrumptious dinner with friends when you organize a progressive dinner party. It involves planning a cooperative meal—preferably with friends who live in close proximity—and eating a different course at each house. You share expenses and prep time. Bon appétit!

PLANNING A SUCCESSFUL PROGRESSIVE DINNER PARTY

- The closer people live to one another the better; a neighborhood block, an apartment building or a condo are ideal settings.

- Plan on three to four courses. Try an appetizer, main meal and dessert, or focus on all appetizers and desserts and limit the celebration to two homes.

- Try not to have more than three changes of locale. Once people are settled it can be difficult to get them to move to the next place.

- Choose recipes that can be made ahead and simply reheated and served when guests arrive so hosts don't have to leave a house early to get ready at their own.

- Ask each host to provide drinks that work best for their course or ask participants who aren't hosting to bring beverages. Or request that everyone bring their own beverage.

- If you are the host at the second or third house, set the table prior to leaving for the party.

- If you have to drive between locations, be sure to appoint a designated driver.

MENU

Apricot Baked Brie **44**

Apricot preserves add a burst of fruitiness that complements the creamy texture of Brie.

Pesto-Glazed Salmon Fillet **55**

Impress dinner guests with this Italian-inspired baked salmon recipe. It's easy, too, with just three ingredients and 5 minutes of prep time. Enjoy!

Gorgonzola Twice-Baked Potatoes with Bacon **76**

Bacon and Gorgonzola make already delicious twice-baked potatoes heavenly.

Green Beans with Lemon-Herb Butter **71**

Here's a new herb and citrus twist to jazz up classic green beans.

Caramel-Pecan Chocolate Dessert **90**

Chocolate chips in the batter and a nutty caramel topping turn basic brownies into a dazzling dessert.

Italian Sausage Kale Soup with Cheesy Crostini

Sausage, kale, Progresso® beans and Progresso™ Recipe Starters™ tomato sauce combine to make this hearty soup for dinner topped with cheesy crostini—ready in 25 minutes.

PREP TIME: 25 MINUTES • **TOTAL TIME:** 25 MINUTES • **MAKES 4 SERVINGS**

Soup

- ½ pound bulk Italian pork sausage
- 1 pound kale, ribs and stems removed and coarsely chopped (about 6 cups)
- 2 cans (18 ounces each) Progresso™ Recipe Starters™ fire roasted tomato cooking sauce
- 1 can (15 ounces) Progresso® cannellini beans, drained, rinsed

Cheesy Crostini

- 8 slices (½ inch thick) baguette French bread
- 1 tablespoon olive oil
- 2 tablespoons shredded Parmesan cheese
- ¼ teaspoon chopped garlic in water (from 4.5-ounce jar) or 1 clove garlic, finely chopped

1. In 3-quart saucepan, cook sausage and kale over medium-high heat 6 to 8 minutes, stirring occasionally, until sausage is no longer pink.

2. Stir in cooking sauces and beans. Heat to boiling; reduce heat. Simmer uncovered 12 to 15 minutes, stirring occasionally, until kale is tender and flavors are blended.

3. Meanwhile, set oven control to broil. Place bread on cookie sheet. Brush lightly with the olive oil; sprinkle with cheese and garlic. Broil with tops 4 to 6 inches from heat 1 to 2 minutes or until edges of bread are golden brown.

4. Spoon soup into serving bowls; top with bread slices.

BETTY'S SUCCESS TIPS

- Spinach leaves can be substituted for the kale. Do not cook with sausage; add with cooking sauces and beans in step 2. Reduce cooking time to 6 to 8 minutes.
- One or two slices per serving of frozen five-cheese or Parmesan Texas toast, heated as directed on package, can be substituted for the baguette, olive oil, Parmesan cheese and garlic. Omit broiler step.

1 SERVING: Calories 490; Total Fat 19g (Saturated Fat 6g); Sodium 1,130mg; Total Carbohydrate 54g (Dietary Fiber 11g); Protein 27g; **Exchanges:** 3 Starch; 1½ Vegetable; 2 Very Lean Meat; 3 Fat; **Carbohydrate Choices:** 3½

Slow Cooker French Onion Soup

This fantastic French onion soup makes a hearty meal. Start the soup in the morning and come home to a no-fuss dinner.

PREP TIME: 15 MINUTES • **TOTAL TIME:** 9 HOURS 50 MINUTES • **MAKES 8 SERVINGS**

Soup

- 3 large onions, sliced (3 cups)
- 3 tablespoons margarine or butter, melted
- 3 tablespoons all-purpose flour
- 1 tablespoon Worcestershire sauce
- 1 teaspoon sugar
- ¼ teaspoon pepper
- 4 cans (14.5 ounces each) ready-to-serve beef broth

Cheesy Broiled French Bread

- 8 slices French bread, 1 inch thick
- ¾ cup shredded mozzarella cheese (3 ounces)
- 2 tablespoons grated or shredded Parmesan cheese

1. Spray slow cooker with cooking spray.

2. In slow cooker, mix onions and margarine.

3. Cover and cook on High heat setting 30 to 35 minutes or until onions begin to slightly brown around edges.

4. Mix flour, Worcestershire sauce, sugar and pepper. Stir flour mixture and broth into onions. Cover and cook on Low heat setting 7 to 9 hours (or High heat setting 3 to 4 hours) or until onions are very tender.

5. Prepare Cheesy Broiled French Bread. Place 1 slice bread on top of each bowl of soup. Serve immediately.

BETTY'S SUCCESS TIPS

- Here's some "broth math" to help you if don't have any ready-to-serve beef broth on hand. You can use three 10½-ounce cans of condensed beef broth with 2½ soup cans of water or 7 cups of your homemade beef broth. Or add 7 cups of water with 7 beef bouillon cubes or 2 heaping tablespoons of beef bouillon granules.
- Vegetarians in your family? Use 4 cans of ready-to-serve vegetable broth instead of the beef broth. The color will not be a rich, deep brown, though, so Golden French Onion Soup may be a more appropriate name!

1 SERVING: Calories 185; Total Fat 8g (Saturated Fat 3g); Sodium 1,240mg; Total Carbohydrate 21g (Dietary Fiber 2g); Protein 9g; **Exchanges:** 1 Starch; 2 Vegetable; 1 Fat; **Carbohydrate Choices:** 1½

Bratwurst and Vegetable Soup

Bratwurst adds a smoky flavor to this simple, hearty soup. It's ready to serve in 35 minutes.

PREP TIME: 35 MINUTES • TOTAL TIME: 35 MINUTES • MAKES 5 SERVINGS

1 teaspoon caraway seed
1 medium baking potato, peeled, cut into $1/2$-inch pieces (1 cup)
$3/4$ cup fresh green beans (about 4 ounces), cut into 1-inch pieces
1 cup ready-to-eat baby-cut carrots
$1/4$ cup chopped fresh parsley
$1/4$ teaspoon pepper
2 cups reduced-sodium beef broth

4 smoked beef bratwurst (from 12-ounce package), cut into $1/2$-inch-thick slices (about $1 1/2$ cups)
1 can (15.5 ounces) great northern beans, drained
1 can (14.5 ounces) Muir Glen® organic diced tomatoes with garlic and onion, undrained

1. In 3-quart saucepan, cook and stir caraway seed 1 to 2 minutes over medium heat until toasted.

2. Stir in remaining ingredients; increase heat to high. Heat to boiling; reduce heat. Cover; simmer 15 to 20 minutes, stirring occasionally, until vegetables are tender.

BETTY'S SUCCESS TIP

Pumpernickel bread or rolls would be perfect to serve with this German-inspired soup.

1 SERVING (About $1 1/3$ Cups): Calories 320; Total Fat 13g (Saturated Fat 5g); Sodium 1,560mg; Total Carbohydrate 33g (Dietary Fiber 8g); Protein 16g; **Exchanges:** 2 Starch; 1 Vegetable; $1 1/2$ Fat; **Carbohydrate Choices:** 2.

Green Beans with Lemon-Herb Butter

Here's a new herb and citrus twist to jazz up classic green beans.

PREP TIME: 10 MINUTES • **TOTAL TIME:** 20 MINUTES • **MAKES 4 SERVINGS**

1 **package (12 ounces) fresh green beans**	1 **teaspoon dried marjoram leaves**
3 **tablespoons butter**	¼ **teaspoon salt**
1 **teaspoon grated lemon peel**	**Lemon slices, if desired**

1. Cook green beans as directed on package; drain.

2. Meanwhile, in 2-quart saucepan, heat butter over medium heat until melted and beginning to brown; immediately remove from heat. Stir in lemon peel, marjoram and salt. Pour over beans; toss to coat. Garnish with lemon slices.

BETTY'S SUCCESS TIPS

- If you can't find a 12-ounce package of fresh green beans, you can purchase them in bulk. To prepare, wash beans, then boil uncovered 6 to 8 minutes or until crisp-tender.
- Be sure to use real butter in this recipe. The toasty flavor that comes from browning is possible only with butter, not margarine. When melting the butter, using a heavy saucepan allows better control over the heat level than a thin pan. Remove the pan from the heat as soon as the butter starts to turn color, as the heat from the pan will continue to brown the butter.

1 SERVING: Calories 110; Total Fat 9g (Saturated Fat 6g); Sodium 220mg; Total Carbohydrate 5g (Dietary Fiber 3g); Protein 1g; **Exchanges:** 1 Vegetable; 2 Fat; **Carbohydrate Choices:** ½

Buttercup Squash with Apples

Enjoy this wonderful side dish made with buttercup and apple that is ready in 45 minutes.

PREP TIME: 5 MINUTES • **TOTAL TIME:** 45 MINUTES • **MAKES 2 SERVINGS**

1 small buttercup or other winter squash, cut in half, seeds and fibers removed (1 pound)

1/2 cup chopped tart apple

2 teaspoons packed brown sugar

2 teaspoons margarine or butter, softened

1/2 teaspoon lemon juice

Dash of ground nutmeg

Heat oven to 400°F. Place squash halves cut sides up in ungreased rectangular baking dish, 11 x 7 x 1 1/2 inches. Mix remaining ingredients; spoon into squash. Cover and bake 30 to 40 minutes or until squash is tender.

1 SERVING: Calories 130; Total Fat 5g (Saturated Fat 1g); Sodium 50mg; Total Carbohydrate 25g (Dietary Fiber 5g); Protein 1g; **Carbohydrate Choices:** 1 1/2

Acorn Squash with Dates

Looking for a vegetable side dish? Then check out this delicious acorn squash recipe with dates that's ready in just 25 minutes.

PREP TIME: 5 MINUTES • **TOTAL TIME:** 25 MINUTES • **MAKES 4 SERVINGS**

1 acorn squash (1½ to 2 pounds)	1½ teaspoons no-trans-fat vegetable oil spread
2 tablespoons chopped dates or raisins	
1 tablespoon packed brown sugar	

1. Pierce squash with knife in several places to allow steam to escape. Place on microwavable paper towel in microwave oven. Microwave uncovered about 5 minutes or until squash feels warm to the touch. Cut in half; remove seeds.

2. In shallow microwavable dish, place squash halves, cut sides down. Cover with microwavable plastic wrap, folding back one edge or corner ¼ inch to vent steam. Microwave on High 5 to 8 minutes, rotating dish every 2 minutes, until tender. Let stand 5 minutes.

3. In small bowl, mix remaining ingredients. Turn squash cut sides up. Spoon date mixture into centers of squash. Microwave uncovered on High about 1 minute or until sugar is melted. Cut each squash half into 2 serving pieces.

BETTY'S SUCCESS TIPS

- You can find a variety of no-trans-fat vegetable oil spreads located in the refrigerated dairy section by the butter.
- Try this with dried cranberries or cherries instead of dates.

1 SERVING: Calories 45; Total Fat 1½g (Saturated Fat 0g); Sodium 20mg; Total Carbohydrate 7g (Dietary Fiber 0g); Protein 0g; **Exchanges:** 1 Vegetable; **Carbohydrate Choices:** ½

Roasted Brussels Sprouts and Cauliflower with Bacon Dressing

Roasted Brussels sprouts feature in this vinaigrette-tossed side dish packed with cauliflower and bacon—a distinctive meal.

PREP TIME: 30 MINUTES • **TOTAL TIME:** 1 HOUR 20 MINUTES • **MAKES 12 SERVINGS**

1½ pounds fresh Brussels sprouts, trimmed, cut in half	1 tablespoon olive oil
2 medium heads cauliflower (about 2 pounds each), cut into florets	2 cloves garlic, finely chopped
¼ cup olive oil	1 teaspoon salt
2 tablespoons sugar	½ teaspoon pepper
10 slices bacon	¾ cup pitted kalamata olives, coarsely chopped
2 tablespoons white wine vinegar	1 tablespoon chopped fresh parsley
	1 teaspoon chopped fresh thyme leaves

1. Heat oven to 450°F. In large roasting pan, toss Brussels sprouts, cauliflower, ¼ cup oil and the sugar. Spread vegetables in single layer.

2. Roast uncovered 45 to 48 minutes, stirring after 30 minutes, until vegetables are tender and browned.

3. Meanwhile, in 12-inch skillet, cook bacon over medium-high heat 15 minutes or until crisp; drain on paper towels. Crumble bacon; set aside. Transfer 2 tablespoons bacon drippings to small bowl; stir in vinegar, 1 tablespoon oil, the garlic, salt and pepper.

4. Drizzle vinaigrette over roasted vegetables. Add bacon, olives, parsley and thyme; toss to coat.

BETTY'S SUCCESS TIP

To make ahead, cut vegetables up to 1 day ahead and store tightly covered in refrigerator.

1 SERVING: Calories 194; Total Fat 15g (Saturated Fat 3g); Sodium 578mg; Total Carbohydrate 12g (Dietary Fiber 4g); Protein 6g; **Exchanges:** 2 Vegetable; ½ High-Fat Meat; 2 Fat; **Carbohydrate Choices:** 1

Gorgonzola Twice-Baked Potatoes with Bacon

Bacon and Gorgonzola make already delicious twice-baked potatoes heavenly.

PREP TIME: 15 MINUTES • **TOTAL TIME:** 1 HOUR 35 MINUTES • **MAKES 8 SERVINGS**

4 **large baking potatoes (8 to 10 ounces each)**	$\frac{1}{2}$ **cup crumbled Gorgonzola or Roquefort cheese**
4 **slices bacon**	4 **medium green onions, sliced ($\frac{1}{4}$ cup)**
$\frac{2}{3}$ **cup milk**	$\frac{1}{2}$ **teaspoon salt**
2 **tablespoons butter or margarine**	

1. Heat oven to 375°F. Gently scrub potatoes, but do not peel. Pierce potatoes several times with fork. Place on oven rack. Bake 1 hour to 1 hour 15 minutes or until tender when pierced in center with fork. Let stand until cool enough to handle.

2. Meanwhile, in 12-inch skillet, cook bacon over medium heat 5 to 6 minutes, turning occasionally, until crisp; drain on paper towels.

3. Cut each potato lengthwise in half; scoop out inside, leaving a thin shell. In medium bowl, mash potatoes, milk and butter with potato masher or electric mixer on low speed until no lumps remain (amount of milk needed will vary depending upon type of potato used). Stir in cheese, green onions and salt. Fill potato shells with mashed potato mixture. Place on ungreased cookie sheet. Crumble bacon onto potatoes.

4. Bake about 20 minutes or until hot. Garnish with additional sliced green onion tops, if desired.

BETTY'S SUCCESS TIPS

- A grapefruit spoon is super for scraping the potato from the shell.
- You can cut down the baking time for the potatoes to about 30 minutes if you microwave them first for 6 minutes before putting them in the oven.
- To make ahead, assemble the potatoes up to 12 hours ahead, cover with plastic wrap or foil and put in the fridge. Then bake as directed in step 4.

1 SERVING: Calories 160; Total Fat 8g (Saturated Fat 4g); Sodium 400mg; Total Carbohydrate 17g (Dietary Fiber 1g); Protein 5g; **Exchanges:** 1 Starch; $1\frac{1}{2}$ Fat; **Carbohydrate Choices:** 1

Crunchy Kale Salad with Yogurt Vinaigrette

Massaging the kale with olive oil softens the texture of the leaves, making them a perfect salad base. Granola gives the salad a pleasantly sweet crunch.

PREP TIME: 10 MINUTES • **TOTAL TIME:** 10 MINUTES • **MAKES 4 SERVINGS**

Kale
- 1 bunch kale with stems removed
- 1/4 cup olive oil
- 1/4 teaspoon salt

Topping
- 1/4 cup Nature Valley® oats 'n honey protein granola
- 1/4 cup dried cranberries

Yogurt Vinaigrette
- 1/4 cup olive oil
- 1/4 cup Yoplait® Greek 100 vanilla yogurt
- 2 tablespoons red wine vinegar
- 1 tablespoon lemon juice
- 2 teaspoons coarse-grained Dijon mustard
- 1 teaspoon finely chopped garlic

1. In large bowl, mix kale, 1/4 cup olive oil and the salt. Massage with your hands 2 to 3 minutes or until kale softens slightly.

2. In blender or food processor, place yogurt vinaigrette ingredients. Cover; blend or process until smooth.

3. Divide kale among 4 plates. Drizzle with vinaigrette; top with granola and dried cranberries. Pass any remaining dressing.

BETTY'S SUCCESS TIP

Make this salad a meal by topping with sliced cooked chicken breast.

1 SERVING: Calories 270; Total Fat 21g (Saturated Fat 3g); Sodium 390mg; Total Carbohydrate 16g (Dietary Fiber 1g); Protein 4g; **Exchanges:** 1 Starch; 4 Fat; **Carbohydrate Choices:** 1

Pomegranate and Almond Salad

Baby greens are sprinkled with tart-sweet pomegranate seeds, almonds, and an easy citrus dressing for a salad that tastes as festive as it looks!

PREP TIME: 20 MINUTES • **TOTAL TIME:** 20 MINUTES • **MAKES 16 SERVINGS**

1 cup sliced almonds
1/3 cup olive or vegetable oil
2 tablespoons fresh lime juice
1 tablespoon sugar
1/4 teaspoon salt
1/8 teaspoon coarsely ground pepper

1 clove garlic, finely chopped
2 bags (5 ounces each) sweet baby lettuces or butter and red leaf lettuce (about 12 cups)
1 pomegranate, seeded (3/4 cup seeds)

1. Sprinkle almonds in ungreased heavy skillet. Cook over medium heat 5 to 7 minutes, stirring frequently until almonds begin to brown, then stirring constantly until light brown. Remove from skillet; set aside.

2. Meanwhile, in small bowl, beat oil, lime juice, sugar, salt, pepper and garlic with wire whisk until smooth.

3. In large serving bowl, mix lettuces and pomegranate seeds. Add dressing; toss to coat. Sprinkle with almonds; toss gently.

BETTY'S SUCCESS TIPS

- To seed a pomegranate, cut the crown end off the pomegranate and then make 4 to 6 lengthwise cuts, 1/4 inch deep, in the rind. Put the pomegranate in a bowl and cover with cool water; let stand 5 minutes. Holding the pomegranate under the water, break it apart into sections, separating the seeds from the pithy white membrane. The edible sacs will sink to the bottom of the bowl and the bitter, inedible membrane will float to the top. Throw out the membrane and the rind. Drain the seeds in a colander; gently pat dry with paper towels. Be careful, as pomegranate juice can stain permanently.
- Substitute your favorite greens for baby greens or butter lettuce, if desired.

1 SERVING: Calories 90; Total Fat 7g (Saturated Fat 1g); Sodium 40mg; Total Carbohydrate 4g (Dietary Fiber 1g); Protein 1g; **Exchanges:** 1/2 Other Carbohydrate; 1 1/2 Fat; **Carbohydrate Choices:** 0

Apple, Cheese and Toasted Walnut Salad

Looking for a signature salad? Try this one and keep it handy in your go-to recipe collection.

PREP TIME: 20 MINUTES • **TOTAL TIME:** 20 MINUTES • **MAKES 10 SERVINGS**

Dressing

- $1/3$ **cup vegetable oil**
- $1/4$ **cup sugar**
- 3 **tablespoons white wine vinegar**
- 1 **tablespoon finely chopped red onion**
- $1/2$ **teaspoon salt**
- $1/2$ **teaspoon ground mustard**
- $1/4$ **to** $1/2$ **teaspoon celery seed**

Salad

- 1 **medium head romaine lettuce, torn into bite-size pieces (about 10 cups)**
- 4 **cups mixed salad greens (from 10-ounce bag)**
- 1 **container (4 ounces) blue or Gorgonzola cheese crumbles**
- 1 **cup walnut halves, toasted**
- 2 **red apples, cut into bite-size pieces**

1. In medium bowl, mix dressing ingredients with wire whisk until sugar is dissolved (dressing will be thick); set aside.

2. In very large bowl (at least 4 quart), gently mix salad ingredients. Just before serving, pour dressing over salad; toss to coat. Serve immediately.

BETTY'S SUCCESS TIPS

- To toast walnut halves, spread on cookie sheet; bake at 350°F for 5 to 7 minutes, stirring occasionally, until golden brown.
- Skim prep time and use a bottled salad dressing.

1 SERVING: Calories 240; Total Fat 17g (Saturated Fat 4g); Sodium 290mg; Total Carbohydrate 17g (Dietary Fiber 3g); Protein 5g; **Exchanges:** 1 Starch; $1/2$ Vegetable; 3 Fat; **Carbohydrate Choices:** 1

Pomegranate and Poppy Seed Salad

Crisp, green romaine is the perfect base for this salad of red onion, pomegranate seeds and a creamy dressing.

PREP TIME: 10 MINUTES • **TOTAL TIME:** 10 MINUTES • **MAKES 12 SERVINGS**

Salad

- 2 heads romaine, torn into bite-size pieces
- 1 medium red onion, sliced
- 2 cups pomegranate seeds

Creamy Poppy Seed Dressing

- 1 cup mayonnaise or salad dressing
- $2/3$ cup sugar
- $1/2$ cup milk
- $1/4$ cup white vinegar
- 2 tablespoons poppy seed

1. In large bowl, mix all salad ingredients.

2. In small bowl, mix all dressing ingredients until well blended. Pour over salad; toss to coat. Serve immediately.

BETTY'S SUCCESS TIPS

- If you can't find pomegranates, you can use 1 cup dried cranberries or sour cherries.
- Pomegranates add more than just great taste and brilliant color to recipes. They're also rich in potassium and contain a good amount of vitamin C.

1 SERVING: Calories 210; Total Fat 15g (Saturated Fat 2g); Sodium 115mg; Total Carbohydrate 18g (Dietary Fiber 1g); Protein 2g; **Exchanges:** 1 Fruit; 1 Vegetable; 3 Fat; **Carbohydrate Choices:** 1

Caesar Salad

Finally, the secret to making a great-tasting Caesar salad at home. This one has olive oil, lemon juice, anchovy paste, romaine and Parmesan cheese—everything you need to capture that classic taste.

PREP TIME: 15 MINUTES • **TOTAL TIME:** 15 MINUTES • **MAKES 6 SERVINGS**

1/3 cup olive or vegetable oil	1 clove garlic, finely chopped
3 tablespoons lemon juice	1 large bunch romaine, torn into bite-size pieces (10 cups)
2 teaspoons anchovy paste	1 cup garlic-flavored croutons
1 teaspoon Worcestershire sauce	1/3 cup grated Parmesan cheese
1/4 teaspoon salt	Freshly ground pepper
1/4 teaspoon ground mustard	

1. Mix oil, lemon juice, anchovy paste, Worcestershire sauce, salt, mustard and garlic in salad bowl.

2. Add romaine; toss until coated. Sprinkle with croutons, cheese and pepper; toss.

BETTY'S SUCCESS TIPS

- If you don't have anchovy paste, you can use 8 anchovy fillets. Just drain, cut them up and mix with the remaining dressing ingredients.
- Jazz up this classic salad with grilled chicken breast. Or for seafood lovers, top the salad with 1 pound cooked peeled deveined large shrimp.

1 SERVING: Calories 175; Total Fat 15g (Saturated Fat 3g); Sodium 430 mg; Total Carbohydrate 7g (Dietary Fiber 2g); Protein 5g; **Exchanges:** 1 1/2 Vegetable; 3 Fat; **Carbohydrate Choices:** 1/2

Apple-Cranberry Salad

Crunchy apple and chewy dried cranberries bring a bit of sweetness to an ordinary green salad.

PREP TIME: 15 MINUTES • **TOTAL TIME:** 15 MINUTES • **MAKES 6 SERVINGS**

5 cups torn romaine lettuce	1/4 cup chopped green onions (4 medium)
1 medium unpeeled apple, diced (1 cup)	1/3 cup refrigerated poppy seed dressing
1/2 cup sweetened dried cranberries	

1. In large serving bowl, place lettuce, apple, cranberries and green onions.

2. Pour dressing over salad; toss to coat.

BETTY'S SUCCESS TIPS

- Use a ripe, red or yellow-green pear instead of the apple.
- Look for refrigerated poppy seed dressing in the produce section of your grocery store.

1 SERVING: Calories 120; Total Fat 6g (Saturated Fat 1/2g); Sodium 140mg; Total Carbohydrate 17g (Dietary Fiber 2g); Protein 0g; **Exchanges:** 1 Other Carbohydrate; 1 1/2 Fat; **Carbohydrate Choices:** 1

Winter Cottage Fruit Salad

Fresh side dish in just 15 minutes! Winter fruits, berries and cottage cheese come together in this delicious salad served over lettuce leaves.

PREP TIME: 15 MINUTES • **TOTAL TIME:** 15 MINUTES • **MAKES 4 SERVINGS**

12 Boston or Bibb lettuce leaves
1 can (15 to 16 ounces) packed in water sliced peaches, chilled and drained
1 can (15 to 16 ounces) sliced pears, chilled and drained
1 cup fresh or frozen raspberries

1 container (16 ounces) reduced-fat small curd cottage cheese
1/2 package (8-ounce size) reduced-fat cream cheese (Neufchâtel), softened
1/4 cup maraschino cherry juice
1/4 cup chopped pecans

1. Divide lettuce among 4 plates. Top with peaches, pears and raspberries. Add 1/2-cup scoop cottage cheese in center of each salad.

2. Mix cream cheese and cherry juice until smooth; drizzle over salads. Sprinkle with pecans.

BETTY'S SUCCESS TIP

For a cool and quick salad or snack, keep canned fruits in the refrigerator. Canned fruits make this the ideal winter salad, but you can also use fresh peaches and pears when they are in season.

1 SERVING: Calories 272; Total Fat 11g (Saturated Fat 4g); Sodium 513mg; Total Carbohydrate 30g (Dietary Fiber 4g); Protein 15g; **Exchanges:** 1 1/2 Fruit; 1 1/2 Lean Meat; 1 1/2 Fat; **Carbohydrate Choices:** 2 1/2

Vanilla-Ginger-Pear Crumble

Bake this cobbler topped with vanilla wafer cookies—a delicious fruit dessert.

PREP TIME: 20 MINUTES • **TOTAL TIME:** 1 HOUR 20 MINUTES • **MAKES 6 SERVINGS**

Pear Mixture

- 6 medium slightly ripe, firm Bartlett pears (about 2³/₄ pounds), peeled, cut into ¹/₂-inch slices (about 6 cups)
- ¹/₄ cup granulated sugar
- 2 tablespoons Gold Medal® all-purpose flour
- 2 teaspoons vanilla
- ¹/₂ to ³/₄ teaspoon ground ginger

Topping

- ¹/₃ cup Gold Medal® all-purpose flour
- ¹/₄ cup packed brown sugar
- ¹/₄ cup cold butter or margarine, cut into pieces
- 12 vanilla wafer cookies, crushed (about ¹/₂ cup)

1. Heat oven to 375°F.

2. In large bowl, mix pear mixture ingredients until evenly coated. Spread in ungreased 8-inch square (2-quart) glass baking dish.

3. In same bowl, mix ¹/₃ cup flour and the brown sugar. Cut in butter, using pastry blender (or pulling 2 table knives through mixture in opposite directions), until mixture looks like coarse crumbs. Stir in crushed cookies. Crumble over pears.

4. Bake 50 to 60 minutes or until pears are tender and topping is golden brown.

BETTY'S SUCCESS TIPS

- The pears in this recipe should be slightly ripe, yet firm. If you need to ripen your pears a bit, place in a sealed paper bag at room temperature.
- For an elegant touch, serve this dessert in a stemmed glass!

1 SERVING: Calories 300; Total Fat 9g (Saturated Fat 5g); Sodium 90mg; Total Carbohydrate 51g (Dietary Fiber 5g); Protein 2g; **Exchanges:** 1 Starch; 1 Fruit; 1¹/₂ Other Carbohydrate; 1¹/₂ Fat; **Carbohydrate Choices:** 3¹/₂

Apple-Fig Bread Pudding Cupcakes with Maple Sauce

For a simple fall or winter dessert, you can't beat bread pudding. Baked in jumbo muffin cups for pretty presentation and served warm with maple sauce, it's delightful.

PREP TIME: 30 MINUTES • **TOTAL TIME:** 1 HOUR 10 MINUTES • **MAKES 6 SERVINGS**

Cupcakes

- 7 cups cubed (1-inch) day-old French or Italian bread (from 1-pound loaf)
- 1 large cooking apple (Braeburn, Cortland or Granny Smith), peeled, chopped (1½ cups)
- ½ cup chopped dried figs
- 1 cup packed brown sugar
- 1 cup milk
- ¼ cup butter or margarine
- 1 teaspoon ground cinnamon
- ½ teaspoon vanilla
- 2 eggs, beaten

Sauce

- ⅓ cup granulated sugar
- ⅓ cup packed brown sugar
- ⅓ cup whipping cream
- ⅓ cup butter or margarine
- ½ teaspoon maple flavor
  Maple candies, if desired

1. Heat oven to 350°F (325°F for dark or nonstick pan). Grease 6 jumbo muffin cups with shortening.

2. In large bowl, mix bread cubes, apple and figs. In small saucepan, cook 1 cup brown sugar, the milk and ¼ cup butter over medium heat until butter is melted. Remove from heat; stir in cinnamon and vanilla. Pour over bread mixture in bowl. Add eggs; toss to coat. Spoon mixture into muffin cups, filling to tops of cups.

3. Bake 30 to 34 minutes or until center is set and apples are tender. Cool while making sauce.

4. In 1-quart saucepan, stir granulated sugar, ⅓ cup brown sugar, the whipping cream and ⅓ cup butter. Heat to boiling over medium heat, stirring occasionally. Remove from heat; stir in maple flavor.

5. Remove warm cupcakes from pan; place on serving plates. Spoon warm sauce over cupcakes. Garnish with maple candies.

BETTY'S SUCCESS TIP

For sweet indulgence, top with whipped cream and a toasted pecan.

1 SERVING (1 Cupcake and About ¼ Cup Sauce): Calories 660; Total Fat 26g (Saturated Fat 16g); Sodium 450mg; Total Carbohydrate 98g (Dietary Fiber 3g); Protein 9g; **Exchanges:** 2½ Starch; ½ Fruit; 3½ Other Carbohydrate; 5 Fat; **Carbohydrate Choices:** 6½

Caramel-Pecan Chocolate Dessert

Chocolate chips in the batter and a nutty caramel topping turn basic brownies into a dazzling dessert.

PREP TIME: 20 MINUTES • **TOTAL TIME:** 5 HOURS 15 MINUTES • **MAKES 12 SERVINGS**

1 package (1 pound 3.8 ounces) Betty Crocker® fudge brownie mix
$^1/_4$ cup water
$^1/_2$ cup vegetable oil
2 eggs
1 cup milk chocolate chips
$^1/_2$ cup whipping (heavy) cream

20 caramels (from 14-ounce bag), unwrapped
1 egg, beaten
1 cup broken pecans
$^3/_4$ cup whipping (heavy) cream
2 tablespoons powdered sugar

1. Heat oven to 350°F (325° for dark or nonstick pan). Grease bottom and side of 10-inch springform pan with shortening. In medium bowl, stir brownie mix, water, oil and 2 eggs until well blended. Stir in chocolate chips. Spread in pan.

2. Bake 50 to 60 minutes or until puffed in center and toothpick inserted near center comes out clean. Cool completely, about 1 hour.

3. Meanwhile, in 1-quart saucepan, heat $^1/_2$ cup whipping cream and the caramels over medium heat, stirring frequently, until caramels are melted. Stir small amount of the hot mixture into beaten egg, then stir egg back into mixture in saucepan. Cook over medium heat 2 to 3 minutes, stirring constantly, until thickened. Stir in pecans. Spread over brownie. Refrigerate uncovered at least 3 hours until chilled.

4. Run metal spatula around side of pan to loosen dessert; remove side of pan. Transfer dessert on pan base to serving plate. In chilled small bowl, beat $^3/_4$ cup whipping cream and the powdered sugar with electric mixer on high speed until stiff peaks form. Spoon whipped cream in 12 dollops around edge of dessert. Cut into wedges to serve. Store covered in refrigerator.

BETTY'S SUCCESS TIPS

- Mark the top of the dessert with a knife before adding the whipped cream garnish. That way, you'll know the whipped cream will be centered on each serving.
- Whipped cream from a spray can works great for this recipe—and saves the time of whipping the cream.
- Make the dessert up to 24 hours ahead and refrigerate. Up to 2 hours before serving, beat the cream with the powdered sugar as directed.

1 SERVING: Calories 600; Total Fat 38g (Saturated Fat 14g); Sodium 85mg; Total Carbohydrate 57g (Dietary Fiber 3g); Protein 7g; **Exchanges:** 2 Starch; 2 Other Carbohydrate; 7 Fat; **Carbohydrate Choices:** 4

Caramel-Drizzled Brownie Hearts

Love brownies? Here's a special way to love every chocolaty crumb.

PREP TIME: 20 MINUTES • TOTAL TIME: 2 HOURS 55 MINUTES • MAKES 8 SERVINGS

1 box (1 pound 2.4 ounces) Betty Crocker® Original Supreme Premium brownie mix
Water, vegetable oil and egg called for on brownie mix box

36 caramels, unwrapped (from 14-ounce bag)
2 tablespoons whipping cream
1/3 cup chopped pecans

1. Heat oven to 350°F (325°F for dark or nonstick pan). Line bottom and sides of 9-inch square pan with foil. Grease bottom only of foil with shortening or cooking spray. Make and bake brownie mix as directed on box. Cool completely, about 1 1/2 hours.

2. Using foil to lift, remove brownie from pan. Remove foil. With deep 3-inch heart-shaped cookie cutter, cut 8 brownies.

3. In medium microwavable bowl, microwave caramels and whipping cream uncovered on High 1 to 2 minutes, stirring every minute, until caramels are melted.

4. Arrange brownies on serving plate. Drizzle caramel mixture over brownies. Sprinkle with pecans.

BETTY'S SUCCESS TIPS

- Make double-chocolate brownie hearts by drizzling with chocolate syrup instead of the caramel.
- Use a deep 2-inch heart-shaped cookie cutter, for 18 smaller brownie hearts.

1 BROWNIE HEART: Calories 490; Total Fat 17g (Saturated Fat 4g); Sodium 290mg; Total Carbohydrate 80g (Dietary Fiber 2g); Protein 4g; **Exchanges:** 2 Starch; 3 1/2 Other Carbohydrate; 3 Fat; **Carbohydrate Choices:** 5

Frosted Bonbons

Delight in a sweet almond surprise baked in the center of frosted bonbons.

PREP TIME: 1 HOUR 40 MINUTES • **TOTAL TIME:** 2 HOURS 10 MINUTES • **MAKES 6 DOZEN**

Bonbons

3	cups Gold Medal® all-purpose flour
1	cup butter or margarine, softened
2/3	cup powdered sugar
1/4	cup milk
1	teaspoon vanilla
1	package (7- or 8-ounce size) almond paste

Vanilla Bonbon Frosting

1	cup powdered sugar
1 1/2	tablespoons milk
1	teaspoon vanilla

Chocolate Bonbon Frosting

1	ounce unsweetened baking chocolate, melted and cooled
1	cup powdered sugar
2	tablespoons milk
1	teaspoon vanilla

Decoration

Betty Crocker® sugar sequins or other decors

1. Heat oven to 375°F. In large bowl, beat all bonbon ingredients except almond paste with electric mixer on medium speed, or mix with spoon, until dough forms.

2. Cut almond paste into 1/4-inch slices; cut each slice into fourths. Shape 1-inch ball of dough around each piece of almond paste. Gently roll to form ball. Place about 1 inch apart on ungreased cookie sheet.

3. Bake 10 to 12 minutes or until set and bottom is golden brown. Remove from cookie sheet to wire rack. Cool completely, about 30 minutes.

4. For vanilla frosting, in small bowl, stir all vanilla bonbon frosting ingredients until smooth.

5. For chocolate frosting, in small bowl, stir all chocolate bonbon frosting ingredients until smooth. If necessary, stir in additional milk, 1 teaspoon at a time, until soft enough to spread.

6. Dip tops of cookies into frostings and sprinkle with decors as desired.

BETTY'S SUCCESS TIPS

● Instead of almond paste, wrap dough around whole almonds, chocolate chunks or dried fruit.

● Serve bonbons in mini paper cupcake liners or fluted bonbon cups.

1 COOKIE: Calories 80; Total Fat 3 1/2 g (Saturated Fat 1 1/2 g); Sodium 20mg; Total Carbohydrate 10g (Dietary Fiber 0g); Protein 0g; **Exchanges:** 1/2 Other Carbohydrate; 1 Fat; **Carbohydrate Choices:** 1/2

Holiday Snickerdoodles

Red and green sugars dress up a best-loved cookie for the holidays.

PREP TIME: 1 HOUR 20 MINUTES • **TOTAL TIME:** 1 HOUR 50 MINUTES • **MAKES 6 DOZEN**

2 tablespoons Betty Crocker® Decors red sugar	1/2 cup butter or margarine, softened
1 tablespoon ground cinnamon	2 eggs
2 tablespoons Betty Crocker® Decors green sugar	2 3/4 cups Gold Medal® all-purpose flour
1 1/2 cups sugar	2 teaspoons cream of tartar
1/2 cup shortening	1 teaspoon baking soda
	1/4 teaspoon salt

1. Heat oven to 400°F. In small bowl, mix red sugar and 1 1/2 teaspoons of the cinnamon; set aside. In another small bowl, mix green sugar and remaining 1 1/2 teaspoons cinnamon; set aside.

2. In large bowl, beat sugar, shortening, butter and eggs with electric mixer on medium speed, or mix with spoon. Stir in flour, cream of tartar, baking soda and salt.

3. Shape dough into 3/4-inch balls. Roll in sugar-cinnamon mixtures. Place about 2 inches apart on ungreased cookie sheet.

4. Bake 8 to 10 minutes or until centers are almost set. Cool 1 minute; remove from cookie sheet to wire rack. Cool completely, about 30 minutes.

BETTY'S SUCCESS TIPS

- Cookie dough can be covered and refrigerated for up to 24 hours before baking. If it's too firm, let stand at room temperature for 30 minutes.
- These rich cinnamon-sugar cookies make a great gift! Place a bag of them in a small basket along with packets of cappuccino or hot chocolate mix.

1 COOKIE: Calories 60; Total Fat 3g (Saturated Fat 1g); Sodium 35mg; Total Carbohydrate 9g (Dietary Fiber 0g); Protein 0g; **Exchanges:** 1/2 Starch; 1/2 Fat; **Carbohydrate Choices:** 1/2

Turtle Shortbread Cookies

Chocolate, caramel and nuts create the classic turtle flavors that are anything but slow in leaving a serving tray.

PREP TIME: 1 HOUR 20 MINUTES • **TOTAL TIME:** 1 HOUR 50 MINUTES • **MAKES 6 DOZEN**

1½ cups butter or stick margarine, softened
½ cup sugar
1 teaspoon almond extract
4 cups Gold Medal® all-purpose flour
½ teaspoon salt
24 caramels, unwrapped

1 bag (6 ounces) semisweet chocolate chips (1 cup)
2 teaspoons shortening
1 cup chopped pecans
6 dozen pecan halves

1. Heat oven to 350°F. In large bowl, mix butter, sugar and almond extract. Stir in flour and salt. (If dough is crumbly, mix in 1 to 2 tablespoons additional softened butter or stick margarine.)

2. Divide dough into 12 equal parts. Roll each part into ¼-inch-thick circle. (If dough is sticky, chill about 15 minutes.) Cut each circle into 6 wedges. Place wedges 1 inch apart on ungreased cookie sheet. Bake 8 to 10 minutes or until set. Immediately remove from cookie sheet to wire rack. Cool completely, about 30 minutes.

3. Meanwhile, in 1-quart saucepan, heat caramels over medium heat about 10 minutes, stirring frequently, until melted. In small microwavable bowl, microwave chocolate chips and shortening uncovered on High 1 to 3 minutes, stirring halfway through heating time, until melted and thin enough to drizzle.

4. Dip 2 straight edges of each cookie into melted caramel, then into chopped pecans. (If caramel thickens, add up to 1 teaspoon water and heat over low heat, stirring constantly, until caramel softens.)

5. Place a dot of melted chocolate on top of each cookie; place pecan half on chocolate. Drizzle remaining chocolate on tops of cookies.

BETTY'S SUCCESS TIPS

- Shortbread comes from Scotland and was originally made as a large round cake with notched "spokes" radiating from the center to symbolize the rays of the sun. In the eighteenth century, the triangular wedges were called "petticoat tails."
- Milk chocolate chips can be substituted for the semisweet chocolate chips.
- Use vanilla instead of the almond extract for a slightly different flavor.

1 COOKIE: Calories 110; Total Fat 7g (Saturated Fat 3g); Sodium 50mg; Total Carbohydrate 11g (Dietary Fiber 0g); Protein 1g; **Exchanges:** ½ Starch; 1½ Fat; **Carbohydrate Choices:** 1

Double-Chocolate and Caramel Bars

Indulge in rich bars that combine favorite caramel and chocolate flavors.

PREP TIME: 30 MINUTES • **TOTAL TIME:** 3 HOURS 5 MINUTES • **MAKES 72 BARS**

3 cups Gold Medal® all-purpose flour
¾ cup packed brown sugar
⅔ cup baking cocoa
1 egg, beaten
1½ cups firm butter or margarine
1½ cups chopped walnuts
1 bag (12 ounces) semisweet chocolate chips (2 cups)
48 caramels, unwrapped
2 cans (14 ounces each) sweetened condensed milk

Chocolate Glaze

1 bag (6 ounces) semisweet chocolate chips (1 cup)
1 teaspoon shortening or vegetable oil

1. Heat oven to 350°F. Line 15 x 10 x 1-inch pan with foil, leaving about 2 inches of foil hanging over sides of pan.

2. In large bowl, stir together flour, brown sugar, cocoa and egg. Cut in 1¼ cups of the butter, using pastry blender (or pulling 2 table knives through ingredients in opposite directions), until crumbly. Stir in walnuts; reserve 3 cups of the crumb mixture. Press remaining mixture firmly in bottom of pan; sprinkle with 2 cups chocolate chips. Bake 15 minutes.

3. Meanwhile, in heavy 2-quart saucepan, melt caramels with sweetened condensed milk and remaining ¼ cup butter over low heat, stirring constantly. Pour over crust. Top with reserved crumb mixture. Bake about 20 minutes longer or until bubbly. Cool completely, about 2 hours.

4. In small microwavable bowl, microwave 1 cup chocolate chips and the shortening uncovered on High 1 to 3 minutes, stirring halfway through heating time, until melted and thin enough to drizzle. Drizzle over bars. For bars, cut into 12 rows by 6 rows.

BETTY'S SUCCESS TIPS

- Place bars in decorative mini muffin cups. It makes serving a snap.
- Instead of walnuts, use pecans for a "turtle" flavor combo bar.
- Bars can also be baked in a 17 x 11 x ¾-inch pan; decrease first bake time to 13 minutes and second bake time to about 18 minutes or until bubbly.

1 BAR: Calories 180; Total Fat 9g (Saturated Fat 4½g); Sodium 60mg; Total Carbohydrate 23g (Dietary Fiber 1g); Protein 3g; **Exchanges:** ½ Starch; 1 Other Carbohydrate; 2 Fat; **Carbohydrate Choices:** 1½

How to Host a Cookie Exchange

Discover an easy, fun way for you, friends and family to get an assortment of fresh, homemade cookies for the holidays while only baking one kind.

DECIDE ON A NUMBER OF GUESTS

- The more guests at the party, the more cookies to exchange—and the more space required. The general rule of thumb is to ask each guest to bring one dozen cookies per attendee, plus another dozen to share at the swap. So if a party has 10 guests, each person should bring 11 dozen cookies.

SEND OUT INVITES EARLY

- Holiday schedules fill up quickly. By sending out an invitation early you'll have time to adjust the guest list based on responses. Ask guests to RSVP with the kind of cookie they're bringing to avoid duplicates.

REMEMBER THE RECIPES

- Along with their cookies, ask each guest to bring copies of their recipe to share. Inexpensive 4 x 6 photo albums work well for organizing recipe cards, plus they make great parting gifts.

WRAP IT UP

- Provide guests with containers for packaging their cookies. Here are a few of our favorite ideas:
- Take lessons from takeout: Think pizza boxes and Chinese cartons.
- Raid the dollar store for tins and trays on the cheap.
- Make cake stands by gluing together mismatched candlesticks and saucers.

MAKE IT SPECIAL

- Turn your gathering into a party with music and food. Think light, festive and fun!

PARTY FOOD

Maple Chicken Drummies **38**

Gorgonzola and Toasted Walnut Spread **43**

Fig and Blue Cheese Appetizer Tarts **39**

Apricot-Glazed Coconut-Chicken Bites **37**

COOKIE EXCHANGE IDEAS

Holiday Snickerdoodles **93**

Double-Chocolate and Caramel Bars **96**

Turtle Shortbread Cookies **94**

Frosted Bonbons **92**

Dark Chocolate Raspberry Fondue

Dip into the dark, rich pleasure of chocolate fondue! Four ingredients are all it takes to make this indulgent treat.

PREP TIME: 15 MINUTES • **TOTAL TIME:** 20 MINUTES • **MAKES 16 SERVINGS**

$2/3$ **cup whipping cream**
$1/3$ **cup seedless raspberry preserves**
1 **tablespoon honey**
1 **bag (12 ounces) semisweet chocolate chunks**

Assorted dippers (fresh fruit pieces, pretzels, shortbread cookies, pound cake cubes or angel food cake cubes), if desired

1. In fondue pot or 2-quart saucepan, mix whipping cream, raspberry preserves and honey. Heat over warm/simmer setting or medium-low heat, stirring occasionally, just until bubbles rise to surface (do not boil).

2. Add chocolate; stir with wire whisk until melted. Keep warm over warm/simmer setting. (If using saucepan, pour into fondue pot and keep warm over warm/simmer setting.) Serve with dippers.

BETTY'S SUCCESS TIPS

- Create a new dip using $1/3$ cup of your favorite fruit preserves, perhaps pineapple or orange marmalade, in place of the raspberry preserves.
- Serve this fruity chocolate sauce warm over a scoop of vanilla ice cream, and top with fresh raspberries.

1 SERVING (2 TABLESPOONS): Calories 170; Total Fat 9g (Saturated Fat 6g); Sodium 10mg; Total Carbohydrate 19g (Dietary Fiber 1g); Protein 1g; **Exchanges:** 1 Other Carbohydrate; 2 Fat; **Carbohydrate Choices:** 1

Caramel-Coffee Fondue

Dunk pieces of fruit and pound cake into a sweet fondue. Fun for all ages!

PREP TIME: 20 MINUTES • **TOTAL TIME:** 20 MINUTES • **MAKES 8 SERVINGS**

¼ cup water	2 apples (1 Braeburn, 1 Granny Smith), cut into ½-inch slices
1 tablespoon instant coffee crystals	2 cups fresh pineapple chunks
1 can (14 ounces) sweetened condensed milk	½ package (16-ounce size) pound cake, cut into 1-inch cubes (about 4 cups)
1 bag (14 ounces) caramels, unwrapped	
½ cup coarsely chopped pecans	

1. In 2-quart nonstick saucepan, heat water over high heat until hot. Dissolve coffee crystals in water.

2. Add milk, caramels and pecans to coffee. Heat over medium-low heat, stirring frequently, until caramels are melted and mixture is hot. Pour mixture into fondue pot and keep warm.

3. Arrange apples, pineapple and cake on serving plate. Use skewers or fondue forks to dip into fondue.

BETTY'S SUCCESS TIP

Use a small slow cooker, uncovered, in place of a fondue pot.

1 SERVING: Calories 590; Total Fat 21g (Saturated Fat 10g); Sodium 210mg; Total Carbohydrate 90g (Dietary Fiber 3g); Protein 9g; **Exchanges:** 3 Starch; 3 Other Carbohydrate; 4 Fat; **Carbohydrate Choices:** 6

Milk Chocolate-Pecan Toffee

Enjoy this toffee that's made with pecans and chocolate—a nutty dessert.

PREP TIME: 20 MINUTES • **TOTAL TIME:** 1 HOUR 20 MINUTES • **MAKES 36 SERVINGS**

1$\frac{1}{2}$ cups sugar	2 tablespoons water
1$\frac{1}{2}$ cups butter or margarine	2 cups chopped pecans, lightly toasted
2 tablespoons light corn syrup	1$\frac{1}{4}$ cups milk chocolate chips

1. Line 17 x 12-inch half-sheet pan with foil; spray foil with cooking spray. In 3-quart heavy saucepan, heat sugar, butter, corn syrup and water to boiling over medium-high heat, stirring constantly. Reduce heat to medium; cook about 10 minutes, stirring constantly, to 300°F on candy thermometer or until small amount of mixture dropped into cup of very cold water separates into hard, brittle threads. (Watch carefully so mixture does not burn.)

2. Stir in 1 cup of the pecans; immediately pour toffee mixture into pan. Quickly spread mixture to $\frac{1}{4}$-inch thickness with rubber spatula. Sprinkle with chocolate chips; let stand about 1 minute or until chips are completely softened. Spread softened chocolate evenly over toffee. Sprinkle with remaining 1 cup pecans.

3. Let stand at room temperature about 1 hour or refrigerate, if desired, until firm. Break into pieces. Store tightly covered.

1 SERVING: Calories 185; Total Fat 14g (Saturated Fat 7g); Sodium 71mg; Total Carbohydrate 15g (Dietary Fiber 1g); Protein 1g; **Exchanges:** 1 Other Carbohydrate; 2$\frac{1}{2}$ Fat; **Carbohydrate Choices:** 1

Rich Chocolate Fudge

Looking for a chocolate dessert? Then check out this rich fudge recipe that's easy enough to be made at home!

PREP TIME: 15 MINUTES • TOTAL TIME: 1 HOUR 45 MINUTES • MAKES 64 CANDIES

1 can (14 ounces) sweetened condensed milk (not evaporated)

1 bag (12 ounces) semisweet chocolate chips (2 cups)

1 ounce unsweetened baking chocolate, chopped, if desired

1 1/2 cups chopped nuts, if desired

1 teaspoon vanilla

1. Grease bottom and sides of 8-inch square pan with butter.

2. In 2-quart saucepan, heat milk, chocolate chips and unsweetened chocolate over low heat, stirring constantly, until chocolate is melted and mixture is smooth. Remove from heat.

3. Quickly stir in nuts and vanilla. Spread in pan. Refrigerate about 1 hour 30 minutes or until firm. Cut into 8 rows by 8 rows to make 1-inch squares.

BETTY'S SUCCESS TIP

Line the pan with foil for super-quick cleanup and to easily lift the fudge out of the pan so you can cut it evenly.

1 CANDY: Calories 60; Total Fat 2 1/2g (Saturated Fat 1 1/2g); Sodium 10mg; Total Carbohydrate 8g (Dietary Fiber 0g); Protein 0g; **Exchanges:** 1/2 Other Carbohydrate; 1/2 Fat; **Carbohydrate Choices:** 1/2

Menus

Christmas Dinner

Sweet Potato Soup 31

Roast Goose with Apple Stuffing 52

Pomegranate and Poppy Seed Salad 83

Apple-Fig Bread Pudding Cupcakes with Maple Sauce 88

Caramel-Pecan Chocolate Dessert 90

New Year's Gathering

Mini Rosemary-Garlic Focaccias 34

Slow Cooker New Hoppin' John 64

Pomegranate and Almond Salad 80

Vanilla-Ginger-Pear Crumble 87

Rich Chocolate Fudge 102

Valentine's Day Dinner

Pomegranate and Almond Salad 80

Beef Tenderloin with Herb-Dijon Crust 50

Gorgonzola Twice-Baked Potatoes with Bacon 76

Caramel-Drizzled Brownie Hearts 91

Spring

Brunch Ham and Egg Muffins

Have leftover ham and hard-cooked eggs? Then you can have this delicious dish finished in even shorter order.

PREP TIME: 45 MINUTES • **TOTAL TIME:** 45 MINUTES • **MAKES 4 SERVINGS**

8 large eggs	1 teaspoon lemon juice
1 package (0.9-ounce) hollandaise sauce mix	1/4 teaspoon dried dill weed
	Dash pepper
1 cup milk	8 ounces sliced cooked ham
1/4 cup butter	4 English muffins, split, toasted

1. Place eggs in single layer in large saucepan or Dutch oven; add enough cold water to cover eggs by 1 inch. Bring to a boil. Immediately remove from heat; cover and let stand 15 minutes. Drain; rinse with cold water. Place eggs in bowl of ice water; let stand 10 minutes. Peel eggs; cut eggs into quarters. Set aside.

2. In medium saucepan, prepare sauce mix with milk and butter as directed on package. Stir in quartered hard-cooked eggs, lemon juice, dill and pepper. Cook and stir 2 to 3 minutes or until thoroughly heated.

3. Place ham on microwavable plate; cover loosely with microwavable plastic wrap. Microwave on Medium for 2 to 3 minutes or until thoroughly heated.

4. Place 2 muffin halves on each serving plate. Arrange ham slices on muffins. Spoon egg mixture over ham.

BETTY'S SUCCESS TIP

This simple recipe makes use of any eggs that are left over from an Easter egg hunt, as well as any leftover ham. If you have hard-cooked eggs on hand, omit the cooking directions in step 1.

1 SERVING: Calories 520; Total Fat 29g (Saturated Fat 13g); Sodium 1,490mg; Total Carbohydrate 32g (Dietary Fiber 2g); Protein 31g; **Exchanges:** 1 Starch; 1 Other Carbohydrate; 1 1/2 Fat; **Carbohydrate Choices:** 2

Armadillo Eggs

Enjoy these cheesy armadillo eggs that are made with jalapeño chiles, sausage and Original Bisquick® mix—tasty appetizers!

PREP TIME: 45 MINUTES • **TOTAL TIME:** 1 HOUR 15 MINUTES • **MAKES 10 SERVINGS**

20 canned whole jalapeño chiles	1 pound bulk mild pork sausage
3 cups shredded sharp Cheddar cheese (12 ounces)	2 cups Original Bisquick® mix
2 cups shredded Monterey Jack cheese (8 ounces)	2 eggs, beaten
	1 package (6 ounces) seasoned coating mix for pork

1. Heat oven to 375°F. Spray 15 x 10-inch pan with cooking spray. Cut lengthwise slit on one side of each chile, leaving other side intact; remove seeds. Stuff each chile with about 2 teaspoons Cheddar cheese. Pinch edges to close; set aside.

2. In large bowl, mix remaining Cheddar cheese, the Monterey Jack cheese, sausage and Bisquick mix. Shape about 2 rounded tablespoonfuls of sausage mixture into ¼-inch-thick patties. Place 1 stuffed chile in center of each patty and wrap mixture around chile. Dip in eggs; roll in coating mix. Place in pan.

3. Bake 30 minutes or until golden.

BETTY'S SUCCESS TIP

To make ahead, unbaked Armadillo Eggs may be refrigerated up to 2 hours before baking or frozen up to 1 month. If frozen, add about 5 minutes to the baking time.

1 SERVING: Calories 535; Total Fat 35g (Saturated Fat 17g); Sodium 1,666mg; Total Carbohydrate 32g (Dietary Fiber 1g); Protein 24g; **Exchanges:** 2 Starch; 2½ High-Fat Meat; 2 Fat; **Carbohydrate Choices:** 2

Gluten-Free Artichoke Basil Frittata

Add something flavorful to your family's Italian meal with this delicious artichoke frittata—ready in just 25 minutes. A perfect recipe for breakfast or dinner!

PREP TIME: 10 MINUTES • **TOTAL TIME:** 25 MINUTES • **MAKES 6 SERVINGS**

1 can (13 to 14.5 ounces) artichoke hearts, drained, or 1 package (12 ounces) frozen artichoke hearts, thawed
1 tablespoon olive oil
½ cup chopped red onion
2 cloves garlic, finely chopped
2 tablespoons chopped fresh or 2 teaspoons dried basil leaves

1 tablespoon chopped fresh parsley
6 eggs
½ teaspoon salt
¼ teaspoon pepper
2 tablespoons gluten-free grated Parmesan cheese

1. Cut artichoke hearts into quarters. In 10-inch ovenproof nonstick skillet, heat oil over medium heat (if not using nonstick skillet, increase oil to 2 tablespoons). Add onion, garlic, basil and parsley; cook 3 minutes, stirring frequently, until onion is tender. Reduce heat to medium-low.

2. In medium bowl, beat eggs, salt and pepper until blended. Pour over onion mixture. Arrange artichokes on top of egg mixture. Cover; cook 7 to 9 minutes or until eggs are set around edge and beginning to brown on bottom (egg mixture will be uncooked on top). Sprinkle with cheese.

3. Set oven control to broil. Broil frittata with top about 5 inches from heat about 3 minutes or until eggs are cooked on top and light golden brown. (Frittata will puff up during broiling but will collapse when removed from broiler.)

BETTY'S SUCCESS TIPS

- The cooked egg under the artichoke pieces may turn light green due to the acid in the artichoke hearts. This will not affect the eating quality or flavor of the frittata.
- Always read labels to make sure each recipe ingredient is gluten free. Products and ingredient sources can change.

1 SERVING: Calories 140; Total Fat 8g (Saturated Fat 2g); Sodium 480mg; Total Carbohydrate 9g (Dietary Fiber 4g); Protein 10g; **Exchanges:** 2 Vegetable; **Carbohydrate Choices:** ½

Spring Frittata

Tender-crisp asparagus and bright-red bell peppers flavor this easy egg dish. A gentle flip at the end of cooking turns both sides golden brown.

PREP TIME: 20 MINUTES • **TOTAL TIME:** 20 MINUTES • **MAKES 4 SERVINGS**

4 teaspoons olive oil	1 tablespoon finely chopped fresh basil
½ pound fresh asparagus spears, trimmed, cut into 1-inch pieces	¼ teaspoon salt
1 small red bell pepper, thinly sliced	
2 cartons (8 ounces each) fat-free, cholesterol-free egg product (2 cups) or 8 eggs, lightly beaten	

1. In 10-inch nonstick skillet, heat 2 teaspoons of the oil over medium-high heat. Add asparagus and bell pepper; cook 3 to 5 minutes, stirring frequently, until crisp-tender. Remove from heat; place cooked vegetables in medium bowl. Stir egg product, basil and salt into vegetables.

2. In same skillet, add remaining 2 teaspoons oil and the egg mixture. Cook over medium heat about 5 minutes or until bottom is lightly browned and top is set, lifting edges occasionally to allow uncooked egg mixture to flow to bottom of skillet.

3. Place skillet-size heatproof plate, upside down, on top of skillet. Turn plate and skillet over; slide frittata back into skillet, browned side up. Cook until bottom is lightly browned. Invert onto serving plate, if desired. Cut into wedges.

BETTY'S SUCCESS TIP

For brunch or lunch, serve this frittata with crusty Italian bread and a tomato and lettuce salad.

1 SERVING: Calories 80; Total Fat 4½g (Saturated Fat ½g); Sodium 260mg; Total Carbohydrate 4g (Dietary Fiber 1g); Protein 7g; **Exchanges:** ½ Other Carbohydrate; 1 Lean Meat; **Carbohydrate Choices:** 0

Springtime Ham and Egg Bake

Spring for a brunch! No last-minute scrambling is needed with this easy egg bake!

PREP TIME: 20 MINUTES • **TOTAL TIME:** 1 HOUR 25 MINUTES • **MAKES 8 SERVINGS**

6 eggs
¾ cup Gold Medal® all-purpose flour
1 teaspoon ground mustard
½ teaspoon seasoned salt
½ teaspoon baking powder
1 container (8 ounces) sour cream
¾ cup milk
2 cups cubed fully cooked ham (12 ounces)

1 cup chopped roma (plum) tomatoes (3 medium)
2 cups shredded Cheddar, Monterey Jack and American cheese blend (8 ounces)
½ cup chopped fresh or 1½ teaspoons freeze-dried chives
Additional roma (plum) tomatoes, thinly sliced, if desired
Additional chives, if desired

1. Heat oven to 350°F. Spray rectangular baking dish, 11 x 7 x 1½ inches, with cooking spray.

2. Beat eggs, flour, mustard, seasoned salt, baking powder, sour cream and milk in large bowl with wire whisk until blended. Fold in ham, chopped tomatoes, cheese and chives. Pour evenly into baking dish.

3. Bake uncovered 50 to 60 minutes or until mixture is set and top is lightly browned. Let stand 5 minutes before cutting. Garnish with tomato slices and chives.

BETTY'S SUCCESS TIPS

- Offer sides of steamed asparagus, fresh fruit and assorted rolls to complement this egg bake.
- You can purchase precubed cooked ham in the refrigerated section of the supermarket where ham is sold.

1 SERVING: Calories 340; Total Fat 22g (Saturated Fat 12g); Sodium 1,020mg; Total Carbohydrate 13g (Dietary Fiber 1g); Protein 24g; **Exchanges:** 1 Starch; 1 Fat; **Carbohydrate Choices:** 1

Smoked Salmon and Asparagus Quiche

An easy pat-in-the-pan crust makes quiche making a snap!

PREP TIME: 20 MINUTES • **TOTAL TIME:** 1 HOUR 30 MINUTES • **MAKES 6 SERVINGS**

1½ **cups Gold Medal® all-purpose flour**

1½ **teaspoons sugar**

1 **teaspoon onion salt**

½ **cup vegetable oil**

2 **tablespoons milk**

1 **package (3.5 to 4.5 ounces) smoked salmon, flaked**

1 **package (10 ounces) frozen asparagus cuts, thawed and drained**

1 **cup shredded Havarti cheese or Monterey Jack cheese (4 ounces)**

3 **eggs**

1 **cup whipping (heavy) cream**

2 **teaspoons chopped fresh or 1 teaspoon dried dill weed**

½ **teaspoon salt**

⅛ **teaspoon pepper**

1. Heat oven to 425°F. Mix flour, sugar and onion salt in medium bowl. Beat oil and milk in measuring cup with fork until creamy. Pour oil mixture over flour mixture; stir until dough forms.

2. Pat dough on bottom and side of ungreased pie plate, 9 x 1¼ inches, or quiche dish, 9 x 1½ inches. Sprinkle salmon over crust. Cut off bottom one-third of each asparagus spear; reserve top spear portions. Chop asparagus ends; sprinkle over salmon. Sprinkle cheese evenly over asparagus.

3. Beat eggs, whipping cream, dill weed, salt and pepper in medium bowl with wire whisk. Slowly pour egg mixture over quiche ingredients. Arrange reserved asparagus in spoke fashion on top of quiche.

4. Bake 15 minutes. Reduce oven temperature to 325°F. Bake 40 to 45 minutes longer or until knife inserted in center comes out clean. If necessary, cover edge of crust with strips of aluminum foil after 10 to 15 minutes of baking to prevent excessive browning. Let stand 10 minutes before cutting.

BETTY'S SUCCESS TIPS

- Substitute 8 ounces of fresh asparagus spears (about 25) for the frozen, blanching the spears first. To blanch, place the spears in boiling water for 2 to 3 minutes or until bright green; immediately rinse with cold water.
- Garnish servings of quiche with additional fresh dill weed.

1 SERVING: Calories 550; Total Fat 41g (Saturated Fat 15g); Sodium 800mg; Total Carbohydrate 29g (Dietary Fiber 2g); Protein 16g; **Exchanges:** 2 Starch; 1½ High-Fat Meat; 5½ Fat; **Carbohydrate Choices:** 2

Asparagus-Potato Brunch Bake

Thanks to leftover ham and frozen vegetables, this comforting casserole is in the oven in only 15 minutes.

PREP TIME: 15 MINUTES • TOTAL TIME: 50 MINUTES • MAKES 8 SERVINGS

1 tablespoon butter or margarine
1 cup sliced green onions
8 eggs
1/2 cup fat-free (skim) milk
3 cups frozen southern-style diced hashbrown potatoes (from 32-ounce bag), thawed

2 cups chopped lean cooked ham (1/2 pound)
1 box (9 ounces) Green Giant® frozen asparagus cuts, thawed, drained
1 cup shredded Cheddar cheese (4 ounces)

1. Heat oven to 350°F. Generously spray 13 x 9-inch (3-quart) baking dish with cooking spray. In 8-inch skillet, melt butter over medium heat. Cook onions in butter 2 to 3 minutes, stirring occasionally, until tender.

2. In large bowl, mix eggs and milk until blended. Stir in cooked onions, potatoes, ham and asparagus. Pour into baking dish. Top with cheese.

3. Bake 30 to 35 minutes or until set. Season to taste with salt and pepper.

BETTY'S SUCCESS TIPS

- This casserole can be covered and refrigerated up to 24 hours before baking. Uncover; bake 40 to 45 minutes or until set.
- Two cartons (8 ounces each) fat-free egg product (2 cups) can be substituted for the 8 eggs. One-eighth of the recipe will yield 220 calories with 8 grams of fat per serving.

1 SERVING: Calories 270; Total Fat 13g (Saturated Fat 6g); Sodium 530mg; Total Carbohydrate 19g (Dietary Fiber 2g); Protein 18g; **Exchanges:** 1 Starch; 1/2 Other Carbohydrate; 1/2 Fat; **Carbohydrate Choices:** 1

Make-Ahead Spring Brunch Bake

Prepared in 25 minutes the night before, this tasty egg casserole serves 12 with ease.

PREP TIME: 25 MINUTES • **TOTAL TIME:** 9 HOURS 45 MINUTES • **MAKES 12 SERVINGS**

2 tablespoons margarine or butter

2 medium leeks, quartered, sliced, using bulb and light green portions (about 2 cups)

8 ounces fresh asparagus spears, trimmed, broken into 1-inch pieces

5 cups frozen southern-style hashbrown potatoes (from 32-ounce package)

1/2 cup roasted red bell pepper strips (from 7.25-ounce jar)

1 teaspoon salt

1 teaspoon dried dill weed

8 eggs

1 pint (2 cups) half-and-half or milk

1 cup finely shredded fresh Parmesan cheese (4 ounces)

1. Spray 13 x 9-inch (3-quart) glass baking dish with cooking spray. Melt margarine in 12-inch skillet over medium-high heat. Add leeks and asparagus pieces; cook and stir 5 to 6 minutes or until crisp-tender.

2. Add potatoes, roasted pepper strips, salt and dill; mix lightly. Spoon evenly into sprayed baking dish.

3. Beat eggs in medium bowl. Add half-and-half; beat well. Add half of the cheese; mix well. Pour over vegetable mixture in baking dish. Sprinkle with remaining half of cheese. Cover with foil; refrigerate at least 8 hours or overnight.

4. Heat oven to 350°F. Bake, covered, 45 minutes. Uncover; bake an additional 20 to 25 minutes or until center is set. Let stand 10 minutes. Cut into squares. If desired, garnish with red bell pepper strips.

BETTY'S SUCCESS TIP

The white bulb and light green portion of a leek are its most tender parts. The dark green leaves are usually tough and should be discarded. Sand and dirt hide between the layers of a leek, so rinse sliced leeks until they are free of any residue.

1 SERVING: Calories 250; Total Fat 13g (Saturated Fat 6g); Sodium 450mg; Total Carbohydrate 22g (Dietary Fiber 2g); Protein 11g; **Exchanges:** 1 1/2 Starch; 1 1/2 Fat; **Carbohydrate Choices:** 1 1/2

Artichoke-Spinach Strata

Perfect for a holiday brunch, this baked egg dish is loaded with fresh and frozen vegetables.

PREP TIME: 20 MINUTES • **TOTAL TIME:** 5 HOURS 30 MINUTES • **MAKES 8 SERVINGS**

2 teaspoons olive or vegetable oil

1 cup finely chopped red bell pepper (1 medium)

1/2 cup finely chopped onion (1 medium)

2 cloves garlic, finely chopped

1 can (14 ounces) quartered artichoke hearts, drained, coarsely chopped (1 1/2 cups)

1 box (9 ounces) Green Giant® frozen spinach, thawed, squeezed to drain

8 cups cubed (1-inch) rustic round bread (about 1 pound)

1 1/2 cups shredded Monterey Jack cheese (6 ounces)

6 eggs

2 1/2 cups milk

1/2 teaspoon ground mustard

1 teaspoon salt

1/4 teaspoon pepper

1/2 cup shredded Parmesan cheese (2 ounces)

1. In 10-inch nonstick skillet, heat oil over medium heat. Add bell pepper, onion and garlic; cook about 6 minutes, stirring occasionally, until tender. Remove from heat. Stir in artichokes and spinach; set aside.

2. Spray 13 x 9-inch (3-quart) glass baking dish with cooking spray. Arrange bread cubes in dish. Spoon vegetable mixture evenly over bread cubes; sprinkle with Monterey Jack cheese.

3. In medium bowl, beat eggs, milk, mustard, salt and pepper with wire whisk until blended; pour evenly over bread, vegetables and Monterey Jack cheese. Sprinkle with Parmesan cheese. Cover tightly with foil; refrigerate at least 4 hours but no longer than 24 hours.

4. Heat oven to 350°F. Bake covered 30 minutes. Uncover; bake 20 to 30 minutes longer or until top is golden brown and knife inserted in center comes out clean. Let stand 10 minutes before cutting.

BETTY'S SUCCESS TIPS

- For added flavor, try using an herb-flavored rustic bread such as oregano or basil.
- Assemble this strata the day before your brunch, then pop it in the oven in time for your guests' arrival.

1 SERVING: Calories 390; Total Fat 17g (Saturated Fat 8g); Sodium 980mg; Total Carbohydrate 35g (Dietary Fiber 7g); Protein 24g; **Exchanges:** 1 Starch; 1 Other Carbohydrate; 1 Vegetable; 1 Fat; **Carbohydrate Choices:** 2

Ham 'n Cheese French Toast

Try classic French toast in a new way! This sweet-savory Bisquick® mix battered and toasted bread, ham and cheese sandwich makes a hearty breakfast or light brunch—ready in 15 minutes.

PREP TIME: 15 MINUTES • **TOTAL TIME:** 15 MINUTES • **MAKES 6 SERVINGS**

1 cup milk
1/3 cup Original Bisquick® mix
2 teaspoons vanilla
4 eggs
6 slices (1 inch thick) day-old ciabatta
or French bread

2 tablespoons Dijon mustard
6 ounces thinly sliced cooked ham
(from deli)
1 1/2 cups shredded mild Cheddar cheese
(6 ounces)
2 tablespoons butter or margarine
Powdered sugar

1. In shallow dish, stir milk, Bisquick mix, vanilla and eggs with fork or whisk until blended. In each slice of bread, cut 3-inch pocket through top crust. Spread about 1 teaspoon mustard in each pocket. Place 1 ounce ham and 1/4 cup cheese in each pocket.

2. Heat griddle or skillet over medium heat (350°F); melt butter on griddle. Dip bread in egg mixture, coating both sides. Place bread on hot griddle; cook about 5 minutes, turning once, until golden brown.

3. Cut French toast in half diagonally; sprinkle with powdered sugar.

BETTY'S SUCCESS TIP

For a sweet and savory taste, serve with your favorite jam or preserves.

1 SERVING: Calories 550; Total Fat 21g (Saturated Fat 12g); Sodium 1,250mg; Total Carbohydrate 62g (Dietary Fiber 2g); Protein 28g; **Exchanges:** 4 Starch; 1/2 Lean Meat; 1 High-Fat Meat; 1 Fat; **Carbohydrate Choices:** 4

Chocolate-Stuffed French Toast

Enjoy this chocolate-stuffed French toast made with an Original Bisquick® mix and eggs mixture. Serve with orange butter at your breakfast.

PREP TIME: 30 MINUTES • **TOTAL TIME:** 30 MINUTES • **MAKES 6 SERVINGS**

Orange Butter
- ½ cup butter, softened
- 2 tablespoons powdered sugar
- 1 tablespoon grated orange peel

French Toast
- 1 cup milk
- ⅓ cup Original Bisquick® mix
- 1 tablespoon vanilla
- 1 teaspoon grated orange peel

- 1 tablespoon fresh orange juice
- 4 eggs
- 6 slices (1 inch thick) day-old French bread
- 6 tablespoons hazelnut spread with cocoa
- 2 tablespoons butter
- Additional powdered sugar, if desired
- Additional hazelnut spread with cocoa, if desired

1. In small bowl, stir orange butter ingredients with wooden spoon until blended. Cover; refrigerate until serving time.

2. In shallow dish, stir milk, Bisquick mix, vanilla, 1 teaspoon orange peel, the orange juice and eggs with fork or whisk until blended. In each slice of bread, cut 3-inch pocket through top crust. Spread 1 tablespoon hazelnut spread in each pocket.

3. Heat griddle or skillet over medium heat (350°F); melt 2 tablespoons butter on griddle. Dip bread in egg mixture, coating both sides. Place bread on hot griddle; cook about 4 minutes, turning once, until golden brown.

4. Sprinkle French toast with additional powdered sugar; top with additional hazelnut spread. Serve with orange butter.

1 SERVING: Calories 477; Total Fat 30g (Saturated Fat 19g); Sodium 490mg; Total Carbohydrate 40g (Dietary Fiber 2g); Protein 11g; **Exchanges:** 1 Starch; 1½ Other Carbohydrate; 5 Fat; **Carbohydrate Choices:** 3½

Red Velvet Pancakes with Cream Cheese Topping

Move over red velvet cake, it's breakfast time with Red Velvet Pancakes made with Bisquick®! But wait, they wouldn't be complete without a wonderful, rich and creamy cream cheese topping—yum!

PREP TIME: 20 MINUTES • **TOTAL TIME:** 20 MINUTES • **MAKES 14 SERVINGS**

Cream Cheese Topping

- 4 ounces (half of 8-ounce package) cream cheese, softened
- 1/4 cup butter, softened
- 3 tablespoons milk
- 2 cups powdered sugar

Pancakes

- 2 cups Original Bisquick® mix
- 1 tablespoon granulated sugar
- 1 tablespoon unsweetened baking cocoa
- 1 cup milk
- 1 to 1 1/2 teaspoons red paste food color*
- 2 eggs
  Powdered sugar, if desired

1. In medium bowl, beat cream cheese, butter and 3 tablespoons milk with electric mixer on low speed until smooth. Gradually beat in 2 cups powdered sugar, 1 cup at a time, on low speed until topping is smooth. Cover; set aside.

2. In large bowl, stir all pancake ingredients except powdered sugar with wire whisk until well blended. Heat griddle or skillet over medium-high heat (375°F). (To test griddle, sprinkle with a few drops of water. If bubbles jump around, heat is just right.) Brush with vegetable oil if necessary or spray with cooking spray before heating.

3. For each pancake, pour slightly less than 1/4 cup batter onto hot griddle. Cook 2 to 3 minutes or until bubbles form on top and edges are dry. Turn; cook other side until golden brown.

4. Spoon cream cheese topping into resealable food-storage plastic bag; seal bag. Cut off tiny corner of bag; squeeze bag to drizzle topping over pancakes. Sprinkle with powdered sugar.

*Liquid food color is not recommended for this recipe.

1 SERVING: Calories 450; Total Fat 19g (Saturated Fat 10g); Sodium 560mg; Total Carbohydrate 62g (Dietary Fiber 1g); Protein 7g; **Exchanges:** 2 1/2 Starch; 1 1/2 Other Carbohydrate; 3 1/2 Fat; **Carbohydrate Choices:** 4

Raspberry-Rhubarb Puff Pancake

There's no need to stand over the stove flipping pancakes when you make this easy oven recipe. Topped with ricotta and fruit, this pretty puff pancake makes a special breakfast or brunch.

PREP TIME: 25 MINUTES • **TOTAL TIME:** 25 MINUTES • **MAKES 4 SERVINGS**

3/4 cup Gold Medal® all-purpose flour
3/4 cup milk
3 eggs
1/2 teaspoon vanilla
2 tablespoons butter
3/4 cup ricotta cheese

2 tablespoons powdered sugar
1 cup chopped fresh or frozen rhubarb
1/4 cup granulated sugar
1/4 cup water
2 teaspoons cornstarch
1 cup fresh or frozen (thawed) raspberries

1. Heat oven to 425°F. In medium bowl, beat flour, milk, eggs and vanilla with wire whisk until combined.

2. In 9½-inch glass deep-dish pie plate, melt butter in oven. Using oven mitts, carefully tilt pie plate to coat bottom with melted butter. Slowly pour batter into hot plate. Bake 18 to 20 minutes or until puffed and deep golden brown (do not underbake).

3. Meanwhile, in small bowl, mix cheese and powdered sugar; set aside. In 1-quart saucepan, cook and stir rhubarb, granulated sugar, water and cornstarch over medium-low heat until rhubarb is tender, about 4 minutes. Cool slightly. Stir in raspberries.

4. Remove pancake from oven. Carefully spread cheese filling over bottom of pancake. Cut into quarters. If necessary, run spatula under pancake to loosen. Top with fruit filling.

BETTY'S SUCCESS TIP

Prepare the cheese and fruit fillings while the pancake bakes so they are ready to use as soon as the pancake comes out of the oven. The "puff" will start to deflate quickly.

1 SERVING: Calories 370; Total Fat 15g (Saturated Fat 8g); Sodium 170mg; Total Carbohydrate 45g (Dietary Fiber 3g); Protein 14g; **Exchanges:** 1½ Starch; 1 Fruit; ½ Other Carbohydrate; 1½ Lean Meat; 2 Fat; **Carbohydrate Choices:** 3

Smoked Salmon and Dill Muffins

These delicious savory smoked salmon, cheese and dill muffins made with Original Bisquick® mix are a gourmet and classy addition to a bread basket.

PREP TIME: 15 MINUTES • **TOTAL TIME:** 40 MINUTES • **MAKES 12 SERVINGS**

3 tablespoons butter or margarine	2 tablespoons chopped fresh dill weed
1 medium onion, finely chopped (¹/₂ cup)	³/₄ teaspoon grated lemon peel
1 package (4.5 ounces) smoked salmon, flaked or finely chopped	¹/₂ cup milk
1¹/₂ cups Original Bisquick® mix	2 tablespoons vegetable oil
1¹/₄ cups shredded Italian cheese blend (5 ounces)	1 egg

1. Heat oven to 425°F. Spray 12 regular-size muffin cups with cooking spray.

2. In 8-inch skillet, melt butter over medium-high heat. Cook onion in butter 3 to 5 minutes, stirring frequently, until tender. Stir in salmon.

3. In large bowl, stir Bisquick mix, ³/₄ cup of the cheese, the dill and lemon peel. In small bowl, stir milk, oil and egg with fork or whisk until blended. Make well in center of Bisquick mixture; stir in egg mixture just until dry ingredients are moistened. Stir in onion and salmon. Divide batter evenly among muffin cups, filling each two-thirds full. Sprinkle evenly with remaining ¹/₂ cup cheese.

4. Bake 18 to 20 minutes or until golden. Cool 2 to 3 minutes; remove from pan. Serve warm.

1 SERVING: Calories 160; Total Fat 10g (Saturated Fat 4g); Sodium 380mg; Total Carbohydrate 11g (Dietary Fiber 0g); Protein 8g; **Exchanges:** 1 Starch; ¹/₂ Lean Meat; 1¹/₂ Fat; **Carbohydrate Choices:** 1

Passover Apple Muffins

Matzo farfel, finely broken matzo, replaces flour in these moist apple-cinnamon muffins.

PREP TIME: 25 MINUTES • **TOTAL TIME:** 50 MINUTES • **MAKES 12 MUFFINS**

2 cups matzo farfel
1/2 cup raisins
4 egg whites
Dash salt
1/4 cup sugar
1 large tart apple, peeled, finely chopped (1 1/3 cups)

1/2 teaspoon ground cinnamon
3 tablespoons butter or margarine, melted
2 teaspoons sugar
1 teaspoon ground cinnamon

1. Heat oven to 375°F. Place paper baking cup in each of 12 regular-size muffin cups.

2. Place matzo farfel in plastic bag; crush lightly with rolling pin. Place in large strainer or colander; moisten well under hot running water until soft. Drain; squeeze out as much water as possible. Rinse raisins with hot water.

3. In large bowl, beat egg whites and salt with electric mixer on high speed until soft peaks form. Gradually add 1/4 cup sugar, beating until stiff peaks form.

4. Sprinkle farfel, raisins, apple and 1/2 teaspoon cinnamon over egg whites. Drizzle with butter; fold in lightly. Divide mixture evenly among muffin cups, packing lightly. (Muffin cups will be full.) In small bowl, mix 2 teaspoons sugar and 1 teaspoon cinnamon; sprinkle about 1/4 teaspoon mixture over each muffin.

5. Bake 20 to 25 minutes or until golden brown. Immediately remove from pan to wire rack. Serve warm.

BETTY'S SUCCESS TIPS

- Tart apples, such as Granny Smith, McIntosh or Haralson, make the most flavorful muffins.
- If you do not have paper muffin cups, grease muffin cups instead.

1 SERVING (1 Muffin): Calories 130; Total Fat 3g (Saturated Fat 2g); Sodium 40mg; Total Carbohydrate 23g (Dietary Fiber 1g); Protein 2g; **Exchanges:** 1/2 Starch; 1 Other Carbohydrate; 1/2 Fat; **Carbohydrate Choices:** 1 1/2

Cheesecake-Poppy Seed Muffins

Treat your family to muffins with a surprise cheesecake filling. It's easy when you start with a no-fail mix.

PREP TIME: 15 MINUTES • **TOTAL TIME:** 50 MINUTES • **MAKES 12 MUFFINS**

1 box Betty Crocker® lemon-poppy seed muffin mix	³/₄ cup milk
1 package (3 ounces) cream cheese, softened	¹/₄ cup vegetable oil
	2 eggs

1. Heat oven to 425°F. Place paper baking cup in each of 12 regular-size muffin cups, or grease bottoms only of muffin cups.

2. Squeeze Glaze packet (from Muffin Mix) about 10 seconds (do not microwave). Cut off tip of 1 corner of packet with scissors. In small bowl, stir together cream cheese and about half of the glaze. Reserve remaining glaze for topping.

3. In medium bowl, stir Muffin Mix, milk, oil and eggs just until blended (batter may be lumpy). Place 1 tablespoonful of batter in each muffin cup. Top batter in each cup with about 1 teaspoon cream cheese mixture. Divide remaining batter among muffin cups (fill each about two-thirds full).

4. Bake 17 to 22 minutes or until golden brown and tops spring back when lightly touched. Cool 5 minutes; remove from pan. Cool 5 minutes longer. Drizzle remaining glaze over muffins; serve warm. Refrigerate any remaining muffins.

BETTY'S SUCCESS TIPS

- Use shiny muffin pans for golden and tender muffin crusts.
- For easy baking and cleanup, use paper baking cups.

1 SERVING (1 Muffin): Calories 230; Total Fat 10g (Saturated Fat 3g); Sodium 230mg; Total Carbohydrate 30g (Dietary Fiber 1g); Protein 4g; **Exchanges:** 1 Starch; 1 Other Carbohydrate; 2 Fat; **Carbohydrate Choices:** 2

Slow Cooker Creamy Ham and Wild Rice Soup

Give traditional wild rice soup a twist with this creamy ham version. It's in your slow cooker, filling the house with that mouthwatering aroma, in just 15 minutes.

PREP TIME: 15 MINUTES • **TOTAL TIME:** 7 HOURS 30 MINUTES • **MAKES 6 SERVINGS**

- 2 cups diced cooked ham
- 1 cup purchased julienne (matchstick-cut) carrots
- ¾ cup uncooked wild rice
- 1 medium onion, chopped (½ cup)
- 1¾ cups Progresso® chicken broth (from 32-ounce carton)
- 1 can (10.75 ounces) reduced-sodium cream of celery soup
- ¼ teaspoon pepper
- 3 cups water
- 1 cup half-and-half
- ¼ cup sliced almonds
- 2 tablespoons dry sherry, if desired
- ¼ cup chopped fresh parsley

1. Spray 3- to 4-quart slow cooker with cooking spray. In cooker, mix all ingredients except half-and-half, almonds, sherry and parsley.

2. Cover; cook on Low heat setting 7 to 8 hours.

3. Stir in remaining ingredients. Increase heat setting to High. Cover; cook 10 to 15 minutes longer or until hot.

BETTY'S SUCCESS TIPS

- For best results, we recommend you do not use canned or quick-cooking wild rice for this recipe.
- Look for a bag of julienne-cut carrots or French-cut cooking carrots in the refrigerated vegetable section of your grocery store.

1 SERVING: Calories 290; Total Fat 12g (Saturated Fat 5g); Sodium 1,190mg; Total Carbohydrate 28g (Dietary Fiber 3g); Protein 17g; **Exchanges:** 1½ Starch; ½ Other Carbohydrate; 2 Lean Meat; 1 Fat; **Carbohydrate Choices:** 2

Spring Arborio Rice and Chicken Soup

Looking for a delicious dinner? Then check out this rice and chicken soup that's ready in 50 minutes.

PREP TIME: 20 MINUTES • **TOTAL TIME:** 50 MINUTES • **MAKES 6 SERVINGS**

2 tablespoons olive or vegetable oil	6 cups ready-to-serve chicken broth
1 small onion, finely chopped ($^1/_4$ cup)	$^1/_4$ cup chopped fresh mint leaves
1 cup cubed cooked chicken	3 tablespoons chopped fresh parsley
1 cup uncooked Arborio or other short-grain rice	1 package (10 ounces) frozen green peas
	Freshly grated Parmesan cheese

1. Heat oil in Dutch oven over medium heat. Cook onion and chicken in oil, stirring frequently for about 5 minutes, or until onion is translucent.

2. Stir in rice. Cook 1 minute over medium heat, stirring frequently, until rice begins to brown. Pour $^1/_2$ cup of the broth over rice mixture. Cook uncovered, stirring frequently, until broth is absorbed. Continue cooking 15 to 20 minutes, adding broth $^1/_2$ cup at a time and stirring frequently, until rice is creamy and almost tender and 3 cups broth have been used.

3. Stir in remaining 3 cups broth, the mint, parsley and frozen peas. Cook over medium heat about 5 minutes or until hot. Serve with cheese.

BETTY'S SUCCESS TIP

Arborio is an Italian-grown rice and its high starch content gives risotto its creamy texture. Like pasta, it is cooked until al dente, meaning "to the tooth," so it isn't overcooked and soft.

1 SERVING: Calories 280; Total Fat 8g (Saturated Fat 1g); Sodium 1,110mg; Total Carbohydrate 36g (Dietary Fiber 3g); Protein 19g; **Exchanges:** 2 Starch; 1 Vegetable; 2 Lean Meat; **Carbohydrate Choices:** 2$^1/_2$

Leek and Potato Soup

This creamy, hearty soup is made with Progresso® chicken broth, refrigerated mashed potatoes and leeks—an easy, one-pot dinner recipe.

PREP TIME: 35 MINUTES • **TOTAL TIME:** 35 MINUTES • **MAKES 4 SERVINGS**

2 leeks
1 package (24 ounces) refrigerated country-style mashed potatoes
2 slices center-cut bacon
1 cup Progresso® reduced sodium chicken broth (from 32-ounce carton)

1/4 teaspoon salt
2 cups milk
1/4 teaspoon freshly ground pepper

1. Remove roots, outer leaves and tops from leeks, leaving only white part. Cut white part in half lengthwise. Cut crosswise into 1/2-inch-thick slices to measure 1 cup. Rinse with cold water; drain.

2. Microwave potatoes as directed on package. Meanwhile, in 3-quart saucepan, cook bacon until crisp; drain on paper towels. Crumble bacon; set aside. Cook leeks in bacon drippings over medium heat 3 minutes, adding 2 tablespoons of the broth to prevent sticking. Cook 4 minutes longer, stirring occasionally, until tender.

3. Stir in remaining broth, scraping pan to loosen brown particles. Stir in potatoes and salt. Gradually add milk, stirring until smooth. Cook uncovered 10 minutes, stirring occasionally, until thoroughly heated. Stir in pepper. Sprinkle individual servings with bacon.

1 SERVING: Calories 240; Total Fat 8g (Saturated Fat 5g); Sodium 620mg; Total Carbohydrate 34g (Dietary Fiber 4g); Protein 9g; **Exchanges:** 1 1/2 Starch; 1/2 Low-Fat Milk; 1 Vegetable; 1 Fat; **Carbohydrate Choices:** 2

Asparagus Soup with Brie Bruschetta

Creamy and delicious describe this fresh asparagus soup blended with Progresso® chicken broth. Serve with crusty bread slices topped and broiled with buttery Brie for a delightful meal.

PREP TIME: 45 MINUTES • **TOTAL TIME:** 45 MINUTES • **MAKES 6 SERVINGS**

Asparagus Soup

- 1 1/2 pounds fresh asparagus, cut into 1/2-inch pieces
- 2 tablespoons extra-virgin olive oil
- 1 tablespoon unsalted butter
- 1 tablespoon minced garlic
- 1 cup diced onion
- 1/2 cup diced celery
- 1 carton (32 ounces) Progresso® reduced sodium chicken broth (4 cups)
- 2 teaspoons finely chopped fresh thyme leaves
- 2 cups loosely packed spinach
- 2 teaspoons freshly grated lemon peel
- 1 cup whipping (heavy) cream or buttermilk (if using buttermilk, cut the lemon peel in half)
- 1/2 teaspoon gray sea salt
- 1/4 teaspoon freshly ground black pepper

Gremolata

- 2 tablespoons butter
- 1/2 cup Progresso® Italian style panko crispy bread crumbs
- 2 tablespoons chopped fresh Italian (flat-leaf) parsley
- Grated peel of 1 medium orange

Bruschetta

- 1/4 cup butter, softened
- 1 loaf crusty French or Italian bread, sliced
- 1 pound Brie cheese, sliced

1. Snap off ends from asparagus and peel any tough skin from the stalks; set aside.

2. In 3-quart saucepan, heat oil and 1 tablespoon unsalted butter over medium-high heat until hot. Add garlic to oil and butter; cook until light brown. Add onion and celery; reduce heat to medium and cook 10 minutes, stirring occasionally, until vegetables are tender.

3. Meanwhile, make the gremolata. In 8-inch skillet, melt 2 tablespoons butter over medium heat. Add bread crumbs to butter; cook until lightly browned, stirring frequently; transfer to small bowl. Stir in the parsley and orange peel; set aside.

4. In saucepan, add asparagus, broth and thyme to vegetable mixture. Heat to boiling; cook about 3 minutes or until asparagus is tender. Stir in spinach and lemon peel (the spinach will wilt in the soup). Pour soup into blender in small batches; cover and puree each batch until smooth. (The soup can be made ahead to this point, cooled, covered, and refrigerated for up to 1 day or frozen for up to 1 month.)

5. Return soup to saucepan and heat over low heat until hot. Stir in the whipping cream, salt and pepper. Ladle into warm bowls. Sprinkle soup with 1 teaspoon gremolata. Pass the remaining gremolata at the table.

6. Set oven control to broil. To make bruschetta, butter bread slices on both sides and top each with several slices of Brie (2 to 3 ounces per bread slice). Broil with tops about 5 inches from heat until cheese is bubbly and slightly browned.

1 SERVING: Calories 880; Total Fat 57g (Saturated Fat 32g); Sodium 1,780mg; Total Carbohydrate 60g (Dietary Fiber 5g); Protein 31g; **Exchanges:** 3 Starch; 2 1/2 Vegetable; 2 1/2 High-Fat Meat; 7 Fat; **Carbohydrate Choices:** 4

Penne and Ham Primavera

Leftover ham goes Italian in this 25-minute meal for four.

PREP TIME: 10 MINUTES • **TOTAL TIME:** 25 MINUTES • **MAKES 4 SERVINGS**

2 cups uncooked penne or mostaccioli pasta (6 ounces)
1 cup sliced zucchini
1 cup sliced yellow summer squash
2 cups cubed fully cooked ham

1/2 cup reduced-fat Italian dressing
1/4 cup chopped fresh basil leaves
1/3 cup shredded Parmesan cheese
Coarsely ground pepper, if desired

1. Cook pasta as directed on package, adding zucchini and yellow squash during last 3 to 4 minutes of cooking; drain.

2. Return pasta mixture to saucepan; add ham and dressing. Cook over medium heat, stirring occasionally, until hot. Sprinkle with basil, cheese and pepper.

BETTY'S SUCCESS TIPS

- We recommend reduced-fat Italian dressing because it clings very well to the pasta, vegetables and ham. In regular Italian dressing, the herbs and spices often separate and sink to the bottom of the bottle.
- Select small zucchini, which are younger, more tender and have thinner skins. Look for skins that are blemish free with a vibrant color.

1 SERVING: Calories 390; Total Fat 14g (Saturated Fat 4g); Sodium 1,360mg; Total Carbohydrate 43g (Dietary Fiber 3g); Protein 26g; **Exchanges:** 2 Starch; 3 Vegetable; 2 Lean Meat; 1 Fat; **Carbohydrate Choices:** 3

Easy Ham and Noodles

With this one-dish meal for four, supper's on the table in 20!

PREP TIME: 20 MINUTES • **TOTAL TIME:** 20 MINUTES • **MAKES 4 SERVINGS**

1 can (14 ounces) chicken broth
1 cup water
3 cups uncooked dumpling egg noodles (5 ounces)

2 boxes (10 ounces each) Green Giant® frozen broccoli, cauliflower, carrots & cheese flavored sauce
2 cups cubed ($\frac{1}{2}$ inch) cooked ham

1. In 3-quart saucepan, heat broth and water to boiling. Add noodles; return to boiling. Reduce heat to medium-low; cook 8 to 10 minutes or until noodles are tender and most of liquid is absorbed, stirring occasionally (do not drain).

2. Meanwhile, cook vegetables as directed on box.

3. Gently stir vegetables in cheese sauce and ham into noodle mixture. Cook over medium-low heat 3 to 4 minutes or until hot, stirring occasionally.

BETTY'S SUCCESS TIP

To save time, look for cubed cooked ham near the lunchmeat products at the supermarket.

1 SERVING: Calories 350; Total Fat 10g (Saturated Fat 3$\frac{1}{2}$g); Sodium 1,960mg; Total Carbohydrate 38g (Dietary Fiber 4g); Protein 25g; **Exchanges:** 2 Starch; 1 Vegetable; 2$\frac{1}{2}$ Lean Meat; $\frac{1}{2}$ Fat; **Carbohydrate Choices:** 2$\frac{1}{2}$

Lemony Leeks and Pasta Salad

Far from ordinary, this salad will impress with its flavorful combination of ingredients.

PREP TIME: 35 MINUTES • **TOTAL TIME:** 1 HOUR 35 MINUTES • **MAKES 8 SERVINGS**

1 large lemon
3 tablespoons olive or vegetable oil
1 cup slivered almonds
3 cups sliced leeks (about 4 leeks)
3 tablespoons capers, drained
$1/_2$ teaspoon salt

$1/_8$ teaspoon pepper
1 large red bell pepper, roasted, cut into strips
1 large yellow bell pepper, roasted, cut into strips
8 ounces (3 $1/_2$ cups) uncooked bow-tie (farfalle) pasta

1. Remove peel from lemon, using zester or grater; set aside. Cut white pith from lemon; discard. Cut lemon into $1/_4$-inch slices; set aside.

2. In 10-inch skillet, heat oil over medium-high heat until hot. Cook and stir almonds in oil about 30 seconds or until light brown. With slotted spoon, remove almonds from skillet; set aside.

3. In same skillet, cook and stir lemon slices, lemon peel, leeks, capers, salt and pepper about 1 minute or until vegetables are crisp-tender. Remove from heat. Remove lemon slices; discard. Stir in bell peppers and almonds. Cover; refrigerate at least 2 hours until chilled.

4. Cook pasta to desired doneness as directed on package. Drain; rinse with cold water to cool. In large serving bowl, gently toss pasta, vegetable mixture and almonds.

BETTY'S SUCCESS TIPS

- Leeks look like giant green onions and are related to both onions and garlic. Choose leeks that are firm and brightly colored, with an unblemished white bulb portion. Smaller leeks will be more tender than larger ones.
- Two 7.25-ounce jars (2 cups) roasted red bell peppers, drained, can be substituted for the roasted red and yellow peppers.

1 SERVING: Calories 290; Total Fat 13g (Saturated Fat $1^1/_2$g); Sodium 350mg; Total Carbohydrate 35g (Dietary Fiber 4g); Protein 8g; **Exchanges:** 2 Starch; 1 Vegetable; $2^1/_2$ Fat; **Carbohydrate Choices:** 2

Ham and Cheddar Torta

Brunch? Serve ham, Cheddar and veggies baked in an easy press-in-the-pan crust.

PREP TIME: 20 MINUTES • **TOTAL TIME:** 1 HOUR 45 MINUTES • **MAKES 6 TO 8 SERVINGS**

1¹⁄₃ cups Original Bisquick® mix
   1 can (15 ounces) Progresso® cannellini beans, drained, rinsed and mashed
 ¹⁄₃ cup Italian dressing
1¹⁄₂ cups diced cooked ham
   1 box (9 ounces) Green Giant® frozen cut broccoli, thawed, drained

1 cup shredded Cheddar cheese (4 ounces)
1 cup milk
2 tablespoons Original Bisquick® mix
3 eggs, slightly beaten

1. Heat oven to 375°F. In small bowl, stir together 1¹⁄₃ cups Bisquick mix, the beans and dressing. Spread in bottom and 2 inches up side of ungreased 9 x 3-inch springform pan. Bake 10 to 12 minutes or until set.

2. Layer ham, broccoli and cheese over crust. In small bowl, stir milk, 2 tablespoons Bisquick mix and the eggs until blended; pour over cheese.

3. Bake 55 to 60 minutes or until golden brown and knife inserted near center comes out clean. Let stand 10 minutes. Loosen edge of torta from side of pan; remove side of pan.

BETTY'S SUCCESS TIP

Bake the crust the day before and store covered in the refrigerator. Or make the torta completely the day before, store covered in the refrigerator and reheat loosely covered in 375°F oven 15 to 20 minutes or until hot.

1 SERVING: Calories 430; Total Fat 19g (Saturated Fat 8g); Sodium 1,160mg; Total Carbohydrate 39g (Dietary Fiber 5g); Protein 26g; **Exchanges:** 1¹⁄₂ Starch; 1 Other Carbohydrate; ¹⁄₂ Fat; **Carbohydrate Choices:** 2¹⁄₂

Spinach and Ham French Bread Pizza

Looking for a hearty Italian dinner? Then check out this delicious spinach and ham pizza made with French bread—ready in 30 minutes.

PREP TIME: 20 MINUTES • **TOTAL TIME:** 30 MINUTES • **MAKES 6 SERVINGS**

1 loaf (1 pound) French bread
3 tablespoons olive or vegetable oil
1 can (8 ounces) pizza sauce
1 cup chopped cooked ham
1 small onion, chopped (¼ cup)

2 tablespoons pine nuts
2 cups chopped fresh spinach (about 2 ounces)
12 slices (1 ounce each) provolone cheese, cut in half

1. Heat oven to 400°F. Cut loaf of bread in half horizontally; cut each half crosswise into thirds. Place cut sides up on ungreased large cookie sheet; brush with oil. Bake 5 to 6 minutes or until tops are slightly toasted. Remove from oven.

2. Spread pizza sauce evenly over cut sides of each piece of bread. Top evenly with ham, onion, nuts and spinach. Place 4 half slices of cheese on top of each.

3. Bake 7 to 10 minutes or until cheese is melted and pizza is hot.

BETTY'S SUCCESS TIPS

- This recipe is a great way to use up leftover ham. Or look for packaged chopped, cooked ham near packaged deli meats and bacon at your grocery store.
- Pine nuts, which have a high fat content, can turn rancid quickly. Store them in an airtight container in the refrigerator up to 3 months or in the freezer up to 9 months.

1 SERVING: Calories 560; Total Fat 27g (Saturated Fat 12g); Sodium 1,400mg; Total Carbohydrate 49g (Dietary Fiber 3g); Protein 30g; **Exchanges:** 2½ Starch; ½ Other Carbohydrate; ½ Vegetable; 3 Lean Meat; 3½ Fat; **Carbohydrate Choices:** 3

Ham and Egg Salad Sandwiches

Try a Betty Crocker sandwich recipe.

PREP TIME: 20 MINUTES • **TOTAL TIME:** 20 MINUTES • **MAKES 4 SANDWICHES**

$^1/_2$ cup chopped fully cooked ham
$^1/_2$ cup chopped broccoli florets
$^1/_2$ cup chopped celery
$^1/_2$ cup mayonnaise or salad dressing
1 tablespoon chopped fresh chives

2 teaspoons chopped fresh or $^3/_4$ teaspoon dried marjoram leaves
$^1/_4$ teaspoon onion salt
3 hard-cooked eggs, chopped
Lettuce leaves
8 slices herb or whole wheat bread

1. In medium bowl, mix all ingredients except lettuce and bread.

2. Place lettuce leaf on 4 of the bread slices. Spoon egg mixture onto lettuce. Top with remaining bread.

BETTY'S SUCCESS TIP

Need a foolproof way to hard-cook eggs? It's easy. Just place eggs in saucepan, and add cold water to cover eggs by 1 inch. Cover; heat to boiling. Remove from heat; let stand covered 15 minutes. Drain. Immediately cool in cold water. Tap egg to crack the shell, roll between hands to loosen, then peel.

1 SERVING (1 Sandwich): Calories 440; Total Fat 29g (Saturated Fat 5g); Sodium 840mg; Total Carbohydrate 29g (Dietary Fiber 4g); Protein 15g; **Exchanges:** 2 Starch; 4 Fat; **Carbohydrate Choices:** 2

Spring Gathering for a Crowd

A shower event, a prom party, a graduation, a farewell or just a friendly get-together demands lots of good food. Follow this make-ahead menu planned for 20 people, and you'll be able to enjoy the party, too!

THAT SPECIAL SOMEONE

- For a special loved one who is moving or for a celebrated individual, place a photo in a 6-inch or wider mat. Have party attendees autograph the mat and send well wishes. After the party, frame the matted photo for a lifetime keepsake.
- Place disposable cameras about the party scene. Guests can capture the moments for you to later compile in a memory book for the star of the party.
- Request guests bring a written memory of the honored individual to be shared with everyone at a planned time. This can replace gifts.

SERVE WITH STYLE

- Buffet service frees the host. Consider using several small tables for a cozier feel. Group desserts on one table, beverages on another.
- Hire high school or college students to serve appetizers for a special touch, or just have them replenish the tables and free yourself to mingle.

DECORATIONS

- Choose a color scheme that fits your party. Check out party stores for paper supplies or linen outlets for less-expensive table linens. Buy inexpensive rubber stamps, and stamp linens or paper if you can't find ready-made themed ware.
- Scatter candles throughout the party area, or string fun lights to match the decor.
- Make a flag to hang outside your home to represent the event. Use colored felts and a wooden dowel found at craft stores.

MENU IDEAS

Sparkling Citrus Punch for a Crowd **154**

Springtime Ham and Egg Bake **111**

Do-Ahead Chicken-Leek Strata **164**

Slow Cooker Southwest Artichoke and Spinach Dip **148**

Elegant Tossed Salad **182**

Festive Fruit Platter **153**

Praline Mini Cakes **193**

Tiramisu Bites **201**

Pistachio Fudge Cups **191**

Smoked Turkey and Creamy Artichoke Sandwiches

Turkey, lettuce and veggies layered between bread slices flavored with artichoke dip makes creamy sandwiches ready in 10 minutes.

PREP TIME: 10 MINUTES • **TOTAL TIME:** 10 MINUTES • **MAKES 4 SANDWICHES**

8 slices marble-rye bread	4 thin slices onion
1/2 cup refrigerated artichoke dip	8 thin slices tomato
1/2 pound thinly sliced smoked turkey (from deli)	4 leaves lettuce

On each of 4 slices bread, spread 2 tablespoons artichoke dip. Layer each with turkey, onion, tomato, lettuce and remaining bread.

BETTY'S SUCCESS TIPS

- Feel free to toast the bread first before assembling the sandwiches.
- Substitute your favorite whole grain or white bread for the rye.

1 SERVING (1 Sandwich): Calories 260; Total Fat 8g (Saturated Fat 3¹/₂g); Sodium 1,230mg; Total Carbohydrate 30g (Dietary Fiber 3g); Protein 16g; **Exchanges:** 2 Starch; ¹/₂ Vegetable 1¹/₂ Lean Meat; ¹/₂ Fat; **Carbohydrate Choices:** 2

Fresh Crab Rolls

Enjoy these crab rolls that are made with yogurt and Progresso® artichoke hearts—a tasty dinner.

PREP TIME: 20 MINUTES • **TOTAL TIME:** 50 MINUTES • **MAKES 6 ROLLS**

1 container (6 ounces) fat-free plain Greek yogurt

3 tablespoons mayonnaise

2 teaspoons chopped fresh tarragon leaves

$1/2$ teaspoon salt

2 cloves garlic, crushed

1 pound fresh Dungeness or white crabmeat, separated into bite-size pieces

1 jar (6 ounces) Progresso® marinated artichoke hearts, drained, chopped

$1/2$ cup chopped celery

$1/4$ cup chopped green onions (4 medium)

1 tablespoon butter, melted

6 brioche or Parker House rolls, split

6 leaves Bibb or butter lettuce

6 lime wedges, if desired

1. In large bowl, mix yogurt, mayonnaise, tarragon, salt and garlic. Stir until well blended. Stir in crab, artichoke hearts, celery and green onions. Cover and refrigerate about 30 minutes to blend flavors.

2. Heat 10-inch skillet over medium-high heat. Brush melted butter on cut sides of rolls. Place cut sides down in skillet; cook about 2 minutes or until toasted.

3. Place rolls on plates; fill with lettuce and crab mixture. Serve with lime wedges.

1 SERVING (1 Crab Roll): Calories 450; Total Fat 20g (Saturated Fat 5g); Sodium 760mg; Total Carbohydrate 43g (Dietary Fiber 2g); Protein 23g; **Exchanges:** $2^{1}/_2$ Starch; $1/2$ Vegetable; 2 Very Lean Meat; $3^{1}/_2$ Fat; **Carbohydrate Choices:** 3

Ham and Cheese Chex® Mix

This salty, cheesy mix was inspired by famous Virginia cured hams.

PREP TIME: 15 MINUTES • **TOTAL TIME:** 15 MINUTES • **MAKES 16 SERVINGS**

6 cups Multi-Bran Chex® cereal	1 teaspoon seasoned salt
2 tablespoons butter or margarine	1 cup cubed cooked ham
1 tablespoon Dijon mustard	4 ounces Swiss cheese, cut into
1 tablespoon honey	¼ x 1-inch sticks

1. In large microwavable bowl, place cereal.

2. In 1-cup microwavable measuring cup, microwave butter, mustard, honey and salt uncovered on High 30 to 40 seconds or until butter is melted and mixture is hot; stir.

3. Pour over cereal, stirring until evenly coated. Microwave uncovered on High 3 to 4 minutes, stirring after every minute.

4. Spread on waxed paper or foil to cool. When mixture is cool, stir in ham and cheese. Store covered in refrigerator.

BETTY'S SUCCESS TIP

Cheddar cheese can be substituted for the Swiss cheese.

1 SERVING: Calories 160; Total Fat 5g (Saturated Fat 2½g); Sodium 400mg; Total Carbohydrate 21g (Dietary Fiber 3g); Protein 6g; **Exchanges:** 1 Starch; ½ Other Carbohydrate; ½ High-Fat Meat; **Carbohydrate Choices:** 1½

Spiced Nuts 'n Chex® Mix

Chili powder and red pepper spice up a party-perfect mix that's ready for munching in 15 minutes!

PREP TIME: 10 MINUTES • **TOTAL TIME:** 10 MINUTES • **MAKES 16 SERVINGS**

¼ cup sugar	2 cups Corn Chex® cereal
1 tablespoon chili powder	2 cups Rice Chex® cereal
¼ teaspoon ground red pepper (cayenne)	2 cups Wheat Chex® cereal
¼ cup butter or margarine	1 can (11.5 ounces) mixed nuts

1. In small bowl, mix sugar, chili powder and red pepper.

2. In large microwavable bowl, microwave butter uncovered on High about 40 seconds or until melted. Stir in cereal and nuts until evenly coated. Stir in sugar mixture until evenly coated.

3. Microwave uncovered on High 4 to 5 minutes, stirring after 2 minutes, until mixture just begins to brown. Spread on waxed paper to cool. Store in airtight container.

BETTY'S SUCCESS TIP

You can use your favorite combo of Chex® cereals that adds up to 6 cups.

1 SERVING: Calories 230; Total Fat 14g (Saturated Fat 3g); Sodium 290mg; Total Carbohydrate 21g (Dietary Fiber 3g); Protein 5g; **Exchanges:** 1½ Starch; 2½ Fat; **Carbohydrate Choices:** 1½

Muffuletta Slices

Feed a crowd in 15 minutes! Sandwich slices are bursting with salami, roasted red peppers and artichoke hearts.

PREP TIME: 15 MINUTES • **TOTAL TIME:** 15 MINUTES • **MAKES 18 SERVINGS**

1 baguette French bread (16 ounces; about 20 inches long), cut in half horizontally

1/4 cup chives-and-onion cream cheese spread (from 8-ounce container)

1 jar (6 1/2 ounces) marinated artichoke hearts, well drained, patted dry and finely chopped

1/4 cup basil pesto

1/2 cup roasted red bell peppers (from 12-ounce jar), patted dry, cut into 1 1/2-inch strips

1/4 pound thinly sliced salami
    Assorted large pitted kalamata and pimiento-stuffed green olives, if desired

1. Remove some of soft bread from center of top half of baguette to make a long, narrow well. If desired, cut off about 1/2 inch of pointed ends of baguette.

2. In small bowl, mix cream cheese spread and artichokes. Generously spread mixture in long, narrow well in top half of baguette. Spread pesto over cream cheese mixture.

3. Place roasted pepper strips on bottom half of baguette. Fold salami slices in half; layer diagonally over peppers, overlapping slices slightly.

4. Place top half of baguette, pesto side down, over salami; press halves together well. Thread olives onto toothpicks or cocktail picks; insert toothpicks through all layers at 1-inch intervals. Cut between toothpicks into 18 slices.

BETTY'S SUCCESS TIPS

- This appetizer loaf can be assembled several hours ahead. Wrap it tightly in plastic wrap and refrigerate until you're ready to cut and serve.
- Substitute thinly sliced turkey or other deli meat for the salami, if you like.

1 SERVING: Calories 140; Total Fat 6g (Saturated Fat 2g); Sodium 380mg; Total Carbohydrate 16g (Dietary Fiber 1g); Protein 5g; **Exchanges:** 1 Starch; 1 Fat; **Carbohydrate Choices:** 1

Artichoke 'n Bacon Crescent Squares

Tasty fresh veggies and crisp bacon add to the flavorful toppings in a crowd-pleasing easy appetizer.

PREP TIME: 20 MINUTES • **TOTAL TIME:** 1 HOUR 5 MINUTES • **MAKES 32 APPETIZERS**

2 cans (8 ounces each) refrigerated seamless crescent dough sheet

1 package (8 ounces) cream cheese, softened

¼ cup shredded Parmesan cheese

1 tablespoon chopped fresh parsley

1 tablespoon mayonnaise or salad dressing

1 cup chopped fresh spinach

2 jars (6 to 7 ounces each) marinated artichoke hearts, drained, coarsely chopped

6 slices bacon, crisply cooked, crumbled

1 cup seeded, diced roma (plum) tomatoes

½ cup diced red bell pepper

1. Heat oven to 375°F. Unroll both cans of dough. Place in ungreased 15 x 10 x 1-inch pan, long sides overlapping to fit pan. Press in bottom and up sides of pan to form crust.

2. Bake 10 to 15 minutes or until golden brown. Cool completely, about 30 minutes.

3. In small bowl, beat cream cheese, Parmesan cheese, parsley and mayonnaise with electric mixer on medium speed until smooth. Spread over cooled crust. Top with remaining ingredients. Serve immediately, or cover and refrigerate up to 2 hours. Cut into 8 rows by 4 rows.

BETTY'S SUCCESS TIP

It's easy to vary the toppings. Add olives and chopped fresh basil for a different twist.

1 SERVING (1 Appetizer): Calories 100; Total Fat 6g (Saturated Fat 3g); Sodium 210mg; Total Carbohydrate 8g (Dietary Fiber 0g); Protein 2g; **Exchanges:** ½ Starch; 1 Fat; **Carbohydrate Choices:** ½

Family-Friendly Fat Tuesday Fun

Give Old Man Winter a nudge with a fun little get-together that can be enjoyed by young and old alike. Whether enjoyed with other neighborhood families or as a family gathering—even for a birthday—this Mardi Gras Carnival celebration is full of surprises!

THE SKINNY ON FAT TUESDAY

- If there's a French speaker in your house, then he or she can tell you that *Mardi* translates to "Tuesday" and *gras* to "fat," giving the origin of the term *Mardi Gras*.
- Parts of the United States originally settled by the French or Spanish—like Louisiana and Alabama—were the first to have celebrations of Mardi Gras. This day prior to Ash Wednesday, the beginning of the Christian season of Lent—46 days before Easter—became a day to eat decadently one more time. During Lent, many Christians fast—refrain from eating meat certain days of the week or rich foods containing eggs, sugar, butter and milk—so the day before Lent starts is one to use up those foods.
- Now, many U.S. cities have Mardi Gras Carnival festivities not only on Fat Tuesday but anytime following the Twelfth Night after Christmas. It's the kind of party that's a cure for the wintertime blues or, as they say in New Orleans, a chance to let the good times roll!
- Other countries call this day by other names such as Shrove Tuesday, Carnival, Fastnacht and many more! If your family's roots are in one of them, explore and celebrate with traditional foods and fun.

MARDI GRAS FAMILY FUN

- Search for family events that are a part of many cities' Mardi Gras festivities. What a fun outing for the family!
- Put kids to work fashioning paper plate masks. Cut eyeholes and attach ribbon for tying on or tape on bamboo sticks for handheld masks before the decorating starts. Supply mask makers with colored paper, stickers, beads and feathers along with scissors and glue. Give several prizes: Most Creative, Best Use of Supplies, Most Ferocious, etc.
- If children have enjoyed big parades like those held in Mardi Gras cities, decorating shoebox floats and staging their own parade can be fun. Give them a variety of craft supplies to work with. Again, prizes are part of the fun!
- Use a doll that represents the baby hidden in the famous King Cake, a Mardi Gras tradition, to play a version of the "hot potato" game.
- Have a scavenger hunt with beads, doubloons and candy hidden throughout the house.

MENU IDEAS

Spiced Nuts 'n Chex® Mix **144**

Chili powder and red pepper spice up a party-perfect mix that's ready for munching in 15 minutes!

Cajun Black Beans with Sausage and Corn **161**

Grab a skillet for easy Cajun cooking! This one-pan meal can be ready to serve in less than 30 minutes.

Corn muffins

Springtime Sprinkles Cake **183**

Easy to decorate in no time! It's delicious, too.

Slow Cooker Southwest Artichoke and Spinach Dip

Standard spinach-artichoke dip gets a Mexican makeover with the addition of chopped green chiles and pepper Jack cheese.

PREP TIME: 10 MINUTES • **TOTAL TIME:** 2 HOURS 15 MINUTES • **MAKES 26 SERVINGS**

- 1 can (14 ounces) artichoke hearts, drained, coarsely chopped
- 1 box (9 ounces) Green Giant® frozen spinach, thawed, squeezed to drain
- 1 package (8 ounces) cream cheese, cubed, softened
- 1 can (4.5 ounces) Old El Paso® chopped green chiles, undrained
- $1/2$ medium red bell pepper, chopped (about $1/2$ cup)
- $1/2$ cup shredded pepper Jack cheese (2 ounces)
- 1 bag (14 ounces) round tortilla chips

1. Spray 1- to $1^1/_2$-quart slow cooker with cooking spray. In medium bowl, mix all ingredients except pepper Jack cheese and tortilla chips; spoon into cooker.

2. Cover; cook on Low heat setting 2 to 3 hours.

3. Stir pepper Jack cheese into artichoke mixture. Cover; cook on Low heat setting about 5 minutes longer or until cheese is melted. Serve with tortilla chips.

BETTY'S SUCCESS TIPS

- Drained, roasted red bell peppers can be substituted for the fresh bell pepper.
- This tasty twist on spinach and artichoke dip can also be served with slices of French bread.

1 SERVING: Calories 130; Total Fat 7g (Saturated Fat 3g); Sodium 150mg; Total Carbohydrate 12g (Dietary Fiber 2g); Protein 2g; **Exchanges:** 1 Starch; 1 Fat; **Carbohydrate Choices:** 1

Black-Eyed Pea and Ham Dip

This easy black-eyed pea and ham dip with tomato, green onions and parsley pairs perfectly with corn chips for a tasty appetizer—ready in just 25 minutes.

PREP TIME: 25 MINUTES • **TOTAL TIME:** 25 MINUTES • **MAKES 24 SERVINGS**

$\frac{1}{2}$ cup diced cooked ham

2 cans (15 ounces each) black-eyed peas, drained, rinsed

$\frac{3}{4}$ cup water

1 large tomato, finely chopped (1 cup)

2 medium green onions, sliced (2 tablespoons)

1 stalk celery, finely chopped ($\frac{1}{2}$ cup)

$\frac{1}{4}$ cup chopped fresh parsley

2 tablespoons olive oil

1 to 2 tablespoons cider vinegar

Corn chips, if desired

1. Spray large skillet with cooking spray; heat over medium-high heat. Add ham; cook 3 to 5 minutes, stirring frequently, until lightly browned. Stir in black-eyed peas and water. Reduce heat to medium; cook 8 minutes, stirring occasionally, until liquid is reduced by three-fourths. Partially mash peas with back of spoon to desired consistency.

2. In small bowl, stir together tomato, onions, celery, parsley, oil and vinegar.

3. Spoon warm pea mixture into serving dish; top with tomato mixture. Serve with corn chips.

1 SERVING: Calories 50; Total Fat: 1$\frac{1}{2}$g (Saturated Fat 0g); Sodium 120mg; Total Carbohydrate 6g (Dietary Fiber 1g); Protein 2g; **Exchanges:** $\frac{1}{2}$ Starch; **Carbohydrate Choices:** 1$\frac{1}{2}$

Smoky Deviled Eggs

Serve your guests these delicious stuffed eggs ready in 25 minutes—perfect for appetizers.

PREP TIME: 25 MINUTES • **TOTAL TIME:** 25 MINUTES • **MAKES 24 SERVINGS**

12 hard-cooked eggs	$1/4$ teaspoon salt
$1/3$ cup mayonnaise	$1/4$ teaspoon pepper
2 medium green onions, chopped (2 tablespoons)	$1/4$ teaspoon smoked paprika
1 teaspoon Dijon mustard	3 slices bacon, crisply cooked, crumbled ($1/4$ cup)
1 teaspoon lemon juice	24 sliced ripe olives (from 2.25-ounce can), chopped

1. Peel eggs; cut lengthwise in half. Slip out yolks into medium bowl; set egg whites aside. Mash yolks with fork until smooth; stir in mayonnaise, 1 tablespoon of the onion, the mustard, lemon juice, salt, pepper and paprika.

2. Fill egg white halves with egg yolk mixture, heaping lightly. Sprinkle with bacon, olives and remaining 1 tablespoon onion. Serve immediately, or cover and refrigerate up to 24 hours.

BETTY'S SUCCESS TIP

Look for peeled hard-cooked eggs in the grocery store dairy case.

1 SERVING: Calories 70; Total Fat 6g (Saturated Fat $1^1/2$g); Sodium 127mg; Total Carbohydrate $1/2$g (Dietary Fiber 0g); Protein $3^1/2$g; **Exchanges:** $1/2$ Fat; **Carbohydrate Choices:** 0

Cheese and Fruit Plate

Turn an ordinary cheese and fruit tray into something more memorable with the addition of a chewy and nutty fig spread.

PREP TIME: 15 MINUTES • **TOTAL TIME:** 15 MINUTES • **MAKES 18 SERVINGS**

Fig Spread

- 1 **bag (9 ounces) dried Mission figs (about 24 medium figs), chopped**
- 1 **bag (2.5 ounces) hazelnuts (filberts), chopped (about $1/3$ cup)**
- 1 **jar (12 ounces) apricot preserves**

Cheese and Fruit

- 1 **piece (8 ounces) Gouda cheese**
- 1 **piece (8 ounces) blue cheese**
- 1 **round (8 ounces) Brie cheese**
- 1 **container (1 pound) fresh strawberries (about 24)**
- 1 **bag (7 ounces) dried apricots**
- 64 **whole wheat crackers**
  Fresh parsley sprigs

1. In small serving bowl, mix spread ingredients until blended.

2. To serve, place cheeses on decorative platter; surround with strawberries, apricots and crackers. Garnish with parsley sprigs. Serve with fig spread.

BETTY'S SUCCESS TIPS

- Don't like figs? Serve with your favorite specialty jelly or jam.
- The fig mixture can be made up to 3 days ahead; store it in an airtight container in the refrigerator. Just remember to bring it to room temperature before serving.

1 SERVING: Calories 330; Total Fat 14g (Saturated Fat 7g); Sodium 460mg; Total Carbohydrate 40g (Dietary Fiber 4g); Protein 11g; **Exchanges:** 1 Starch; 1 Fruit; $1/2$ Other Carbohydrate; 1 High-Fat Meat; 1 Fat; **Carbohydrate Choices:** $2^{1}/_{2}$

Hosting a Cheese Tasting

Turn a boring appetizer platter with some chunks of hastily arranged cheese into something special. Let a cheese tasting take an evening with friends in an exciting direction. You'll not only enjoy your friends, you'll enlighten them.

Discover just how to organize the cheese tasting and weigh up the differences in the cheeses you choose to taste. And, naturally, we have some easy ideas for hosting tasting parties with all kinds of themes, any time of year!

CHEESE 101

- Take time to learn about cheese. Our "All About Cheese" (http://www.bettycrocker.com/how-to/tipslibrary /ingredients/all-about-cheese) is one way. Attending a class or reading up on cheese from a book or online is another.
- Decide what cheese you think your guests would enjoy and like to learn about. One variety, from different places? Cheese from your favorite part of the world—or where you'd love to travel? Make choices by the season: Cheddars in the fall, blue-veined cheese in winter, chèvre (goat) cheese in warmer months.
- Create a well-balanced cheese plate with three varieties of cheese, chosen for appearance, taste and texture. Include at least one sure to be enjoyed by even the pickiest of eaters.
- Try the wonderful artisan cheeses available at reasonable prices in groceries, specialty shops, at farmers' markets and online.

HOW MUCH IS ENOUGH?

- Plan to serve 1 to 2 ounces of cheese per guest for appetizers, 2 to 3 ounces per guest for heartier eating—when cheese and its accompaniments replace a meal.
- If your guest list isn't too large, plan these tastings for your dining table. Cheeses can be portioned out on large dinner plates, tasted in order from mildest to most pungent. Add some of the accompaniments and have others to pass. This plan makes it easier to have a discussion and share what you've learned about the cheese chosen.
- For a more informal tasting buffet, arrange cheese with creative food label cards naming them and their characteristics. Provide a separate serving knife or cutter for each type of cheese.

TASTING NOTES

- Most cheeses should stand at room temperature for 30 minutes to an hour before serving. Keep covered until serving to prevent drying out.
- Compare each cheese based on these five characteristics:
  - Appearance/Aroma: first impression of the look and smell before tasting.
  - Texture: the feel of the cheese in your mouth as you chew it.
  - Flavor: the total impression of aroma and texture combined with the flavors you discover as your taste buds are stimulated. Identify specific taste attributes: earthy, buttery, sharp, caramel-like, nutty, milky, peppery, herbal, tart, pungent, grassy and smoky flavors.
  - Finish: the flavors that remain after tasting. The big question: Do you like it?

Festive Fruit Platter

Have a big party coming up? Keep dessert simple by serving this eye-catching platter of fresh fruit and a sour cream dip.

PREP TIME: 35 MINUTES • **TOTAL TIME:** 35 MINUTES • **MAKES 32 SERVINGS**

2 pounds seedless green or red grapes, cut into small bunches

2 pints strawberries (4 cups)

1 honeydew melon, peeled and sliced

1 cantaloupe, peeled and sliced

6 medium apricots, pitted and cut in half

4 medium kiwifruit, peeled and sliced

2 cups sour cream

1/2 cup packed brown sugar

Fresh white currants, if desired

1. Arrange fruit on large platter.

2. Mix sour cream and brown sugar. Garnish with currants. Serve with fruit.

BETTY'S SUCCESS TIPS

- The sour cream-brown sugar "dip" will keep for about a week when refrigerated.
- Go with the seasons! Vary the fruit you use depending on what looks good in the grocery store or at the farmers' market.

1 SERVING: Calories 90; Total Fat 3g (Saturated Fat 2g); Sodium 15mg; Total Carbohydrate 17g (Dietary Fiber 2g); Protein 1g; **Exchanges:** 1 Fruit; 1/2 Fat; **Carbohydrate Choices:** 1

Sparkling Citrus Punch for a Crowd

Easy to make, this recipe makes plenty—enough to quench the thirst of a large gathering of friends and family!

PREP TIME: 5 MINUTES • **TOTAL TIME:** 5 MINUTES • **MAKES 30 SERVINGS**

8 cups cold water

2 cans (12 ounces each) frozen tangerine or orange juice concentrate, thawed

2 cans (12 ounces each) frozen grapefruit concentrate

2 bottles (1 liter each) sparkling water, chilled

1. Mix all ingredients in punch bowl.

2. Serve over ice.

BETTY'S SUCCESS TIPS

- Make an easy ice ring using a ring mold or bundt cake pan that fits inside your punch bowl. Arrange sliced fruit or berries and mint leaves in the mold. Add water to fill three-fourths full; freeze until solid, then unmold.
- Using fruit-flavored sparkling water brings another level of flavor to this sensational sparkling punch.
- For fruity ice cubes, drop small strawberry slices and mint leaves into a filled ice-cube tray before the water is frozen.
- Add fruity cubes to the pitcher or punch bowl just before serving. Chill the pitcher or punch bowl, and fill with citrus punch just as your guests arrive.

1 SERVING: Calories 85; Total Fat 0g (Saturated Fat 0g); Sodium 0mg; Total Carbohydrate 20g (Dietary Fiber 0g); Protein 1g; **Exchanges:** 1½ Fruit; **Carbohydrate Choices:** 1

Two Favorite Cheese-Tasting Party Plans

WARM HEARTS, COLD NIGHT: CHEESE PLATE WITH NO-FUSS DINNER

Selection of Wisconsin natural cheeses (many are Italian style)

Warm roasted pecans

Dried fruits—including cranberries and cherries

Cracker assortment

Ale-style beer, wine matched to cheese

Beet and Arugula Salad **181**

Slow Cooker Creamy Ham and Wild Rice Soup **127**

Garlic bread

Praline Mini Cakes **193**

Tiramisu Bites **201**

WARM HEARTS, WARM NIGHT: CHEESE TASTING WITH APPETIZERS

Selection of French or French-style soft cheeses

Baguette-style French bread

Olives

Melon and prosciutto

Elegant Tossed Salad **182**

Sparkling water, white wine—could be sparkling—matched to cheeses

MAKE IT SPECIAL!

- Cheese is an essential element of the Spanish cocktail hour custom of tapas. Is there a tapas gathering in your plans?
- Have your camera handy. It's the perfect kind of party for snapping photos of friends. And another reason to "say cheese."

Colada Cooler Punch

Keep guests cool with an easy-to-make punch of juice and soda pop.

PREP TIME: 10 MINUTES • **TOTAL TIME:** 10 MINUTES • **MAKES 24 SERVINGS**

2 cans (12 ounces each) frozen piña colada mix concentrate, thawed

2 cans (12 ounces each) frozen white grape juice concentrate, thawed

6 cups cold water

6 cups (about 1 liter) lemon-lime soda pop
Lemon and lime slices

1. In large glass or plastic container, mix piña colada and juice concentrates. Stir in water.

2. Just before serving, pour into punch bowl. Add soda pop and lemon and lime slices. Serve over ice.

BETTY'S SUCCESS TIP

Make grape ice cubes by putting 1 or 2 grapes in each section of an ice-cube tray. Cover with water and freeze.

1 SERVING: Calories 120; Total Fat 0g (Saturated Fat 0g); Sodium 15mg; Total Carbohydrate 30g (Dietary Fiber 0g); Protein 0g; **Exchanges:** 2 Other Carbohydrate; **Carbohydrate Choices:** 2

Leg of Lamb with Garlic and Herbs

Looking for a delicious alternative to your regular Sunday roast? Try a succulent leg of lamb; it's easy to season and roast to perfection.

PREP TIME: 20 MINUTES • **TOTAL TIME:** 3 HOURS 10 MINUTES • **MAKES 8 SERVINGS**

1 leg of lamb (5 pounds)	1 teaspoon dried rosemary leaves, crushed
3 cloves garlic, cut into slivers	
3 teaspoons dried dill weed	1/2 teaspoon pepper
1 1/2 teaspoons salt	

1. Heat oven to 325°F. Do not remove fell (paperlike covering) from lamb. Make 10 or 12 small slits in lamb with tip of knife. Insert slivers of garlic into slits. Mix remaining ingredients; rub over lamb.

2. Place lamb, fat side up, on rack in shallow roasting pan. Insert meat thermometer so tip is in center of thickest part of lamb and does not touch bone or rest in fat. Do not add water.

3. Roast uncovered to desired doneness: for medium-rare, 1 hour 40 minutes to 2 hours 5 minutes or until thermometer reads 140°F; for medium, 2 hours 5 minutes to 2 hours 30 minutes or until thermometer reads 155°F.

4. Cover lamb with tent of aluminum foil and let stand 15 to 20 minutes. Temperature will continue to rise about 5°F (to 145°F for medium-rare; to 160°F for medium) and lamb will be easier to carve as juices set up. Remove foil.

BETTY'S SUCCESS TIPS

- Let color guide you when purchasing lamb. In general, the lighter the color, the younger and more tender the meat. Other things to look for are a fine-grained flesh and a creamy white fat. Follow time and temperature guidelines exactly so you don't overcook the meat.
- Remember this recipe the next time lamb goes on sale.
- Not a camper? A tent of aluminum foil loosely covers a roast and is folded to hold in as much heat and steam as possible.

1 SERVING: Calories 275; Total Fat 13g (Saturated Fat 5g); Sodium 540mg; Total Carbohydrate 1g (Dietary Fiber 0g); Protein 39g; **Exchanges:** 6 Lean Meat; 1 1/2 Fat; **Carbohydrate Choices:** 0

Grilled Mint-Wine Lamb Chops

Just three ingredients plus salt and pepper turn lamb chops into an elegant and easy dinner.

PREP TIME: 25 MINUTES • **TOTAL TIME:** 25 MINUTES • **MAKES 4 SERVINGS**

8 lamb rib chops or lamb loin chops, about 1 inch thick (about 2 pounds)

2 tablespoons dry white wine or apple juice

2 tablespoons honey

1 teaspoon chopped fresh or ¼ teaspoon dried mint leaves

¼ teaspoon salt

⅛ teaspoon pepper

1. Heat coals or gas grill for direct heat. Remove excess fat from lamb. In small bowl, mix remaining ingredients.

2. Place lamb on grill over medium heat; brush with wine mixture. Cover and grill 9 to 11 minutes for medium doneness, turning once and brushing with wine mixture. Discard any remaining wine mixture.

BETTY'S SUCCESS TIPS

- One teaspoon chopped fresh or ¼ teaspoon dried thyme leaves can be substituted for the mint.
- Brush ½-inch-thick slices of a small onion with vegetable oil and grill for 5 to 10 minutes. Place a couple of the onion rings on the bone of each chop. Thread fresh mint sprigs through the onion rings.
- Place on a platter for serving.

1 SERVING: Calories 210; Total Fat 10g (Saturated Fat 3½g); Sodium 210mg; Total Carbohydrate 9g (Dietary Fiber 0g); Protein 20g; **Exchanges:** ½ Other Carbohydrate; 3 Lean Meat; **Carbohydrate Choices:** ½

Apricot-Bourbon Glazed Ham

Combine three ingredients to create a simply delicious basting sauce for baked ham.

PREP TIME: 10 MINUTES • **TOTAL TIME:** 1 HOUR 55 MINUTES • **MAKES 10 SERVINGS**

$\frac{1}{2}$ cup apricot preserves
2 teaspoons ground ginger

$\frac{1}{4}$ cup bourbon or pineapple juice
6 to 8 pounds fully cooked smoked bone-in ham

1. Heat oven to 325°F. In small bowl, mix preserves, ginger and bourbon until smooth.

2. Place ham on rack in shallow roasting pan. Make cuts about $\frac{1}{2}$ inch apart and $\frac{1}{4}$ inch deep in diamond pattern around top and sides of ham. Brush with 3 tablespoons of the preserves mixture. Insert ovenproof meat thermometer in thickest part of ham.

3. Bake uncovered 45 minutes. Brush remaining preserves mixture over ham. Bake about 45 minutes longer or until thermometer reads 140°F. Remove ham from oven, cover with tent of foil and let stand 10 to 15 minutes for easier carving.

BETTY'S SUCCESS TIP

Scoring the ham allows the flavors of the glaze to seep into the meat.

1 SERVING: Calories 250; Total Fat 8g (Saturated Fat 2$\frac{1}{2}$g); Sodium 1,770mg; Total Carbohydrate 13g (Dietary Fiber 0g); Protein 31g; **Exchanges:** 1 Other Carbohydrate; 4$\frac{1}{2}$ Very Lean Meat; 1 Fat; **Carbohydrate Choices:** 1

Love Your Ham Leftovers

Ham leftovers? Therein lie delicious possibilities.

Congratulations. The ham dinner was delicious. With every diner plus the carving board full, now what? Read through the following tips to help you savor every last delicious scrap of leftover ham.

REDEFINE HAM LEFTOVERS

- To keep meals fresh, imagine all the ways to incorporate your leftover ham into mouthwatering dishes that look absolutely nothing like that original ham dinner. Chop it up for hearty handhelds, such as Ham and Egg Salad Sandwiches (page 138) or Spinach and Ham French Bread Pizza (page 137). Cube it to toss into crisp green salads, baked ham dishes like Asparagus-Potato Brunch Bake (page 114), warming soups or fresh pasta dishes and salads, including those jump-started with Suddenly Salad.™ Consider classic favorites, such as Springtime Ham and Egg Bake (page 111), or adding ham to Betty Crocker® scalloped or au gratin potatoes or ham soup, such as Slow Cooker Creamy Ham and Wild Rice Soup (page 127). Find plenty more new and delicious ham recipe options by searching "ham" at BettyCrocker.com.

FREEZE!

- Be realistic. Not ready to prepare all your ham leftovers within the next few days? No problem. That's what the freezer is for. Slice or cube your leftover ham and portion it out into usable amounts, such as a sandwich's, omelet's or casserole's worth. Put your portions in airtight freezer-safe bags or containers—"freezer-safe" is the key phrase here—and label each package with today's date and the ham's prospective use. Note that according to the USDA Food Safety and Inspection Service, well-packaged cooked ham and other meats retain their quality best if properly thawed and used within 2 to 3 months of freezing, though food frozen constantly at 0°F remains safe indefinitely.

USE THE BONE

- Hold on to that ham bone! Preferably with all those tasty remnants still clinging to it. The ham bone is full of flavor, making it the ideal soup-starter ingredient. Use it right away, or seal it in a labeled freezer-safe bag and toss in the freezer for when you're ready to fill your home with the tantalizing, smoky aroma of simmering ham soup down the road. Of course, split pea soup is one delicious favorite, but options include quick ham and cauliflower, plus you can always fortify any veggie or cheese-based soup or stew with cubed ham. Keep Green Giant™ frozen and canned veggies on hand to help make quick work of any soup, ham or otherwise, and remember: Simply adding bread, and perhaps a small green salad, makes your soup a meal. Homemade biscuits require just two ingredients—Bisquick™ baking mix and milk.

Cajun Black Beans with Sausage and Corn

Grab a skillet for easy Cajun cooking! This one-pan meal can be ready to serve in less than 30 minutes.

PREP TIME: 25 MINUTES • **TOTAL TIME:** 25 MINUTES • **MAKES 4 SERVINGS**

- 2 tablespoons vegetable oil
- 2 cloves garlic, finely chopped
- 1 cup frozen bell pepper and onion stir-fry (from 1-pound bag)
- 1½ cups Green Giant® Valley Fresh Steamers™ Niblets® frozen corn
- 8 ounces smoked kielbasa sausage, coarsely chopped

- ½ teaspoon salt
- ½ teaspoon dried thyme leaves
- ¼ teaspoon black and red pepper blend
- 1½ cups chopped fresh tomatoes
- 1 can (15 ounces) Progresso® black beans, drained, rinsed

1. In 10-inch skillet, heat oil over medium-high heat. Add garlic; cook and stir 1 minute. Add bell pepper and onion stir-fry; cook and stir 2 to 3 minutes or until crisp-tender.

2. Stir in corn, sausage, salt, thyme and pepper blend. Cook 3 to 5 minutes, stirring occasionally, until corn is tender.

3. Stir in tomatoes and beans; cook 3 to 5 minutes, stirring occasionally, until hot.

BETTY'S SUCCESS TIP

Garlic, thyme and pepper are traditional flavors of Cajun foods.

1 SERVING: Calories 450; Total Fat 24g (Saturated Fat 7g); Sodium 830mg; Total Carbohydrate 44g (Dietary Fiber 12g); Protein 17g; **Exchanges:** 2 Starch; ½ Other Carbohydrate; 1 Vegetable; 1½ High-Fat Meat; 2 Fat; **Carbohydrate Choices:** 3

Grilled Shrimp Kabobs with Orange Spinach Salad

Grilled shrimp, oranges and onion make a tasty trio to top spinach greens. An orange-ginger mix marinates the shrimp and dresses the salad.

PREP TIME: 30 MINUTES • **TOTAL TIME:** 45 MINUTES • **MAKES 8 SERVINGS**

Shrimp Kabobs

- 4 navel oranges
- 1 pound uncooked, peeled deveined large shrimp, thawed if frozen
- 1 small red onion, cut in half
- 1 package (10 ounces) fresh spinach

Orange Marinade and Dressing

- ³/₄ cup orange juice
- ¹/₃ cup light sesame or olive oil
- ¹/₂ teaspoon ground ginger
- 1 teaspoon garlic salt
- ¹/₄ teaspoon pepper
- 4 medium green onions, chopped (¹/₄ cup)

1. Cut 2 of the oranges into 8 wedges each. Peel and section remaining 2 oranges; reserve sections. Mix all orange marinade and dressing ingredients; reserve half for dressing. In shallow glass or plastic dish or heavy-duty resealable food-storage plastic bag, place shrimp and remaining marinade. Cover dish or seal bag and refrigerate 15 minutes.

2. Heat coals or gas grill for direct heat. Cut one onion half into wedges; separate into pieces. Thinly slice remaining onion half; separate into pieces and set aside. Remove shrimp from marinade; reserve marinade for basting. Thread shrimp, orange wedges and onion wedges alternately on each of eight 8-inch or four 15-inch metal skewers, leaving space between each piece.

3. Grill kabobs uncovered 4 to 6 inches from medium heat 6 to 8 minutes, turning frequently and brushing with reserved basting marinade, until shrimp are pink and firm. Discard any remaining basting marinade.

4. In large bowl, gently toss spinach, reserved orange sections, reserved thinly sliced onion and reserved dressing. Serve with kabobs.

BETTY'S SUCCESS TIPS

- Use a small sharp knife to peel the orange, starting at the top; be sure to remove all the white pith from the fruit. To section an orange, gently slice on both sides of the orange section membrane.
- The shrimp, orange wedges and onion wedges can be grilled in a grill basket instead of on skewers.
- The orange marinade and dressing can be prepared 1 day ahead; cover and refrigerate.

1 SERVING: Calories 330; Total Fat 30g (Saturated Fat 3g); Sodium 490mg; Total Carbohydrate 21g (Dietary Fiber 5g); Protein 2g; **Exchanges:** 1 Fruit; 1 Vegetable; 3 Lean Meat; 1 Fat; **Carbohydrate Choices:** 1¹/₂

Pan-Seared Parmesan Scallops

Tender seared scallops are simple to make and delightful to eat. Serve them with risotto, polenta, or your favorite hot cooked pasta and grilled asparagus spears or steamed green beans.

PREP TIME: 10 MINUTES • **TOTAL TIME:** 20 MINUTES • **MAKES 4 SERVINGS**

16 **large sea scallops (about 1¹⁄₂ pounds)**	1 **tablespoon butter**
¹⁄₂ **cup grated Parmesan cheese (2 ounces)**	**Coarse ground black pepper**
1 **tablespoon olive or vegetable oil**	**Chopped fresh chives or parsley**

1. Pat scallops dry with paper towels. Place cheese in shallow dish or resealable food-storage plastic bag. Coat scallops with cheese. Discard any remaining cheese.

2. Heat oil and butter in 12-inch nonstick skillet over medium-high heat. Cook half of the scallops at a time in oil 3 to 6 minutes, turning once, until golden brown on outside and white and opaque inside. Sprinkle with pepper and chives.

BETTY'S SUCCESS TIP

For Pan-Seared Asiago Scallops, substitute Asiago cheese for the Parmesan.

1 SERVING: Calories 170; Total Fat 11g (Saturated Fat 4¹⁄₂g); Sodium 410mg; Total Carbohydrate 0g (Dietary Fiber 0g); Protein 19g; **Exchanges:** 2 Very Lean Meat; ¹⁄₂ Lean Meat; 1¹⁄₂ Fat; **Carbohydrate Choices:** 0

Do-Ahead Chicken-Leek Strata

Save time on cooking! This chicken and leek strata recipe can be done ahead and requires only baking to serve anytime.

PREP TIME: 20 MINUTES • **TOTAL TIME:** 5 HOURS 35 MINUTES • **MAKES 12 SERVINGS**

2 tablespoons butter or margarine
2 cups sliced leeks (about 2 pounds)
24 slices French bread, each ½ inch thick (from 1-pound loaf)
2 cups chopped cooked chicken or turkey
2 tablespoons chopped fresh or 2 teaspoons dried dill weed

3 cups shredded mozzarella cheese (12 ounces)
8 eggs, beaten
4 cups milk
1 teaspoon salt
¼ teaspoon pepper

1. In 2-quart saucepan, melt butter over medium heat. Add leeks; cook about 3 minutes, stirring frequently, until softened. Remove from heat.

2. Line bottom of ungreased 13 x 9-inch (3-quart) glass baking dish with half of the bread slices. Sprinkle with chicken and dill weed; layer with leeks. Sprinkle 2 cups of the cheese over leeks. Top with remaining bread slices; sprinkle with remaining 1 cup cheese.

3. In medium bowl, mix remaining ingredients; pour over bread mixture. Cover tightly; refrigerate at least 4 hours but no longer than 24 hours.

4. About 1 hour 15 minutes before serving, heat oven to 325°F. Uncover dish; bake 1 hour to 1 hour 5 minutes or until knife inserted in center comes out clean. Let stand 10 minutes before serving.

BETTY'S SUCCESS TIPS

- Instead of chicken or turkey, use a 14.75-ounce can of red or pink salmon, drained and flaked.
- Purchase leeks with brightly colored leaves and an unblemished white portion. The smaller the leek, the more tender it will be. Refrigerate in a plastic bag up to 5 days. Before using, trim the root and leaf ends. Slit the leeks from top to bottom and wash thoroughly to remove dirt trapped between leaf layers.

1 SERVING: Calories 340; Total Fat 15g (Saturated Fat 8g); Sodium 670mg; Total Carbohydrate 26g (Dietary Fiber 1g); Protein 25g; **Exchanges:** 2 Starch; **Carbohydrate Choices:** 2

Primavera Pie

Enjoy this cheesy pie made using Original Bisquick® mix topped with veggies—a tasty Italian dinner.

PREP TIME: 20 MINUTES • **TOTAL TIME:** 1 HOUR 25 MINUTES • **MAKES 8 SERVINGS**

2¹/₂ cups Original Bisquick® mix
6 tablespoons cold butter
¹/₄ cup boiling water
1 cup grated Parmesan cheese
8 ounces asparagus, trimmed, cut into 1¹/₂-inch pieces
³/₄ cup chopped roasted red bell peppers (from 7.25-ounce jar)
2 teaspoons chopped fresh oregano leaves

1 tablespoon vegetable oil
1 medium zucchini, sliced
1 medium yellow squash, sliced
1 cup half-and-half
¹/₂ teaspoon salt
¹/₂ teaspoon freshly ground pepper
4 eggs
2 tablespoons bread crumbs

1. Heat oven to 350°F. Spray 9¹/₂-inch glass deep-dish pie plate with cooking spray. In medium bowl, place Bisquick mix; cut in butter, using pastry blender or fork, until crumbly. Add boiling water; stir vigorously until soft dough forms. Using fingers dipped in Bisquick mix, press dough on bottom and up side of pie plate, forming edge on rim of plate. Sprinkle ¹/₂ cup of the cheese over bottom of crust. Arrange asparagus in even layer over cheese; top with roasted peppers and oregano. In 12-inch skillet, heat oil over medium-high heat. Add zucchini and yellow squash; cook 2 minutes or just until tender. Layer over mixture in pie plate, overlapping slightly.

2. In medium bowl, beat half-and-half, salt, pepper and eggs with wire whisk. Pour over vegetables. Sprinkle with remaining ¹/₂ cup cheese and the bread crumbs. Bake 45 to 50 minutes or until knife inserted in center comes out clean. Let stand 15 minutes.

1 SERVING: Calories 400; Total Fat 25g (Saturated Fat 12g); Sodium 1,018mg; Total Carbohydrate 31g (Dietary Fiber 2g); Protein 14g; **Exchanges:** 2 Starch; ¹/₂ Vegetable; 3¹/₂ Fat; **Carbohydrate Choices:** 2

Asparagus and Goat Cheese Quiche

Bake the pie crust topped with asparagus and goat cheese to make this delicious quiche for dinner—a perfect French cuisine recipe.

PREP TIME: 20 MINUTES • **TOTAL TIME:** 1 HOUR 15 MINUTES • **MAKES 6 SERVINGS**

1 refrigerated pie crust, softened as directed on box

1 tablespoon butter

1/2 pound fresh asparagus spears, trimmed, cut into 1-inch pieces

1/2 cup chopped onion (1 medium)

1/2 cup chopped drained roasted red bell peppers (from a jar)

1 log (4 ounces) chèvre (goat) cheese, crumbled

1 cup half-and-half

1/2 teaspoon salt

1/2 teaspoon freshly ground pepper

3 eggs

1/2 cup freshly shredded Parmesan cheese (2 ounces)

1. Heat oven to 375°F. Spray 9-inch glass pie plate with cooking spray. Place pie crust in pie plate as directed on box for One-Crust Filled Pie; flute edges.

2. In 12-inch skillet, melt butter over medium-high heat. Cook asparagus and onion in butter 5 to 8 minutes, stirring occasionally, until asparagus is crisp-tender. Spoon vegetables into crust-lined plate. Top with roasted peppers and goat cheese.

3. In large bowl, beat half-and-half, salt, pepper and eggs with whisk. Pour over ingredients in crust. Sprinkle with Parmesan cheese.

4. Place pie plate on lowest oven rack; bake 35 to 45 minutes or until knife inserted in center comes out clean. Let stand 10 minutes before cutting.

1 SERVING: Calories 360; Total Fat 24g (Saturated Fat 15g); Sodium 650mg; Total Carbohydrate 15g (Dietary Fiber 1g), Protein 15g; **Exchanges:** 1 Starch; 1/2 Vegetable; 1 High-Fat Meat; 2 Fat; **Carbohydrate Choices:** 1

Niçoise French Bread Pizza

Dinner ready in just 40 minutes! Enjoy this French-style bread pizza topped with roasted vegetables, eggs, olives and cheese.

PREP TIME: 15 MINUTES • **TOTAL TIME:** 40 MINUTES • **MAKES 4 SERVINGS**

4 roma (plum) tomatoes, cut into ¼-inch slices

1 medium green bell pepper, cut into ¼-inch rings

1 large onion, thinly sliced

½ cup Italian dressing

½ loaf (1-pound size) French bread, cut horizontally in half

2 hard-cooked eggs, sliced

¼ cup sliced ripe olives

1 cup finely shredded mozzarella cheese (4 ounces)

1. Heat oven to 450°F. Line jelly roll pan, 15½ x 10½ x 1 inch, with aluminum foil. Spread tomatoes, bell pepper and onion on foil. Brush both sides of vegetables with about half of the dressing. Bake uncovered 12 to 15 minutes or until onion is crisp-tender.

2. Reduce oven temperature to 375°F. Remove vegetables and foil from pan. Place bread halves, cut sides up, in pan. Brush with remaining dressing. Top evenly with roasted vegetables, eggs, olives and cheese.

3. Bake 8 to 10 minutes or until cheese is melted. Cut into 2-inch slices.

BETTY'S SUCCESS TIPS

- Salade Niçoise is a salad from the French city of Nice, perched on the glamorous French Riviera. The salad is often served with crusty French bread so a French bread pizza is a perfect adaptation.

- For do-ahead convenience, bake the vegetables and refrigerate them up to 2 days before preparing the pizza.

- Niçoise Tuna French Bread Pizza—Add 1 can (6 ounces) white tuna in water, drained, with the roasted vegetables in step 2. Continue as directed.

1 SERVING: Calories 320; Total Fat 16g (Saturated Fat 5g); Sodium 620mg; Total Carbohydrate 34g (Dietary Fiber 3g); Protein 13g; **Exchanges:** 2 Starch; 1 Vegetable; 1½ Medium-Fat Meat; 1½ Fat; **Carbohydrate Choices:** 2

Artichoke-Spinach Lasagna

Try a new lasagna that features a creamy sauce, veggies and two cheeses.

PREP TIME: 20 MINUTES • **TOTAL TIME:** 1 HOUR 30 MINUTES • **MAKES 8 SERVINGS**

1 medium onion, chopped ($^1/_2$ cup)
4 cloves garlic, finely chopped
1 can (14 ounces) vegetable broth
1 tablespoon chopped fresh or 1 teaspoon dried rosemary leaves
1 can (14 ounces) artichoke hearts, drained, coarsely chopped
1 box (9 ounces) Green Giant® frozen chopped spinach, thawed, squeezed to drain

1 jar (15 to 17 ounces) roasted garlic Parmesan or Alfredo pasta sauce
9 uncooked lasagna noodles
3 cups shredded mozzarella cheese (12 ounces)
1 package (4 ounces) crumbled herb-and-garlic feta cheese (1 cup)
Rosemary sprigs, if desired
Lemon wedges, if desired

1. Heat oven to 350°F. Spray 13 x 9-inch (3-quart) glass baking dish with cooking spray.

2. Spray 12-inch skillet with cooking spray; heat over medium-high heat. Add onion and garlic; cook about 3 minutes, stirring occasionally, until onion is crisp-tender. Stir in broth and rosemary. Heat to boiling. Stir in artichokes and spinach; reduce heat. Cover; simmer 5 minutes. Stir in pasta sauce.

3. Spread one-quarter of the artichoke mixture in bottom of baking dish; top with 3 noodles. Sprinkle with $^3/_4$ cup of the mozzarella cheese. Repeat layers twice. Spread with remaining artichoke mixture; sprinkle with remaining mozzarella cheese. Sprinkle with feta cheese.

4. Cover and bake 40 minutes. Uncover and bake about 15 minutes longer or until noodles are tender and lasagna is bubbly. Let stand 10 to 15 minutes before cutting. Garnish with rosemary sprigs and lemon wedges.

BETTY'S SUCCESS TIPS

- Warm focaccia or pita bread and a tossed salad with tomatoes would be nice partners to this lasagna.
- Stir in $^1/_2$ cup cut-up pitted kalamata, Greek or ripe olives with the pasta sauce.

1 SERVING: Calories 350; Total Fat 13g (Saturated Fat 8g); Sodium 950mg; Total Carbohydrate 38g (Dietary Fiber 5g); Protein 20g; **Exchanges:** 2 Starch; 1 Vegetable; 1 Fat; **Carbohydrate Choices:** $2^1/_2$

Praline Bacon

A sweet, crunchy layer of pecans and brown sugar takes bacon to a whole new level.

PREP TIME: 15 MINUTES • **TOTAL TIME:** 1 HOUR 5 MINUTES • **MAKES 8 SERVINGS**

$\frac{1}{2}$ **pound bacon (8 slices)**
$\frac{1}{4}$ **cup packed brown sugar**
$\frac{1}{4}$ **cup finely chopped pecans**

1. Heat oven to 350°F. Line cookie sheet with foil. Place wire rack on foil.

2. Arrange bacon in single layer on rack. Bake 20 minutes. Meanwhile, in small bowl, stir together brown sugar and pecans.

3. Turn bacon over; sprinkle with brown sugar mixture. Bake 10 to 15 minutes longer or until golden brown. Remove from rack. Cool completely, about 15 minutes.

BETTY'S SUCCESS TIPS

- "Praline" most commonly refers to pecans or almonds coated with caramelized sugar. This treat is thought to have originated from Louisiana, where spices are not an uncommon addition to this sweet, crunchy delight.
- Light or dark brown sugar can be used in this recipe. The dark brown sugar will give the bacon a deeper, more caramelized flavor.

1 SERVING: Calories 90; Total Fat 6g (Saturated Fat 1$\frac{1}{2}$g); Sodium 190mg; Total Carbohydrate 7g (Dietary Fiber 0g); Protein 3g; **Exchanges:** $\frac{1}{2}$ Other Carbohydrate; $\frac{1}{2}$ High-Fat Meat; $\frac{1}{2}$ Fat; **Carbohydrate Choices:** $\frac{1}{2}$

French Onion Scalloped Potatoes

Jazz up oven-baked Betty Crocker® potatoes with ranch dressing, rich cream and crunchy French-fried onion rings.

PREP TIME: 15 MINUTES • **TOTAL TIME:** 60 MINUTES • **MAKES 8 SERVINGS**

- 2 boxes (4.7 ounces each) Betty Crocker® scalloped potatoes
- 1 package (1 ounce) ranch salad dressing and seasoning mix (milk recipe)
- 3½ cups boiling water

- 2 cups half-and-half
- ¾ cup chopped red bell pepper
- 1 can (2.8 ounces) French-fried onions
- 2 tablespoons chopped fresh parsley, if desired

1. Heat oven to 400°F.

2. In 13 x 9-inch (3-quart) glass baking dish, stir together both Sauce Mixes (from potato boxes), the dressing mix, boiling water and half-and-half with wire whisk. Stir in both Potatoes pouches and the bell pepper. Bake uncovered 35 minutes or until potatoes are tender.

3. Top with onions; bake 10 minutes longer. Sprinkle with parsley before serving. Let stand 5 minutes before serving (sauce will thicken as it stands).

BETTY'S SUCCESS TIP

No red pepper? Use green peppers instead.

1 SERVING: Calories 270; Total Fat 12g (Saturated Fat 5g); Sodium 1,120mg; Total Carbohydrate 36g (Dietary Fiber 2g); Protein 5g; **Exchanges:** 2 Starch; ½ Other Carbohydrate; 2 Fat; **Carbohydrate Choices:** 2½

Leek and Garlic Mashed Potatoes

Mashed potatoes become even more mouthwatering with the addition of whipping cream, garlic and leek.

PREP TIME: 25 MINUTES • **TOTAL TIME:** 45 MINUTES • **MAKES 10 SERVINGS**

3 pounds potatoes (about 8 medium), peeled and cut into pieces

2 cups sliced leek with some of green top (about 1 medium)

4 cloves garlic, peeled

¾ teaspoon salt

1 cup Progresso® chicken broth (from 32-ounce carton)

¼ cup whipping (heavy) cream

1 tablespoon butter or margarine

Additional whipping (heavy) cream, heated, if desired

1 tablespoon chopped fresh chives

1. In 3-quart saucepan, place potatoes, leek, garlic, salt and broth. Cover and heat to boiling; reduce heat. Simmer covered 20 to 25 minutes or until tender (do not drain). Mash potato mixture with potato masher or electric mixer on low speed.

2. In 1-quart saucepan, heat ¼ cup whipping cream and the butter over medium heat, stirring occasionally, until butter is melted. Add cream mixture to potato mixture; continue mashing until potatoes are light and fluffy. Add additional heated whipping cream for desired consistency. Stir in chives.

BETTY'S SUCCESS TIPS

- Don't have whipping cream? Milk works just fine in this recipe, and it trims some of the calories, too.
- Leeks are usually grown in sand, which can become embedded in the tight rings. So separate the slices into rings and rinse well before cooking.
- Make the potatoes ahead of time and put them in your slow cooker on the Low heat setting to keep warm for up to 2 hours.

1 SERVING: Calories 160; Total Fat 3½g (Saturated Fat 2g); Sodium 300mg; Total Carbohydrate 29g (Dietary Fiber 3g); Protein 3g; **Exchanges:** 1 Starch; 1 Other Carbohydrate; ½ Fat; **Carbohydrate Choices:** 2

Roasted Garlic Mashed Potatoes with Toppings

Wow your guests by serving mashed potatoes in martini glasses!

PREP TIME: 10 MINUTES • **TOTAL TIME:** 15 MINUTES • **MAKES 16 SERVINGS**

6 cups hot water
2 cups milk
$\frac{1}{2}$ cup butter or margarine
2 packages (7.2 ounces each) Betty Crocker® roasted garlic mashed potatoes

Assorted toppings (shredded cheese; cooked bacon pieces; chopped bell peppers, broccoli, avocado, green onions; sliced ripe olives; sour cream)

1. Heat water, milk and butter to boiling in 4-quart Dutch oven; remove from heat.

2. Stir in 4 pouches Potatoes and Seasoning just until moistened. Let stand about 1 minute or until liquid is absorbed. Whip with fork until smooth.

3. Spray inside of $3\frac{1}{2}$-quart slow cooker with cooking spray. Spoon mashed potatoes into slow cooker; keep warm over Low heat setting. Serve with toppings.

BETTY'S SUCCESS TIPS

- Keeping the mashed potatoes warm in a slow cooker is the perfect solution for buffets and office parties. The mashed potatoes will hold up to 2 hours.
- Turn this appetizer idea into a main-dish masterpiece. Serve the mashed potatoes in martini glasses (oversized ones work really well), and for toppings, offer beef stroganoff, chicken à la king or your favorite chili.
- Add a salad and crusty bread to create a showstopper with rave reviews!

1 SERVING: Calories 205; Total Fat 12g (Saturated Fat 6g); Sodium 510mg; Total Carbohydrate 21g (Dietary Fiber 2g); Protein 5g; **Exchanges:** 1 Starch; 1 Vegetable; 2 Fat; **Carbohydrate Choices:** $1\frac{1}{2}$

Leeks au Gratin

Mild-flavored leeks and Gruyère cheese offer a refreshing taste variation in this baked side dish usually reserved for potatoes and Cheddar cheese.

PREP TIME: 15 MINUTES • **TOTAL TIME:** 50 MINUTES • **MAKES 8 SERVINGS**

8 medium leeks with tops (3 pounds)
2 tablespoons butter or margarine
2 tablespoons plus 2 teaspoons Gold Medal® all-purpose flour
1/2 teaspoon salt
1/8 teaspoon pepper

1 1/3 cups milk
1 cup shredded Gruyère cheese (4 ounces)
1/4 cup Progresso® dry bread crumbs (any flavor)
2 teaspoons butter or margarine, melted

1. Heat oven to 325°F. Grease bottom and side of shallow 2-quart casserole. Cut leeks into 1/2-inch pieces. In 3-quart saucepan, heat 2 inches water to boiling. Add leeks. Cover and cook over medium heat about 5 minutes or until crisp-tender; drain.

2. In 2-quart saucepan, melt 2 tablespoons butter over low heat. Cook flour, salt and pepper over low heat, stirring constantly, until smooth and bubbly; remove from heat. Gradually stir in milk. Heat to boiling, stirring constantly. Boil and stir 1 minute. Stir in cheese until melted. Stir in leeks. Pour into casserole.

3. In small bowl, mix bread crumbs and 2 teaspoons butter until crumbly. Sprinkle evenly over casserole.

4. Bake uncovered about 25 minutes or until golden brown.

BETTY'S SUCCESS TIPS

- To clean leeks, cut stalks lengthwise in half; rinse under cold water, separating leaves to remove sand and dirt.
- When you're looking for leeks, choose those that have a crisp, bright green top and blemish-free white bulb.

1 SERVING: Calories 160; Total Fat 9g (Saturated Fat 5g); Sodium 270mg; Total Carbohydrate 13g (Dietary Fiber 2g); Protein 8g; **Exchanges:** 3 Vegetable; 2 Fat; **Carbohydrate Choices:** 1

Roasted Parmesan Asparagus

Simple seasonings and Parmesan cheese enhance the flavors of naturally delicious asparagus. It's ready in 30 minutes!

PREP TIME: 10 MINUTES • **TOTAL TIME:** 30 MINUTES • **MAKES 6 SERVINGS**

1½ pounds fresh asparagus	½ teaspoon garlic pepper blend
2 tablespoons olive or vegetable oil	½ teaspoon dried oregano leaves
½ teaspoon seasoned salt	2 tablespoons shredded Parmesan cheese

1. Heat oven to 425°F. Spray 15 x 10 x 1-inch pan with cooking spray. Wash asparagus; break off tough ends where stalks snap easily. If desired, peel stems of spears.

2. In shallow bowl, mix remaining ingredients except cheese; toss with asparagus to coat. Spread in pan.

3. Roast uncovered 10 minutes. Sprinkle with cheese; toss to coat. Roast uncovered 5 to 8 minutes longer or until asparagus is crisp-tender.

BETTY'S SUCCESS TIP

Substitute ¼ teaspoon each garlic powder and coarse ground pepper for the garlic pepper blend.

1 SERVING: Calories 60; Total Fat 5g (Saturated Fat 1g); Sodium 150mg; Total Carbohydrate 2g (Dietary Fiber 0g); Protein 2g; **Exchanges:** 1 Fat; **Carbohydrate Choices:** 0

Layered Ham Salad

Give taco salad a new twist with ham. With precooked meat, shredded cheese and a simple mayo dressing, this recipe saves time without compromising great flavor.

PREP TIME: 25 MINUTES • **TOTAL TIME:** 25 MINUTES • **MAKES 8 SERVINGS**

Salad

- 1 bag (10 ounces) mixed salad greens
- 6 medium roma (plum) tomatoes, chopped (2 cups)
- 1 can (11 ounces) Green Giant® SteamCrisp® Mexicorn® whole kernel corn with red and green peppers, drained
- 2 cups cubed ($^1/_2$ inch) cooked ham
- $^1/_4$ cup chopped red onion
- 2 cups shredded Mexican cheese blend (8 ounces)

Dressing

- 1 cup mayonnaise or salad dressing
- $^1/_4$ cup taco sauce
- 2 tablespoons honey

1. In 5-quart glass salad bowl or 13 x 9-inch (3-quart) glass baking dish, spread salad greens.

2. Layer remaining salad ingredients except cheese over greens.

3. In small bowl, mix dressing ingredients. Spread dressing evenly over salad. Sprinkle cheese over dressing. Cover; refrigerate up to 3 hours before serving.

BETTY'S SUCCESS TIPS

- You can choose to serve this make-ahead salad in its layered form or toss it all together just before serving.
- If you don't have Mexican cheese blend, use Cheddar, Colby or Monterey Jack cheese.

1 SERVING: Calories 450; Total Fat 34g (Saturated Fat 10g); Sodium 1,050mg; Total Carbohydrate 18g (Dietary Fiber 3g); Protein 16g; **Exchanges:** $^1/_2$ Starch; $^1/_2$ Other Carbohydrate; 1 Vegetable; 2 High-Fat Meat; $3^1/_2$ Fat; **Carbohydrate Choices:** 1

Ham and Smoked Gouda Salad

Ready in 25 minutes! Mild Gouda pairs well with salty ham in a pasta salad topped with a creamy honey-mustard dressing.

PREP TIME: 25 MINUTES • **TOTAL TIME:** 25 MINUTES • **MAKES 4 SERVINGS**

2 **cups uncooked rotini pasta (6 ounces)**
¼ **cup mayonnaise or salad dressing**
3 **tablespoons honey**
2 **tablespoons Dijon mustard**

2 **cups cubed fully cooked ham**
2 **medium stalks celery, sliced (¾ cup)**
1 **cup cubed smoked Gouda cheese (5 ounces)**

1. Cook and drain pasta as directed on package. Rinse with cold water; drain.

2. Mix mayonnaise, honey and mustard in small bowl. Place pasta, ham, celery and cheese in large bowl. Add mayonnaise mixture; toss to coat.

BETTY'S SUCCESS TIPS

- Smoked Cheddar can be used instead of smoked Gouda, or if you prefer a cheese without the smoke flavor, substitute regular Gouda, Cheddar or Swiss.
- Turkey ham or reduced-fat ham delivers great taste with less fat. Go ahead and use reduced-fat mayonnaise instead of the regular.
- Smoked Gouda has a creamy yellow color slightly tinged with tan and light brown hues. The texture is smooth and creamy with a smoky yet mild flavor.

1 SERVING: Calories 574; Total Fat 29g (Saturated Fat 11g); Sodium 1,504mg; Total Carbohydrate 47g (Dietary Fiber 2g); Protein 31g; **Exchanges:** 2 Starch; 1 Other Carbohydrate; 2 Lean Meat; 3 Fat; **Carbohydrate Choices:** 3

Green Garden Fries

Fast food meets the backyard! These crispy green "fries" are made from fresh garden veggies. Oven fried and served with a lemony Greek yogurt dipping sauce, they are the perfect summer side dish.

PREP TIME: 20 MINUTES • **TOTAL TIME:** 40 MINUTES • **MAKES 6 SERVINGS**

Dip

- 1 container (6 ounces) fat-free plain Greek yogurt
- 1 tablespoon olive oil
- 1 tablespoon lemon juice
- 1 clove garlic, finely chopped
- $1/2$ teaspoon salt
- 2 tablespoons fresh herbs (basil, dill, oregano and/or thyme)

Vegetable Fries

- 1 cup Progresso® panko bread crumbs
- $1/2$ cup finely shredded Parmesan cheese
- 1 tablespoon fresh herbs (basil, dill, oregano and/or thyme)
- $1/4$ teaspoon salt
- 3 tablespoons all-purpose flour
- 2 eggs, beaten
- $1^1/2$ pounds sugar snap peas, broccolini, asparagus and/or zucchini
- 2 tablespoons butter, melted

1. In small bowl, mix dip ingredients. Cover and refrigerate.

2. Heat oven to 400°F. Line large cookie sheet with foil and spray with cooking spray; set aside.

3. In small bowl, mix bread crumbs, Parmesan cheese, 1 tablespoon fresh herbs and the salt. Line up 3 baking dishes or shallow bowls. Place flour in first dish. Place eggs in second dish. Place bread crumb mixture in third dish. Dip and roll vegetables into flour to coat, dip into eggs, then coat with bread crumb mixture. Place coated vegetables on cookie sheet. Sprinkle any remaining crumb mixture over vegetables. Drizzle with melted butter.

4. Bake 18 to 20 minutes or until vegetables are tender and coating is light golden brown. Serve with dip.

1 SERVING: Calories 260; Total Fat 12g (Saturated Fat 5g); Sodium 560mg; Total Carbohydrate 24g (Dietary Fiber 2g); Protein 12g; **Exchanges:** 1 Starch; 2 Vegetable; $1/2$ Lean Meat; 2 Fat; **Carbohydrate Choices:** $1^1/2$

Beet and Arugula Salad

Embellish dinner with a beautiful and flavorful salad.

PREP TIME: 20 MINUTES • **TOTAL TIME:** 4 HOURS 40 MINUTES • **MAKES 4 SERVINGS**

6 **medium beets (4 to 6 ounces each)**	2 **cups arugula leaves, watercress or bite-size pieces salad greens**
1/4 **cup olive or vegetable oil**	1/2 **cup crumbled chèvre (goat) cheese (2 ounces)**
2 **tablespoons red wine vinegar or cider vinegar**	1 **tablespoon chopped walnuts, toasted, if desired**
1 **tablespoon Dijon mustard**	
1 **teaspoon sugar**	

1. Remove greens from beets, leaving about 1/2 inch of stem. Do not trim or cut root. Wash beets well. Place beets in 2-quart saucepan; add enough water to cover. Cover and heat to boiling; reduce heat. Simmer 40 to 50 minutes or until tender; drain.

2. Cool beets 1 hour. Remove skins from beets under running water; drain beets on paper towels. Cut beets into julienne strips; place in shallow glass or plastic dish.

3. In tightly covered container, shake oil, vinegar, mustard and sugar. Pour half of the mixture over beets. Cover and refrigerate at least 2 hours but no longer than 12 hours. Let stand at room temperature 30 minutes before preparing salad.

4. Arrange beets on 4 salad plates. Top with arugula and cheese. Drizzle with remaining oil mixture if desired. Sprinkle with walnuts. Serve immediately.

BETTY'S SUCCESS TIPS

- Substitute 1 can (16 ounces) julienne beets for the cooked fresh beets. Marinate as directed in step 3.
- Beets range in color from the common deep garnet to white and gold. Although any color beet can be used in this salad, marinate each color separately because beets have a tendency to "bleed."
- Chèvre is a white goat's milk cheese with a mildly tart flavor. If you prefer a slightly more assertive flavor, try a blue cheese such as Gorgonzola or Roquefort.
- To toast nuts, bake uncovered in ungreased shallow pan in 350°F oven about 10 minutes, stirring occasionally, until golden brown. Or cook in ungreased heavy skillet over medium-low heat 5 to 7 minutes, stirring frequently until browning begins, then stirring constantly until golden brown.

1 SERVING: Calories 255; Total Fat 20g (Saturated Fat 6g); Sodium 250mg; Total Carbohydrate 15g (Dietary Fiber 3g); Protein 7g; **Exchanges:** 3 Vegetable; 4 Fat; **Carbohydrate Choices:** 1

Elegant Tossed Salad

Impress someone special with this delightful salad of greens, mushrooms and leeks with a homemade Parmesan-Dijon dressing.

PREP TIME: 25 MINUTES • **TOTAL TIME:** 1 HOUR 25 MINUTES • **MAKES 2 SERVINGS**

2 tablespoons olive or vegetable oil
1 tablespoon red wine vinegar
2 teaspoons grated Parmesan cheese
2 teaspoons Dijon mustard
1/4 teaspoon salt

2 cups assorted bite-size pieces salad greens (2 ounces)
1/2 cup sliced fresh mushrooms
1/4 cup thinly sliced leek
Croutons, if desired

1. In tightly covered container, shake oil, vinegar, cheese, mustard and salt until well blended. Refrigerate at least 1 hour.

2. In large bowl, place salad greens, mushrooms and leek. Add dressing; toss to coat. Garnish with croutons.

BETTY'S SUCCESS TIPS

- Experiment with salad greens! The produce and deli areas in many supermarkets have a vast assortment. Splurge on a mixture of organic salad greens.
- Leery of leeks? Thinly sliced red onions make an attractive and flavorful stand-in.

1 SERVING: Calories 155; Total Fat 15g (Saturated Fat 2g); Sodium 470mg; Total Carbohydrate 4g (Dietary Fiber 2g); Protein 3g; **Exchanges:** 1 Vegetable; 3 Fat; **Carbohydrate Choices:** 0

Springtime Sprinkles Cake

Easy to decorate in no time! It's delicious, too.

PREP TIME: 25 MINUTES • **TOTAL TIME:** 1 HOUR 20 MINUTES • **MAKES 16 SERVINGS**

1 box Betty Crocker® SuperMoist® white cake mix
   Water, butter and egg whites called for on cake mix box

1 container Betty Crocker® Rich & Creamy vanilla frosting
   Betty Crocker® Decorating Decors orange, blue and purple sugars

1. Heat oven to 350°F (325°F for dark or nonstick pan). Make, bake and cool cake as directed on box for 13 x 9-inch pan.

2. Frost with frosting.

3. To decorate: Gently press cookie cutter into frosting on cake where you want sugar design; remove cutter and dip bottom edge into one of the sugars, then gently press cutter back into same stamped image on cake; remove. Continue with other remaining sugars and different sizes of cookie cutters as desired. Store loosely covered.

BETTY'S SUCCESS TIPS

- Pressing the clean cookie cutter into frosting before dipping in sugar will help the sugar adhere to the cutter. It's important only for the first dip.
- Use a set of nested cookie cutters (same shape, different sizes) to give a fun look to the decorations.

1 SERVING: Calories 260; Total Fat 10g (Saturated Fat 2g); Sodium 270mg; Total Carbohydrate 42g (Dietary Fiber 0g); Protein 2g; **Exchanges:** 1 Starch; 2 Other Carbohydrate; 1½ Fat; **Carbohydrate Choices:** 3

Strawberry Rhubarb Chiffon Cake

A vintage-inspired pretty-in-pink chiffon cake with fresh strawberry and rhubarb is the perfect way to celebrate.

PREP TIME: 55 MINUTES • **TOTAL TIME:** 3 HOURS 55 MINUTES • **MAKES 20 SERVINGS**

Strawberry Chiffon Cake
- 1¾ cups Gold Medal® all-purpose flour
- 2 teaspoons baking powder
- 1 teaspoon salt
- 1¼ cups granulated sugar
- ½ cup vegetable oil
- 6 egg yolks
- 10 strawberries, pureed in blender or food processor (about ¾ cup)
- 22 drops red liquid food color
- 6 egg whites
- ½ teaspoon cream of tartar

Filling and Glaze
- 1 cup frozen cut rhubarb, thawed, drained or chopped fresh rhubarb
- 2 teaspoons grated lemon peel
- ¼ cup granulated sugar
- 1 tablespoon water
- 1½ cups quartered strawberries
- 1 cup whipping (heavy) cream
- 1½ cups powdered sugar

1. Heat oven to 350°F. In large bowl, mix flour, baking powder, salt and ½ cup of the granulated sugar until blended. Add oil, egg yolks, pureed strawberries and food color. Beat with electric mixer on medium speed about 2 minutes or until blended; set aside.

2. Wash and dry beaters. In medium bowl, beat egg whites and cream of tartar with electric mixer on medium speed about 1 minute 30 seconds or until soft peaks form. Gradually add the remaining ¾ cup granulated sugar. Beat until stiff peaks form. Fold one-third of the egg white mixture into the egg yolk batter gently but thoroughly. Fold in remaining egg white mixture. Pour into ungreased 10-inch angel food (tube) cake pan. Tap pan on counter to remove air bubbles.

3. Bake 50 to 60 minutes or until toothpick inserted in center comes out clean. Immediately turn pan upside down onto heatproof bottle or funnel. Let hang about 2 hours or until cake is completely cool.

4. Meanwhile, in 1-quart saucepan, heat rhubarb, lemon peel, ¼ cup granulated sugar and the water to boiling over medium heat. Reduce heat to medium-low; simmer until soft and cooked through, about 3 minutes. Remove from heat; set aside to cool, about 30 minutes. Stir in quartered strawberries.

5. In medium bowl, beat ½ cup of the whipping cream and 1 tablespoon of the powdered sugar until stiff peaks form. Fold in ½ cup of the cooled strawberry-rhubarb mixture. Reserve remaining mixture for top of cake.

6. Place cake top side down on serving platter. Cut 1-inch layer off top of cake; set aside. Cut tunnel into cake 1 inch deep and 1 inch wide; discard tunnel scraps. Fill tunnel with strawberry-rhubarb cream mixture. Replace top of cake.

7. To make glaze, stir together remaining $1/2$ cup whipping cream and remaining powdered sugar (almost $1^1/2$ cups) in medium bowl until smooth. Spoon glaze over top of cake, letting it run down side. Top with reserved strawberry-rhubarb mixture just before serving.

BETTY'S SUCCESS TIPS

- Short on time? Make the strawberry-rhubarb mixture (step 4) up to 2 days ahead of time. Store covered in refrigerator until ready to use.
- Rhubarb and strawberries are a refreshing pair for spring. To prepare fresh rhubarb, trim the ends and discard all traces of the leaves (rhubarb leaves are poisonous). Scrub the stalks and cut into pieces about 1 inch in length.

1 SERVING: Calories 270; Total Fat 12g (Saturated Fat 4g); Sodium 190mg; Total Carbohydrate 38g (Dietary Fiber 1g); Protein 3g; **Exchanges:** 1 Starch; $1^1/2$ Other Carbohydrate; $2^1/2$ Fat; **Carbohydrate Choices:** $2^1/2$

Luscious Lemon Meringue Pie

Taste a classic recipe! This pie is bursting with fresh lemon taste and a sweet, creamy real meringue topping.

PREP TIME: 30 MINUTES • **TOTAL TIME:** 3 HOURS 45 MINUTES • **MAKES 8 SERVINGS**

Pastry

1	cup Gold Medal® all-purpose flour
1/2	teaspoon salt
1/3	cup plus 1 tablespoon shortening
2	to 3 tablespoons cold water

Meringue

3	egg whites
1/4	teaspoon cream of tartar
6	tablespoons sugar
1/2	teaspoon vanilla

Filling

3	egg yolks
1 1/2	cups sugar
1/3	cup plus 1 tablespoon cornstarch
1 1/2	cups water
3	tablespoons butter or margarine
2	teaspoons grated lemon peel
1/2	cup lemon juice
2	drops yellow food color, if desired

1. In medium bowl, mix flour and salt. Cut in shortening, using pastry blender (or pulling 2 table knives through ingredients in opposite directions), until particles are size of small peas. Sprinkle with cold water, 1 tablespoon at a time, tossing with fork until all flour is moistened and pastry almost cleans side of bowl (1 to 2 teaspoons more water can be added if necessary).

2. Gather pastry into a ball. Shape into flattened round on lightly floured surface. Wrap in plastic wrap; refrigerate about 45 minutes or until dough is firm and cold, yet pliable. This allows the shortening to become slightly firm, which helps make the baked pastry more flaky. If refrigerated longer, let pastry soften slightly before rolling.

3. Heat oven to 475°F. With floured rolling pin, roll pastry into round 2 inches larger than upside-down 9-inch glass pie plate. Fold pastry into fourths; place in pie plate. Unfold and ease into plate, pressing firmly against bottom and side. Trim overhanging edge of pastry 1 inch from rim of pie plate. Fold and roll pastry under, even with plate; flute as desired. Prick bottom and side of pastry thoroughly with fork. Bake 8 to 10 minutes or until light brown; cool on cooling rack.

4. Reduce oven temperature to 400°F. In small bowl, beat egg yolks with fork. In 2-quart saucepan, mix sugar and cornstarch; gradually stir in water. Cook over medium heat, stirring constantly, until mixture thickens and boils. Boil and stir 1 minute.

5. Immediately stir at least half of hot mixture into egg yolks; stir back into hot mixture in saucepan. Boil and stir 2 minutes; remove from heat. Stir in butter, lemon peel, lemon juice and food color. Pour into pie crust.

6. In medium bowl, beat egg whites and cream of tartar with electric mixer on high speed until foamy. Beat in sugar, 1 tablespoon at a time; continue beating until stiff and glossy. Do not underbeat. Beat in vanilla. Spoon onto hot pie filling. Spread over filling, carefully sealing meringue to edge of crust to prevent shrinking or weeping.

7. Bake 8 to 12 minutes or until meringue is light brown. Cool away from draft 2 hours. Cover and refrigerate cooled pie until serving. Store in refrigerator.

BETTY'S SUCCESS TIPS

- For the best meringue, be sure not to get any egg yolks into the egg whites while separating the eggs, because even a speck of yolk will prevent the whites from beating properly.
- Substitute Betty Crocker® pie crust mix for the scratch pie crust in this recipe and save time.

1 SERVING: Calories 430; Total Fat 16g (Saturated Fat 6g); Sodium 210mg; Total Carbohydrate 66g (Dietary Fiber 0g); Protein 4g; **Exchanges:** 1 Starch; 3½ Other Carbohydrate; 3 Fat; **Carbohydrate Choices:** 4½

Salted Caramel Stout and Chocolate Cheesecake

Chocolate, beer and cheesecake—can't go wrong with that!

PREP TIME: 15 MINUTES • **TOTAL TIME:** 7 HOURS 45 MINUTES • **MAKES 16 SERVINGS**

Crust and Filling

- 1 package (9 ounces) thin chocolate wafer cookies, crushed (2 cups)
- 6 tablespoons butter or margarine, melted
- 2 packages (8 ounces each) cream cheese, softened
- $2/3$ cup granulated sugar
- 3 eggs
- 1 bag (12 ounces) semisweet chocolate chips (2 cups), melted
- $1/4$ cup whipping (heavy) cream
- $3/4$ cup stout beer
- 2 tablespoons butter or margarine, melted
- 1 teaspoon vanilla

Beer Sauce and Salt

- $1/2$ cup butter
- $1 1/4$ cups packed brown sugar
- 2 tablespoons stout beer
- $1/2$ cup whipping (heavy) cream
- $1 1/2$ teaspoons sea salt flakes

1. Heat oven to 325°F. In medium bowl, mix crust ingredients; reserve 1 tablespoon crumbs for garnish. Press remaining crumbs in bottom and 2 inches up side of ungreased 10-inch springform pan. Wrap foil around pan to catch drips. Refrigerate while making filling.

2. In large bowl, beat cream cheese and granulated sugar with electric mixer on medium speed until smooth. Beat in eggs, one at a time, until well blended, scraping bowl after each addition. Add melted chocolate; beat well. Add remaining filling ingredients; beat until smooth. Pour into crust-lined pan.

3. Bake 60 to 70 minutes or until edges are set; center of cheesecake will be soft. (To minimize cracking, place shallow pan half full of hot water on lower oven rack during baking.) Turn off oven; leave cheesecake in oven 30 minutes longer.

4. Carefully run small metal spatula around edge of springform pan. Cool completely, about 2 hours. Refrigerate at least 4 hours or overnight.

5. In 2-quart saucepan, melt $1/2$ cup butter over medium heat. Add brown sugar and 2 tablespoons stout beer. Heat to boiling; cook and stir about 1 minute or until sugar dissolves. Stir in $1/2$ cup whipping cream; return to boiling. Remove from heat. Cool 10 minutes.

6. To serve, run small metal spatula around edge of springform pan again; carefully remove foil and side of pan. Cut cheesecake into slices. Drizzle sauce over slices; sprinkle with salt. Garnish with reserved crumbs. Cover and refrigerate any remaining cheesecake.

BETTY'S SUCCESS TIP

Don't worry about the center of the cheesecake being soft when you take it out of the oven; it becomes firm as it cools. To cut cheesecake easily, dip the knife into water and clean it off after every cut.

1 SERVING: Calories 540; Total Fat 35g (Saturated Fat 20g); Sodium 550mg; Total Carbohydrate 52g (Dietary Fiber 1g); Protein 5g; **Exchanges:** $1 1/2$ Starch; 2 Other Carbohydrate; 7 Fat; **Carbohydrate Choices:** $3 1/2$

Chocolate Pecan Bourbon Cake

A cake that's worthy of a celebration is worth making for everyday enjoyment. Indulge yourself!

PREP TIME: 20 MINUTES • **TOTAL TIME:** 2 HOURS 30 MINUTES • **MAKES 16 SERVINGS**

Cake

2	cups Gold Medal® all-purpose flour
2	cups granulated sugar
1/2	cup butter or margarine, softened
3/4	cup buttermilk
1/2	cup water
1/4	cup bourbon or water
1	teaspoon baking soda
1	teaspoon vanilla
1/2	teaspoon baking powder
1/2	teaspoon salt
2	eggs
4	ounces unsweetened baking chocolate, melted, cooled
1	cup chopped pecans

Chocolate Glaze

1	ounce unsweetened baking chocolate
1	teaspoon butter or margarine
1	cup powdered sugar
5	to 6 teaspoons boiling water

1. Heat oven to 350°F. Grease and flour 10-inch angel food cake (tube) pan or 12-cup fluted tube cake pan.

2. In large bowl, beat all cake ingredients except pecans with electric mixer on low speed 30 seconds, scraping bowl constantly. Beat on high speed 3 minutes, scraping bowl occasionally. Stir in pecans. Pour into pan.

3. Bake 60 to 65 minutes or until toothpick inserted in center comes out clean. Cool 10 minutes; remove from pan to wire rack. Cool completely, about 1 hour.

4. In 2-quart saucepan, melt 1 ounce chocolate and 1 teaspoon butter over low heat, stirring occasionally. Stir in powdered sugar and water until smooth and thin enough to drizzle. Drizzle cooled cake with chocolate glaze.

BETTY'S SUCCESS TIPS

- No buttermilk? Measure 2 1/4 teaspoons vinegar into measuring cup; add enough milk to make 3/4 cup. Stir and let sit a few minutes.
- Sprinkle cake top with additional chopped nuts for a special touch.

1 SERVING: Calories 360; Total Fat 17g (Saturated Fat 7g); Sodium 220mg; Total Carbohydrate 48g (Dietary Fiber 2g); Protein 4g; **Exchanges:** 1 Starch; 2 Other Carbohydrate; 3 1/2 Fat; **Carbohydrate Choices:** 3

Pistachio Fudge Cups

These dainty treats showcase a fudgy filling nestled in a tender cream-cheese crust.

PREP TIME: 25 MINUTES • **TOTAL TIME:** 45 MINUTES • **MAKES 24 CUPS**

Crust

- 1/4 **cup butter or margarine, softened**
- 1 **package (3 ounces) cream cheese, softened**
- 3/4 **cup Gold Medal® all-purpose flour**
- 1/4 **cup powdered sugar**
- 2 **tablespoons unsweetened baking cocoa**
- 1/2 **teaspoon vanilla**

Pistachio Fudge Filling

- 2/3 **cup granulated sugar**
- 2/3 **cup chopped pistachio nuts**
- 1/3 **cup unsweetened baking cocoa**
- 2 **tablespoons butter or margarine, softened**
- 1 **egg**

1. Heat oven to 350°F. In large bowl, beat butter and cream cheese with electric mixer on medium speed, or mix with spoon. Stir in remaining crust ingredients until well blended.

2. Divide dough into 24 equal pieces. Press each piece in bottom and up side of ungreased mini muffin cup.

3. In medium bowl, mix all filling ingredients until well blended. Spoon about 2 teaspoons filling into each cup.

4. Bake 18 to 20 minutes or until almost no indentation remains when filling is touched lightly. Cool slightly; loosen from muffin cups with tip of knife. Remove from pan to cooling rack.

BETTY'S SUCCESS TIPS

- Bake these gems in sparking gold or silver baking cups, and swirl on your favorite chocolate frosting.
- Pistachio problems? Try Coconut Fudge Cups instead: Just use 2/3 cup flaked coconut in place of the pistachio nuts.

1 SERVING (1 Cup): Calories 105; Total Fat 6g (Saturated Fat 2g); Sodium 45mg; Total Carbohydrate 12g (Dietary Fiber 1g); Protein 2g; **Exchanges:** 1 Starch; 1/2 Fat; **Carbohydrate Choices:** 1

Praline Mini Cakes

Family and friends will go crazy for mini cakes! Toffee bits add sweet flavor and crunch.

PREP TIME: 20 MINUTES • **TOTAL TIME:** 1 HOUR 55 MINUTES • **MAKES 12 MINI CAKES**

Cakes
- 1 **box Betty Crocker® SuperMoist® yellow cake mix**
- 1 **cup water**
- 1/2 **cup vegetable oil**
- 3 **eggs**
- 1/2 **cup chopped pecans**
- 1/2 **cup toffee bits**

Glaze and Garnish
- 1/4 **cup butter (do not use margarine)**
- 1/2 **cup packed brown sugar**
- 2 **tablespoons corn syrup**
- 2 **tablespoons milk**
- 1 **cup powdered sugar**
- 1 **teaspoon vanilla**
- 1/4 **cup toffee bits**

1. Heat oven to 350°F (325°F for dark or nonstick pans). Generously grease and lightly flour 12 mini fluted tube cake pans or 12 jumbo muffin cups (do not spray with cooking spray).

2. In large bowl, beat cake mix, water, oil and eggs with electric mixer on low speed 30 seconds, then on medium speed 2 minutes, scraping bowl occasionally. Fold in pecans and 1/2 cup toffee bits. Divide batter evenly among mini pans.

3. Bake 18 to 23 minutes or until toothpick inserted in center of cake comes out clean. Cool 10 minutes; remove from pans to cooling rack. Cool completely, about 1 hour.

4. In 1-quart saucepan, melt butter over medium-high heat. Stir in brown sugar, corn syrup and milk. Heat to rolling boil over medium-high heat, stirring frequently; remove from heat. Immediately beat in powdered sugar and vanilla with whisk until smooth. Immediately drizzle about 1 tablespoon glaze over each cake; sprinkle each with 1 teaspoon toffee bits. Store loosely covered.

BETTY'S SUCCESS TIPS

- Almond lovers can get a fix by substituting almonds for the pecans and almond extract for the vanilla.
- To keep the cakes from sticking to the cake pans, be sure to generously grease and flour the pans.

1 SERVING (1 Mini Cake): Calories 470; Total Fat 24g (Saturated Fat 8g); Sodium 310mg; Total Carbohydrate 62g (Dietary Fiber 1g); Protein 3g; **Exchanges:** 1 Starch; 3 Other Carbohydrate; 4 1/2 Fat; **Carbohydrate Choices:** 4

Butterfly Cupcake Petits Fours

These little gems are perfect for a spring or summer gathering, or a baby or bridal shower. They're sure to fly off the dessert table!

PREP TIME: 2 HOURS 30 MINUTES • **TOTAL TIME:** 3 HOURS 20 MINUTES • **MAKES 72 CUPCAKES**

Cupcakes
- 2³/₄ cups Gold Medal® all-purpose flour
- 3 teaspoons baking powder
- ¹/₂ teaspoon salt
- ³/₄ cup shortening
- 1²/₃ cups granulated sugar
- 5 egg whites
- 2¹/₂ teaspoons vanilla
- 1¹/₄ cups milk

Glaze
- 8 cups powdered sugar
- ¹/₂ cup water
- ¹/₂ cup light corn syrup
- 2 teaspoons almond extract

Decorations
- Pastel-colored miniature mint candy drops
- Yogurt- or white chocolate-covered small pretzel twists
- Pastel-colored chocolate-covered candy pieces
- Black string licorice, cut into ¹/₂-inch pieces

1. Heat oven to 350°F. Place mini paper baking cup in each of 24 mini muffin cups. In medium bowl, mix flour, baking powder and salt; set aside.

2. In large bowl, beat shortening with electric mixer on medium speed 30 seconds. Gradually add granulated sugar, about ¹/₃ cup at a time, beating well after each addition and scraping bowl occasionally. Beat 2 minutes longer. Add egg whites, one at a time, beating well after each addition. Beat in vanilla. On low speed, alternately add flour mixture, about one-third at a time, and milk, about half at a time, beating just until blended.

3. Fill each cup with about 1 tablespoon plus 1 teaspoon batter or until about two-thirds full. (Cover and refrigerate remaining batter until ready to bake; cool pan 15 minutes before reusing.)

4. Bake 18 to 20 minutes or until toothpick inserted in center comes out clean. Cool 5 minutes. Remove cupcakes from pans; place on cooling racks. Cool completely, about 15 minutes. Repeat with remaining batter to make an additional 48 mini cupcakes. When cupcakes are cool, remove paper baking cups.

5. In 2¹/₂ quart saucepan, beat glaze ingredients until smooth. Heat over low heat just until lukewarm. Remove from heat. If necessary, add hot water, a few drops at a time, until glaze is pourable.

6. Working in small batches, place cupcakes upside down on cooling rack over large bowl. Pour enough glaze over tops to cover tops and sides. (Reheat glaze, if necessary.)

7. Place 3 mint candy drops in a row and next to each other in center of each cupcake. Press 2 pretzels, one on each side of row of mint drops, to look like butterfly wings. Use pastel candy pieces for heads and licorice pieces for antennae.

BETTY'S SUCCESS TIP

For sparkly butterfly wings, brush pretzels with a little of the glaze, then sprinkle with colored sugar.

1 SERVING (1 Cupcake): Calories 120; Total Fat 2¹/₂g (Saturated Fat ¹/₂g); Sodium 45mg; Total Carbohydrate 24g (Dietary Fiber 0g); Protein 1g; **Exchanges:** ¹/₂ Starch; 1 Other Carbohydrate; ¹/₂ Fat; **Carbohydrate Choices:** 1¹/₂

Pink Champagne Cupcakes

Tiny bubbles. Beautiful cupcakes. Super easy!

PREP TIME: 25 MINUTES • **TOTAL TIME:** 1 HOUR 15 MINUTES • **MAKES 24 CUPCAKES**

Champagne Cupcakes

1	box Betty Crocker® SuperMoist® white cake mix
1¼	cups champagne
⅓	cup vegetable oil
3	egg whites
4 to 5	drops red food color

Champagne Frosting

½	cup butter or margarine, softened
4	cups powdered sugar
¼	cup champagne
1	teaspoon vanilla
4 to 5	drops red food color

Garnishes

Betty Crocker® pink decorating sugar
Edible pink pearls

1. Heat oven to 350°F (325°F for dark or nonstick pan). Place paper baking cup in each of 24 regular-size muffin cups.

2. In large bowl, mix dry cake mix and champagne. Add oil, egg whites and food color. Beat with electric mixer on medium speed 2 minutes. Divide batter evenly among muffin cups.

3. Bake 17 to 22 minutes or until toothpick inserted in center comes out clean. Cool 10 minutes; remove from pan to cooling rack. Cool completely, about 30 minutes.

4. In medium bowl, beat frosting ingredients with electric mixer on medium speed until smooth. Frost cupcakes. Sprinkle with garnishes. Store loosely covered.

BETTY'S SUCCESS TIPS

- Champagne is a sparkling wine, and while many expensive champagnes are available, this is one time you might choose less expensive champagne. Have the champagne at room temperature when preparing the cake.
- For pink decorator sugar crystals, edible pink pearls and decorative cupcake liners, check out fancyflours.com.
- Sprinkle garnishes on cupcakes just before serving to maximize sparkle and keep them from absorbing moisture and melting into frosting.

1 SERVING (1 Cupcake, Cake and Frosting Only): Calories 250; Total Fat 8g (Saturated Fat 3½g); Sodium 170mg; Total Carbohydrate 40g (Dietary Fiber 0g); Protein 1g; **Exchanges:** 3 Other Carbohydrate; 1½ Fat; **Carbohydrate Choices:** 2½

Bread Pudding with Bourbon Sauce

A classic recipe for bread pudding lovers everywhere!

PREP TIME: 15 MINUTES • **TOTAL TIME:** 1 HOUR 10 MINUTES • **MAKES 8 SERVINGS**

Bread Pudding

- 2 cups milk
- 1/4 cup butter or margarine
- 1/2 cup granulated sugar
- 1 teaspoon ground cinnamon or nutmeg
- 1/4 teaspoon salt
- 2 eggs, slightly beaten
- 6 cups dry bread cubes (8 slices)
- 1/2 cup raisins, if desired

Bourbon Sauce

- 1 cup packed brown sugar
- 1/2 cup butter or margarine
- 2 tablespoons whipping cream
- 3 to 4 tablespoons bourbon or 2 teaspoons brandy extract

1. Heat oven to 350°F. In 2-quart saucepan, heat milk and 1/4 cup butter over medium heat until butter is melted and milk is hot.

2. In large bowl, mix granulated sugar, cinnamon, salt and eggs with wire whisk until well blended. Stir in bread cubes and raisins. Stir in milk mixture. Pour into ungreased 8-inch square (2-quart) glass baking dish or 1 1/2-quart casserole. Place casserole in 13 x 9-inch pan; pour boiling water into pan until 1 inch deep.

3. Bake uncovered 40 to 45 minutes or until knife inserted 1 inch from edge of baking dish comes out clean.

4. In 1-quart heavy saucepan, heat all sauce ingredients to boiling over medium heat, stirring constantly, until sugar is dissolved. Serve sauce over warm bread pudding. Store in refrigerator.

BETTY'S SUCCESS TIPS

- Be sure to set aside a serving (or two) of this mouthwatering bread pudding so you can enjoy it for tomorrow's breakfast!
- Eliminate an ingredient by using 8 slices of cinnamon-raisin bread and leaving out the 1/2 cup raisins.

1 SERVING: Calories 450; Total Fat 22g (Saturated Fat 13g); Sodium 430mg; Total Carbohydrate 56g (Dietary Fiber 0g); Protein 6g; **Exchanges:** 1 1/2 Starch; 2 Other Carbohydrate; 4 1/2 Fat; **Carbohydrate Choices:** 4

Country Rhubarb Crostata

A rustic no-fuss crust and a simple custard filling, yet springtime special!

PREP TIME: 20 MINUTES • **TOTAL TIME:** 4 HOURS 20 MINUTES • **MAKES 8 SERVINGS**

Crust
- 1 box refrigerated pie crusts, softened as directed on box

Filling
- 1 cup sugar
- 3 tablespoons all-purpose flour
- ½ teaspoon grated orange peel
- 3 eggs, slightly beaten
- ½ cup sour cream
- 3½ cups sliced fresh or frozen rhubarb

Topping
- ¼ cup sugar
- ¼ cup all-purpose flour
- 2 tablespoons butter or margarine, softened

1. Heat oven to 375°F. Place pie crust in 9-inch glass pie plate as directed on box for One-Crust Filled Pie (do not trim or flute crust).

2. In medium bowl, mix 1 cup sugar, 3 tablespoons flour and the orange peel. Stir in eggs and sour cream. Add rhubarb; toss gently. Spoon into crust-lined pie plate. Fold edges of crust over filling, ruffling decoratively.

3. In small bowl, mix topping ingredients until crumbly. Sprinkle over filling.

4. Bake 50 to 60 minutes or until crust is light golden brown. Cool 3 hours before serving. Cover and refrigerate any remaining tart.

BETTY'S SUCCESS TIPS
- Frozen rhubarb can be used in this pie—there's no need to thaw.
- The grated orange peel adds zip to this tart, but feel free to leave it out if you don't care for it.

1 SERVING: Calories 350; Total Fat 14g (Saturated Fat 7g); Sodium 190mg; Total Carbohydrate 52g (Dietary Fiber 1g); Protein 4g; **Exchanges:** ½ Starch; 1 Fruit; 2 Other Carbohydrate; 3 Fat; **Carbohydrate Choices:** 3½

Traditional Spring Celebration Brownies

Jazz up brownies for spring with marshmallows and pretty pastels—super easy!

PREP TIME: 15 MINUTES • **TOTAL TIME:** 1 HOUR 45 MINUTES • **MAKES 24 BROWNIES**

1 box Betty Crocker® fudge brownie mix
Water, vegetable oil and eggs called for on brownie mix box
3 cups miniature marshmallows

1 cup pastel-colored chocolate candies
$1/4$ cup semisweet or milk chocolate chips
$1/4$ teaspoon shortening

1. Heat oven to 350°F. Grease bottom only of 13 x 9-inch pan with cooking spray or shortening. Make brownies as directed on box for 13 x 9-inch pan, using water, oil and eggs.

2. Bake 23 minutes. Sprinkle with marshmallows; bake 5 minutes longer or until marshmallows are puffed and golden. Sprinkle with candies.

3. In small microwavable bowl, microwave chips and shortening uncovered on High 15 seconds; stir. Drizzle over bars. Cool completely, about 1 hour. For easier cutting, use plastic knife dipped in hot water. For bars, cut into 6 rows by 4 rows.

BETTY'S SUCCESS TIP

To easily remove and cut the bars, line pan with foil before spraying, allowing foil to extend over sides. Just lift out of the pan after cooling.

1 SERVING (1 Brownie): Calories 200; Total Fat 6g (Saturated Fat $2^1/_2$g); Sodium 90mg; Total Carbohydrate 34g (Dietary Fiber 1g); Protein 1g; **Exchanges:** 1 Starch; $1^1/_2$ Other Carbohydrate; 1 Fat; **Carbohydrate Choices:** 2

Tiramisu Bites

Spoon a creamy mocha filling on top of mini pound cake circles for a decadent dessert.

PREP TIME: 1 HOUR • **TOTAL TIME:** 5 HOURS • **MAKES 24 SERVINGS**

12 slices (¼ inch thick) frozen (thawed) pound cake (from 10-ounce package)
¼ cup water
1½ teaspoons instant coffee granules
1½ teaspoons rum extract
1 container (8 ounces) mascarpone cheese

¼ cup powdered sugar
½ cup whipping (heavy) cream
½ ounce semisweet baking chocolate
24 espresso coffee beans, if desired

1. Line 24 mini muffin cups with petit four paper cups. Cut two 1¼-inch rounds from each cake slice. Place 1 cake round in bottom of each cup.

2. In small bowl, mix water, coffee granules and ½ teaspoon of the rum extract. Drizzle about ½ teaspoon of the coffee mixture over cake in each muffin cup. Set aside.

3. In medium bowl, beat cheese, powdered sugar and remaining 1 teaspoon rum extract with electric mixer on medium speed until creamy. In another medium bowl, beat whipping cream on high speed until soft peaks form. On low speed, beat cheese mixture into whipped cream. Spoon or pipe a rounded tablespoon whipped cream mixture into each cup, covering cake.

4. Grate semisweet chocolate over each cup. Top each with coffee bean. Refrigerate at least 4 hours to blend flavors. Store covered in refrigerator.

BETTY'S SUCCESS TIPS

- Although these yummy little bites are ready to serve in 5 hours, the flavor and texture actually improve with longer standing. Make a day ahead, and let them mellow in the refrigerator.
- Garnish with chocolate-covered espresso coffee beans.

1 SERVING: Calories 110; Total Fat 8g (Saturated Fat 4½g); Sodium 15mg; Total Carbohydrate 9g (Dietary Fiber 0g); Protein 1g; **Exchanges:** ½ Starch; 1½ Fat; **Carbohydrate Choices:** ½

Lemon Crème Brûlée

The addition of lemon peel gives this version of a classic dessert a little lighter flavor.

PREP TIME: 30 MINUTES • **TOTAL TIME:** 6 HOURS • **MAKES 4 SERVINGS**

6 egg yolks	1 tablespoon grated lemon peel
2 cups whipping (heavy) cream	8 teaspoons sugar
1/3 cup sugar	1/2 cup fresh raspberries
1 teaspoon vanilla	

1. Heat oven to 350°F. In small bowl, slightly beat egg yolks with wire whisk. In large bowl, stir whipping cream, 1/3 cup sugar, the vanilla and lemon peel until well mixed. Add egg yolks to cream mixture; beat with wire whisk until evenly colored and well blended.

2. In 13 x 9-inch pan, place four 6-ounce ceramic ramekins.* Pour cream mixture evenly into ramekins.

3. Carefully place pan with ramekins in oven. Pour enough boiling water into pan, being careful not to splash water into ramekins, to cover two-thirds of the height of the ramekins.

4. Bake 30 to 40 minutes or until top is light golden brown and sides are set (centers will be jiggly).

5. Carefully transfer ramekins to wire rack, grasping tops of ramekins with pot holder. Cool no longer than 1 hour or until room temperature. Cover tightly with plastic wrap; refrigerate until chilled, at least 4 hours but no longer than 2 days.

6. Uncover ramekins; gently blot any condensation on custards with paper towel. Sprinkle 2 teaspoons sugar over each custard. Holding kitchen torch 3 to 4 inches from custard, caramelize sugar on each custard by heating with torch about 2 minutes, moving flame continuously over sugar in circular motion, until sugar is melted and light golden brown. (To caramelize sugar in the broiler, see Betty's Success Tip.) Place 2 tablespoons raspberries over each custard. Serve immediately, or refrigerate up to 8 hours before serving.

Do not use glass custard cups or glass pie plates; they cannot withstand the heat from the kitchen torch or broiler and may break.

BETTY'S SUCCESS TIP

The sugar topping can be caramelized in the broiler. Sprinkle 2 teaspoons brown sugar over each chilled custard. Place ramekins on cookie sheet with sides. Broil with tops 4 to 6 inches from heat 5 to 6 minutes or until sugar is melted and forms a glaze.

1 SERVING: Calories 550; Total Fat 44g (Saturated Fat 25g); Sodium 55mg; Total Carbohydrate 32g (Dietary Fiber 1g); Protein 7g; **Exchanges:** 2 Other Carbohydrate; 1 High-Fat Meat; 7 Fat; **Carbohydrate Choices:** 2

Chocolate Cherry Mini Lava Cakes

Try this decadent dessert with a molten center—all without the guilt!

PREP TIME: 20 MINUTES • **TOTAL TIME:** 45 MINUTES • **MAKES 12 CAKES**

Cakes

- 1 teaspoon shortening
- 2 tablespoons plus 2 teaspoons unsweetened baking cocoa
- 1/2 cup plus 1 teaspoon Gold Medal® all-purpose flour
- 1/2 cup semisweet chocolate chips
- 1 tablespoon vegetable oil
- 1 cup powdered sugar
- 1/2 cup fat-free egg product
- 1 container (5.3 ounces) Yoplait® Greek 100 Fat Free black cherry yogurt

Toppings, If Desired

- 1 tablespoon powdered sugar
- 12 cherries, with stems

1. Heat oven to 350°F. Lightly grease 12 regular-size muffin cups with shortening. In small bowl, stir together 2 teaspoons of the baking cocoa and 1 teaspoon of the flour; lightly sprinkle in muffin cups.

2. In medium bowl, microwave chocolate chips and oil uncovered on High 1 to 2 minutes, stirring every 30 seconds, until mixture is melted and smooth. Stir in 1 cup powdered sugar and the egg product with whisk until blended. Stir in 2 tablespoons baking cocoa, the yogurt and 1/2 cup flour. Spoon batter evenly into muffin cups, filling each about two-thirds full.

3. Bake 9 to 10 minutes, or until sides are firm (centers will still be soft). Let stand 2 minutes. Place serving platter upside down on muffin pan. Turn platter and muffin pan over; remove muffin pan. Sprinkle cakes with powdered sugar, and top each with a cherry. Serve immediately.

1 SERVING (1 Cake): Calories 130; Total Fat 4g (Saturated Fat 1 1/2 g); Sodium 25mg; Total Carbohydrate 20g (Dietary Fiber 1g); Protein 3g; **Exchanges:** 1 Starch; 1/2 Other Carbohydrate; 1/2 Fat; **Carbohydrate Choices:** 1

Menus

Springtime Alfresco Lunch

Leek and Potato Soup 129

Smoked Turkey and Creamy Artichoke Sandwiches 141

Festive Fruit Platter 153

Country Rhubarb Crostata 199

Easter Dinner

Smoky Deviled Eggs 150

Apricot-Bourbon Glazed Ham 159

French Onion Scalloped Potatoes 171

Roasted Parmesan Asparagus 175

Springtime Sprinkles Cake 183

Mother's Day Brunch

Colada Cooler Punch 156

Chocolate-Stuffed French Toast 119

Strawberry Rhubarb Chiffon Cake 184

Summer

Cheesy Spinach and Egg Hashbrowns Skillet

Enjoy breakfast for dinner, or any other time of the day, with this cheesy hashbrowns skillet with eggs and spinach.

PREP TIME: 30 MINUTES • **TOTAL TIME:** 30 MINUTES • **MAKES 4 SERVINGS**

$1/2$ pound lean (at least 80%) ground beef or ground Italian pork sausage
$1^2/_3$ cups hot water
2 tablespoons butter or margarine
$1/4$ teaspoon salt
1 box Hamburger Helper® cheesy hashbrowns

1 to 2 cups baby spinach leaves
4 eggs
$2/_3$ cup milk
2 tablespoons shredded Parmesan cheese, if desired
Additional salt and ground black pepper, if desired

1. In 12-inch nonstick skillet, cook beef over medium-high heat, stirring frequently, until brown; drain. Stir in hot water, butter, salt and potatoes (from Hamburger Helper box). Heat to boiling over high heat, stirring constantly, until butter is melted.

2. Reduce heat to medium; press potato mixture evenly with back of spatula. Cook uncovered 6 minutes, without stirring, until liquid is absorbed. Add spinach to skillet; stir until spinach is wilted slightly. Use spatula to make four holes in mixture; crack 1 egg into each hole. Cover; cook 10 to 12 minutes or until egg whites and yolks are firm, not runny, and potatoes are crispy. Meanwhile, in medium bowl, mix milk and topping mix (from Hamburger Helper box).

3. Remove skillet from heat. Top eggs with cheese, salt and pepper. Serve with topping mixture.

BETTY'S SUCCESS TIP

Use shredded Cheddar cheese in place of the Parmesan cheese.

1 SERVING: Calories 460; Total Fat 20g (Saturated Fat 9g); Sodium 1,400mg; Total Carbohydrate 48g (Dietary Fiber 2g); Protein 21g; **Exchanges:** $2^1/2$ Starch; $1/2$ Other Carbohydrate; 1 Lean Meat; 2 Fat; **Carbohydrate Choices:** 3

"Berry Good" French Toast Bake

Easy does it! You can make this blueberry munch the night before you serve breakfast or brunch.

PREP TIME: 15 MINUTES • **TOTAL TIME:** 40 MINUTES • **MAKES 8 SERVINGS**

½ cup Gold Medal® all-purpose flour
1½ cups milk
1 tablespoon sugar
½ teaspoon vanilla
¼ teaspoon salt
6 eggs
10 slices (1 inch thick) French bread, cut into 1-inch cubes

1 package (3 ounces) cream cheese, cut into ½-inch cubes
1 cup fresh or frozen (thawed) blueberries
½ cup chopped nuts
Powdered sugar, if desired
Blueberry or maple syrup, if desired

1. Generously grease 2½-quart casserole or rectangular baking dish, 13 x 9 x 2 inches. Beat flour, milk, sugar, vanilla, salt and eggs in large bowl with hand beater until smooth. Stir in bread cubes until coated.

2. Pour bread mixture into casserole. Top evenly with cream cheese, blueberries and nuts. Cover and refrigerate at least 1 hour but no longer than 24 hours.

3. Heat oven to 400°F. Uncover and bake 20 to 25 minutes or until golden brown. Sprinkle with powdered sugar. Serve with syrup.

BETTY'S SUCCESS TIPS

- Hunting for blueberries? Look for plump, firm berries that are bluish black with a hint of silvery gray.
- Blueberries are best when you store them in a moisture-proof container (if possible, in a single layer) in the refrigerator no longer than 5 days. Wash and dry the berries with paper towels just before you use them.

1 SERVING: Calories 315; Total Fat 15g (Saturated Fat 5g); Sodium 360mg; Total Carbohydrate 30g (Dietary Fiber 2g); Protein 12g; **Exchanges:** 1 Starch; 1 Fruit; 2 Fat; **Carbohydrate Choices:** 2

Ooey-Gooey Pancake S'mores

Camping out? Breakfast on these s'mores pancake treats!

PREP TIME: 10 MINUTES • TOTAL TIME: 13 MINUTES • MAKES 7 SERVINGS

2 cups Original Bisquick® mix	1 egg
1⅓ cups milk	⅓ cup graham cracker crumbs
2 tablespoons sugar	7 tablespoons marshmallow creme
1 teaspoon vanilla	7 tablespoons milk chocolate chips

1. Heat griddle or skillet; grease if necessary. Stir Bisquick mix, milk, sugar, vanilla and egg until blended. Pour batter by slightly less than ¼ cupfuls onto hot griddle.

2. Cook until bubbles break on surface. Sprinkle about 1 teaspoon cracker crumbs over each pancake. Turn; cook until golden. Remove from griddle.

3. Spread about 1 tablespoon marshmallow creme over the crumbs side of each of 7 pancakes; sprinkle about 1 tablespoon chocolate chips over marshmallow creme on each. Top with another pancake, crumbs side down.

BETTY'S SUCCESS TIP

Instead of pancake s'mores, spread cooked pancakes with process American cheese spread (as much as you like) from an 8-ounce aerosol can, and top with Bac~Os® bacon flavor bits.

1 SERVING: Calories 280; Total Fat 10g (Saturated Fat 4g); Sodium 530mg; Total Carbohydrate 41g (Dietary Fiber 1g); Protein 6g; **Exchanges:** 2½ Starch; 2 Fat; **Carbohydrate Choices:** 3

Cheesecake Pancakes

Make restaurant-inspired cream cheese pancakes at home and there's no limit to how many you can have.

PREP TIME: 30 MINUTES • TOTAL TIME: 8 HOURS 30 MINUTES • MAKES 5 SERVINGS

Pancakes
- 1 package (8 ounces) cream cheese
- 2 cups Original Bisquick® mix
- 1/2 cup graham cracker crumbs
- 1/4 cup sugar
- 1 cup milk
- 2 eggs

Strawberry Syrup
- 1 cup sliced fresh strawberries
- 1/2 cup strawberry syrup for pancakes

1. Slice cream cheese lengthwise into four pieces. Place on ungreased cookie sheet; cover and freeze 8 hours or overnight.

2. Brush griddle or skillet with vegetable oil, or spray with cooking spray; heat griddle to 375°F or heat skillet over medium heat.

3. Cut cream cheese into bite-size pieces; set aside. In large bowl, stir Bisquick mix, graham cracker crumbs, sugar, milk and eggs with whisk or fork until blended. Stir in cream cheese.

4. For each pancake, pour slightly less than 1/3 cup batter onto hot griddle. Cook until edges are dry. Turn; cook other side until golden brown.

5. In small bowl, mix strawberries and syrup; top pancakes with strawberry mixture.

BETTY'S SUCCESS TIP

Use your favorite fruit or offer a variety.

1 SERVING: Calories 580; Total Fat 26g (Saturated Fat 12g); Sodium 830mg; Total Carbohydrate 75g (Dietary Fiber 2g); Protein 11g; **Exchanges:** 2½ Starch; 2½ Other Carbohydrate; ½ High-Fat Meat; 4 Fat; **Carbohydrate Choices:** 5

Berry Breakfast Quinoa

A perfect mix of breakfast flavors in one powerful little cup. So many layers to love: yogurt, chia seeds, quinoa, fresh berries, almonds, cinnamon. Make it the night before and grab some extra zzzzs.

PREP TIME: 10 MINUTES • **TOTAL TIME:** 10 MINUTES • **MAKES 4 SERVINGS**

$^1/_4$ **cup milk**

2 **containers (6 ounces each) Yoplait®
Original 99% Fat Free French vanilla,
strawberry or harvest peach yogurt**

4 **teaspoons chia seed**

1 **cup cooled cooked quinoa
($^1/_4$ cup uncooked)**

2 **cups fresh fruit (mixed berries or
chopped peaches)**

$^1/_4$ **cup coarsely chopped toasted almonds
or pecans**

$^1/_8$ **teaspoon ground cinnamon**

1. In medium bowl, stir together milk, yogurt and chia seed until blended. Evenly divide mixture among 4 glasses. Spoon $^1/_4$ cup cooled cooked quinoa on top of yogurt layer on each.

2. Top each with a layer of fruit and almonds. Sprinkle with cinnamon. Let stand 5 minutes, or cover and refrigerate overnight.

BETTY'S SUCCESS TIPS

- Chia seed is a delicious addition to this recipe. It thickens the yogurt mixture and adds a nice crunch.
- Quinoa (KEEN-wah) has the highest protein content of all the grains. Its flavor is mild, like that of rice or couscous. Rinse the grain before cooking to remove any lingering traces of its bitter-tasting coating.
- To toast almonds or pecans, sprinkle in ungreased heavy skillet. Cook over medium-low heat 5 to 7 minutes, stirring frequently until browning begins, then stirring constantly until golden brown.

1 SERVING: Calories 260; Total Fat 8g (Saturated Fat 1$^1/_2$g); Sodium 80mg; Total Carbohydrate 40g (Dietary Fiber 4g); Protein 8g; **Exchanges:** 2 Starch; $^1/_2$ Fruit; 1$^1/_2$ Fat; **Carbohydrate Choices:** 2$^1/_2$

Chocolate and Toasted Coconut Yogurt Bowl

This quick and easy breakfast idea delivers big flavor in a flash!

PREP TIME: 10 MINUTES • **TOTAL TIME:** 10 MINUTES • **MAKES 2 SERVINGS**

2 containers (5.3 ounces each) Yoplait® Greek 100 vanilla yogurt

1 cup Nature Valley® oats 'n dark chocolate protein granola

1 cup fresh blueberries

¼ cup shredded coconut, toasted

1. Divide yogurt, granola and berries between 2 bowls.

2. Top with toasted coconut.

BETTY'S SUCCESS TIPS

- Use your favorite flavor of yogurt in place of the vanilla yogurt.
- To toast coconut, sprinkle in ungreased heavy skillet. Cook over medium-low heat 6 to 14 minutes, stirring frequently until browning begins, then stirring constantly until golden brown.
- Toast coconut in advance, and store in resealable container.

1 SERVING: Calories 420; Total Fat 9g (Saturated Fat 5g); Sodium 230mg; Total Carbohydrate 59g (Dietary Fiber 4g); Protein 24g; **Exchanges:** 3½ Starch; ½ Fruit; **Carbohydrate Choices:** 4

Breakfast Kabobs with Yogurt Dip

Begin the day a whole new way with breakfast on a stick! Bread, meat, cheese and fruit are ready for dipping.

PREP TIME: 25 MINUTES • **TOTAL TIME:** 25 MINUTES • **MAKES 4 SERVINGS**

8 (8-inch) wooden skewers
2 ounces thinly sliced hard salami, folded into quarters
4 ounces Muenster cheese, cubed
2 cups cantaloupe cubes
1 cup fresh strawberries, halved

4 slices ($^1/_2$ inch thick) French bread, cut into cubes
1 cup Yoplait® 99% Fat Free creamy harvest peach, creamy strawberry or creamy strawberry banana yogurt (from 2-pound container)

1. Onto wooden skewers, thread salami, cheese, fruit and bread.

2. Serve kabobs with yogurt as a dip.

BETTY'S SUCCESS TIP

Thread the kabobs the night before, leaving a little space between each ingredient. Cover tightly and refrigerate.

1 SERVING: Calories 330; Total Fat 15g (Saturated Fat 8g); Cholesterol 40mg; Sodium 630mg; Total Carbohydrate 34g (Dietary Fiber 2g); Protein 15g; **Exchanges:** $1^1/_2$ Starch; 1 Fruit; $2^1/_2$ Other Carbohydrate; $1^1/_2$ High-Fat Meat; ; **Carbohydrate Choices:** 2

Peach-Berry Smoothies

Blend and enjoy a delicious beverage for four in 5 minutes!

PREP TIME: 5 MINUTES • **TOTAL TIME:** 5 MINUTES • **MAKES 4 SERVINGS**

2 containers (6 ounces each) Yoplait® Original 99% Fat Free strawberry yogurt
1 cup sliced fresh or frozen peaches or nectarines

1 cup sliced fresh strawberries
1 cup crushed ice

1. In blender, place all ingredients. Cover; blend on high speed 30 to 60 seconds or until smooth.

2. Pour into 4 glasses. Serve immediately.

BETTY'S SUCCESS TIPS

- Serve this energizing fruit shake as a quick breakfast or as an after-school snack.
- Frozen whole strawberries, slightly thawed, can be substituted for the fresh.

1 SERVING: Calories 120; Total Fat 1g (Saturated Fat $^1/_2$g); Sodium 40mg; Total Carbohydrate 24g (Dietary Fiber 1g); Protein 3g; **Exchanges:** 1 Fruit; $^1/_2$ Skim Milk; **Carbohydrate Choices:** $1^1/_2$

Summer's Bounty Smoothies

Turn a plain ol' banana into an energizing breakfast drink.

PREP TIME: 10 MINUTES • **TOTAL TIME:** 10 MINUTES • **MAKES 2 SERVINGS**

1 ripe banana, peeled, cut into chunks

1 ripe nectarine, peeled, pitted and quartered

4 to 5 large fresh strawberries, cut in half

1 cup strawberry frozen yogurt

1. In blender or food processor, place all ingredients. Cover; blend on high speed 20 to 30 seconds or until smooth.

2. Pour into 2 glasses. Serve immediately.

BETTY'S SUCCESS TIP

One tablespoon wheat germ or Fiber One® cereal can be added to this recipe. Garnish each serving with a whole strawberry, if desired.

1 SERVING: Calories 240; Total Fat 2$\frac{1}{2}$g (Saturated Fat 1$\frac{1}{2}$g); Sodium 75mg; Total Carbohydrate 47g (Dietary Fiber 3g); Protein 7g; **Exchanges:** 2$\frac{1}{2}$ Fruit; 1 Skim Milk; **Carbohydrate Choices:** 3

Gazpacho with Basil Crème Fraîche

Nothing feels, tastes or shouts summer more than this refreshing melange of tomatoes with just a touch of other veggies.

PREP TIME: 45 MINUTES • **TOTAL TIME:** 6 HOURS 45 MINUTES • **MAKES 4 SERVINGS**

Gazpacho

- 4 large tomatoes, seeded, chopped (4 cups)
- 2 large red bell peppers, chopped (3 cups)
- 2 medium cucumbers, peeled, chopped (2 cups)
- 2 medium celery stalks, diagonally sliced (1 cup)
- 8 medium green onions, sliced ($1/2$ cup)
- 4 cups tomato juice
- $1/4$ cup red wine vinegar
- 2 to 3 teaspoons red pepper sauce
- $1/2$ teaspoon freshly ground pepper
- $1/2$ teaspoon Worcestershire sauce
- 2 cloves garlic, finely chopped
- 2 cans (15 ounces each) Progresso® black beans, drained, rinsed
- $1/2$ cup herb-flavored croutons, if desired

Basil Crème Fraîche

- $2/3$ cup crème fraîche or sour cream
- $1/4$ cup chopped fresh or 2 teaspoons dried basil leaves

1. In large bowl, mix all gazpacho ingredients except croutons until well blended. Cover and refrigerate 4 to 6 hours to blend flavors, stirring occasionally.

2. In small bowl, mix crème fraîche and basil. Stir gazpacho; ladle into serving dishes. Top each serving with basil crème fraîche and croutons.

BETTY'S SUCCESS TIPS

- A real tomato lover must have invented this dish. It's brimming with so many tomatoes and fresh vegetables that there's little room for any fat.
- For a delicious change of pace, serve this soup hot.
- If you serve this as an appetizer instead of a main dish, it will serve about 8.

1 SERVING: Calories 240; Total Fat 5g (Saturated Fat 3g); Sodium 950mg; Total Carbohydrate 46g (Dietary Fiber 10g); Protein 13g; **Exchanges:** 9 Vegetable; $1/2$ Fat; **Carbohydrate Choices:** 3

Pesto, Mozzarella and Tomato Panini

Dinner ready in 20 minutes! Enjoy a classic grilled tomato and cheese sandwich with an Italian twist—a wonderful meal.

PREP TIME: 20 MINUTES • **TOTAL TIME:** 20 MINUTES • **MAKES 4 SANDWICHES**

4 **ciabatta sandwich rolls**	1 **medium tomato, cut into 8 thin slices**
2 **tablespoons olive oil**	$1/2$ **teaspoon salt**
$1/2$ **cup basil pesto**	$1/4$ **teaspoon pepper**
8 **slices mozzarella cheese**	

1. Heat closed contact grill 5 minutes.

2. Cut each roll in half horizontally; brush outside of each half with oil. Spread pesto on inside of both halves. Layer each sandwich with cheese and tomato. Sprinkle with salt and pepper.

3. When grill is heated, place sandwiches on grill. Close grill; grill 4 minutes or until bread is toasty and cheese is melted. Slice sandwiches on diagonal and serve warm.

BETTY'S SUCCESS TIPS

- If you can't find ciabatta rolls, you can substitute focaccia or 8 slices of country bread.
- This sandwich is especially delicious when made with large beefsteak tomatoes at their peak of ripeness.
- When ripe tomatoes are not available, try using chopped cherry tomatoes. They are more reliably flavorful no matter what the season.
- Fresh mozzarella can be used instead of the slices.

1 SANDWICH: Calories 430; Total Fat 30g (Saturated Fat 8g); Sodium 950mg; Total Carbohydrate 26g (Dietary Fiber 2g); Protein 15g; **Exchanges:** $1^1/2$ Starch; $1^1/2$ High-Fat Meat; $3^1/2$ Fat; **Carbohydrate Choices:** 2

Creamy Tomato Basil Soup with Mini Grilled Cheese Sandwiches

You'll love the rich creaminess of this delicious soup with Greek yogurt!

PREP TIME: 40 MINUTES • **TOTAL TIME:** 40 MINUTES • **MAKES 9 SERVINGS**

Tomato Soup

- ¼ cup olive oil
- 1 medium onion, chopped (½ cup)
- 1 clove garlic, finely chopped
- 2 cans (14.5 ounces each) diced tomatoes, undrained
- 1 container (5.3 ounces) Liberté® Greek plain yogurt
- ¼ cup grated Parmesan cheese (1 ounce)
- 2 tablespoons chopped fresh basil leaves
- ½ teaspoon salt
- ¼ teaspoon pepper

Sandwiches

- 3 tablespoons butter or margarine, softened
- 6 slices (½ inch thick) whole grain bread
- 3 slices (1 ounce each) Cheddar cheese, cut in half
- 1 tablespoon chopped fresh basil leaves
- 9 (4-inch) wooden skewers

1. In 4-quart saucepan, heat oil, onion and garlic over medium-low heat 5 to 10 minutes, stirring frequently, until onion is soft and translucent.

2. Add tomatoes; heat to boiling. Reduce heat; simmer 30 minutes, stirring occasionally. Remove from heat; add yogurt, Parmesan cheese, 2 tablespoons basil leaves, the salt and pepper. In blender, place soup mixture. Cover; puree until smooth.

3. Spread butter on 1 side of each bread slice. Arrange 3 slices bread, buttered side down, on work surface, and place 2 slices cheese and 1 teaspoon of the basil leaves on each bread slice. Top with remaining 3 bread slices, buttered sides up. In 10-inch nonstick skillet, cook 3 sandwiches at a time over medium heat, turning once, until golden brown and cheese just melts. Cut each sandwich into 6 squares. Place 2 sandwich squares onto each skewer.

4. To serve, spoon soup into small cups; place sandwich skewer on top of cup.

BETTY'S SUCCESS TIP

Prepare the soup 1 day ahead, cover and refrigerate. Reheat over medium-low heat, stirring occasionally, 5 to 8 minutes or until thoroughly heated.

1 SERVING: Calories 220; Total Fat 14g (Saturated Fat 6g); Sodium 500mg; Total Carbohydrate 14g (Dietary Fiber 2g); Protein 8g; **Exchanges:** 1 Starch; ½ Lean Meat; 2½ Fat; **Carbohydrate Choices:** 1

Bacon, Tomato and Avocado Sandwich with Chipotle Aioli

Yogurt provides a wonderful addition to the chipotle aioli that's spread in this sandwich. A tasty dinner made with bacon, tomatoes and avocados—ready in just 15 minutes.

PREP TIME: 15 MINUTES • **TOTAL TIME:** 15 MINUTES • **MAKES 6 SERVINGS**

Chipotle Aioli

- 1 container (6 ounces) fat-free plain Greek yogurt
- 2 tablespoons mayonnaise
- 2 cloves garlic, finely chopped
- 1 chipotle chile in adobo sauce, chopped

Sandwich

- 1 loaf (14 ounces) ciabatta bread (about 12 inches), split horizontally
- 2 medium tomatoes, sliced
- 2 medium avocados, pitted, peeled and sliced
- 1/2 pound sliced pepper bacon, crisply cooked

1. In small bowl, mix chipotle aioli ingredients. Cover and refrigerate until ready to serve.

2. Spread bottom half of loaf with aioli. Top with tomatoes, avocados and bacon. Top with other half of loaf. To serve, cut into slices 2 inches thick.

1 SERVING: Calories 340; Total Fat 17g (Saturated Fat 3g); Sodium 620mg; Total Carbohydrate 36g (Dietary Fiber 5g); Protein 11g; **Exchanges:** 1 1/2 Starch; 1/2 Fruit; 1/2 Other Carbohydrate; 1 High-Fat Meat; 1 1/2 Fat; **Carbohydrate Choices:** 2 1/2

Antipasto Focaccia Sandwich Wedges

Get a taste of Italy in this super-simple sandwich, perfect for a summer lunch gathering.

PREP TIME: 15 MINUTES • **TOTAL TIME:** 15 MINUTES • **MAKES 6 SERVINGS**

$1/2$ **cup creamy Italian or regular Italian dressing**	$1/2$ **cup roasted red bell peppers (from a jar), cut into 2 x $1/4$-inch strips**
1 **focaccia bread (8 to 10 inches), cut in half horizontally**	1 **package (6 ounces) deli sliced provolone cheese**
4 **leaves romaine or iceberg lettuce**	6 **ounces thinly sliced hard salami**

1. Spread $1/4$ cup of the dressing on bottom half of focaccia bread. Layer lettuce, roasted peppers, cheese and salami over dressing.

2. Spread cut side of top half of bread with remaining $1/4$ cup dressing; place dressing side down over salami. Cut sandwich into wedges to serve.

BETTY'S SUCCESS TIPS

- Anchor each stacked sandwich wedge with a long toothpick or small skewer.
- For fun, add cherry tomatoes, banana peppers or olives to each toothpick before skewering the wedges.

1 SERVING: Calories 450; Total Fat 30g (Saturated Fat 10g); Sodium 1,350mg; Total Carbohydrate 27g (Dietary Fiber 1g); Protein 18g; **Exchanges:** 2 Starch; 2 High-Fat Meat; 2 Fat; **Carbohydrate Choices:** 2

Easy Backyard Cookout

Celebrate in your backyard with sensational new sliders and easy sips. With our easy tips, you'll be able to enjoy your own party.

FIRE UP THE GRILL EARLY

- Get the coals hot or preheat the grill before guests arrive.

MAKE SOME APPE-TEASERS

- Grilled food can take time to cook. So, prepare appetizers for folks to snack on while they're milling around waiting for the main course.

KEEP ESSENTIAL TOOLS HANDY

- A lighter, tongs, grill and basting brushes and a spray bottle for taming the flame—having these at the ready will make your life easier.

HAVE A PLAN B

- Make sure your house is ready for company just in case the weather turns and you have to bring the party indoors.

MENU

Mini Greek Burgers **246**

Grilled Baby Burgers **232**

Cajun Sweet Potato Fries with Yogurt Dipping Sauce **268**

Vegetable Kabobs with Mustard Dip **267**

Cashew-Fudge-Caramel Ice Cream Pie **287**

Chai iced tea

Hoagie Sandwiches on the Grill

This hefty meat-and-cheese sandwich cooks on the grill for delicious flavor and easy cleanup.

PREP TIME: 25 MINUTES • **TOTAL TIME:** 25 MINUTES • **MAKES 8 SANDWICHES**

8 soft hoagie buns (6 to 7 inches), split
3/4 cup creamy Dijon mustard–mayonnaise spread
8 slices (1 3/4 ounces each) provolone or mozzarella cheese, each cut into 4 pieces

1/2 pound thinly sliced salami or summer sausage
1 pound thinly sliced cooked turkey or chicken
1 medium green bell pepper, cut into thin bite-size strips

1. Heat gas or charcoal grill. Cut 8 (12 x 12-inch) sheets of heavy-duty foil. Spread cut sides of buns with mustard-mayonnaise spread.

2. On bottom halves of buns, layer cheese, salami, turkey and bell pepper. Cover with top halves of buns. Place sandwiches on foil. Wrap each packet securely using double-fold seals, allowing room for heat expansion.

3. Place packets on grill. Cover grill; cook over medium heat 8 to 10 minutes or until thoroughly heated. Carefully open packets to allow steam to escape.

BETTY'S SUCCESS TIP

Set out the ingredients for these hoagies and let guests prepare their own. Include extra mustards, mayonnaise and garnishes such as pickles and olives.

1 SANDWICH: Calories 560; Total Fat 25g (Saturated Fat 12g); Sodium 1,540mg; Total Carbohydrate 43g (Dietary Fiber 2g); Protein 39g; **Exchanges:** 2 1/2 Starch; 1/2 Other Carbohydrate; **Carbohydrate Choices:** 3

Super Summer Subs

Pick up a rotisserie chicken from the deli so you can assemble sub sandwiches in less than half an hour.

PREP TIME: 20 MINUTES • **TOTAL TIME:** 20 MINUTES • **MAKES 6 SANDWICHES**

Club-Style Filling, Mediterranean Filling or Western Barbecue Filling (below)

3 **cups shredded roasted chicken (from a deli rotisserie chicken)**

6 **soft hoagie or crusty submarine sandwich rolls (about 6 inches), split**

1. Choose one or more of the fillings and layer with chicken on rolls.

2. Club-Style Filling: Spread ¹/₂ cup honey mustard on cut sides of rolls. Layer with 4 ounces thinly sliced cooked roast beef or fully cooked ham. Top with chicken. Add 6 tablespoons sliced ripe or pimiento-stuffed olives; 2 medium tomatoes, sliced; and, if desired, spinach leaves. Mediterranean Filling: Spread ¹/₂ cup hummus on cut sides of rolls. Layer with 1 small red onion, thinly sliced; 2 ounces feta cheese, crumbled (¹/₂ cup); 24 spinach leaves and the chicken. Western Barbecue Filling: Spread ¹/₂ cup guacamole on cut sides of rolls. Layer with chicken. Drizzle with ¹/₄ cup barbecue sauce. Add 1 small green bell pepper, thinly sliced.

1 SANDWICH: Calories 390; Total Fat 12g (Saturated Fat 3g); Sodium 810mg; Total Carbohydrate 41g (Dietary Fiber 4g); Protein 32g; **Exchanges:** 2 Starch; ¹/₂ Other Carbohydrate; 3¹/₂ Very Lean Meat; **Carbohydrate Choices:** 3

Chili Dog Tacos

Here's a playful twist on hot dogs in a bun. Use prepared chunky salsa and canned pinto beans for fast toppings that don't skimp on flavor.

PREP TIME: 20 MINUTES • **TOTAL TIME:** 20 MINUTES • **MAKES 10 TACOS**

½ **pound lean (at least 80%) ground beef**	10 **hot dogs**
½ **cup Old El Paso® Thick 'n Chunky salsa**	1¼ **cups shredded Cheddar cheese (5 ounces)**
1 **can (16 ounces) pinto beans, drained**	¼ **cup finely chopped onion**
10 **Old El Paso® taco shells (from 4.6-ounce box)**	

1. Heat oven to 375°F. In 8-inch nonstick skillet, cook ground beef over medium-high heat 5 to 7 minutes, stirring occasionally, until thoroughly cooked; drain. Stir in salsa and beans. Cook until thoroughly heated.

2. Meanwhile, heat taco shells as directed on box.

3. In 10-inch nonstick skillet, cook hot dogs over medium-high heat 2 to 3 minutes, turning frequently, until browned.

4. Place hot dogs in taco shells; top each with ground beef mixture, cheese and onion.

BETTY'S SUCCESS TIP

Some kids don't like pinto beans. To keep everyone happy, heat the beans separately and let diners add them to their tacos if they wish.

1 TACO: Calories 300; Total Fat 20g (Saturated Fat 7g); Sodium 770mg; Total Carbohydrate 21g (Dietary Fiber 4g); Protein 14g; **Exchanges:** 1 Starch; ½ Other Carbohydrate; 2 Fat; **Carbohydrate Choices:** 1½

Fish Tacos with Pico de Gallo

Enjoy these tacos made with fish, pico de gallo salsa and Old El Paso® flour tortillas—a tasty Mexican dinner that's ready in 25 minutes.

PREP TIME: 25 MINUTES • **TOTAL TIME:** 25 MINUTES • **MAKES 12 TACOS**

1 1/2 pounds firm white fish fillets (halibut, cod, red snapper), cut into 1-inch pieces
2 tablespoons olive oil
1 teaspoon ground cumin
1/2 teaspoon coarse (kosher or sea) salt
1/4 teaspoon pepper
2 cloves garlic, finely chopped

2 tablespoons fresh lemon juice
1 package (8.2 ounces) Old El Paso® flour tortillas for soft tacos & fajitas (6 inch), warmed
1/2 cup pico de gallo salsa
Sour cream, chopped avocado, chopped tomatoes, chopped lettuce, if desired

1. Brush fish fillets with 1 tablespoon of the olive oil; sprinkle with cumin, salt and pepper. Set aside.

2. In 12-inch skillet, heat remaining 1 tablespoon olive oil over medium-high heat. Stir in garlic; cook 1 minute. Add fish fillets; cook 5 to 7 minutes or until fish flakes easily with fork. Drizzle with lemon juice.

3. Spoon fish onto each tortilla; top with pico de gallo. Roll up tortillas. Serve with remaining ingredients.

1 TACO: Calories 120; Total Fat 5g (Saturated Fat 1g); Sodium 320mg; Total Carbohydrate 11g (Dietary Fiber 0g); Protein 8g; **Exchanges:** 1/2 Starch; 1 Very Lean Meat; 1 Fat; **Carbohydrate Choices:** 1

Chicken Nopales Tacos with Chipotle

Treat your family with these tacos made with nopales, chicken, Old El Paso® salsa and tortillas—a delicious Mexican dinner that's ready in just 15 minutes.

PREP TIME: 15 MINUTES • TOTAL TIME: 15 MINUTES • MAKES 12 TACOS

3 tablespoons olive oil

1 cup thinly sliced onion

3 cloves garlic, finely chopped

1 jar (30 ounces) nopales, drained, or 1 pound fresh nopales (3 or 4), cleaned and cut into strips

4 cups shredded cooked chicken

1 jar (16 ounces) Old El Paso® Thick 'n Chunky salsa

1 tablespoon adobo sauce (from 7-ounce can chipotle chiles in adobo sauce)

1/3 cup chopped fresh cilantro

1 package (8.2 ounces) Old El Paso® flour tortillas for soft tacos & fajitas (6 inch), warmed

1. In 12-inch skillet, heat oil over medium-high heat. Stir in onion and garlic; cook and stir about 5 minutes or until onion is tender.

2. Stir in nopales, chicken, salsa and adobo sauce. Cook and stir about 3 minutes or until mixture is hot. Stir in cilantro.

3. Spoon about 1/3 cup chicken mixture onto each tortilla. Roll up tortillas.

1 TACO: Calories 200; Total Fat 9g (Saturated Fat 2g); Sodium 510mg; Total Carbohydrate 16g (Dietary Fiber 1g); Protein 15g; **Exchanges:** 1/2 Starch; 1 1/2 Vegetable; 1/2 Very Lean Meat; 1 Lean Meat; 1 Fat; **Carbohydrate Choices:** 1

No Bake Salad Pizza

No cooking required! Enjoy dinner with this chicken and veggies salad served on a prebaked Italian pizza crust—ready in just 10 minutes!

PREP TIME: 10 MINUTES • **TOTAL TIME:** 10 MINUTES • **MAKES 6 SERVINGS**

1 cup spinach dip	1 cup cubed cooked chicken
1 package (10 ounces) prebaked thin Italian pizza crust (12 inch)	3 tablespoons sliced green onions (3 medium)
1 cup coarsely chopped fresh broccoli	1 small tomato, seeded, chopped ($\frac{1}{2}$ cup)

1. Spread spinach dip evenly over pizza crust to within $\frac{1}{2}$ inch of edge.

2. Top with remaining ingredients. Cut into 6 wedges.

BETTY'S SUCCESS TIP

Use other vegetables that you have on hand to vary the topping on this pizza, such as chopped ready-to-eat baby-cut carrots, shredded lettuce or sliced olives.

1 SERVING: Calories 260; Total Fat 11g (Saturated Fat 3½g); Sodium 500mg; Total Carbohydrate 26g (Dietary Fiber 2g); Protein 13g; **Exchanges:** 2 Starch; 1 Fat; **Carbohydrate Choices:** 2

Food on a Roll

The food truck phenomenon is sweeping the nation. Chefs from New York to L.A. (and everywhere in between) are taking to the streets, trading in full-sized kitchens for close quarters on the open road. And Americans are eating it up!

Food is made fresh, fast and on the spot—which may or may not be the same from day to day. For some patrons, using Twitter to track down their favorite food truck is half the fun. The other half, of course, is the food.

As for food truck fare, the only rule seems to be that there is no rule; anything goes. Taking our cues from international flavors and regional favorites, we've created five recipes that are sure to have your friends and family lined up around the block!

Grilled Baby Burgers

Seasonings, cheese, tomatoes and pickles give bite-size burgers big flavor. Make them in 30 minutes!

PREP TIME: 30 MINUTES • **TOTAL TIME:** 30 MINUTES • **MAKES 16 BURGERS**

1 pound lean (at least 80%) ground beef
2 teaspoons dried minced onion
1 teaspoon parsley flakes
$3/4$ teaspoon seasoned salt
4 slices (1 ounce each) American cheese, cut into quarters
8 slices white bread, toasted, crusts trimmed, cut into quarters

16 thin slices roma (plum) tomatoes (2 small), if desired
16 thin hamburger-style dill pickle slices, if desired
   Ketchup, if desired
   Mustard, if desired

1. Heat gas or charcoal grill. In medium bowl, mix beef, onion, parsley and seasoned salt. Divide into 16 portions. Shape each portion into a ball and flatten to $1/2$-inch-thick patty, about $1 1/2$ inches in diameter. On each of 4 (12-inch) metal skewers, thread 4 patties horizontally, leaving space between each.

2. Place patties on grill. Cover grill; cook over medium heat 8 to 10 minutes, turning once, until patties are no longer pink in center (160°F).

3. Top each burger with cheese piece. Place each burger on toast square. Top with tomato slice and another toast square. Place pickle slice on top; spear with toothpick to hold layers together. Serve with ketchup and mustard for dipping.

BETTY'S SUCCESS TIPS

- These cute little burgers can be mixed and shaped ahead of time. Just cover and refrigerate them until you are ready to grill.
- Some plum tomatoes are quite large. Select smaller tomatoes for this recipe so they are about the same size as the burgers.

1 BURGER: Calories 110; Total Fat 6g (Saturated Fat $2 1/2$g); Sodium 270mg; Total Carbohydrate 7g (Dietary Fiber 0g); Protein 8g; **Exchanges:** $1/2$ Starch; **Carbohydrate Choices:** $1/2$

Grilled Antipasti Platter with Lemon Aioli

Serve your family with grilled vegetables placed upon salami sprinkled with cheese and served with lemon aioli—tasty appetizers ready in just an hour.

PREP TIME: 35 MINUTES • **TOTAL TIME:** 1 HOUR 5 MINUTES • **MAKES 10 SERVINGS**

Lemon Aioli

- 1 cup mayonnaise or salad dressing
- 1 teaspoon grated lemon peel
- 2 tablespoons fresh lemon juice
- 1 to 2 cloves garlic, finely chopped

Antipasti

- 1 medium zucchini, cut into 4-inch sticks
- 1 medium yellow summer squash or crookneck squash, cut into 4-inch sticks
- 1 medium red bell pepper, cut into 2-inch pieces
- 2 cups cherry tomatoes
- 1 cup small whole mushrooms
- 1 medium red onion, cut into $1/2$-inch wedges
- 2 tablespoons olive or vegetable oil
- 1 teaspoon salt
- 20 thin slices hard salami (about $1/4$ pound)
- $1/2$ pound mozzarella cheese, cut into $1/2$-inch cubes

1. In small bowl, stir all aioli ingredients until well mixed. Cover and refrigerate at least 1 hour before serving.

2. Heat coals or gas grill for direct heat.

3. In large bowl, toss vegetables with oil and salt. Heat grill basket (grill "wok") on grill until hot. Add vegetables to grill basket. Cover and grill vegetables 6 to 10 minutes, shaking basket or stirring vegetables occasionally, until vegetables are crisp-tender and lightly charred.

4. Arrange salami around edge of large serving platter. Mound grilled vegetables onto center of serving platter. Sprinkle cheese cubes over vegetables. Serve with aioli for dipping.

BETTY'S SUCCESS TIP

Omit grilling step. Add 1 cup pitted whole ripe olives and 10 pepperoncini peppers (bottled Italian peppers), drained, with the cheese cubes.

1 SERVING: Calories 320; Total Fat 28g (Saturated Fat 7g); Sodium 690mg; Total Carbohydrate 7g (Dietary Fiber 1g); Protein 9g; **Exchanges:** 1 Vegetable; 1 High-Fat Meat; 4 Fat; **Carbohydrate Choices:** $1/2$

Basil- and Crabmeat-Topped Cucumbers

Crisp cucumber slices are topped with a creamy crabmeat spread for a colorful, appetizing snack.

PREP TIME: 40 MINUTES • **TOTAL TIME:** 40 MINUTES • **MAKES 36 APPETIZERS**

1 medium English cucumber	2 teaspoons grated lemon peel
1 package (3 ounces) cream cheese, softened	1 cup frozen cooked crabmeat, thawed, flaked
2 tablespoons mayonnaise or salad dressing	2 tablespoons capers, if desired
1/4 cup chopped fresh basil leaves	Small basil leaves or chopped fresh basil, if desired
2 tablespoons finely chopped red onion	

1. Score cucumber lengthwise with tines of fork if desired. Cut into 36 (1/4-inch) slices.

2. In small bowl, beat cream cheese with electric mixer on low speed until creamy. Beat in mayonnaise until well blended. Stir in 1/4 cup chopped basil, onion, lemon peel and crabmeat.

3. Spread or pipe about 1 teaspoon crabmeat mixture on each cucumber slice. Sprinkle with capers. Garnish with basil leaves.

BETTY'S SUCCESS TIPS

- English cucumbers, also called hothouse cucumbers, have very small seeds and thin skins that don't require peeling, so they work well for this appetizer.
- If you can't find frozen crabmeat, use a 6-ounce can of crabmeat, well drained.

1 APPETIZER: Calories 18; Total Fat 1 1/2 g (Saturated Fat 1/2 g); Sodium 25mg; Total Carbohydrate 0g (Dietary Fiber 0g); Protein 1g; **Exchanges:** 0; **Carbohydrate Choices:** 0

Hawaiian Appetizer Quesadillas

Combine Canadian bacon, pineapple and cheese for a savory snack, hot out of the oven.

PREP TIME: 20 MINUTES • **TOTAL TIME:** 35 MINUTES • **MAKES 32 APPETIZERS**

1 package (11.5 ounces) Old El Paso® flour tortillas for burritos (8 tortillas)

1 cup finely chopped cooked Canadian bacon (about 5 ounces)

½ cup crushed pineapple (from 8-ounce can), well drained

1 cup finely shredded Mexican cheese blend (4 ounces)

½ cup mango or peach salsa, if desired

1. Move oven rack to lowest position; heat oven to 400°F. Spray one side of 4 tortillas with cooking spray. On large cookie sheet, place tortillas, sprayed sides down, overlapping in center so tortillas do not hang over edge of sheet. Top evenly with bacon, pineapple, cheese and remaining tortillas. Spray tops of tortillas with cooking spray. Place another cookie sheet on top of tortillas; press down.

2. Bake on bottom oven rack 8 to 10 minutes or until bottom tortillas are golden brown. Turn cookie sheets and quesadillas over. Bake about 5 minutes longer or until bottoms are golden brown and cheese is melted. Cut each quesadilla into 8 small wedges; serve warm with salsa.

BETTY'S SUCCESS TIPS

- Feel free to use any kind of shredded cheese you like in these tropical quesadillas.
- Stir fresh mango or peach pieces into purchased salsa if you can't find mango or peach salsa.

1 APPETIZER: Calories 60; Total Fat 2½g (Saturated Fat 1g); Sodium 160mg; Total Carbohydrate 6g (Dietary Fiber 0g); Protein 3g; **Exchanges:** ½ Starch; ½ Fat; **Carbohydrate Choices:** ½

Farmer's Crostini

Appetizer ready in 40 minutes! Try this tasty bread topped with a cucumber and tomato mixture layered with cheese.

PREP TIME: 40 MINUTES • **TOTAL TIME:** 40 MINUTES • **MAKES 20 SERVINGS**

1 baguette (14 ounces), cut into 40 (1/4-inch) slices

2 packages (3 ounces each) cream cheese, softened

1/4 cup crumbled blue cheese (from 5-ounce container)

1/4 cup mayonnaise or salad dressing

1/4 teaspoon garlic powder

1/4 teaspoon salt

1/8 teaspoon pepper

1/2 medium cucumber, finely chopped

1 small ripe tomato, finely chopped

1/2 medium red or yellow bell pepper, cut into matchsticks

Fresh flat-leaf (Italian) parsley leaves, if desired

1. Heat oven to 325°F. Place bread slices on ungreased cookie sheet; spray lightly with cooking spray. Bake 6 to 9 minutes or until crispy. Remove to wire rack; cool completely.

2. In medium bowl, beat cream cheese, blue cheese, mayonnaise, garlic powder, salt and pepper with electric mixer on medium speed until well blended.

3. In small bowl, stir together cucumber, tomato and bell pepper.

4. Spread about 1 teaspoon cheese mixture on top of each slice of baguette. Top with cucumber and tomato mixture. Garnish with parsley.

BETTY'S SUCCESS TIPS

- Substitute vegetables, as desired. Other fresh vegetable options might include tiny broccoli florets, sliced fresh mushrooms, shredded carrot or sliced green onions.
- Garnish with fresh dill sprigs or fresh thyme sprigs.
- Grilled vegetables including grilled zucchini or summer squash, red onion strips, or peppers are great on these crostini. Allow grilled vegetables to cool slightly before placing on cheese mixture.

2 CROSTINI: Calories 120; Total Fat 6g (Saturated Fat 2 1/2 g); Sodium 230mg; Total Carbohydrate 12g (Dietary Fiber 0g); Protein 3g; **Exchanges:** 1 Starch; 1 Fat; **Carbohydrate Choices:** 1

Pizza-Filled Pretzels

Add these pretzels that are made using pizza crust and filled with pepperoni to your bread basket.

PREP TIME: 30 MINUTES • **TOTAL TIME:** 45 MINUTES • **MAKES 4 PRETZELS**

Pizza Filling

- 1/2 cup finely shredded mozzarella cheese (2 ounces)
- 1/2 cup finely chopped pepperoni
- 2 tablespoons pizza sauce

Pretzels

- 1 can (13.8 ounces) refrigerated classic pizza crust
- 2 cups water
- 1/4 cup baking soda
- 1 egg
- 1 tablespoon water
- Coarse (kosher or sea) salt
- Pizza sauce, as desired

1. Heat oven to 400°F. In small bowl, mix pizza filling ingredients; set aside. Line large cookie sheet with cooking parchment paper. Unroll pizza crust dough onto lightly floured surface; roll into 14 x 12-inch rectangle. Using pizza cutter, cut dough lengthwise into 4 strips.

2. Spoon about 1/4 cup of the filling onto long edge of each dough strip. Stretch dough over filling; brush edges with water, and pinch to seal. Pick up ends of filled dough, and stretch to make 24-inch rope.

3. To make pretzel shape, form each rope into U shape. Twist ends twice. Press down where dough overlaps in an "X" to hold shape. Pick up ends and fold over so they rest over bottom of U shape.

4. In medium microwavable bowl, microwave 2 cups water uncovered on High about 2 minutes or until hot. Add baking soda; stir until dissolved. Dip each pretzel, one at a time, into water mixture. Immediately remove from water with large pancake turner; let stand about 5 minutes. In small bowl, beat egg and 1 tablespoon water with whisk; brush pretzels with egg mixture.

5. Place pretzels on cookie sheet; sprinkle with salt. Bake 11 to 15 minutes or until tops of pretzels are dark golden brown. Serve with pizza sauce.

1 PRETZEL: Calories 360; Total Fat 11g (Saturated Fat 3 1/2 g); Sodium 1,670mg; Total Carbohydrate 50g (Dietary Fiber 2g); Protein 13g; **Exchanges:** 2 Starch; 1 1/2 Other Carbohydrate; 1 High-Fat Meat; 1/2 Fat; **Carbohydrate Choices:** 3

Fresh Tomato-Basil Caprese Kabobs

Fancy Italian skewers will earn raves at any gathering. Assemble them in only 30 minutes!

PREP TIME: 30 MINUTES • **TOTAL TIME:** 1 HOUR 30 MINUTES • **MAKES 34 KABOBS**

1/4 cup extra-virgin olive oil

2 tablespoons lemon juice

2/3 cup coarsely chopped fresh basil or lemon basil leaves

1/4 teaspoon salt

1/4 teaspoon freshly ground black pepper

1 pint red cherry tomatoes

1 pint yellow cherry tomatoes

2 medium zucchini or yellow squash, cubed

1 pound fresh mozzarella cheese, cubed

34 (6-inch) bamboo skewers

Fresh basil leaves, if desired

1. In large bowl, mix oil, lemon juice, basil, salt and pepper, using wire whisk. Add tomatoes, zucchini and cheese. Cover and refrigerate about 30 minutes.

2. Drain vegetables, reserving olive oil mixture. Thread skewers alternately with tomatoes, zucchini and cheese; top with basil leaf. Serve kabobs with reserved olive oil mixture.

BETTY'S SUCCESS TIPS

- Virtually any skewer-able vegetable will work in this recipe. Try red, green or yellow bell pepper pieces or fresh pea pods.
- Thread the vegetables and cheese between large leaves of fresh basil for a different look.

1 KABOB: Calories 60; Total Fat 4 1/2 g (Saturated Fat 2g); Sodium 90mg; Total Carbohydrate 2g (Dietary Fiber 0g); Protein 4g; **Exchanges:** 1/2 Fat; **Carbohydrate Choices:** 0

Elderflower-White Wine Sangria

A quick, refreshing, fruity and lightly floral summer drink.

PREP TIME: 10 MINUTES • **TOTAL TIME:** 40 MINUTES • **MAKES 8 SERVINGS**

1 bottle (750 milliliters) white wine	½ orange, thinly sliced
1½ cups elderflower liqueur	1 cup berries (raspberries and blackberries)
1 ripe medium mango, seed removed, peeled and chopped (1 cup)	1 bottle (1 liter) sparkling water, chilled
½ lime, thinly sliced	Ice

1. In pitcher, stir together all ingredients except sparkling water and ice. Refrigerate at least 30 minutes or until ready to serve.

2. Just before serving, pour sparkling water into pitcher to fill. Stir gently to mix. Fill glasses with ice; pour mixture over ice. Top with remaining sparkling water.

BETTY'S SUCCESS TIPS

- You can make everything up to 1 day ahead—just wait until 30 minutes before serving to assemble.
- Mix up the fruit; use whatever is your favorite or is in season!

1 SERVING: Calories 170; Total Fat 0g (Saturated Fat 0g); Sodium 0mg; Total Carbohydrate 24g (Dietary Fiber 2g); Protein 0g; **Exchanges:** 0; **Carbohydrate Choices:** 1½

Frozen Mango COCOritas

Blend up fruity margaritas made with sweet mango, fresh lime juice and coconut water.

PREP TIME: 10 MINUTES • **TOTAL TIME:** 2 HOURS 10 MINUTES • **MAKES 4 SERVINGS**

1½ cups coconut water	2 tablespoons light agave nectar
3 ounces blanco tequila	1½ cups chopped fresh mango
1 ounce clear orange-flavored liqueur	Mango or lime slices, if desired for garnish
1 ounce fresh lime juice	

1. Pour coconut water into standard ice cube tray. Place in freezer until frozen, about 2 hours.

2. In blender, add tequila, orange-flavored liqueur, lime juice, agave nectar and chopped mango. Cover; blend until smooth. Add coconut water ice cubes; blend until smooth.

3. Pour into 4 glasses. Garnish as desired.

1 SERVING: Calories 160; Total Fat 0g (Saturated Fat 0g); Sodium 95mg; Total Carbohydrate 23g (Dietary Fiber 2g); Protein 1g; **Exchanges:** 0; **Carbohydrate Choices:** 1½

Summer Luau

Have some laid-back fun this summer by hosting a backyard bash with a wink to the tropics. Keep the party casual yet festive with beachy music, fruity cocktails and a flip-flops-required dress code.

THE SETUP

- Favors: Welcome guests with plastic or floral leis as they come through the door or back gate.
- Footwear: Fill a basket with inexpensive, colorful flip-flops for everyone to wear. Set out a few markers so that people can decorate or sign each other's pairs.
- Décor: Light a few tiki torches or a bonfire, hang colorful paper lanterns or streamers, and set out plenty of chairs and benches.
- Playlist: Go throwback with the Beach Boys or Frankie Avalon. Any classic surf songs will fit the bill.
- Games: Channel the beach party mood with a limbo contest once the party is in full swing.
- Movies: Play old beach movies like *Back to the Beach* if you have a projector and an open wall for screening.

MENU IDEAS

Frozen Mango COCOritas **242**

Blend up fruity margaritas made with sweet mango, fresh lime juice and coconut water.

Hawaiian Appetizer Quesadillas **235**

Pair Canadian bacon, pineapple and cheese for a savory snack, hot out of the oven.

Grilled Spicy Garlic Shrimp, Pepper and Pineapple Kabobs **252**

Make sensational shrimp! The secret is the peppy citrus marinade that goes together in minutes.

Maui Dogs **260**

Looking for dinner with a tropical twist? Then check out these grilled beef hot dogs placed in hoagie buns spooned with pineapple salsa—ready in just 15 minutes!

Flip-Flop Fun Cookies **296**

Transform purchased peanut butter cookies into adorable summertime treats . . . you'll flip over how simple they are to make!

Mai Tai Tiki Pops **308**

These rum-spiked frozen treats take the flavors of a well-known tiki cocktail—the Mai Tai—and turn them into a fruity (and boozy) ice pop.

Grilled Ribs with Cherry Cola Barbecue Sauce

Lick-your-fingers good! Baby back ribs are a fantastic summertime supper.

PREP TIME: 30 MINUTES • **TOTAL TIME:** 2 HOURS • **MAKES 6 SERVINGS**

5 to 6 pounds pork baby back ribs	1 can (12 ounces) cherry cola
1 teaspoon seasoned salt	1/4 cup cherry preserves
1 teaspoon garlic pepper blend	1/2 teaspoon ground mustard
1/2 teaspoon ground ginger	1 to 2 teaspoons buffalo wing hot sauce or other hot sauce
1 cup barbecue sauce	

1. Heat oven to 350°F. Cut ribs into serving-size sections. Rub ribs with seasoned salt, garlic pepper and ginger. Place ribs in 15 x 10 x 1-inch pan, overlapping slightly. Bake uncovered about 1 hour 30 minutes or until tender.

2. Meanwhile, in 2-quart saucepan, mix barbecue sauce, cola, preserves, mustard and buffalo wing sauce. Heat to boiling; reduce heat to medium-low. Simmer uncovered 30 to 40 minutes, stirring occasionally, until flavors are blended and sauce is slightly thickened.

3. Heat coals or gas grill for direct heat. Cover and grill ribs over medium heat 10 to 15 minutes, turning and brushing occasionally with barbecue sauce mixture to glaze.

4. Heat remaining barbecue sauce mixture to boiling; boil and stir 1 minute. Serve sauce with ribs.

BETTY'S SUCCESS TIPS

- Precooking the ribs in the oven or microwave shortens the grilling time, helps tenderize the meat and removes some of the fat.
- You can use regular cola instead of the cherry cola if you like.

1 SERVING: Calories 830; Total Fat 55g (Saturated Fat 20g); Sodium 840mg; Total Carbohydrate 31g (Dietary Fiber 0g); Protein 53g; **Exchanges:** 2 Other Carbohydrate; 1/2 Fat; **Carbohydrate Choices:** 2

Mini Greek Burgers

Take a taste trip to the Mediterranean in 30 minutes! Mini burgers are topped with a creamy yogurt sauce, cucumber and onion.

PREP TIME: 30 MINUTES • **TOTAL TIME:** 30 MINUTES • **MAKES 16 SANDWICHES**

Sauce

- $3/4$ cup Yoplait® Fat Free plain yogurt (from 2-pound container)
- 1 teaspoon grated lemon peel
- 1 clove garlic, finely chopped
- $1/4$ teaspoon salt
- $1/4$ teaspoon dried dill weed

Burgers

- 1 pound lean (at least 80%) ground beef
- $1/4$ cup Progresso® plain bread crumbs
- 1 tablespoon balsamic vinegar
- 2 teaspoons finely grated lemon peel
- 2 teaspoons fresh lemon juice
- 1 teaspoon dried oregano leaves
- 1 teaspoon dried thyme leaves
- $1/2$ teaspoon salt
- 3 cloves garlic, finely chopped

Breads and Toppings

- 16 mini ($2^1/2$-inch) pita breads (from one 7-ounce bag)
- $1/2$ medium cucumber, cut into very thin slices
- $1/4$ small red onion, cut into bite-size strips

1. In small bowl, mix sauce ingredients. Cover; refrigerate until ready to use.

2. In large bowl, mix burger ingredients until well mixed. Shape beef mixture into 16 patties, about $1/4$ inch thick.

3. Place 8 patties in 12-inch nonstick skillet; cook over medium-low heat about 3 minutes. Turn patties; cook 2 to 4 minutes longer or until meat thermometer inserted in center of patties reads 160°F. Remove patties from skillet; cover to keep warm. Repeat with remaining patties.

4. With serrated knife, cut pita breads in half horizontally. Place patties on bottom halves of breads. Top each patty with about 2 teaspoons sauce, several slices of cucumber and strips of onion. Cover with top halves of breads. Serve immediately.

BETTY'S SUCCESS TIP

- If you can't find mini pita breads, purchase regular-size ones and cut into quarters.
- Look for mini pitas in the deli or bakery section of your local grocery store.

1 SANDWICH: Calories 90; Total Fat $3^1/2$g (Saturated Fat $1^1/2$g); Sodium 190mg; Total Carbohydrate 8g (Dietary Fiber 0g); Protein 6g; **Exchanges:** $1/2$ Starch; **Carbohydrate Choices:** $1/2$

Grilled Herb Chicken on a Can

The secret to perfectly tender and exceptionally juicy chicken is balancing a bird on a beer can. Don't worry; it's easier than it looks!

PREP TIME: 10 MINUTES • **TOTAL TIME:** 1 HOUR 55 MINUTES • **MAKES 6 SERVINGS**

1 **tablespoon paprika**	¹/₂ **teaspoon pepper**
2 **teaspoons salt**	1 **whole chicken (4 to 4¹/₂ pounds)**
¹/₂ **teaspoon garlic powder**	1 **can (12 ounces) regular or**
¹/₂ **teaspoon onion powder**	**nonalcoholic beer**

1. If using charcoal grill, place drip pan directly under grilling area, and arrange coals around edge of firebox. Heat coals or gas grill for indirect heat. In small bowl, mix paprika, salt, garlic powder, onion powder and pepper.

2. Fold wings of chicken across back with tips touching. Sprinkle paprika mixture inside cavity and over outside of chicken; rub with fingers.

3. Pour ¹/₂ cup of beer from can. Hold chicken upright, with opening of body cavity down; insert beer can into cavity. Insert barbecue meat thermometer so tip is in thickest part of inside thigh muscle and does not touch bone.

4. Cover and grill chicken upright over drip pan or over unheated side of gas grill over medium heat 1 hour 15 minutes to 1 hour 30 minutes or until thermometer reads 180°F and juice is no longer pink when center of thigh is cut.

5. Using tongs, carefully lift chicken and place in 13 x 9-inch pan, holding large metal spatula under beer can for support. Let stand 15 minutes before carving. Remove beer can; discard.

BETTY'S SUCCESS TIP

Use a 12-ounce can of lemon-lime soda pop instead of the beer. The flavor will be slightly different, but the chicken will be tender and juicy.

1 SERVING: Calories 320; Total Fat 18g (Saturated Fat 5g); Sodium 500mg; Total Carbohydrate 4g (Dietary Fiber 0g); Protein 35g; **Exchanges:** 5 Lean Meat; 1 Fat; **Carbohydrate Choices:** 0

Grilled Firecracker Chicken Drummies

Serve sour cream on the side to cut the heat of chicken drummies seasoned with chili powder and cayenne pepper.

PREP TIME: 35 MINUTES • **TOTAL TIME:** 1 HOUR 35 MINUTES • **MAKES 20 APPETIZERS**

2 tablespoons chili powder	1 teaspoon pepper
1½ teaspoons dried oregano leaves	2 packages (1 pound each) chicken wing drummettes
1¼ teaspoons ground red pepper (cayenne)	Sour cream, if desired
1 teaspoon garlic salt	Paprika, if desired
1 teaspoon ground cumin	

1. In 1-gallon resealable food-storage plastic bag, place all ingredients except chicken, sour cream and paprika. Seal bag; shake to blend seasonings. Add chicken; seal bag and shake until chicken is coated with seasonings. Refrigerate at least 1 hour to marinate but no longer than 24 hours.

2. Heat gas or charcoal grill. Place chicken in grill basket (grill "wok"). Place basket on grill over medium heat. Cover grill; cook 20 to 25 minutes, shaking basket to turn chicken after 10 minutes, until juice of chicken is clear when thickest part is cut to bone and thermometer reads 180°F.

3. Serve chicken with sour cream sprinkled with paprika.

BETTY'S SUCCESS TIPS

- Purchased blue cheese dressing can be served instead of the sour cream and paprika.
- Grill baskets (grill "woks") are available at discount stores or in kitchen specialty shops.

1 APPETIZER: Calories 50; Total Fat 2½g (Saturated Fat 1g); Sodium 70mg; Total Carbohydrate 0g (Dietary Fiber 0g); Protein 6g; **Exchanges:** 1 Lean Meat; **Carbohydrate Choices:** 0

Grilled Barbecue Chicken Kabobs

Simply delicious chicken and veggie skewers with a tangy citrus sauce go from the grill to the table in no time.

PREP TIME: 45 MINUTES • **TOTAL TIME:** 45 MINUTES • **MAKES 4 SERVINGS**

1/2 cup barbecue sauce
1/4 cup orange marmalade
1 pound boneless skinless chicken breasts, cut into 3/4-inch pieces
1/2 medium red onion, cut into 1-inch chunks

1 medium red bell pepper, cut into 1-inch chunks
2 tablespoons olive or vegetable oil
1 teaspoon seasoned salt

1. Heat gas or charcoal grill. In small microwavable bowl, mix barbecue sauce and marmalade. Remove 1/4 cup of the sauce mixture to small dish; set aside.

2. On each of 4 (11-inch) metal skewers, thread chicken pieces, leaving 1/4-inch space between each piece. On 4 additional skewers, thread onion and bell pepper chunks, leaving 1/4-inch space between each piece. Brush chicken and vegetables with oil; sprinkle with seasoned salt.

3. Place kabobs on grill over medium heat. Cover grill; cook 10 to 15 minutes, turning kabobs 2 or 3 times and brushing chicken and vegetables with reserved 1/4 cup sauce mixture during last 5 to 8 minutes of grilling, until chicken is no longer pink in center.

4. Microwave remaining barbecue sauce mixture uncovered on High 20 to 30 seconds or until thoroughly heated. Serve sauce with kabobs.

BETTY'S SUCCESS TIPS

- Serve kabobs with coleslaw and baked beans for a down-home dinner.
- Barbecue sauces vary widely in flavor, from a manufacturer's original flavor to hickory, mesquite, honey, spicy, honey-mustard, sweet, sassy and low-sodium varieties. Experiment to find your favorite.

1 SERVING: Calories 320; Total Fat 11g (Saturated Fat 2g); Sodium 740mg; Total Carbohydrate 30g (Dietary Fiber 1g); Protein 25g; **Exchanges:** 2 Other Carbohydrate; 3 1/2 Lean Meat; **Carbohydrate Choices:** 2

Grilled Spicy Garlic Shrimp, Pepper and Pineapple Kabobs

Make sensational shrimp! The secret is the peppy citrus marinade that goes together in minutes.

PREP TIME: 25 MINUTES • **TOTAL TIME:** 40 MINUTES • **MAKES 4 KABOBS**

Pineapple-Lime Marinade
- 2 tablespoons olive or vegetable oil
- 1 teaspoon grated lime peel
- 2 tablespoons lime juice
- 2 tablespoons reserved pineapple juice from can of pineapple
- $1/4$ teaspoon salt
- $1/4$ teaspoon red pepper sauce
- 2 cloves garlic, finely chopped

Kabobs
- $3/4$ pound uncooked peeled, deveined large shrimp, thawed if frozen
- 1 can (8 ounces) pineapple chunks in juice, drained, 2 tablespoons juice reserved for marinade
- 1 orange bell pepper, cut into 12 pieces
- 4 medium green onions, cut into $1^1/_2$-inch pieces

1. In shallow glass or plastic dish or resealable food-storage plastic bag, mix marinade ingredients. Add shrimp, pineapple, bell pepper and onions; stir to coat. Cover dish or seal bag; refrigerate 15 to 30 minutes, turning once or twice.

2. Heat gas or charcoal grill. Carefully brush vegetable oil on grill rack. On each of 4 (12- to 14-inch) metal skewers, thread shrimp, pineapple, bell pepper and onions alternately, leaving small space between each piece. Reserve marinade.

3. Place kabobs on grill over medium heat. Cover grill; cook 5 to 7 minutes, turning and brushing with marinade once, until shrimp are pink and vegetables are tender. Discard any remaining marinade.

BETTY'S SUCCESS TIPS

- Marinating for a little longer will intensify the flavor slightly, but don't marinate for more than 2 hours. The marinade will start to break down the tissues in the shrimp, and the bell pepper will not be as pretty.
- This marinade is also delicious on chicken breasts. Marinate as directed, then grill until the juice of the chicken is clear when center of thickest part is cut and thermometer reads 170°F.

1 KABOB: Calories 100; Total Fat $2^1/_2$g (Saturated Fat 0g); Sodium 135mg; Total Carbohydrate 11g (Dietary Fiber 1g); Protein 9g; **Exchanges:** 1 Other Carbohydrate; 1 Lean Meat; **Carbohydrate Choices:** 1

Grilled Honey-Cumin BBQ Pork Packs

Peek into a packet of power-packed pork! You'll find a whole meal with saucy veggies!

PREP TIME: 20 MINUTES • **TOTAL TIME:** 40 MINUTES • **MAKES 4 SERVINGS**

$1/2$ cup barbecue sauce

$1/4$ cup honey

2 teaspoons ground cumin

4 pork boneless rib or loin chops, $3/4$ to 1 inch thick ($1 1/4$ pounds)

2 large ears corn, each cut into 6 pieces

1 cup baby-cut carrots, cut lengthwise in half

2 cups (from 1-pound 4-ounce bag) refrigerated cooked new potato wedges

1 teaspoon salt

1. Heat coals or gas grill for direct heat. Spray half of one side of four 18 x 12-inch sheets of heavy-duty aluminum foil with cooking spray.

2. Mix barbecue sauce, honey and cumin in small bowl. Place 1 pork chop, 3 pieces corn, $1/4$ cup carrots and $1/2$ cup potato wedges on center of each sprayed foil sheet; sprinkle with $1/4$ teaspoon salt. Spoon 3 tablespoons sauce mixture over pork and vegetables on each sheet.

3. Fold foil over pork and vegetables so edges meet. Seal edges, making tight $1/2$-inch fold; fold again. Allow space on sides for circulation and expansion.

4. Grill packets 4 to 6 inches from medium heat 15 to 20 minutes, turning once, until pork is slightly pink in center. Place packets on plates. Cut large X across top of each packet; fold back foil.

BETTY'S SUCCESS TIPS

- Look for the cooked potato wedges in the refrigerated section of the supermarket.
- You can use fresh potatoes in place of the refrigerated ones. Cut 2 medium potatoes into wedges and place in a microwavable bowl. Cover and microwave on High for about 5 minutes or until crisp-tender. Place potatoes in packet and grill as directed.

1 SERVING: Calories 435; Total Fat 8g (Saturated Fat 3g); Sodium 960mg; Total Carbohydrate 72g (Dietary Fiber 5g); Protein 24g; **Exchanges:** 4 Starch; 2 Vegetable; 1 Lean Meat; **Carbohydrate Choices:** 5

Grilled Salmon Paella Packs

This meal-in-a-bundle has all the flavors of the Spanish classic without all the work.

PREP TIME: 1 HOUR 15 MINUTES • **TOTAL TIME:** 1 HOUR 30 MINUTES • **MAKES 8 SERVINGS**

- $3/4$ teaspoon saffron threads, if desired
- 4 large green onions, finely chopped ($1/3$ cup)
- 4 large cloves garlic, finely chopped
- 3 tablespoons fresh lemon juice
- 3 tablespoons extra-virgin olive oil
- 1 tablespoon sweet smoky Spanish paprika or any sweet paprika
- 2 teaspoons salt
- $1/2$ teaspoon freshly ground black pepper

- 8 skinless salmon fillets (5 ounces each)
- 1 can (14 ounces) chicken broth
- 8 servings cooked instant brown rice
- 1 package (12 ounces) fully cooked linguiça or andouille sausage links
- 4 medium roma (plum) tomatoes, seeded, chopped
- 2 medium red bell peppers, diced $1/4$ inch
- 1 cup lightly packed fresh Italian (flat-leaf) parsley, chopped

1. Soak saffron in 2 teaspoons hot water; set aside 30 minutes.

2. To make salmon marinade, in small bowl, mix onions, garlic, lemon juice, 2 tablespoons of the oil, the paprika, salt and pepper. In 13 x 9-inch (3-quart) glass baking dish, arrange salmon; spoon marinade over salmon, turning to evenly coat. Cover; refrigerate 20 minutes.

3. Cut 8 (18 x 12-inch) sheets of heavy-duty foil. Grease with remaining 1 tablespoon oil.

4. Add water to broth to measure amount of water called for on rice package for 8 servings. Make 8 servings rice as directed on package, using broth and water mixture for the water.

5. Meanwhile, cut sausages in half lengthwise. Cut crosswise into thin slices; stir into rice along with tomatoes, bell peppers and saffron threads with soaking liquid. Use fork to mix ingredients and separate saffron.

6. Mound generous 1 cup rice mixture on center of each piece of foil. Top with 1 salmon fillet, and drizzle with a spoonful of marinade. Spoon any remaining marinade over fillets. Bring up long sides of foil together so edges meet. Seal edges, making tight $1/2$-inch fold; fold again, allowing space for heat circulation and expansion. Fold other sides to seal.

7. Heat gas or charcoal grill. Place packets on grill over low heat, allowing space around packets for circulation. Cover grill; cook 10 minutes for salmon that is opaque with a deeper pink center, or about 15 minutes until fish flakes easily with fork. Place packets on plates. Carefully unfold foil away from face. Sprinkle each serving with parsley.

1 SERVING: Calories 620; Total Fat 27g (Saturated Fat 7g); Sodium 1,430mg; Total Carbohydrate 49g (Dietary Fiber 4g); Protein 44g; **Exchanges:** $2^1/2$ Starch; $1/2$ Other Carbohydrate; 1 Vegetable; 5 Lean Meat; 2 Fat; **Carbohydrate Choices:** 3

Grilled Seafood Packs with Lemon-Chive Butter

Looking for a grilled seafood recipe? Then check out these shrimp, clam, scallop and vegetable packs drizzled with butter—a wonderful dinner topped with chives.

PREP TIME: 40 MINUTES • **TOTAL TIME:** 40 MINUTES • **MAKES 8 SERVINGS**

Seafood Packets
- 32 shell clams (littlenecks or cherrystones)
- 32 uncooked medium shrimp in shells (about 1 1/4 pounds), thawed if frozen
- 32 sea scallops (about 2 1/2 pounds)
- 4 ears fresh sweet corn, husks removed, cleaned, cut into fourths
- 32 large cherry tomatoes

Lemon-Chive Butter
- 1/3 cup butter or margarine, melted
- 2 teaspoons grated lemon peel
- 2 teaspoons chopped fresh or 1/2 teaspoon freeze-dried chives
- Fresh chive stems or chopped fresh chives, if desired

1. Heat gas or charcoal grill. Cut 8 (18 x 12-inch) sheets of heavy-duty foil (and cooking parchment, if desired); spray with cooking spray.

2. Place 4 clams, shrimp and scallops in center of each sheet; top each with 2 pieces of corn and 4 tomatoes. In small bowl, mix butter, lemon peel and 2 teaspoons fresh chives. Drizzle about 2 teaspoons butter mixture over seafood and vegetables in each packet.

3. Bring up 2 sides of foil so edges meet. Seal edges, making tight 1/2-inch fold; fold again, allowing space for heat circulation and expansion. Fold other sides to seal.

4. Place packets on grill over medium heat. Cover grill; cook 15 to 20 minutes, rotating packets a half turn after 10 minutes, or until clam shells have opened, shrimp are pink, and scallops are white and opaque. (Cooking time may vary depending on ingredients selected.) Discard any clams that don't open.

5. To serve, cut large X across top of each packet; carefully fold back foil to allow steam to escape. Top with fresh chive stems.

BETTY'S SUCCESS TIP

Mussels can be substituted for the clams. If your guests don't care for either clams or mussels, you may double the amount of shrimp or scallops instead.

1 SERVING: Calories 300; Total Fat 10g (Saturated Fat 5g); Sodium 350mg; Total Carbohydrate 17g (Dietary Fiber 3g); Protein 33g; **Exchanges:** 1 Starch; 4 Lean Meat; **Carbohydrate Choices:** 1

Maui Dogs

Looking for dinner with a tropical twist? Then check out these grilled beef hot dogs placed in hoagie buns spooned with pineapple salsa—ready in just 15 minutes!

PREP TIME: 15 MINUTES • **TOTAL TIME:** 15 MINUTES • **MAKES 8 SERVINGS**

8 beef hot dogs	1 cup pineapple salsa
8 small hoagie buns, unsliced	2 medium green onions, sliced (2 tablespoons)

1. Heat gas or charcoal grill.

2. Place hot dogs on grill over medium heat. Cook uncovered 10 to 15 minutes, turning frequently, until hot.

3. Using handle of wooden spoon, poke a hole through center of each bun lengthwise to make hole for hot dog.

4. In small bowl, mix salsa and green onions; spoon 2 tablespoons salsa mixture into hole in each bun. Place hot dog in each bun; top with additional salsa, if desired.

BETTY'S SUCCESS TIP

To broil hot dogs, set oven control to broil. Spray cookie sheet with cooking spray. Place hot dogs on cookie sheet. Broil with tops 4 to 6 inches from heat 4 to 5 minutes or until hot.

1 SERVING: Calories 340; Total Fat 16g (Saturated Fat 6g); Sodium 1,020mg; Total Carbohydrate 36g (Dietary Fiber 2g); Protein 11g; **Exchanges:** 2½ Starch; 2½ Fat; **Carbohydrate Choices:** 2½

Blue Cheese Deviled Dogs

Grilled hot dogs become "devilish" with the addition of blue cheese, hard-cooked eggs and a spicy hint of Sriracha sauce. Devilishly delicious!

PREP TIME: 15 MINUTES • **TOTAL TIME:** 15 MINUTES • **MAKES 8 SERVINGS**

8 beef hot dogs	4 hard-cooked eggs, peeled, sliced, cut in half
1/2 cup mayonnaise or salad dressing	
1 tablespoon Sriracha sauce	1/2 cup crumbled blue cheese
8 hot dog buns, split, toasted	2 medium green onions, sliced (2 tablespoons)

1. Heat gas or charcoal grill.

2. Place hot dogs on grill over medium heat. Cook uncovered 10 to 15 minutes, turning frequently, until hot.

3. Stir together mayonnaise and Sriracha sauce; spread about 1 tablespoon mayonnaise mixture on each toasted bun. Place hot dogs on buns. Top with eggs, blue cheese and onions.

BETTY'S SUCCESS TIP

- Sriracha sauce can be found in the Asian or international aisle of the grocery store.

1 SERVING: Calories 430; Total Fat 31g (Saturated Fat 10g); Sodium 950mg; Total Carbohydrate 24g (Dietary Fiber 1g); Protein 14g; **Exchanges:** 1 1/2 Starch; 4 1/2 Fat; **Carbohydrate Choices:** 1 1/2

Chicago-Style Stand 'N Stuff Hot Dog Tacos

Try a traditional favorite Chicago treat using an Old El Paso® Stand 'N Stuff® soft taco shell! They are the perfect vessel for holding all the delicious toppings of a Chicago-style hot dog. Don't forget the mustard!

PREP TIME: 15 MINUTES • **TOTAL TIME:** 20 MINUTES • **MAKES 8 TACOS**

Tacos

- 8 all-beef kosher hot dogs
- 1 package (6.7 ounces) Old El Paso® Stand 'N Stuff® soft flour tortillas

Toppings

- 2 teaspoons poppy seed, if desired
- 2 whole kosher dill pickles, each cut into 4 spears
- ¹/₂ cup chopped onion
- 1 cup pickled sport peppers (from a jar)
- 2 tomatoes, halved and sliced
- ¹/₂ cup sweet pickle relish
- ¹/₄ cup yellow mustard
- ¹/₂ teaspoon celery salt

1. Add ¹/₂ inch water to 10-inch skillet. Heat over medium-high heat until simmering. Place hot dogs in skillet. Cover; steam 10 minutes.

2. Meanwhile, heat tortillas as directed on package.

3. Place poppy seed on plate, and dip cut edges of kosher dill pickles into seed. Place hot dogs in tortillas. Top with pickles and remaining toppings.

BETTY'S SUCCESS TIP

Make it your own! Try mixing it up with different toppings and condiments if you prefer a different variation of hot dog; the result will be just as delicious.

1 TACO: Calories 280; Total Fat 17g (Saturated Fat 6g); Sodium 1,140mg; Total Carbohydrate 24g (Dietary Fiber 1g); Protein 7g; **Exchanges:** 1¹/₂ Starch; 3¹/₂ Fat; **Carbohydrate Choices:** 1¹/₂

Country "Fried" Chicken

Moist inside and crispy outside—this is country "fried" chicken made in the oven without the greasy mess.

PREP TIME: 15 MINUTES • **TOTAL TIME:** 1 HOUR 10 MINUTES • **MAKES 4 SERVINGS**

$^1/_2$ cup buttermilk
1 cup Progresso® plain panko crispy bread crumbs
1 teaspoon garlic salt
1 teaspoon paprika

$^1/_2$ teaspoon pepper
$^1/_4$ teaspoon poultry seasoning
1 cut-up whole chicken (3 to 3$^1/_2$ pounds; 8 pieces), skin removed
2 tablespoons butter or margarine, melted

1. Heat oven to 400°F. Spray broiler pan with cooking spray. In shallow bowl, place buttermilk. In another shallow bowl, mix bread crumbs, garlic salt, paprika, pepper and poultry seasoning.

2. Dip chicken pieces in buttermilk; coat with crumb mixture. Place on broiler pan. Discard any remaining buttermilk and coating mixture. Drizzle chicken with butter.

3. Bake 45 to 55 minutes or until juice of chicken is clear when thickest pieces are cut to bone and thermometer reads 165°F.

BETTY'S SUCCESS TIP

A perfect choice for picnics, this crisp and flavorful chicken is great paired with black bean and corn salad or cool, creamy potato salad from the deli for an easy, no-fuss meal.

1 SERVING: Calories 390; Total Fat 17g (Saturated Fat 6g); Sodium 470mg; Total Carbohydrate 21g (Dietary Fiber 0g); Protein 37g; **Exchanges:** 1$^1/_2$ Starch; 4$^1/_2$ Lean Meat; $^1/_2$ Fat; **Carbohydrate Choices:** 1$^1/_2$

Arepas with Corn and Pulled Pork

Looking for a classic dinner that's ready in 20 minutes? Then check out these pork arepas featuring Betty Crocker® cornbread & muffin mix and Green Giant® SteamCrisp® Niblets® corn.

PREP TIME: 15 MINUTES • **TOTAL TIME:** 20 MINUTES • **MAKES 6 SERVINGS**

1 pouch (6.5 ounces) Betty Crocker® cornbread & muffin mix
½ cup shredded Monterey Jack cheese (2 ounces)
3 tablespoons butter, melted
3 tablespoons milk
1 can (11 ounces) Green Giant® SteamCrisp® Niblets® whole kernel sweet corn, drained

1½ cups cooked pulled pork
⅓ cup crumbled queso fresco cheese
Chopped fresh cilantro, if desired
Lime wedges, if desired

1. In medium bowl, mix cornbread mix, Monterey Jack cheese, melted butter and milk until well blended. Stir in ⅓ cup of the corn; reserve remaining corn.

2. To make arepas, heat 12-inch heavy skillet or electric griddle on medium-high heat. Shape cornbread mixture into small patties, about 2 inches in diameter. Cook 2 to 3 minutes on each side, turning once, until golden brown.

3. To serve, place 1 arepa on plate; top with about ¼ cup pulled pork, 3 tablespoons reserved corn and 1 tablespoon queso fresco. Sprinkle with cilantro, and serve with lime wedge.

1 SERVING: Calories 330; Total Fat 15g (Saturated Fat 7g); Sodium 490mg; Total Carbohydrate 32g (Dietary Fiber 0g); Protein 16g; **Exchanges:** 1½ Starch; ½ Other Carbohydrate; ½ Vegetable; ½ Lean Meat; 1 High-Fat Meat; 1 Fat; **Carbohydrate Choices:** 2

Fresh Flounder Rolls

Yogurt provides a wonderful addition to the cucumber sauce that's used in these fish rolls that are made with Progresso® bread crumbs—a tasty dinner that's ready in 30 minutes.

PREP TIME: 30 MINUTES • **TOTAL TIME:** 30 MINUTES • **MAKES 12 ROLLS**

Cucumber Sauce

- 1 container (6 ounces) fat-free plain Greek yogurt
- 3 tablespoons mayonnaise
- 1 medium cucumber, peeled, seeded, coarsely grated
- 3 tablespoons chopped fresh dill weed
- 1 tablespoon chopped green onion (1 medium)
- 1 tablespoon lemon juice
- 1/2 teaspoon salt

Flounder and Buns

- 2 pounds fresh flounder, halibut or cod fillets, skin removed
- 1/2 cup milk
- 1 egg
- 1 cup Progresso® panko bread crumbs
- 1 teaspoon salt
- 2 tablespoons vegetable oil
- 2 tablespoons butter, melted
- 12 hot dog buns, split
  Lemon slices, if desired
  Sprigs fresh dill weed, if desired

1. In medium bowl, mix cucumber sauce ingredients. Cover and refrigerate until ready to serve.

2. Cut fish fillets into 12 serving pieces. In pie plate or shallow pan, mix milk and egg. In another pie plate or shallow pan, mix bread crumbs and salt. Dip fillets into milk mixture; roll in bread crumbs. Shake off excess crumbs.

3. In 12-inch skillet, heat oil over medium-high heat. Cook fish fillets in oil 10 to 12 minutes, turning once, until fish flakes easily with fork. Keep warm.

4. Heat 10-inch skillet over medium heat. Brush melted butter on cut sides of buns. Place cut sides down in skillet; cook about 3 minutes or until toasted. Place buns on plates; fill each with fish fillet and about 3 tablespoons sauce. Serve with lemon slices and fresh dill.

1 FISH ROLL: Calories 280; Total Fat 11g (Saturated Fat 3g); Sodium 630mg; Total Carbohydrate 30g (Dietary Fiber 1g); Protein 15g; **Exchanges:** 1 1/2 Starch; 1/2 Other Carbohydrate; 1 1/2 Very Lean Meat; 2 Fat; **Carbohydrate Choices:** 2

Savory Corn on a Stick

Bottled Italian dressing and fresh Parmesan cheese jazz up corn on the cob. Who needs butter?

PREP TIME: 35 MINUTES • **TOTAL TIME:** 40 MINUTES • **MAKES 4 SERVINGS**

4 **ears fresh corn**	2 **tablespoons zesty Italian dressing**
8 **(6-inch) bamboo skewers**	2 **tablespoons shredded fresh Parmesan cheese**

1. Husk corn, remove silk and cut each ear in half. Use metal skewer or ice pick to make a hole through center of one end of each piece of corn. Insert bamboo skewers through corn.

2. Brush corn with Italian dressing. Place corn in rectangular microwavable dish, 11 x 7 x 1½ inches. Cover with plastic wrap, folding back one corner to vent.

3. Microwave on High 9 to 14 minutes, rotating dish a quarter turn every 5 minutes, until tender. Let stand 5 minutes. Sprinkle with cheese before serving.

BETTY'S SUCCESS TIPS

- Rely on frozen ears of Green Giant® corn for yearlong enjoyment.
- Refrigerate unhusked corn until ready to use.
- Corn is best when eaten as soon as possible after picking.
- Husk ears and remove silk just before cooking.

1 SERVING: Calories 155; Total Fat 5g (Saturated Fat 1g); Sodium 120mg; Total Carbohydrate 26g (Dietary Fiber 3g); Protein 5g; **Exchanges:** 1½ Starch; 1 Fat; **Carbohydrate Choices:** 2

Vegetable Kabobs with Mustard Dip

Grilling adds great outdoor flavor to fresh veggies. Pick and dip away!

PREP TIME: 35 MINUTES • **TOTAL TIME:** 1 HOUR 35 MINUTES • **MAKES 9 SERVINGS**

Dip

- $^2/_3$ cup Yoplait® Fat Free plain yogurt (from 2-pound container)
- $^1/_3$ cup fat-free sour cream
- 1 tablespoon finely chopped fresh parsley
- 1 tablespoon Dijon mustard
- 1 teaspoon onion powder
- 1 teaspoon garlic salt

Kabobs

- 1 medium bell pepper, cut into 6 strips, then cut into thirds (18 pieces)
- 1 medium zucchini, cut diagonally into $^1/_2$-inch slices
- 1 package (8 ounces) fresh whole mushrooms
- 9 large cherry tomatoes
- 2 tablespoons olive or vegetable oil

1. In small bowl, mix dip ingredients. Cover; refrigerate at least 1 hour.

2. Heat gas or charcoal grill. On 5 (12-inch) metal skewers, thread vegetables so that one kind of vegetable is on the same skewer (use 2 skewers for mushrooms); leave space between each piece. Brush vegetables with oil.

3. Place skewers of bell pepper and zucchini on grill over medium heat. Cover grill; cook 2 minutes. Add skewers of mushrooms and tomatoes. Cover grill; cook 4 to 5 minutes, carefully turning skewers every 2 minutes, until vegetables are tender. Remove vegetables from skewers to serving plate. Serve with dip.

BETTY'S SUCCESS TIPS

- No metal skewers? Grill the vegetable pieces in a grill basket (grill "wok"). Place the bell pepper and zucchini in the basket first and grill as directed, then add the mushrooms and cherry tomatoes.
- Choose red bell pepper for beautiful color and a sweeter flavor than green bell pepper.

1 SERVING: Calories 70; Total Fat $3^1/_2$g (Saturated Fat $^1/_2$g); Sodium 180mg; Total Carbohydrate 8g (Dietary Fiber 1g); Protein 2g; **Exchanges:** 1 Vegetable; 1 Fat; **Carbohydrate Choices:** $^1/_2$

Cajun Sweet Potato Fries with Yogurt Dipping Sauce

Tired of French fries? Switch to spiced-up sweet potato fries for your next burger or barbecue meal.

PREP TIME: 20 MINUTES • **TOTAL TIME:** 1 HOUR • **MAKES 6 SERVINGS**

Fries

- 3 **large dark-orange sweet potatoes (3 pounds), peeled**
- 2 **teaspoons Cajun seasoning**
- 1 **teaspoon ground cumin**

Sauce

- $2/3$ **cup Yoplait® Fat Free plain yogurt (from 2-pound container)**
- $1/4$ **cup chili sauce**
- 1 **teaspoon soy sauce**

1. Heat oven to 425°F. Cut each potato crosswise into about 4-inch chunks, then cut lengthwise into $1/2$ x $1/2$-inch strips.

2. In large resealable food-storage plastic bag, mix Cajun seasoning and cumin. Add potatoes; toss until evenly coated. In ungreased 15 x 10 x 1-inch pan, arrange potatoes in single layer.

3. Bake 35 to 40 minutes, turning once, until potatoes are lightly browned and tender. Meanwhile, in small bowl, mix all sauce ingredients. Serve sauce with fries.

BETTY'S SUCCESS TIPS

- Health twist—Just one 4-ounce sweet potato exceeds the Daily Value for vitamin A and provides fiber to boot!
- A hot oven and placement of the potatoes in a single layer on a shallow pan are important for the crispiest potatoes. If potatoes are layered, they'll steam and will be soft.

1 SERVING: Calories 150; Total Fat 0g (Saturated Fat 0g); Sodium 460mg; Total Carbohydrate 33g (Dietary Fiber 5g); Protein 5g; **Exchanges:** 1 Starch; 1 Other Carbohydrate; **Carbohydrate Choices:** 2

Baked Basil Fries

A fresh potato twist on French fries with basil and Parmesan cheese.

PREP TIME: 15 MINUTES • TOTAL TIME: 50 MINUTES • MAKES 6 SERVINGS

2 **pounds fresh russet potatoes (about 2 large)**

$^1/_4$ **cup (1 ounce) grated Parmesan cheese**

1 **tablespoon olive oil**

1 **tablespoon dried basil leaves**

$^1/_2$ **teaspoon salt**

$^1/_4$ **teaspoon garlic powder**

1. Heat oven to 425°F. Cut potatoes into $^1/_4$-inch-thick strips. In medium bowl, mix remaining ingredients. Toss potatoes with mixture.

2. Spray large cookie sheet with cooking spray. Place potatoes on cookie sheet in single layer. Bake 15 minutes; turn potatoes, and bake 15 to 20 minutes longer or until tender.

1 SERVING: Calories 160; Total Fat 3$^1/_2$g (Saturated Fat 1g); Sodium 270mg; Total Carbohydrate 26g (Dietary Fiber 3g); Protein 4g; **Exchanges:** 1 Starch; $^1/_2$ Other Carbohydrate; $^1/_2$ Vegetable; $^1/_2$ Fat; **Carbohydrate Choices:** 2

Slow Cooker Baked Beans

Don't heat up the whole house for baked beans—slow-cook them with this extra-easy version of everyone's favorite summer side dish.

PREP TIME: 10 MINUTES • **TOTAL TIME:** 5 HOURS 10 MINUTES • **MAKES 12 SERVINGS**

3 cans (28 ounces each) vegetarian baked beans, drained

1 medium onion, chopped ($^{1}/_{2}$ cup)

$^{2}/_{3}$ cup barbecue sauce

$^{1}/_{2}$ cup packed brown sugar

2 tablespoons ground mustard

1. Mix all ingredients in $3^{1}/_{2}$- to 6-quart slow cooker.

2. Cover and cook on Low heat setting 4 to 5 hours (or High heat setting 2 hours to 2 hours 30 minutes) or until desired consistency.

Note: *This recipe was tested in slow cookers with heating elements in the side and bottom of the cooker, not in cookers that stand only on a heated base. For slow cookers with just a heated base, follow the manufacturer's directions for layering ingredients and choosing a temperature.*

BETTY'S SUCCESS TIPS

- Sprinkle beans with Betty Crocker® Bac~Os® bacon-flavor bits just before serving for that great smoky flavor that goes so well with baked beans.
- You decide! Change the flavor of your baked beans by changing your barbecue sauce. Sweet, smoky sauces lend a smoother taste, and spicy or bold sauces give your beans a zesty taste.

1 SERVING: Calories 200; Total Fat 1g (Saturated Fat 0g); Sodium 1,170mg; Total Carbohydrate 51g (Dietary Fiber 9g); Protein 12g; **Exchanges:** 3 Starch; **Carbohydrate Choices:** $3^{1}/_{2}$

Tuscan-Style Tomato Pasta Salad

Add spinach and tomatoes to Betty Crocker® Suddenly Salad® mix to make this cheesy pasta salad that's ready in just 15 minutes—a perfect Italian side dish.

PREP TIME: 15 MINUTES • **TOTAL TIME:** 15 MINUTES • **MAKES 6 SERVINGS**

1 box Betty Crocker® Suddenly Salad®
Tuscan style tomato pasta salad mix
Water and olive oil called for on box
2 tablespoons fresh lemon juice

2 cups baby spinach leaves
1 cup grape tomatoes, halved
1 cup cubed fresh mozzarella cheese
1/4 cup chopped fresh basil leaves

1. Empty contents of pasta mix (from Suddenly Salad box) into 3-quart saucepan two-thirds full of boiling water. Gently boil uncovered 12 minutes, stirring occasionally.

2. Drain pasta; rinse with cold water. Shake well. In medium bowl, stir seasoning mix, water, olive oil and lemon juice until well blended. Stir in pasta, spinach, tomatoes and cheese; top with basil. Refrigerate until ready to serve. Cover and refrigerate any remaining salad.

1 SERVING: Calories 230; Total Fat 7g (Saturated Fat 3g); Sodium 730mg; Total Carbohydrate 30g (Dietary Fiber 1g); Protein 10g; **Exchanges:** 1 1/2 Starch; 1 Vegetable; 1/2 High-Fat Meat; 1/2 Fat; **Carbohydrate Choices:** 2

Layered Mexican Party Salad

You're 30 minutes away from a fiesta of flavors in a big bowl of luscious layered salad.

PREP TIME: 20 MINUTES • **TOTAL TIME:** 30 MINUTES • **MAKES 12 SERVINGS**

1 box Betty Crocker® Suddenly Salad® classic pasta salad mix

2 tablespoons vegetable oil

3 tablespoons water

1 teaspoon ground cumin

1 can (15 ounces) Progresso® black beans, drained, rinsed

1 can (15.25 ounces) Green Giant® whole kernel corn, drained

4 cups torn romaine lettuce

1 container (12 ounces) refrigerated guacamole dip

1½ cups (6 ounces) finely shredded Mexican 4-cheese blend

3 roma (plum) tomatoes, chopped

1 can (2.25 ounces) sliced ripe olives, drained

3 cups nacho-flavored tortilla chips

1. Empty pasta mix into 3-quart saucepan two-thirds full of boiling water. Gently boil uncovered 12 minutes, stirring occasionally.

2. Drain pasta; rinse with cold water. Shake to drain well. In medium bowl, stir together seasoning mix, oil, water and cumin. Stir in pasta, beans and corn.

3. In 4-quart glass salad bowl or 13 x 9-inch glass baking dish, layer lettuce and pasta mixture. Spread guacamole evenly over top. Sprinkle with cheese and tomatoes; top with olives.

4. Just before serving, arrange chips around edge of bowl. Serve immediately, or refrigerate.

BETTY'S SUCCESS TIPS

- Purchase a bag of ready-to-eat torn romaine lettuce to save time.
- Make this salad up to 24 hours before serving.

1 SERVING: Calories 300; Total Fat 13g (Saturated Fat 4g); Sodium 700mg; Total Carbohydrate 36g (Dietary Fiber 7g); Protein 9g; **Exchanges:** 1½ Starch; 1 Other Carbohydrate; ½ High-Fat Meat; 1½ Fat; **Carbohydrate Choices:** 2½

Ranch Spinach Pasta Salad

Grilling tonight? Add a veggie-rich 15-minute pasta salad that gets its start from a Suddenly Salad® mix.

PREP TIME: 15 MINUTES • **TOTAL TIME:** 15 MINUTES • **MAKES 6 SERVINGS**

1 box Betty Crocker® Suddenly Salad® classic pasta salad mix
$^1/_2$ cup ranch dressing
1 tablespoon fresh lemon juice
2 cups baby spinach leaves or small broccoli florets

$^3/_4$ cup grape tomatoes, halved
$^1/_2$ cup sliced cucumber, halved
$^1/_2$ cup julienne (matchstick-cut) carrots
2 tablespoons chopped fresh or 1 teaspoon dried basil leaves

1. Empty contents of pasta mix (from Suddenly Salad box) into 3-quart saucepan two-thirds full of boiling water. Gently boil uncovered 12 minutes, stirring occasionally.

2. Drain pasta; rinse with cold water. Shake to drain well.

3. In medium bowl, stir contents of seasoning mix (from Suddenly Salad box), the dressing and lemon juice until blended. Stir in pasta and remaining ingredients. Cover; refrigerate until ready to serve. Store any remaining salad covered in the refrigerator.

BETTY'S SUCCESS TIP

Make it a dinner salad. Just stir in 1$^1/_2$ cups cut-up cooked chicken or ham.

1 SERVING: Calories 220; Total Fat 10g (Saturated Fat 1g); Sodium 830mg; Total Carbohydrate 28g (Dietary Fiber 2g); Protein 5g; **Exchanges:** 1$^1/_2$ Starch; $^1/_2$ Other Carbohydrate; 2 Fat; **Carbohydrate Choices:** 2

Corn and Black Bean Salad with Tortilla Wedges

Dinner made ready in 20 minutes! Enjoy this delicious black bean and veggies salad served with tortilla wedges—a hearty meal!

PREP TIME: 15 MINUTES • TOTAL TIME: 20 MINUTES • MAKES 4 SERVINGS

4 fat-free flour tortillas (8 to 10 inches in diameter)

2 teaspoons margarine or butter, softened

1 can (15 to 16 ounces) whole kernel corn, drained

1 can (15 ounces) black beans, rinsed and drained

1 medium red bell pepper, chopped (1 cup)

1 small jicama, peeled and diced (2 cups)

1/2 cup fat-free Italian dressing

1/2 teaspoon salt

1/4 teaspoon pepper
Red leaf lettuce

1/4 cup pine nuts, toasted

1. Heat oven to 400°F. Spread tortillas with margarine; cut into fourths. Place on ungreased cookie sheet. Bake 4 to 5 minutes or until golden brown.

2. Toss remaining ingredients except lettuce and nuts until mixture is coated with dressing.

3. Serve salad on leaf lettuce; sprinkle with nuts. Serve with tortilla wedges.

BETTY'S SUCCESS TIPS

- If you're eliminating all animal products from your diet, be certain to check tortilla labels; some tortillas may contain lard, which is animal fat.
- Whole wheat tortillas also make tasty wedges to serve with this salad.
- Diagonally slice 4 grilled boneless skinless chicken breast halves. Arrange chicken on salad in step 3. Continue as directed.

1 SERVING: Calories 320; Total Fat 10g (Saturated Fat 1g); Sodium 1,004mg; Total Carbohydrate 53g (Dietary Fiber 7g); Protein 10g; **Exchanges:** 1 1/2 Starch; 1/2 Vegetable; 1 1/2 Fat; **Carbohydrate Choices:** 3 1/2

Super-Simple Picnic Potato Salad

Frozen hashbrowns are the key to this convenient recipe. No picnic is complete without potato salad!

PREP TIME: 45 MINUTES • **TOTAL TIME:** 5 HOURS 45 MINUTES • **MAKES 16 SERVINGS**

1 bag (32 ounces) frozen southern-style diced hashbrown potatoes	¼ teaspoon pepper
¼ cup water	5 eggs
2 tablespoons cider vinegar	1 cup mayonnaise or salad dressing
1 tablespoon yellow mustard	½ cup chopped celery
1½ teaspoons salt	⅓ cup chopped onion
	Paprika, if desired

1. In ungreased 3-quart microwavable bowl, mix frozen potatoes and water; spread evenly in bowl. Cover tightly with microwavable plastic wrap. Microwave on High 15 to 20 minutes or until potatoes are hot and tender, stirring once halfway through cooking.

2. Add vinegar, mustard, salt and pepper to hot potatoes; mix well. Spread evenly in bowl. Cover, refrigerate at least 5 hours or until completely cold.

3. Meanwhile, in 2-quart saucepan, place eggs in single layer. Add enough water to cover eggs by 1 inch. Heat to boiling. Immediately remove from heat; cover and let stand 15 minutes. Drain; rinse with cold water. Place eggs in bowl of ice water; let stand 10 minutes. Drain. Peel eggs. Reserve 1 egg for garnish; chop remaining 4 eggs.

4. Stir mayonnaise into cold potato mixture. Add celery, onion and chopped eggs; toss gently to mix. Spoon mixture into large serving bowl. Slice reserved hard-cooked egg; arrange on top of salad. Sprinkle with paprika. Serve immediately, or cover and refrigerate until serving time.

BETTY'S SUCCESS TIP

The flavors in this potato salad will improve in the refrigerator. Prepare the salad a day in advance; cover and refrigerate it until serving time.

1 SERVING: Calories 200; Total Fat 13g (Saturated Fat 2g); Sodium 350mg; Total Carbohydrate 17g (Dietary Fiber 2g); Protein 3g; **Exchanges:** 1 Starch; 2½ Fat; **Carbohydrate Choices:** 1

Fresh Sriracha Refrigerator Pickles

Add a new twist to classic refrigerator pickles with a hot, Thai-inspired sauce that spices up your garden bounty. Best of all, this "can-do" project requires no special canning equipment!

PREP TIME: 20 MINUTES • **TOTAL TIME:** 1 HOUR 20 MINUTES • **MAKES 8 SERVINGS**

6 to 8 red Fresno chiles (4 ounces), coarsely chopped
1 cup unseasoned rice vinegar
3 cloves garlic
2 tablespoons sugar
1 teaspoon grated gingerroot, if desired

1 teaspoon coarse (kosher or sea) salt
1 English (seedless) cucumber, unpeeled, very thinly sliced (about 2 cups)
1/2 cup thinly sliced white onion (1 medium)
1/4 cup fresh cilantro leaves

1. In food processor bowl, place chiles, vinegar, garlic, sugar, gingerroot and salt. Cover; process with on-and-off pulses about 1 minute or until well combined.

2. In medium bowl, place cucumber, onion and cilantro. Pour chili mixture over cucumber mixture; toss to coat. Cover; refrigerate at least 1 hour or overnight before serving. Store covered in refrigerator up to 1 week.

BETTY'S SUCCESS TIP

Heat can be varied in the recipe by seeding the peppers. For medium heat, just remove seeds from half of the peppers used.

1 SERVING: Calories 40; Total Fat 0g (Saturated Fat 0g); Sodium 300mg; Total Carbohydrate 8g (Dietary Fiber 1g); Protein 1g; **Exchanges:** 1/2 Other Carbohydrate; **Carbohydrate Choices:** 1/2

Red, White and Blueberry Salad

Put a colorful and tasty spin on a traditional green salad by tossing in jicama, watermelon and blueberries with a creamy yogurt dressing.

PREP TIME: 15 MINUTES • **TOTAL TIME:** 15 MINUTES • **MAKES 8 SERVINGS**

1 container (6 ounces) Yoplait® Original Key lime pie yogurt	1 bag (10 ounces) chopped or hearts of romaine lettuce (6 cups)
4 teaspoons honey	2½ cups cubed (¾-inch) seedless watermelon
¼ teaspoon salt	1 cup fresh blueberries
½ jicama, peeled, cut into ¼-inch slices	

1. In small bowl, mix yogurt, honey and salt; set aside. Cut jicama slices into star shapes using a small (1-inch) star-shaped canapé cutter.

2. In large bowl, toss remaining ingredients. Pour dressing over salad mixture; toss until well coated. Sprinkle jicama stars over top. Serve immediately.

BETTY'S SUCCESS TIPS

- You can tote this easy salad to a potluck. Pack the dressing and the salad separately, then pour on the dressing just before serving.
- Refrigerate unused jicama in a resealable plastic bag for up to 1 week to use in any summer salad.

1 SERVING: Calories 70; Total Fat 0g (Saturated Fat 0g); Sodium 90mg; Total Carbohydrate 16g (Dietary Fiber 2g); Protein 2g; **Exchanges:** ½ Starch; ½ Fruit; **Carbohydrate Choices:** 1

Nutty Chocolate Chip Picnic Cake

With a sweet and nutty chocolate baked-on topping, here's a cake that's ready to go. No frosting needed.

PREP TIME: 15 MINUTES • **TOTAL TIME:** 1 HOUR 50 MINUTES • **MAKES 15 SERVINGS**

- $\frac{1}{2}$ **cup miniature semisweet chocolate chips**
- $\frac{1}{3}$ **cup packed brown sugar**
- $\frac{1}{3}$ **cup chopped pecans**

- 1 **box Betty Crocker® SuperMoist® devil's food cake mix**
- **Water, vegetable oil and eggs called for on cake mix box**

1. Heat oven to 350°F (325°F for dark or nonstick pan). Grease or spray bottom only of 13 x 9-inch pan. Mix chocolate chips, brown sugar and pecans; set aside.

2. Bake and cool cake as directed on box for 13 x 9-inch pan—except sprinkle chocolate chip mixture on batter in pan before baking.

3. Store tightly covered.

BETTY'S SUCCESS TIPS

- Planning a party? Serve this take-along cake with your favorite ice cream. Chocolate, vanilla and caramel are just a few delicious possibilities.
- For an extra dose of decadence, drizzle the cake with caramel or hot fudge topping and your favorite ice cream.

1 SERVING: Calories 260; Total Fat 13g (Saturated Fat 3$\frac{1}{2}$g); Sodium 260mg; Total Carbohydrate 32g (Dietary Fiber 1g); Protein 3g; **Exchanges:** 1 Starch; 1 Other Carbohydrate; 2$\frac{1}{2}$ Fat; **Carbohydrate Choices:** 2

Chocolate Chip-Caramel Poke Cake

Enjoy this delicious caramel-topped chocolate cake made using Betty Crocker® SuperMoist® cake mix and frosting—a perfect dessert.

PREP TIME: 30 MINUTES • **TOTAL TIME:** 2 HOURS 45 MINUTES • **MAKES 15 SERVINGS**

1 box Betty Crocker® SuperMoist® devil's food cake mix
1 1/3 cups buttermilk
1/2 cup vegetable oil
3 eggs

1 bag (12 ounces) semisweet chocolate chips (2 cups)
1 cup caramel topping
1/2 cup Betty Crocker® Rich & Creamy vanilla frosting

1. Heat oven to 350°F (325°F for dark or nonstick pan). Spray bottom only of 13 x 9-inch pan with baking spray with flour.

2. In large bowl, beat cake mix, buttermilk, oil and eggs with electric mixer on low speed 30 seconds, then on medium speed 2 minutes, scraping bowl occasionally. Pour into pan. Sprinkle with chocolate chips; press gently into batter.

3. Bake 35 to 43 minutes or until toothpick inserted in center comes out clean. Cool 30 minutes. Spray meat fork or other long-tined fork with cooking spray. Poke warm cake every inch with fork tines. Pour caramel topping over cake. Cool completely, about 1 hour.

4. In medium microwavable bowl, microwave frosting 15 to 30 seconds; stir until very soft. Spoon frosting into 1-quart resealable food-storage plastic bag. Cut tip off 1 corner of bag. Drizzle frosting across top of cake. For easy cutting, dip knife in hot water. Store covered.

1 SERVING: Calories 420; Total Fat 18g (Saturated Fat 7g); Sodium 370mg; Total Carbohydrate 59g (Dietary Fiber 2g); Protein 4g; **Exchanges:** 1 1/2 Starch; 2 1/2 Other Carbohydrate; 3 1/2 Fat; **Carbohydrate Choices:** 4

Giant Ganache-Topped Whoopie Pie

Looking for a chocolaty dessert using Betty Crocker® SuperMoist® cake mix? Then try this luscious cake that's topped with ganache and filled with marshmallow creme.

PREP TIME: 25 MINUTES • **TOTAL TIME:** 1 HOUR 25 MINUTES • **MAKES 12 SERVINGS**

Cake

- ½ box Betty Crocker® SuperMoist® devil's food cake mix (about 1²/₃ cups)
- ½ cup water
- ¼ cup vegetable oil
- 2 eggs

Filling

- ¾ cup butter or margarine, softened
- 1 jar (7 ounces) marshmallow creme
- 1 cup powdered sugar
- 1 teaspoon vanilla

Ganache

- ½ cup whipping (heavy) cream
- 4 ounces semisweet baking chocolate, chopped

1. Heat oven to 350°F (325°F for dark or nonstick pans). Spray bottoms and sides of two 8-inch round cake pans with baking spray with flour. In large bowl, beat cake mix, water, oil and eggs with electric mixer on low speed until moistened, then on medium speed 2 minutes, scraping bowl occasionally. Pour into pans. Bake 14 to 20 minutes or until toothpick inserted in center comes out clean. Cool 10 minutes. Remove from pans to cooling racks. Cool completely, about 1 hour.

2. In large bowl, beat filling ingredients with electric mixer on high speed until light and fluffy. On serving plate, place 1 cake layer, rounded side down. Spread filling over cake, spreading slightly over edge. Top with second layer, rounded side up.

3. In 1-quart saucepan, heat whipping cream over low heat until hot but not boiling. Remove from heat; stir in chocolate until melted. Cool about 10 minutes. Pour ganache onto top of cake; spread with spatula so it just begins to flow over edge of cake. Store loosely covered.

BETTY'S SUCCESS TIP

A 1-inch-wide metal spatula works well for spreading glazes, fillings and frostings.

1 SERVING: Calories 410; Total Fat 26g (Saturated Fat 14g); Sodium 260mg; Total Carbohydrate 41g (Dietary Fiber 2g); Protein 3g; **Exchanges:** 1 Starch; 1½ Other Carbohydrate; 5 Fat; **Carbohydrate Choices:** 3

Sparkling 4th of July Cake

Add even more fun to your festivities by making a spirited white cake decorated with red and blue.

PREP TIME: 40 MINUTES • **TOTAL TIME:** 2 HOURS 20 MINUTES • **MAKES 15 SERVINGS**

1 box Betty Crocker® SuperMoist® white cake mix
   Water, vegetable oil and egg whites called for on cake mix box
½ teaspoon red food color
½ teaspoon blue food color

1 container Betty Crocker® Whipped fluffy white or whipped cream frosting
1 tablespoon Betty Crocker® blue sugar
2 tablespoons Betty Crocker® red sugar
   White star candies, if desired
   4th of July candles

1. Heat oven to 350°F (325°F for dark or nonstick pan). Spray bottom only of 13 x 9-inch pan with baking spray with flour. Place paper baking cup in 1 regular-size muffin cup.

2. Make cake batter as directed on box. In small bowl, place ½ cup batter; stir in red food color. In another small bowl, place ½ cup batter; stir in blue food color.

3. Fill muffin cup two-thirds full with white batter; set aside. Pour remaining white batter into 13 x 9-inch pan. Randomly drop generous teaspoonfuls of red and blue batters over white batter in pan. For swirled design, cut through batters with knife in S-shaped curves in one continuous motion; turn pan a quarter turn and repeat.

4. Place muffin pan and cake pan in oven. Bake muffin cup 12 to 13 minutes or until toothpick inserted in center comes out clean; place pan on cooling rack. Continue baking 13 x 9-inch cake 14 to 18 minutes longer or until toothpick inserted in center comes out clean. Cool cake in pan 10 minutes. Remove cake and cupcake from pans to cooling rack. Cool completely, about 1 hour.

5. Reserve 2 tablespoons frosting. Frost cake with remaining frosting. In upper left-hand corner of cake, lightly score 5 x 3½-inch rectangle in frosting for blue area of flag; sprinkle with blue sugar. Cut 2 strips of clean white paper, 13 inches long and 1½ inches wide. Cut a third strip, 8 inches long and 1½ inches wide. Place strips lightly on cake to cover area for white stripes. Sprinkle red sugar on cake for red stripes. Remove paper strips. Top blue sugar with candy stars.

6. Frost cupcake with reserved frosting; place in center of cake. Arrange candles in and around cupcake. Store loosely covered.

BETTY'S SUCCESS TIPS

- The star candies are available on shopbakersnook.com.
- Create an attractive display by covering a piece of sturdy cardboard with wrapping paper, then plastic food wrap. Stretch and secure with tape. Or cover cardboard with foil or cooking parchment paper.

1 SERVING: Calories 270; Total Fat 11g (Saturated Fat 3g); Sodium 250mg; Total Carbohydrate 41g (Dietary Fiber 0g); Protein 2g; **Exchanges:** ½ Starch; 2 Other Carbohydrate; 2 Fat; **Carbohydrate Choices:** 3

Cashew-Fudge-Caramel Ice Cream Pie

Crush cookies for an easy crust, then fill with a sultry blend of ice cream, nuts and ready-made chocolate topping.

PREP TIME: 25 MINUTES • **TOTAL TIME:** 5 HOURS 30 MINUTES • **MAKES 8 SERVINGS**

30 vanilla wafer cookies	2 pints (4 cups) dulce de leche ice cream, softened
³⁄₄ cup cashew halves and pieces	
¹⁄₄ cup butter, melted	1 cup chocolate fudge ice cream topping

1. Heat oven to 350°F. In food processor bowl with metal blade, combine vanilla wafers and ¹⁄₂ cup of the cashews; process until finely ground. Add butter; process just until crumbly. Press mixture in bottom and up side of 9-inch glass pie pan.

2. Bake at 350°F for 10 to 12 minutes or until edges are light golden brown. Refrigerate crust for 20 minutes or until completely cooled.

3. Spread 1 pint of the ice cream in cooled crust. Spoon or drizzle ¹⁄₂ cup of the ice cream topping over ice cream. Freeze about 30 minutes or until partially frozen.

4. Top pie with remaining pint ice cream, spreading evenly. Freeze at least 4 hours or until firm.

5. To serve, let pie stand at room temperature for 15 minutes. Cut into wedges; place on individual dessert plates. Top with remaining ice cream topping and cashew halves.

BETTY'S SUCCESS TIPS

- We've called for dulce de leche (caramel) ice cream in this recipe, but you can use any caramel-flavored ice cream.
- To speed up cooling of the crust, we placed it in the refrigerator until completely cooled. You can choose to cool at room temperature; allow 45 to 60 minutes.
- If your fudge topping is too thick, microwave it for 30 to 60 seconds to soften it. If it gets too warm, let it cool for a minute or two.

1 SERVING: Calories 465; Total Fat 25g (Saturated Fat 12g); Sodium 370mg; Total Carbohydrate 53g (Dietary Fiber 1g); Protein 7g; **Exchanges:** 2 Starch; 1¹⁄₂ Other Carbohydrate; 5 Fat; **Carbohydrate Choices:** 3¹⁄₂

Frosty French Silk Pie

Love the classic decadent French silk pie? Try a frosty version. You can sneak a piece from the freezer any time you crave it.

PREP TIME: 30 MINUTES • **TOTAL TIME:** 6 HOURS 20 MINUTES • **MAKES 12 SERVINGS**

Chocolate Pat-in-Pan Pie Crust

- ³/₄ **cup butter or margarine, softened**
- ¹/₃ **cup sugar**
- ¹/₄ **cup unsweetened baking cocoa**
- 1¹/₄ **cups Gold Medal® all-purpose flour**
- ¹/₄ **cup finely chopped nuts**

Filling

- ¹/₄ **cup butter or margarine**
- 3 **ounces unsweetened baking chocolate**
- 1 **cup sugar**
- 2 **tablespoons cornstarch**
- 3 **eggs**
- 1 **teaspoon vanilla**
- 1 **cup whipping (heavy) cream**

Garnish, If Desired

Whipped cream
Sliced almonds, toasted

1. Heat oven to 325°F. In large bowl, beat ³/₄ cup butter and ¹/₃ cup sugar with electric mixer on medium speed 1 minute. Stir in cocoa and flour until mixture is crumbly. Press firmly and evenly against bottom and side of 9¹/₂-inch deep-dish glass pie plate or 10-inch regular glass pie plate. Sprinkle with chopped nuts. Bake 20 to 25 minutes or until edge appears dry. Cool completely, about 45 minutes.

2. In 2-quart saucepan, melt ¹/₄ cup butter and the chocolate over low heat, stirring occasionally; remove from heat. In small bowl, mix 1 cup sugar and the cornstarch with wire whisk; stir into chocolate mixture.

3. In small bowl, beat eggs with electric mixer on medium speed about 5 minutes or until thick and lemon colored; stir into chocolate mixture. Cook chocolate mixture over medium heat 5 minutes, stirring constantly, until thick and glossy. Stir in vanilla. Cool 10 minutes, stirring occasionally.

4. In medium bowl, beat whipping cream with electric mixer on high speed until stiff. Fold chocolate mixture into whipped cream. Pour over crust. Cover; freeze about 4 hours or until firm. Remove from freezer; let stand 30 minutes before cutting. Top with whipped cream; sprinkle with almonds. Store covered in freezer.

BETTY'S SUCCESS TIPS

- Unsweetened baking chocolate contains 50 to 58 percent cocoa butter. Bitter in flavor, it's used primarily in baking. You'll find it in the supermarket in a rectangular box containing packages of 1-ounce squares or bars.
- Dried chocolate liquor, with the cocoa butter removed, is ground into unsweetened baking cocoa. Cocoa drink mixes that contain added powdered milk and sugar should not be substituted for baking cocoa.

1 SERVING: Calories 430; Total Fat 29g (Saturated Fat 17g); Sodium 135mg; Total Carbohydrate 38g (Dietary Fiber 2g); Protein 5g; **Exchanges:** 1¹/₂ Starch; 1 Other Carbohydrate; 5¹/₂ Fat; **Carbohydrate Choices:** 2¹/₂

Boozy Bourbon Chocolate Cupcakes

Taste for yourself what the buzz is all about! A bit of bourbon, a hit of coffee liqueur and some vanilla vodka-spiked frosting make these sophisticated chocolate cupcakes the ultimate "holiday helpers."

PREP TIME: 40 MINUTES • **TOTAL TIME:** 1 HOUR 45 MINUTES • **MAKES 24 CUPCAKES**

Cupcakes
- 1 box Betty Crocker® SuperMoist® devil's food cake mix
- 1 cup water
- 1/3 cup vegetable oil
- 1/4 cup bourbon whiskey
- 3 eggs
- 1 teaspoon vanilla

Filling
- 3/4 cup whipping (heavy) cream
- 6 ounces semisweet baking chocolate, finely chopped
- 1/3 cup butter, softened
- 3 tablespoons coffee liqueur

Frosting
- 1 jar (7 ounces) marshmallow creme (1 3/4 cups)
- 1 cup butter, softened
- 2 tablespoons vanilla-flavored vodka
- 3 cups powdered sugar

Garnish
- 1/4 cup coffee liqueur

1. Heat oven to 350°F (325°F for dark or nonstick pan). Generously spray 24 regular-size muffin cups with cooking spray. Make cake batter as directed on box, using cake mix, water, oil, bourbon, eggs and vanilla. Divide batter evenly among muffin cups (fill about two-thirds full).

2. Bake 20 to 22 minutes or until toothpick inserted in center comes out clean. Cool in pans 10 minutes; remove from pans to cooling rack. Cool completely, about 30 minutes.

3. Meanwhile, for filling, in medium microwavable bowl, microwave whipping cream uncovered on High 1 minute 30 seconds or until boiling. Stir in remaining filling ingredients until chocolate is melted and smooth. If necessary, microwave on High an additional 15 to 30 seconds until mixture can be stirred smooth. Cover; refrigerate about 1 hour or until spreading consistency.

4. For frosting, in large bowl, beat marshmallow creme, 1 cup butter and the vodka with electric mixer on medium speed until blended. Beat in the powdered sugar until fluffy. If necessary, beat in additional powdered sugar until piping consistency.

5. To assemble, cut tops off each cupcake horizontally. Spread about 1 tablespoon filling onto bottom of each cupcake; add cupcake top. Pipe frosting on cupcake tops. Just before serving, drizzle each cupcake with 1/2 teaspoon coffee liqueur.

BETTY'S SUCCESS TIP

For the full tipsy effect, place the cupcake top at a slight angle.

1 CUPCAKE: Calories 340; Total Fat 19g (Saturated Fat 10g); Sodium 230mg; Total Carbohydrate 38g (Dietary Fiber 1g); Protein 3g; **Exchanges:** 1 Starch; 1 1/2 Other Carbohydrate; 3 1/2 Fat; **Carbohydrate Choices:** 2 1/2

Peanut Butter Truffle Brownies

Craving chocolate and sweet peanut butter all wrapped up into one indulgent bar? Start with a no-fail brownie mix, then add layers of peanut butter and melted chocolate chips. Yum.

PREP TIME: 20 MINUTES • **TOTAL TIME:** 2 HOURS 40 MINUTES • **MAKES 24 BROWNIES**

Brownie Base

1 box (1 pound 2.4 ounces) Betty Crocker® Original Supreme Premium brownie mix

Water, vegetable oil and egg called for on brownie mix box

Filling

$\frac{1}{3}$ cup butter, softened

$\frac{1}{3}$ cup creamy peanut butter

$1\frac{1}{3}$ cups powdered sugar

$1\frac{1}{2}$ teaspoons milk

Topping

$\frac{3}{4}$ cup semisweet chocolate chips

3 tablespoons butter

1. Heat oven to 350°F (325°F for dark or nonstick pan). Grease bottom only of 8-inch or 9-inch square pan with cooking spray or shortening. (For easier cutting, line pan with foil, then grease foil on bottom only of pan.) Make brownies as directed on box. Cool completely, about 1 hour.

2. In medium bowl, beat filling ingredients with electric mixer on medium speed until smooth. Spread mixture evenly over brownie base.

3. In small microwavable bowl, microwave topping ingredients uncovered on High 30 to 60 seconds; stir until smooth. Cool 10 minutes; spread over filling. Refrigerate about 30 minutes or until set. For brownies, cut into 6 rows by 4 rows. Store covered in refrigerator.

BETTY'S SUCCESS TIP

Cut brownies into bite-size treats for a dessert buffet.

1 BROWNIE: Calories 220; Total Fat 11g (Saturated Fat 4$\frac{1}{2}$); Sodium 120mg; Total Carbohydrate 29g (Dietary Fiber 1g); Protein 2g; **Exchanges:** $\frac{1}{2}$ Starch; 1$\frac{1}{2}$ Other Carbohydrate; 2 Fat; **Carbohydrate Choices:** 2

Double-Stack S'more

How could a s'more get any better? Make it bigger and drizzle it with chocolate. Just 5 minutes to total decadence.

PREP TIME: 5 MINUTES • **TOTAL TIME:** 5 MINUTES • **MAKES 1 SERVING**

> **Large marshmallows**
> **Nature Valley® dark chocolate granola thins**
> **Chocolate-flavor syrup**

1. Spear 2 large marshmallows on long-handled fork; toast over campfire coals or over grill on low heat.

2. For each s'more, place 1 toasted marshmallow on chocolate side of each of 2 granola thins.

3. Place 1 additional granola thin between the marshmallows, and press together. Top with 1 teaspoon chocolate syrup.

BETTY'S SUCCESS TIP

If campfire or grill is not available for toasting marshmallows, place marshmallow on microwavable plate; microwave 10 to 12 seconds or until marshmallow doubles in size.

1 SERVING: Calories 320; Total Fat 12g (Saturated Fat 4½g); Sodium 240mg; Total Carbohydrate 49g (Dietary Fiber 1g); Protein 3g; **Exchanges:** 1 Starch; 2½ Other Carbohydrate; 2 Fat; **Carbohydrate Choices:** 3

Chocolate Peanut Butter Cloud Cookies

Looking for a chocolate cookie using Betty Crocker® SuperMoist® chocolate fudge cake mix? Look no further!

PREP TIME: 40 MINUTES • **TOTAL TIME:** 1 HOUR 20 MINUTES • **MAKES** 4¹/₂ DOZEN

Cookies

1 box Betty Crocker® SuperMoist® chocolate fudge cake mix
³/₄ cup creamy peanut butter
¹/₄ cup water
1 teaspoon vanilla
3 eggs
1¹/₂ cups semisweet chocolate chips

Frosting

1¹/₂ containers Betty Crocker® Whipped fluffy white frosting
³/₄ cup creamy peanut butter
2 teaspoons milk

1. Heat oven to 375°F (350°F for dark or nonstick cookie sheet). Spray cookie sheet with cooking spray.

2. In large bowl, beat cake mix, ³/₄ cup peanut butter, the water, vanilla and eggs with electric mixer on medium speed about 1 minute or until blended. Gently stir in chocolate chips. Onto cookie sheet, drop dough by rounded teaspoonfuls about 2 inches apart.

3. Bake 7 to 9 minutes or until set. Cool 1 minute; remove from cookie sheet to cooling rack. Cool completely, about 10 minutes.

4. In medium bowl, stir together frosting ingredients. Frost cookies with frosting. Store covered.

BETTY'S SUCCESS TIPS

- For a decorative touch, spoon frosting into pastry bag fitted with star tip, then squirt frosting on each cookie. You can also use a star tip inside a food-storage plastic bag!
- The secret ingredient in this recipe, cake mix, makes these cookies very light and the perfect chocolate base for the creamy frosting.

1 COOKIE: Calories 150; Total Fat 8g (Saturated Fat 2¹/₂g); Sodium 115mg; Total Carbohydrate 17g (Dietary Fiber 1g); Protein 2g; **Exchanges:** ¹/₂ Starch; ¹/₂ Other Carbohydrate; 1¹/₂ Fat; **Carbohydrate Choices:** 1

Flip-Flop Fun Cookies

Transform purchased peanut butter cookies into adorable summertime treats . . . you'll flip over how simple they are to make!

PREP TIME: 35 MINUTES • **TOTAL TIME:** 35 MINUTES • **MAKES 12 COOKIES**

4 rectangles (1$\frac{1}{2}$ x 1 inch each) vanilla-flavored candy coating (almond bark) (from 20-ounce package)

1 roll Fruit by the Foot® chewy fruit snack (from 6-roll box)

12 peanut butter sandwich cookies (from 1-pound package)

12 miniature candy-coated chocolate baking bits
Brown sugar, if desired

1. In 1-quart saucepan, melt candy coating over low heat, stirring occasionally.

2. Meanwhile, unroll fruit snack roll. Using kitchen scissors, cut 12 (4$\frac{1}{2}$ x $\frac{1}{4}$-inch) strips from fruit snack roll. Remove paper. Fold each strip in half, forming a V shape.

3. Dip tops and sides of cookies into melted candy coating; lift out with fork or tongs, letting excess drip off. Place cookies, coated side up, on cookie sheets. Before coating sets, carefully attach fruit snack pieces to make tops of flip-flop sandals, placing point of V shape near one end of cookie, and ends at other end of cookie. Place baking bit at tip of V shape. Let stand until set, about 10 minutes.

4. Spoon brown sugar onto tray to look like sand; arrange cookies on brown sugar.

BETTY'S SUCCESS TIP

Personalize this fun food by decorating with your own unique candy selection. Add a few drops of food color to the vanilla-flavored candy coating to tint the flip-flops to your liking.

1 COOKIE: Calories 130; Total Fat 6g (Saturated Fat 3g); Sodium 60mg; Total Carbohydrate 16g (Dietary Fiber 0g); Protein 1g; **Exchanges:** $\frac{1}{2}$ Starch; $\frac{1}{2}$ Other Carbohydrate; 1 Fat; **Carbohydrate Choices:** 1

Dulce de Leche Cheesecake Pops

Your favorite dessert has hit the freezer just in time for the dog days of summer. Decadent cheesecake takes pop form with layer after layer of dulce de leche and crunchy cinnamon cereal.

PREP TIME: 25 MINUTES • TOTAL TIME: 6 HOURS 25 MINUTES • MAKES 8 POPS

1   **package (8 ounces) cream cheese, softened**
1/2 **cup sugar**
1/2 **cup sour cream**
1   **cup half-and-half**

2/3 **cup dulce de leche (caramelized sweetened condensed milk) (from 13.4-ounce can)**
2   **tablespoons milk**
1/2 **cup Cinnamon Toast Crunch® cereal, coarsely crushed**

1. In medium bowl, beat cream cheese and sugar with electric mixer on medium speed until smooth. Beat in sour cream and half-and-half. Spoon 1/4 cup mixture into each of eight 5-ounce paper cups. Cover cups with foil; insert craft stick into center of each pop. Freeze about 2 hours or until frozen. Cover and refrigerate remaining cream cheese mixture.

2. In small bowl, mix dulce de leche and milk. Place 1/3 cup dulce de leche mixture in small resealable food-storage plastic bag; cover and refrigerate remaining mixture. Cut off one small corner of bag; squeeze small amounts over frozen cream cheese layer in each cup. Pour remaining cream cheese mixture over dulce de leche layer in cups. Return foil to pops to support sticks. Freeze about 4 hours or until frozen.

3. About 30 minutes before serving, remove reserved dulce de leche mixture from refrigerator; let stand at room temperature to soften. Remove pops from freezer and paper cups. Dip top of each pop in reserved dulce de leche mixture; dip in cereal.

BETTY'S SUCCESS TIP

The yummy, sticky dulce de leche layer may stick to pop molds, so it's best to freeze in paper cups that can easily be peeled off the pops.

1 POP: Calories 310; Total Fat 18g (Saturated Fat 11g); Sodium 170mg; Total Carbohydrate 32g (Dietary Fiber 0g); Protein 5g; **Exchanges:** 1/2 Starch; 1 Other Carbohydrate; 1/2 Skim Milk; 3 1/2 Fat; **Carbohydrate Choices:** 2

Double-Chocolate Swirl Pops

Look out, fudge pops—there's a new icy treat in town and it's doubly delicious. White and dark chocolate swirl together for an indulgent new twist on the classic fudge pop.

PREP TIME: 35 MINUTES • **TOTAL TIME:** 7 HOURS 35 MINUTES • **MAKES 9 POPS**

White Chocolate Yogurt

- 4 ounces white chocolate baking bars or squares, finely chopped
- 1 cup half-and-half
- 1 container (6 ounces) Yoplait® Original 99% Fat Free French vanilla yogurt

Dark Chocolate Yogurt

- 1 cup semisweet chocolate chips
- 1 cup half-and-half
- 1 container (6 ounces) Yoplait® Original 99% Fat Free French vanilla yogurt

1. In 2-quart saucepan, heat white chocolate and 1 cup half-and-half over medium-low heat, stirring with whisk, until melted and smooth. Pour mixture into medium bowl. Beat in 1 container yogurt with whisk. Cover and refrigerate.

2. In same saucepan, heat semisweet chocolate chips and 1 cup half-and-half over medium-low heat, stirring with whisk, until melted and smooth. If necessary, pour mixture through a fine mesh strainer into another medium bowl. Beat in 1 container yogurt with whisk. Cover and refrigerate both yogurt mixtures 1 hour.

3. Alternately spoon both yogurt mixtures, 1 tablespoon at a time, into nine 5-ounce paper cups. Use a knife or craft stick to gently swirl mixtures together. Cover cups with foil; insert craft stick into center of each pop. (Or fill ice pop molds according to manufacturer's directions.) Freeze about 6 hours or until frozen.

BETTY'S SUCCESS TIP

Look for wide craft sticks in specialty cookware stores.

1 POP: Calories 280; Total Fat 16g (Saturated Fat 10g); Sodium 60mg; Total Carbohydrate 29g (Dietary Fiber 1g); Protein 5g; **Exchanges:** 1½ Starch; ½ Other Carbohydrate; 3 Fat; **Carbohydrate Choices:** 2

Mai Tai Tiki Pops

These rum-spiked frozen treats take the flavors of a well-known tiki cocktail—the mai tai—and turn it into a fruity (and boozy) ice pop.

PREP TIME: 20 MINUTES • **TOTAL TIME:** 11 HOURS 20 MINUTES • **MAKES 6 POPS**

Coconut Colada Layer

- 1 container (6 ounces) Yoplait® Original 99% Fat Free piña colada or Key lime pie yogurt
- ¼ cup canned coconut milk, well stirred (not cream of coconut)
- 1 teaspoon dark rum

Mango Mai Tai Layer

- 1 fresh mango, peeled, pitted and cubed (about 1 cup)
- 3 tablespoons sugar
- ¾ cup mango nectar, chilled
- 2 tablespoons dark rum
- 2 tablespoons light rum
- 2 tablespoons fresh lime juice
- 1 tablespoon orange liqueur
- 1 teaspoon amaretto liqueur

1. In small bowl, beat coconut colada layer ingredients with whisk until smooth. Divide mixture among six 5-ounce paper cups. Cover with foil; insert craft stick (flat wooden stick with round ends) through foil into center of pop. Freeze 2 to 3 hours or until frozen.

2. Meanwhile, in blender, place mango mai tai layer ingredients. Cover; blend on medium speed about 45 seconds, stopping frequently to scrape sides, until smooth. Cover and refrigerate while waiting for first layer to freeze.

3. When first layer is frozen, remove foil from pops. Pour mango mixture over frozen layer. Return foil to pops to help support sticks. Freeze about 8 hours or until frozen before serving. Store remaining pops covered in freezer.

BETTY'S SUCCESS TIPS

- Be sure to allow the coconut colada layer to freeze completely before adding the mango mai tai layer.
- Be patient when freezing these spiked ice pops. They take longer to freeze because of the alcohol, but they are worth the wait.

1 POP: Calories 140; Total Fat 2½g (Saturated Fat 2g); Sodium 15mg; Total Carbohydrate 22g (Dietary Fiber 0g); Protein 1g; **Exchanges:** ½ Starch; 1 Other Carbohydrate; ½ Fat; **Carbohydrate Choices:** 1½

Watermelon Pops

Enjoy these watermelon pops made with chocolate, Betty Crocker® SuperMoist® cake mix and Rich & Creamy vanilla frosting—a beautiful dessert.

PREP TIME: 1 HOUR **TOTAL TIME:** 3 HOURS 10 MINUTES • **MAKES 32 POPS**

1   **box Betty Crocker® SuperMoist® white cake mix**
    Water, vegetable oil and egg whites called for on cake mix box
¼ **teaspoon pink paste food color**
¾ **cup Betty Crocker® Rich & Creamy vanilla frosting (from 16-ounce container)**
¾ **cup miniature semisweet chocolate chips**

32 **paper lollipop sticks**
1   **bag (16 ounces) white candy melts or coating wafers, melted**
1   **large block white plastic foam**
1   **bag (16 ounces) green candy melts or coating wafers, melted**
1   **cup light green candy melts (from 16-ounce bag), melted**

1. Heat oven to 350°F. Spray 13 x 9-inch pan with cooking spray. Make and bake cake mix as directed on box for 13 x 9-inch pan, using water, oil and egg whites and adding pink paste food color. Cool completely.

2. Line cookie sheet with waxed paper. Crumble cake into large bowl. Add frosting and chocolate chips; mix well. Shape into 32 oblong balls; place on cookie sheet. Freeze until firm. When cake balls are firm, transfer to refrigerator.

3. Remove several cake balls from refrigerator at a time. Dip tip of 1 lollipop stick ½ inch into melted white candy and insert stick into 1 cake ball no more than halfway. Dip each cake ball into melted candy to cover; tap off excess. Poke opposite end of stick into foam block. Let stand until set. Dip each cake ball into melted green candy to cover; tap off excess. Return sticks to foam block. Let stand until set. With toothpick, decorate cake balls with light green candy to look like watermelons. Let stand until set.

1 POP: Calories 351; Total Fat 17g (Saturated Fat 10g); Sodium 119mg; Total Carbohydrate 49g (Dietary Fiber 0g); Protein 1g; **Exchanges:** ½ Starch; 2½ Other Carbohydrate; 3½ Fat; **Carbohydrate Choices:** 3

Lemon Meringue Pie Pops

What could be better than a slice of pie? Pie pops! Our frozen take on lemon meringue pie has a graham cracker crust, creamy lemon filling and a fluffy topping. Basically it's your own little piece of heaven—on a stick!

PREP TIME: 25 MINUTES • **TOTAL TIME:** 6 HOURS 25 MINUTES • **MAKES 7 POPS**

1 box (4-serving size) lemon instant pudding and pie filling mix
1½ cups half-and-half
¼ cup fresh lemon juice
1 container (6 ounces) Yoplait® Original 99% Fat Free lemon burst yogurt

7 tablespoons coarsely crushed graham crackers
¼ cup marshmallow creme
½ cup whipping (heavy) cream

1. In medium bowl, beat pudding mix and half-and-half with whisk 2 minutes. Beat in lemon juice and yogurt.

2. Pour about ⅓ cup mixture into each of seven 5-ounce paper cups. Sprinkle each with 1 tablespoon graham crackers. Cover cups with foil; insert craft stick into center of each pop. (Or fill ice pop molds according to manufacturer's directions.) Freeze about 6 hours or until frozen.

3. When ready to serve pops, in small bowl, beat marshmallow creme and 1 tablespoon of the whipping cream with electric mixer on low speed until smooth. Add remaining whipping cream, increase speed to high and beat until stiff peaks form. Remove each pop from cup. Spread top of each with about 2 tablespoons marshmallow mixture, forming meringue peaks.

BETTY'S SUCCESS TIP

If you can't find lemon burst yogurt, you can substitute French vanilla.

1 POP: Calories 240; Total Fat 13g (Saturated Fat 8g); Sodium 270mg; Total Carbohydrate 28g (Dietary Fiber 0g); Protein 3g; **Exchanges:** 1 Starch; 1 Other Carbohydrate; 2½ Fat; **Carbohydrate Choices:** 2

Menus

Fire Up the Grill for Father's Day

Grilled Ribs with Cherry Cola Barbecue Sauce 244

Savory Corn on a Stick 266

Slow Cooker Baked Beans 271

Boozy Bourbon Chocolate Cupcakes 290

Betty's Best 4th of July

Grilled Firecracker Chicken Drummies 249

Corn and Black Bean Salad with Tortilla Wedges 275

Red, White and Blueberry Salad 278

Sparkling 4th of July Cake 284

Perfect Picnic

Fresh Sriracha Refrigerator Pickles 277

Country "Fried" Chicken 263

Super-Simple Picnic Potato Salad 276

Nutty Chocolate Chip Picnic Cake 279

Fall

Slow Cooker Apple-Cranberry Oatmeal

Prepare this delicious fruity oatmeal porridge for breakfast in a snap by putting your slow cooker to work overnight!

PREP TIME: 10 MINUTES • **TOTAL TIME:** 6 HOURS 10 MINUTES • **MAKES 6 SERVINGS**

6 cups water	2 tablespoons butter or margarine, melted
3 cups old-fashioned oats	$\frac{1}{2}$ teaspoon ground cinnamon
2 apples, peeled, chopped	$\frac{1}{4}$ teaspoon salt
$\frac{1}{2}$ cup sweetened dried cranberries or raisins	

1. Spray $3\frac{1}{2}$- to 4-quart slow cooker with cooking spray. In slow cooker, mix all ingredients.

2. Cover; cook on Low heat setting 6 to 8 hours. Serve porridge with brown sugar and milk or cream, as desired.

1 SERVING: Calories 250; Total Fat 7g (Saturated Fat 3g); Sodium 135mg; Total Carbohydrate 41g (Dietary Fiber 5g); Protein 6g; **Exchanges:** $1\frac{1}{2}$ Starch; 1 Other Carbohydrate; $1\frac{1}{2}$ Fat; **Carbohydrate Choices:** 3

Baking with Apples

Confession: We're apple lovers to our core. Tart, crisp, red or yellow, we've got recipes for every flavor, and baking tips, too! So forget an ordinary apple a day—indulge in a daily apple recipe instead.

Cookies, cakes, salads and sauces, they're all here! And, of course, apple pies—because what would fall be without them?

WHAT ARE THE BEST APPLES TO USE IN PIES?

- For apple pies, apple crisps and other baked apple items, apples need to be firm enough to hold their shape. We recommend: Braeburn, Cortland, Fuji, Gala, Granny Smith, Haralson, Newtown Pippin.

WHAT ABOUT OTHER BAKED APPLE TREATS?

- Chopped or sliced apples for cakes and sauces can be less firm than apples used in pies. Choose the sweetest variety available for the best flavor. We recommend: Braeburn, Gala, Golden Delicious, Honey Gold, Jonathan, McIntosh.

HOW MANY APPLES DO I NEED FOR MOST PIES?

- You will need 5 to 6 cups of sliced or chopped apples for a 9- or 10-inch pie.

I NEED AN EASY WAY TO CONVERT MY APPLE MEASUREMENTS.

- For chopped or sliced apples, 2 to $2\frac{1}{2}$ cups are equivalent to 3 three medium apples, or about 1 pound.
- 3 medium apples are roughly equivalent to 2 large apples or 4 small apples.

HOW SHOULD APPLES BE STORED?

- Refrigerate apples for full flavor and crunch.
- The perfect temperature is between 32°F and 40°F.
- Store in perforated plastic bags/containers that allow airflow to prevent drying.
- Apples keep in the refrigerator for up to 2 weeks.

HOW SHOULD I PREPARE MY APPLES BEFORE I START COOKING OR BAKING?

- Always peel your apples. The skin becomes tough and it will not break down when cooked.
- Use a vegetable peeler instead of a knife—it's faster and removes less flesh.
- Cut peeled apples into fourths, removing the core.
- Toss cut pieces with water and lemon juice to prevent browning.
- Use overripe or bruised apples for sauce.

ANY OTHER TIPS?

- Select apple varieties that are in season. If the apples are out of season, they may have been in storage and will not be as flavorful and juicy as fresh-picked apples.
- Choose apples that look fresh, are bright in color and have a fresh apple aroma.
- Don't choose unripe apples that are hard and have too much green or yellow color for their variety.

Apple Breakfast Wedges

Slice into a warm apple breakfast or brunch treat. All you need is 15 minutes of prep, and it's in the oven.

PREP TIME: 15 MINUTES • **TOTAL TIME:** 40 MINUTES • **MAKES 6 SERVINGS**

¼ cup packed brown sugar	2 tablespoons butter or margarine
¼ teaspoon ground cinnamon	½ cup Original Bisquick® mix
2 medium cooking apples, peeled, thinly sliced (about 2 cups)	2 eggs
⅓ cup water	Maple-flavored syrup, if desired

1. Heat oven to 400°F. Generously grease 9-inch glass pie plate with shortening or cooking spray. In medium bowl, mix brown sugar and cinnamon. Add apples; toss to coat. Set aside.

2. In 2-quart saucepan, heat water and butter to boiling. Reduce heat to low. Add Bisquick mix; stir vigorously until mixture forms a ball. Remove from heat. Beat in eggs, one at a time; continue beating until smooth.

3. Spread batter in bottom of pie plate. Arrange apples on top to within 1 inch of edge of pie plate.

4. Bake about 23 minutes or until puffed and edges are golden brown. Serve immediately. Drizzle with syrup.

BETTY'S SUCCESS TIP

Use slightly tart apples with a crisp texture, such as Haralson apples. If you like a sweeter apple, choose Fuji, Prairie Spy or Gala.

1 SERVING: Calories 160; Total Fat 7g (Saturated Fat 3½g); Sodium 170mg; Total Carbohydrate 20g (Dietary Fiber 0g); Protein 3g; **Exchanges:** 1 Starch; ½ Other Carbohydrate; 1 Fat; **Carbohydrate Choices:** 1

Apple Oven Pancake

Here's a sweet pancake made with apples and Original Bisquick® mix and served with maple-flavored syrup.

PREP TIME: 25 MINUTES • **TOTAL TIME:** 55 MINUTES • **MAKES 8 SERVINGS**

3 tablespoons butter or margarine

4 medium cooking apples, peeled, thinly sliced (about 6 cups)

1/4 cup packed brown sugar

2 teaspoons ground cinnamon

1 1/2 cups Original Bisquick® mix

1/4 cup granulated sugar

1 cup buttermilk

1 tablespoon fresh lemon juice

1 teaspoon vanilla

2 eggs

1 tablespoon cinnamon-sugar
   Maple-flavored syrup, if desired

1. Heat oven to 450°F. In oven, melt butter in 10-inch ovenproof or cast-iron skillet, about 2 minutes. Add apples, brown sugar and cinnamon; toss to coat apples. (Pan will be very hot.) Bake 2 minutes longer; stir. Bake 3 minutes longer; stir again. Reduce oven temperature to 400°F.

2. In large bowl, beat Bisquick mix, granulated sugar, buttermilk, lemon juice, vanilla and eggs with whisk or fork until blended. Pour over apples.

3. Bake 25 to 30 minutes or until golden brown. Sprinkle with cinnamon-sugar. Cut into wedges. Drizzle with syrup. Serve immediately.

BETTY'S SUCCESS TIPS

- Wondering which apples are best for baking? The best baking apples are slightly tart. Top choices are Braeburn, Granny Smith, Cortland, Northern Spy and Rome Beauty.
- Make weekend mornings special by serving this oven pancake with sausage or bacon.

1 SERVING: Calories 280; Total Fat 9g (Saturated Fat 4 1/2 g); Sodium 370mg; Total Carbohydrate 43g (Dietary Fiber 2g); Protein 5g; **Exchanges:** 1 Starch; 1/2 Fruit; 1 1/2 Other Carbohydrate; 1 1/2 Fat; **Carbohydrate Choices:** 3

Bacon and Hashbrown Egg Bake

Brunch? Mix up breakfast favorites of bacon and hashbrowns in a make-ahead egg bake.

PREP TIME: 30 MINUTES • TOTAL TIME: 9 HOURS 40 MINUTES • MAKES 12 SERVINGS

1 pound bacon, cut into 1-inch pieces
1 medium onion, chopped (¹/₂ cup)
1 medium red bell pepper, chopped (³/₄ cup)
1 package (8 ounces) sliced fresh mushrooms
2 tablespoons Dijon mustard
¹/₂ teaspoon salt

¹/₂ teaspoon pepper
³/₄ cup milk
12 eggs
1 package (2 pounds) frozen hashbrowns, thawed
2 cups shredded Cheddar cheese (16 ounces)

1. In 12-inch skillet, cook bacon until crisp. Using slotted spoon, remove from pan to small bowl. Cover and refrigerate. Drain drippings, reserving 1 tablespoon in pan. Add onion, bell pepper and mushrooms; cook 4 minutes over medium heat, stirring occasionally. Stir in mustard, salt and pepper. In large bowl, beat milk and eggs with wire whisk.

2. Spray 13 x 9-inch (3-quart) baking dish with cooking spray. Spread half of hashbrowns in baking dish. Spread onion mixture evenly on top. Sprinkle with 1 cup of the cheese. Spread remaining hashbrowns over top. Pour egg mixture on top. Cover; refrigerate 8 hours or overnight.

3. Heat oven to 325°F. Uncover; bake 50 to 60 minutes or until thermometer inserted in center reads 160°F. Sprinkle with remaining 1 cup cheese and the bacon. Bake 3 to 5 minutes longer or until knife inserted in center comes out clean, top is puffed and cheese is melted. Let stand 5 minutes.

BETTY'S SUCCESS TIPS

- Substitute Monterey Jack, Colby or Swiss for the Cheddar cheese.
- Serve with assorted breads and fresh fruit.

1 SERVING: Calories 410; Total Fat 24g (Saturated Fat 12g); Sodium 740mg; Total Carbohydrate 25g (Dietary Fiber 3g); Protein 22g; **Exchanges:** 1¹/₂ Starch; 2¹/₂ High-Fat Meat; 1 Fat; **Carbohydrate Choices:** 1¹/₂

Monkey Tail Bread

Go bananas with banana bread, and frost it with the favorite flavors of chocolate and peanut butter.

PREP TIME: 15 MINUTES • **TOTAL TIME:** 2 HOURS 35 MINUTES • **MAKES 1 LOAF**

<table>
<tr><td>

1/2 **cup shortening**
1 **cup sugar**
2 **eggs**
1 **cup mashed banana (3 medium)**
2 **cups Gold Medal® all-purpose flour**
1 **teaspoon baking powder**
1/2 **teaspoon baking soda**
1/2 **teaspoon salt**

</td><td>

1/2 **cup chopped peanuts**
1/2 **cup miniature semisweet chocolate chips**
2 **tablespoons Betty Crocker® Rich & Creamy ready-to-spread chocolate frosting**
1 **tablespoon creamy peanut butter**

</td></tr>
</table>

1. Heat oven to 350°F. Grease bottom only of loaf pan, 9 x 5 x 3 inches, with shortening.

2. Beat 1/2 cup shortening and the sugar in large bowl with electric mixer on medium speed until fluffy. Beat in eggs and bananas until smooth. Beat in flour, baking powder, baking soda and salt just until mixed. Stir in peanuts and chocolate chips. Pour into pan.

3. Bake 1 hour to 1 hour 10 minutes or until toothpick inserted in center comes out clean. Cool in pan 10 minutes; remove from pan to wire rack. Cool completely, about 1 hour.

4. Place frosting in small plastic food-storage bag. Microwave on High 6 to 10 seconds or until pourable. Add peanut butter to bag; gently squeeze bag until peanut butter and frosting are well blended. Cut off tiny corner of bag. Squeeze bag to drizzle chocolate mixture over bread.

BETTY'S SUCCESS TIP

A monkey tail is a carnival treat made of a frozen banana on a stick that's dipped in chocolate and rolled in peanuts.

1 SLICE: Calories 265; Total Fat 12g (Saturated Fat 4g); Sodium 180mg; Total Carbohydrate 34g (Dietary Fiber 2g); Protein 4g; **Exchanges:** 1 Starch; 1 Fruit; 2 1/2 Fat; **Carbohydrate Choices:** 2

Candied Ginger Pumpkin Pancakes

Wake up sleepyheads with warm, spicy pumpkin pancakes! Pass the warm syrup, please.

PREP TIME: 30 MINUTES • **TOTAL TIME:** 30 MINUTES • **MAKES 16 SERVINGS**

2 cups Original Bisquick® mix
2 teaspoons pumpkin pie spice
1 1/2 cups buttermilk
1 cup canned pumpkin (not pumpkin pie mix)
2 eggs
1/4 cup toasted pecan halves, finely chopped

1 tablespoon finely chopped crystallized ginger
Pecan halves, if desired
Butter, if desired
Maple-flavored syrup, if desired

1. In large bowl, stir Bisquick mix, pumpkin pie spice, buttermilk, pumpkin and eggs with whisk or fork until blended. Stir in chopped pecans and ginger.

2. Brush nonstick griddle or nonstick skillet with vegetable oil; heat griddle to 350°F or heat skillet over medium heat.

3. For each pancake, pour 1/4 cup of batter onto hot griddle. Cook until edges are dry. Turn; cook other sides until golden brown. Serve topped with remaining ingredients.

BETTY'S SUCCESS TIPS

- To toast pecans, sprinkle in ungreased heavy skillet. Cook over medium heat 5 to 7 minutes, stirring frequently until pecans begin to brown, then stirring constantly until light brown.
- No pumpkin pie spice? Use 1 teaspoon ground cinnamon and 1/2 teaspoon each of ground nutmeg and ground ginger.

1 PANCAKE: Calories 110; Total Fat 4 1/2g (Saturated Fat 1g); Sodium 210mg; Total Carbohydrate 14g (Dietary Fiber 1g); Protein 3g; **Exchanges:** 1 Starch; 1 Fat; **Carbohydrate Choices:** 1

Gingerbread Coffee Cake

Betty Crocker® gingerbread cookie mix makes these flavorful coffee cakes—a perfect addition to your bread basket.

PREP TIME: 20 MINUTES • **TOTAL TIME:** 1 HOUR 40 MINUTES • **MAKES 12 SERVINGS**

- 1 box Betty Crocker® gingerbread cake and cookie mix
- 1/4 cup hot water
- 2 tablespoons butter, melted
- 1 teaspoon grated gingerroot
- 1 container (8 ounces) sour cream
- 1 egg
- 1/3 cup Gold Medal® all-purpose flour

- 1/3 cup sugar
- 1/4 teaspoon ground ginger
- 1/4 teaspoon ground cinnamon
- 1/3 cup butter, softened
- 3/4 cup crushed gingersnap cookies (about 12 cookies)
- 1/2 cup chopped walnuts

1. Heat oven to 350°F. Spray bottom only of 8-inch square pan with cooking spray. In medium bowl, beat cake and cookie mix, hot water and 2 tablespoons butter with electric mixer on medium speed until blended. Add gingerroot, sour cream and egg; beat until blended. Pour batter into pan.

2. In medium bowl, mix flour, sugar, ginger and cinnamon. Add 1/3 cup softened butter; pinch with fingers until clumps form. Stir in crushed cookies and walnuts. Sprinkle over batter.

3. Bake 48 to 50 minutes or until toothpick inserted in center comes out clean. Cool in pan on cooling rack 30 minutes. Serve warm, or cool completely.

BETTY'S SUCCESS TIP

For best results, work the softened butter into the streusel using your fingers to form large clumps.

1 SERVING: Calories 340; Total Fat 18g (Saturated Fat 8g); Sodium 350mg; Total Carbohydrate 41g (Dietary Fiber 1g); Protein 4g; **Exchanges:** 1 Starch; 1 Other Carbohydrate; 3½ Fat; **Carbohydrate Choices:** 2

Pear and Ginger Muffins

Enjoy these sweet muffins made using Bisquick Heart Smart® mix, pear and ginger—a delicious way to start the day.

PREP TIME: 15 MINUTES • **TOTAL TIME:** 35 MINUTES • **MAKES 12 MUFFINS**

2 cups Bisquick Heart Smart® mix	2 tablespoons vegetable oil
$2/3$ cup milk	1 teaspoon ground cinnamon
1 egg	1 teaspoon grated gingerroot
$1/3$ cup packed brown sugar	1 cup chopped unpeeled pear

1. Heat oven to 400°F. Place paper baking cup in each of 12 regular-size muffin cups.

2. In medium bowl, mix all ingredients except pear. Fold in pear. Divide batter evenly among muffin cups.

3. Bake 17 to 20 minutes or until golden brown. Immediately remove from pan to wire rack. Serve warm, if desired.

BETTY'S SUCCESS TIPS

- Gingerroot can be found in the produce section at the grocery store. Peel before grating. Wrap the unused portion tightly in foil and store in the freezer.
- Freeze leftover muffins and reheat in the microwave when ready to eat.

1 MUFFIN: Calories 140; Total Fat $4^1/_2$g (Saturated Fat $^1/_2$g); Sodium 180mg; Total Carbohydrate 22g (Dietary Fiber 0g); Protein 2g; **Exchanges:** 1 Starch; $^1/_2$ Other Carbohydrate; 1 Fat; **Carbohydrate Choices:** $1^1/_2$

Streusel Pumpkin Muffins

*Enjoy breakfast with these delightful pumpkin-gingersnaps muffins made using Gold Medal®
all-purpose flour—ready in 45 minutes.*

PREP TIME: 20 MINUTES • **TOTAL TIME:** 45 MINUTES • **MAKES 12 MUFFINS**

1½ cups Gold Medal® all-purpose flour
1 cup packed brown sugar
1 teaspoon baking soda
1 teaspoon pumpkin pie spice
¼ teaspoon salt
1 cup canned pumpkin (not pumpkin pie mix)
½ cup buttermilk
2 tablespoons vegetable oil

1 egg
¾ cup crushed gingersnaps (about 13 cookies)
3 tablespoons Gold Medal® all-purpose flour
3 tablespoons packed brown sugar
3 tablespoons butter, softened
Sliced almonds, if desired

1. Heat oven to 350°F. Place paper baking cup in each of 12 regular-size muffin cups. Spray baking cups with cooking spray.

2. In large bowl, mix 1½ cups flour, 1 cup brown sugar, the baking soda, pumpkin pie spice and salt. Stir in pumpkin, buttermilk, oil and egg just until moistened. Divide batter evenly among muffin cups.

3. In small bowl, mix gingersnaps, 3 tablespoons flour, 3 tablespoons brown sugar and the butter with fork until crumbly. Sprinkle evenly over batter in each cup.

4. Bake 24 minutes or until toothpick inserted in center comes out clean. Remove muffins from pan to cooling rack. Sprinkle with sliced almonds. Serve warm.

1 MUFFIN: Calories 218; Total Fat 6g (Saturated Fat 2g); Sodium 213mg; Total Carbohydrate 38g (Dietary Fiber 1g); Protein 3g; **Exchanges:** 1 Starch; 1 Other Carbohydrate; 1 Fat; **Carbohydrate Choices:** 2

Hot Chocolate Pancakes

Hot chocolate with a twist—in pancakes, that is! Bisquick®, chocolate milk, baking cocoa and a bit of sugar make them extra easy. Add your favorite hot chocolate toppings for an awesome breakfast or brunch treat.

PREP TIME: 10 MINUTES • **TOTAL TIME:** 20 MINUTES • **MAKES 16 SERVINGS**

2 **cups Original Bisquick® mix**	**Toppings, If Desired**
1/4 **cup sugar**	**Chocolate-flavored syrup, warmed**
2 **tablespoons unsweetened baking cocoa**	**Sweetened whipped cream**
1 **cup chocolate milk**	**Miniature marshmallows**
1 **teaspoon vanilla**	**Chocolate candy sprinkles**
2 **eggs**	

1. In large bowl, stir all ingredients except toppings with wire whisk until well blended. Heat nonstick griddle to 375°F or 12-inch skillet over medium-high heat. (To test griddle, sprinkle with a few drops of water. If bubbles jump around, heat is just right.) Brush with vegetable oil if necessary or spray with cooking spray before heating.

2. For each pancake, pour slightly less than 1/4 cupful batter onto hot griddle. Cook 2 to 3 minutes or until bubbly on top and dry around edges. Turn; cook other side until light golden brown around edges.

3. Drizzle pancakes with chocolate-flavored syrup; top with whipped cream. Sprinkle with marshmallows and chocolate candy sprinkles.

1 SERVING: Calories 97; Total Fat 3g (Saturated Fat 1g); Sodium 204mg; Total Carbohydrate 15g (Dietary Fiber 1g); Protein 3g; **Exchanges:** 1 Starch; 1/2 Other Carbohydrate; 1/2 Fat; **Carbohydrate Choices:** 1

German Sausage and Cabbage Soup

Make a hearty sausage soup in about 30 minutes, just right for mopping up with crusty dark bread.

PREP TIME: 30 MINUTES • **TOTAL TIME:** 30 MINUTES • **MAKES 5 SERVINGS**

1 tablespoon butter or margarine
3 cups coleslaw mix (from 16-ounce bag)
1 medium onion, coarsely chopped (1/2 cup)
1 stalk celery, sliced (1/2 cup)
1/2 teaspoon caraway seed
3/4 pound cooked kielbasa, quartered lengthwise, then cut into 1/2-inch slices

3 cups frozen southern-style diced hashbrown potatoes (from 32-ounce bag)
3 1/2 cups Progresso® chicken broth (from 32-ounce carton)
1/4 teaspoon coarse ground black pepper

1. In large saucepan or Dutch oven, melt butter over medium heat. Cook coleslaw mix, onion, celery and caraway seed in butter 2 to 3 minutes, stirring frequently, until vegetables are crisp-tender.

2. Stir in remaining ingredients. Heat to boiling; reduce heat. Cover; simmer 5 to 10 minutes, stirring occasionally, until potatoes are tender and soup is thoroughly heated.

BETTY'S SUCCESS TIPS

- You can substitute 2 1/2 cups shredded cabbage and 1/2 cup shredded carrots for the coleslaw mix.
- Reduce the fat and sodium in this soup by using low-fat turkey kielbasa and choosing fat-free chicken broth with one-third less sodium.

1 SERVING: Calories 370; Total Fat 21g (Saturated Fat 8g); Sodium 1,600mg; Total Carbohydrate 32g (Dietary Fiber 4g); Protein 12g; **Exchanges:** 1 Starch; 1/2 Other Carbohydrate; 2 Vegetable; 3 Fat; **Carbohydrate Choices:** 2

Sweet Potato-Peanut Soup with Ham Croutons

Progresso® chicken broth provides a flavorful addition to this sweet potato and peanut soup topped with ham—a delicious dinner.

PREP TIME: 40 MINUTES • **TOTAL TIME:** 1 HOUR 20 MINUTES • **MAKES 10 SERVINGS**

$1/4$ cup butter or margarine
1 medium onion, chopped ($1/2$ cup)
$3/4$ cup chopped celery
2 cloves garlic, finely chopped
6 cups Progresso® chicken broth (from two 32-ounce cartons)
3 large sweet potatoes (about 3 pounds), peeled, coarsely chopped

1 tablespoon chopped fresh rosemary leaves
2 cups cubed cooked ham
$2/3$ cup creamy peanut butter
1 cup whipping (heavy) cream
$3/4$ teaspoon salt
$1/4$ teaspoon freshly ground pepper
Fresh rosemary sprigs, if desired

1. In 4- to 5-quart Dutch oven, melt butter over medium heat. Cook onion, celery and garlic in butter 10 minutes, stirring occasionally, until tender. Add broth, sweet potatoes and chopped rosemary. Heat to boiling; reduce heat. Cover; simmer 25 minutes or until potatoes are very tender. Remove from heat; cool 15 minutes.

2. Meanwhile, heat 10-inch nonstick skillet over medium-high heat. Add ham; cook until browned and crisp on all sides. Drain on paper towels; cover to keep warm.

3. In blender or food processor, place one-third of the potato mixture. Cover; blend on medium speed until smooth. Pour into large bowl. Repeat twice with remaining potato mixture. Return pureed mixture to Dutch oven; stir in peanut butter. Cook over medium-low heat, stirring often, until soup is smooth. Stir in whipping cream, salt and pepper; cook until thoroughly heated. Top individual servings with ham. Garnish with rosemary sprigs.

1 SERVING: Calories 344; Total Fat 22g (Saturated Fat 10g); Sodium 831mg; Total Carbohydrate 29g (Dietary Fiber 5g); Protein 11g; **Exchanges:** $1^{1}/_{2}$ Starch; $1/2$ Other Carbohydrate; 1 High-Fat Meat; 3 Fat; **Carbohydrate Choices:** 2

Autumn Gumbo

Enjoy this Cajun-style autumn gumbo made with Muir Glen® organic diced tomatoes, chicken and veggies—a wonderful dinner dish served with rice.

PREP TIME: 45 MINUTES • **TOTAL TIME:** 45 MINUTES • **MAKES 6 SERVINGS**

¹/₃ cup vegetable oil

¹/₃ cup Gold Medal® all-purpose flour

1 package (10 ounces) frozen diced celery, onion, and red and green bell peppers, thawed, squeezed to drain

4 cloves garlic, finely chopped

2 cups cubed butternut squash

1 can (28 ounces) Muir Glen® organic diced tomatoes, undrained

2 to 2¹/₂ cups Progresso® chicken broth (from 32-ounce carton)

1¹/₂ teaspoons Creole seasoning

3 cups shredded cooked chicken

1¹/₂ cups frozen cut okra, thawed

2 pouches (8.5 ounces each) ready-to-serve Cajun-style rice

6 slices bacon, crisply cooked, coarsely crumbled

1. In small microwavable bowl, stir oil and flour with whisk. Microwave uncovered on High about 4 minutes, stirring every 45 seconds, until caramel colored.

2. Carefully pour roux mixture into 4-quart Dutch oven. Heat over medium heat until hot. Add bell pepper mix and garlic. Cook 2 to 3 minutes, stirring frequently. Add squash; cook 5 minutes.

3. Stir in tomatoes, 2 cups broth and Creole seasoning. Heat to boiling; reduce heat. Cover; simmer 20 minutes, stirring occasionally and adding ¹/₂ cup more broth if needed. Stir in chicken and okra; simmer 5 to 10 minutes longer.

4. Meanwhile, cook rice in microwave as directed on package. Serve gumbo with rice. Sprinkle with bacon.

1 SERVING: Calories 453; Total Fat 19g (Saturated Fat 2.5g); Sodium 1,472mg; Total Carbohydrate 45g (Dietary Fiber 4g); Protein 24g; **Exchanges:** 2¹/₂ Starch; 2 Vegetable; 2 Very Lean Meat; 3 Fat; **Carbohydrate Choices:** 3

Slow Cooker Reuben Sandwiches

Easy enough to make for a weeknight meal or a friendly Oktoberfest gathering. Bring on the beer and the oompah band!

PREP TIME: 15 MINUTES • **TOTAL TIME:** 11 HOURS 15 MINUTES • **MAKES 8 SANDWICHES**

- 1 **package (2 pounds) refrigerated sauerkraut**
- 1 **package (2 to 3 pounds) corned beef brisket**

- 1 **cup Thousand Island dressing**
- 16 **slices pumpernickel rye bread, toasted**
- 8 **slices (1 ounce each) Swiss cheese**

1. Place sauerkraut in 3- to 4-quart slow cooker. Place beef brisket on sauerkraut. (If brisket includes packet of spices, sprinkle spices over brisket.)

2. Cover and cook on Low heat setting 9 to 11 hours.

3. Remove beef from cooker; place on cutting board. Cut beef into slices. To serve, spread 1 tablespoon dressing on each toast slice. Using slotted spoon to remove sauerkraut from cooker, top 8 slices toast with $1/2$ cup sauerkraut each. Top sauerkraut with beef slices and cheese slice. Top with remaining toast.

Note: *This recipe was tested in slow cookers with heating elements in the side and bottom of the cooker, not in cookers that stand only on a heated base. For slow cookers with just a heated base, follow the manufacturer's directions for layering ingredients and choosing a temperature.*

BETTY'S SUCCESS TIPS

- These sandwiches cry out for a good garlic dill pickle, purchased German potato salad or crunchy potato chips and a side of deli slaw.
- To make this a portable potluck sandwich, stir the sliced beef into the sauerkraut. Place the dressing in a squeeze bottle (like for ketchup), and set out a basket of rye buns and smaller slices of Swiss cheese to make it easy for guests to make their own sandwiches.
- Need a hearty party snack? Build the sandwiches on slices of party rye for a three-bite treat.

1 SANDWICH: Calories 540; Total Fat 35g (Saturated Fat 12g); Sodium 2,390mg; Total Carbohydrate 33g (Dietary Fiber 6g); Protein 29g; **Exchanges:** 2 Starch; 1 Vegetable; 3 High-Fat Meat; 1 Fat; **Carbohydrate Choices:** 2

Grilled Mustard Italian Sausages

Brush mustard over sausages and top with a tangy tomato relish for best-on-the-block grilling.

PREP TIME: 45 MINUTES • **TOTAL TIME:** 45 MINUTES • **MAKES 6 SANDWICHES**

Two-Tomato Relish

- 2 medium tomatoes, finely chopped (1 1/2 cups)
- 2 medium yellow pear tomatoes, finely chopped (1/2 cup)
- 1 tablespoon red wine vinegar
- 1 teaspoon chopped fresh or 1/4 teaspoon dried oregano leaves

Sandwiches

- 1/4 cup Dijon mustard
- 2 teaspoons chopped fresh or 1/2 teaspoon dried oregano leaves
- 6 fresh sweet Italian sausages or turkey Italian sausages (about 1 1/4 pounds)
- 6 bratwurst buns, split

1. Heat gas or charcoal grill. In small bowl, mix relish ingredients; cover and refrigerate until serving.

2. In another small bowl, mix mustard and oregano; set aside.

3. Place sausages on grill over medium heat. Cover grill; cook 10 minutes, turning occasionally. Continue grilling 8 to 10 minutes longer, turning and brushing occasionally with mustard mixture, until no longer pink in center. Discard any remaining mustard mixture.

4. Serve sausages on buns with relish.

BETTY'S SUCCESS TIPS

- If yellow pear tomatoes aren't available, substitute your favorite tomatoes or tomatillos.
- If you like spicy food, try using hot Italian sausages.

1 SANDWICH: Calories 460; Total Fat 26g (Saturated Fat 9g); Sodium 1,530mg; Total Carbohydrate 34g (Dietary Fiber 2g); Protein 22g; **Exchanges:** 1 1/2 Starch; 1/2 Other Carbohydrate; 2 1/2 High-Fat Meat; 1 Fat; **Carbohydrate Choices:** 2

Grilled Ham, Cheddar and Chutney Sandwich

Enjoy this cheesy ham sandwich that's grilled to perfection in just 25 minutes—ideal for dinner.

PREP TIME: 25 MINUTES • **TOTAL TIME:** 25 MINUTES • **MAKES 4 SANDWICHES**

3 tablespoons butter, softened
8 slices whole grain bread
6 tablespoons mango chutney

8 ounces extra-sharp Cheddar cheese, sliced
12 ounces thinly sliced smoked ham

1. Heat griddle or 12-inch nonstick skillet over medium heat.

2. Spread butter on one side of each bread slice. Spread a heaping tablespoon of the chutney on unbuttered side of 4 of the bread slices. Top each with one-fourth of the cheese and ham. Top with remaining bread slices, buttered side up.

3. Place sandwiches in skillet. Cook uncovered about 3 minutes or until cheese is slightly melted and bread is browned. Turn sandwiches over; cook 3 minutes longer or until cheese is melted and sandwich is golden brown.

BETTY'S SUCCESS TIPS

- Chutney can be found in the jams and jellies section of the grocery store.
- Some varieties of deli ham can be overly sweet. To get the desired effect of sweetness from the chutney and salty, savory flavors from the cheese and ham, use Black Forest deli ham, which is smoked, but not too sweet.

1 SANDWICH: Calories 600; Total Fat 34g (Saturated Fat 19g); Sodium 1,770mg; Total Carbohydrate 35g (Dietary Fiber 4g); Protein 39g; **Exchanges:** 1^1/$_2$ Starch; 1 Other Carbohydrate; 4^1/$_2$ Lean Meat; 4 Fat; **Carbohydrate Choices:** 2

Hearty Ham and Pear Panini

Pear provides a simple addition to this hearty grilled ham sandwich—a wonderful dinner ready in just 20 minutes. Perfect if you love Italian cuisine.

PREP TIME: 20 MINUTES • **TOTAL TIME:** 20 MINUTES • **MAKES 4 SANDWICHES**

2 **tablespoons yellow mustard**	1 **medium pear, peeled, thinly sliced**
½ **loaf focaccia bread (13 to 15 inches long), cut in half horizontally**	1 **cup shredded mozzarella cheese (4 ounces)**
8 **slices (2 ounces each) ham**	1 **tablespoon olive oil or vegetable oil**

1. Heat closed contact grill 5 minutes.

2. Spread mustard on bottom half of bread; layer with ham, pear and cheese. Cover with top half of bread. Lightly brush top of bread with oil. Cut sandwich into fourths.

3. When grill is heated, place sandwiches on grill. Close grill; grill 4 to 6 minutes or until cheese is melted and bread is golden brown.

1 SANDWICH: Calories 540; Total Fat 23g (Saturated Fat 7g); Sodium 2,230mg; Total Carbohydrate 45g (Dietary Fiber 3g); Protein 36g; **Exchanges:** 3 Starch; 4 Lean Meat; 2 Fat; **Carbohydrate Choices:** 3

Stromboli Hero

Looking for a hero to answer your dinner dilemma? Look no further than this recipe for Stromboli Hero!

PREP TIME: 15 MINUTES • **TOTAL TIME:** 15 MINUTES • **MAKES 6 SERVINGS**

1 **round focaccia bread (8 or 9 inches in diameter)**	1/4 **pound sliced fully cooked ham**
1/4 **cup Italian dressing**	1/4 **pound sliced salami**
4 **to 5 leaves leaf lettuce**	8 **pepperoncini peppers (bottled Italian peppers), drained and cut lengthwise in half**
1/4 **pound sliced provolone cheese**	

1. Cut bread horizontally in half. Drizzle dressing evenly over cut sides of bread.

2. Layer lettuce, cheese, ham, salami and peppers on bottom half of bread. Top with top half. Secure loaf with toothpicks or small skewers. Cut into 6 wedges.

BETTY'S SUCCESS TIPS

- You can use an unsliced 8- or 10-inch round loaf of Italian or sourdough bread instead of the focaccia.
- If you don't have pepperoncini peppers, use sliced tomatoes, sliced red onion or bell pepper rings.
- You can make this hero up to 6 hours ahead; just wrap it (uncut) securely with plastic wrap and refrigerate.

1 SERVING: Calories 310; Total Fat 18g (Saturated Fat 6g); Sodium 1,070mg; Total Carbohydrate 23g (Dietary Fiber 1g); Protein 15g; **Exchanges:** 1 1/2 Starch; 1 1/2 High-Fat Meat; 1 Fat; **Carbohydrate Choices:** 1 1/2

Country Chicken Sandwiches with Maple-Mustard Spread

This thumbs-up sandwich has chicken, avocado, and Swiss cheese accented with a mustard-maple-mayo spread.

PREP TIME: 15 MINUTES • **TOTAL TIME:** 15 MINUTES • **MAKES 4 SERVINGS**

3 tablespoons mayonnaise or salad dressing

2 tablespoons country-style Dijon mustard

2 tablespoons real maple syrup

1 small shallot, finely chopped (about 3 tablespoons)

8 slices rustic bread

4 slices (1 ounce each) Swiss cheese

2 cups sliced deli rotisserie chicken (from 2- to 2½-pound chicken)

1 medium ripe avocado, pitted, peeled and sliced

1. In small bowl, mix mayonnaise, mustard, maple syrup and shallot. Spread on all 8 slices of bread.

2. Top 4 slices of bread with cheese, chicken and avocado. Top with remaining bread slices.

BETTY'S SUCCESS TIPS

- Shallots are in the onion family but have a milder flavor than onions. They are usually purplish in color and add a sweet yet savory zing to this sandwich.
- Avocados are often sold when underripe. Plan ahead for this recipe; if your avocado doesn't yield to gentle pressure from your finger, leave it on your countertop for a few days to completely ripen.

1 SERVING: Calories 460; Total Fat 23g (Saturated Fat 5g); Sodium 660mg; Total Carbohydrate 37g (Dietary Fiber 4g); Protein 26g; **Exchanges:** 2½ Starch; 2½ Lean Meat; 2½ Fat; **Carbohydrate Choices:** 2½

Harvest Torte

Imagine all of your favorite fall foods combined in one dish, and you have this heavenly pasta- and ham-based entrée. Yum!

PREP TIME: 25 MINUTES • **TOTAL TIME:** 1 HOUR 40 MINUTES • **MAKES 8 SERVINGS**

Butternut Squash Sauce

- $1/2$ butternut squash ($2^1/_2$ pounds), peeled and cut into 1-inch pieces (4 cups)
- 1 medium onion, coarsely chopped ($1/2$ cup)
- 2 cloves garlic
- 1 cup water
- 1 tablespoon butter or margarine
- $1/2$ teaspoon salt
- $1/4$ teaspoon ground nutmeg
- $1/8$ teaspoon pepper
- $1/2$ cup milk

Torte

- 1 package (12 ounces) angel hair (capellini) pasta
- 2 cups diced cooked ham (12 ounces)
- $1^1/_2$ cups shredded fresh mozzarella cheese (6 ounces)
- $3/4$ cup dried cranberries
- $1/2$ cup sliced green onions (5 medium)
- 1 tablespoon chopped fresh or 1 teaspoon dried rosemary leaves
- 2 eggs, slightly beaten

1. In 3-quart saucepan, mix all sauce ingredients except milk. Heat to boiling; reduce heat to low. Cover and simmer about 20 minutes or until squash is tender. Carefully spoon squash and cooking liquid into blender. Add milk. Cover and blend on medium speed until smooth.

2. Heat oven to 375°F. Grease and flour 10-inch springform pan. Cook and drain pasta as directed on package. Return pasta to saucepan. Add remaining torte ingredients and sauce; stir to mix. Spoon into pan. Cover with foil.

3. Bake covered 45 to 50 minutes or until hot. Uncover; cool in pan on cooling rack 10 minutes; remove side of pan. Cut into wedges.

BETTY'S SUCCESS TIPS

- Select butternut squash that have hard, tough rinds and are heavy for their size.
- You can use almost any winter squash instead of the butternut. Try buttercup, acorn, kabocha or Hubbard for variety.

1 SERVING: Calories 410; Total Fat 11g (Saturated Fat 5g); Sodium 800mg; Total Carbohydrate 59g (Dietary Fiber 4g); Protein 23g; **Exchanges:** 3 Starch; 3 Vegetable; 1 High-Fat Meat; **Carbohydrate Choices:** 4

Cranberry-Orange Chex® Mix

Give the gift of a homemade snack mix. This one may be the "berry" best you'll make!

PREP TIME: 10 MINUTES • TOTAL TIME: 55 MINUTES • MAKES 20 SERVINGS

3 cups Corn Chex® cereal
3 cups Rice Chex® cereal
3 cups Wheat Chex® cereal
1 cup sliced almonds
$1/4$ cup butter or margarine, melted

$1/4$ cup packed brown sugar
$1/4$ cup frozen (thawed) orange juice concentrate
$1/2$ cup dried cranberries

1. Heat oven to 300°F. In large bowl, mix cereals and almonds.

2. In microwavable measuring cup, mix butter, brown sugar and juice concentrate. Microwave uncovered on High 30 seconds; stir. Pour over cereal mixture, stirring until evenly coated. Pour into ungreased large roasting pan.

3. Bake uncovered 30 minutes, stirring after 15 minutes. Stir in cranberries. Cool completely, about 15 minutes. Store in airtight container.

BETTY'S SUCCESS TIPS

- Having an extra set of hands is especially helpful when pouring the sauce over the cereal so that one person can pour and one can stir.
- Party stores carry cellophane bags designed for all seasons. Keep these bags on hand to give Chex® mixes any time of year.

1 SERVING: Calories 140; Total Fat 5g (Saturated Fat 1$1/2$g); Sodium 170mg; Total Carbohydrate 22g (Dietary Fiber 2g); Protein 3g; **Exchanges:** $1/2$ Starch; 1 Other Carbohydrate; 1 Fat; **Carbohydrate Choices:** 1$1/2$

Potato and Sage Fritters with Lemon Aioli

Light potato fritters with a lemony sauce—serve for a party appetizer.

PREP TIME: 45 MINUTES • **TOTAL TIME:** 3 HOURS 30 MINUTES • **MAKES 15 SERVINGS**

Fritters

- 1/4 cup warm water
- 2 tablespoons Gold Medal® all-purpose flour
- 1 package regular active dry yeast
- 1 pound Betty Crocker® fresh russet potatoes, peeled, cut into 1-inch cubes (about 3 cups)
- 2 eggs
- 1/2 cup olive oil
- 3/4 teaspoon salt
- 1/2 teaspoon pepper
- 2 teaspoons grated lemon peel
- 1 tablespoon finely chopped fresh sage leaves
- 2 cups Gold Medal® all-purpose flour
  Vegetable oil for frying

Lemon Aioli

- 2/3 cup mayonnaise
- 2 large cloves garlic, finely chopped
- 2 tablespoons lemon juice

1. In small bowl, mix warm water, 2 tablespoons flour and the yeast. Stir; let stand in warm place about 30 minutes or until small bubbles form.

2. Meanwhile, in small bowl, mix aioli ingredients. Cover; refrigerate until ready to serve.

3. In 3-quart saucepan, cover potatoes with water; lightly salt. Heat to boiling; reduce heat to medium-low. Cover; cook potatoes about 20 minutes or until tender. Drain; mash potatoes with fork. Cool about 10 minutes.

4. In small bowl, beat eggs and olive oil with whisk; stir in salt, pepper, lemon peel and sage. Set aside.

5. In large bowl, mix mashed potatoes with yeast mixture and 2 cups flour. Stir in egg mixture until well blended. Cover with towel and set in warm place about 1 1/2 hours or until potato mixture is double in size.

6. In deep fryer or 4-quart Dutch oven, heat vegetable oil (2 to 3 inches) to 350°F. Drop potato mixture by tablespoonfuls into hot oil. Fry 3 to 4 minutes, turning once, until golden brown. Drain on paper towels; serve warm with aioli.

1 SERVING: Calories 240; Total Fat 17g (Saturated Fat 2 1/2 g); Sodium 180mg; Total Carbohydrate 20g (Dietary Fiber 1g); Protein 3g; **Exchanges:** 1 Starch; 1/2 Other Carbohydrate; 3 Fat; **Carbohydrate Choices:** 1

Brat- and Sauerkraut-Filled Pretzels

Enjoy these tasty pretzels made using pizza crust. These bread options are filled with bratwurst and sauerkraut.

PREP TIME: 30 MINUTES • **TOTAL TIME:** 45 MINUTES • **MAKES 4 PRETZELS**

2 cooked bratwurst (from 14-ounce package), finely chopped
$1/2$ cup sauerkraut, squeezed dry, chopped
1 can (13.8 ounces) refrigerated pizza crust
2 cups water

$1/4$ cup baking soda
1 egg
1 tablespoon water
$1/2$ teaspoon caraway seed
Mustard, as desired

1. Heat oven to 400°F. Line large cookie sheet with cooking parchment paper.

2. In small bowl, mix bratwurst and sauerkraut; set aside. Unroll dough onto lightly floured surface; roll into 14 x 12-inch rectangle. Using pizza cutter, cut dough lengthwise into 4 strips.

3. Spoon about $1/4$ cup of the bratwurst mixture onto long edge of each dough strip. Stretch dough over bratwurst filling; brush edges with water, and pinch to seal. Pick up ends of filled dough and stretch to make 24-inch rope.

4. To make pretzel shape, form each rope into U shape. Twist ends twice. Press down where dough overlaps in an "X" to hold shape. Pick up ends and fold over so they rest over bottom of U shape.

5. In medium microwavable bowl, microwave 2 cups water uncovered on High about 2 minutes or until hot. Add baking soda; stir until dissolved. Dip each pretzel, one at a time, into water mixture. Immediately remove from water with large pancake turner; let stand about 5 minutes. In small bowl, beat egg and 1 tablespoon water with whisk; brush pretzels with egg mixture.

6. Place pretzels on cookie sheet; sprinkle with caraway seed. Bake 11 to 15 minutes or until tops of pretzels are dark golden brown. Serve with mustard.

1 PRETZEL: Calories 400; Total Fat 16g (Saturated Fat 6g); Sodium 1,940mg; Total Carbohydrate 49g (Dietary Fiber 2g); Protein 14g; **Exchanges:** $3^1/2$ Other Carbohydrate; 2 High-Fat Meat; **Carbohydrate Choices:** 3

Taco Salad Dip

Traditional taco salad ingredients are transformed into an ever-so-easy microwaved munchie.

PREP TIME: 20 MINUTES • TOTAL TIME: 20 MINUTES • MAKES 28 SERVINGS

$1/2$ **pound lean (at least 80%) ground beef**
$1/4$ **cup finely chopped green bell pepper**
1 **small onion, finely chopped ($1/4$ cup)**
1 **can (16 ounces) Old El Paso® refried beans**
1 **can (8 ounces) tomato sauce**
1 **package (1 ounce) Old El Paso® taco seasoning mix**
2 **drops red pepper sauce**

1 **clove garlic, finely chopped**
$1/2$ **cup sour cream**
1 **tablespoon shredded Cheddar cheese**
$1/8$ **teaspoon chili powder**
Finely shredded lettuce, if desired
Additional shredded Cheddar cheese, if desired
Corn chips, if desired

1. In $1^1/2$-quart microwavable casserole, crumble beef. Cover loosely; microwave on High 2 minutes 30 seconds to 3 minutes 30 seconds or until beef is thoroughly cooked. Stir and drain.

2. Stir in bell pepper, onion, beans, tomato sauce, seasoning mix, pepper sauce and garlic. Cover tightly; microwave on High 3 minutes. Stir; spread mixture in 9-inch microwavable pie plate. Cover; microwave on High 3 to 4 minutes or until hot and bubbly.

3. In small bowl, mix sour cream, 1 tablespoon Cheddar cheese and the chili powder. Spread over beef mixture. Sprinkle with lettuce and additional Cheddar cheese. Serve with corn chips.

BETTY'S SUCCESS TIPS

- Bored with iceberg lettuce? Switch to crispy romaine, a dark leafy green regarded as a good source of vitamin A and folate.
- Lighten up this taco treat with fat-free sour cream and reduced-fat Cheddar cheese.

1 SERVING: Calories 45; Total Fat 2g (Saturated Fat 1g); Sodium 250mg; Total Carbohydrate 4g (Dietary Fiber 1g); Protein 3g; **Exchanges:** $1/2$ High-Fat Meat; **Carbohydrate Choices:** 0

Beer Queso Nachos

Nachos smothered with beer-spiked queso dip are sure to be a hit at any party.

PREP TIME: 20 MINUTES • **TOTAL TIME:** 30 MINUTES • **MAKES 12 SERVINGS**

8 cups tortilla chips
½ cup lager beer, such as a Boston lager
2 cups shredded American cheese (8 ounces)
1 cup shredded mild Cheddar cheese (4 ounces)
1 can (4.5 ounces) Old El Paso® chopped green chiles, drained

1 can (15 ounces) Progresso® black beans, drained, rinsed
½ cup Old El Paso® Thick 'n Chunky salsa
1 medium avocado, pitted, peeled and chopped
1 medium tomato, seeded, chopped
2 tablespoons chopped fresh cilantro

1. Heat oven to 350°F.

2. Line large cookie sheet with cooking parchment paper. Arrange tortilla chips on cookie sheet. Bake 5 minutes to warm chips.

3. Meanwhile, in 2-quart saucepan, heat beer over medium heat until just starting to simmer. Slowly add the cheeses in small amounts, stirring constantly with whisk, until melted. Stir in chiles.

4. In medium bowl, mix beans and salsa. Microwave uncovered on High 2 to 3 minutes or until hot.

5. To serve, pour half of the cheese sauce over warm chips; top with half of the bean mixture. Top with remaining cheese mixture and remaining bean mixture. Serve with remaining ingredients.

BETTY'S SUCCESS TIPS

- Nachos are easy to customize. Reduce the fat by using baked tortilla chips.
- Add extra flavor by piling on the vegetables.

1 SERVING: Calories 280; Total Fat 16g (Saturated Fat 7g); Sodium 580mg; Total Carbohydrate 23g (Dietary Fiber 4g); Protein 10g; **Exchanges:** 1 Starch; ½ Other Carbohydrate; 1 High-Fat Meat; 1½ Fat; **Carbohydrate Choices:** 1½

Baked Spinach-Artichoke Dip

Wow your friends with an easy but elegant hot dip you can make ahead.

PREP TIME: 10 MINUTES • **TOTAL TIME:** 30 MINUTES • **MAKES 24 SERVINGS**

1 cup mayonnaise or salad dressing

1 cup freshly grated Parmesan cheese (4 ounces)

1 can (about 14 ounces) artichoke hearts, drained and coarsely chopped

1 box (9 ounces) Green Giant® frozen chopped spinach, thawed and squeezed to drain

$^1/_2$ cup chopped red bell pepper

$^1/_4$ cup shredded Monterey Jack or mozzarella cheese (1 ounce)

Toasted baguette slices or assorted crackers, if desired

1. Heat oven to 350°F. Mix mayonnaise and Parmesan cheese. Stir in artichokes, spinach and bell pepper.

2. Spoon mixture into 1-quart casserole. Sprinkle with Monterey Jack cheese.

3. Cover and bake about 20 minutes or until cheese is melted. Serve warm with baguette slices.

BETTY'S SUCCESS TIPS

- One cup loosely packed, coarsely chopped fresh spinach leaves can be substituted for the frozen spinach.

- Make and refrigerate this sensational, simple-to-prepare dip up to 24 hours ahead. Bake as directed.

1 SERVING: Calories 100; Total Fat 9g (Saturated Fat 2g); Sodium 190mg; Total Carbohydrate 3g (Dietary Fiber 1g); Protein 3g; **Exchanges:** 1 Vegetable; 1$^1/_2$ Fat; **Carbohydrate Choices:** 0

Chorizo con Queso

Enjoy this Tex-Mex appetizer made using sausage and Progresso™ Recipe Starters™ cheese sauce served with tortilla chips—ready in just 15 minutes.

PREP TIME: 15 MINUTES • **TOTAL TIME:** 15 MINUTES • **MAKES 14 SERVINGS**

1 **pound bulk chorizo sausage**	1 **cup shredded Cheddar cheese (4 ounces)**
½ **cup diced red bell pepper**	70 **tortilla chips**
¼ **cup sliced green onions (4 medium)**	
1 **can (18 ounces) Progresso™ Recipe Starters™ creamy three cheese cooking sauce**	**Garnish, If Desired**
	Chopped fresh cilantro

1. In 10-inch nonstick skillet, cook sausage, bell pepper and green onions over medium-high heat 6 to 8 minutes, stirring occasionally and breaking up sausage with spoon, until sausage is thoroughly cooked. Drain on paper towels.

2. Return sausage mixture to skillet; stir in cooking sauce. Heat to boiling, stirring occasionally. Reduce heat to low; simmer uncovered 5 minutes, stirring occasionally. Remove from heat; stir in cheese until melted. Sprinkle with cilantro. Serve warm with tortilla chips.

BETTY'S SUCCESS TIP

Uncooked chorizo sausage links, casings removed, can be substituted.

1 SERVING: Calories 280; Total Fat 21g (Saturated Fat 8g); Sodium 630mg; Total Carbohydrate 12g (Dietary Fiber 0g); Protein 11g; **Exchanges:** 1 Starch; 1 High-Fat Meat; 2½ Fat; **Carbohydrate Choices:** 1

Sausage Cheese Balls

These little appetizers make a big hit with any crowd. They continue to be one of our most-requested recipes!

PREP TIME: 20 MINUTES • **TOTAL TIME:** 45 MINUTES • **MAKES 102 CHEESE BALLS**

3 cups Original Bisquick® mix
1 pound uncooked bulk pork sausage
4 cups shredded Cheddar cheese (16 ounces)
1/2 cup grated Parmesan cheese (2 ounces)
1/2 cup milk

1/2 teaspoon dried rosemary leaves, crushed
1 1/2 teaspoons chopped fresh or 1/2 teaspoon dried parsley flakes
Barbecue sauce or chili sauce, if desired

1. Heat oven to 350°F. Lightly grease bottom and sides of jelly roll pan, 15 1/2 x 10 1/2 x 2 x 1 inch.

2. In large bowl, stir together all ingredients except barbecue sauce, using hands or spoon. Shape mixture into 1-inch balls. Place in pan.

3. Bake 20 to 25 minutes or until brown. Immediately remove from pan. Serve warm with sauce for dipping.

BETTY'S SUCCESS TIPS

- Want to make these savory cheese balls ahead? Your options are many! You can:
  - Cover and refrigerate unbaked balls up to 24 hours. Bake as directed.
  - Cover and freeze unbaked balls up to 1 month. Heat oven to 350°F. Place frozen balls on ungreased cookie sheet. Bake 25 to 30 minutes or until brown.
  - Bake as directed; cover and freeze up to 1 month. Heat oven to 350°F. Place frozen balls on ungreased cookie sheet. Bake 10 to 12 minutes or until heated through.
  - Bake as directed; cover and freeze up to 1 month. Place 6 frozen balls on microwavable plate. Loosely cover with waxed paper. Microwave on High 45 seconds to 1 minute or until heated through.
- The recipe is correct as written—the mixture is made with uncooked sausage.

1 CHEESE BALL: Calories 40; Total Fat 2 1/2g (Saturated Fat 1 1/2g); Sodium 95mg; Total Carbohydrate 2g (Dietary Fiber 0g); Protein 2g; **Exchanges:** 1/2 High-Fat Meat; **Carbohydrate Choices:** 0

Cheddar Cheese Apples

Surprise them with the fun Cheddar and cream cheese spread that you shape to look like an apple!

PREP TIME: 20 MINUTES • TOTAL TIME: 2 HOURS 20 MINUTES • MAKES 24 SERVINGS

2 packages (3 ounces each) cream cheese, softened

2 tablespoons finely chopped onions

1 teaspoon Worcestershire sauce

1/4 teaspoon ground mustard

2 cups shredded Cheddar cheese (8 ounces)

Paprika

Cinnamon sticks and fresh sage leaves, if desired

Assorted crackers, if desired

1. Beat cream cheese, onion, Worcestershire sauce and mustard in large bowl until blended. Mix in Cheddar cheese. Cover and refrigerate about 2 hours or until firm enough to shape.

2. Divide cheese mixture in half. Shape 1 half into a ball on waxed paper. Sprinkle another piece of waxed paper with paprika. Roll cheese ball in paprika, coating thoroughly. Mold into apple shape. Repeat with remaining cheese mixture.

3. To garnish, make small depression in stem ends of apples. Cut 2 small pieces from cinnamon stick. Insert cinnamon stick pieces for stems. Insert sage leaves. Serve cheese balls with crackers.

BETTY'S SUCCESS TIPS

- Sliced apples make a fun addition to this appetizer. Toss them with lemon juice to prevent browning.
- Cheese balls can be stored tightly covered in the refrigerator up to 2 weeks or in freezer up to 4 weeks. Thaw frozen cheese balls in the refrigerator about 6 hours before serving.

1 SERVING: Calories 45; Total Fat 4g (Saturated Fat 3g); Sodium 60mg; Total Carbohydrate 2g (Dietary Fiber 0g); Protein 2g; **Exchanges:** 1 Fat; **Carbohydrate Choices:** 0

Spinach-Cheese Balls

Make a veggie lover's version of our classic and highly rated Sausage Cheese Balls appetizer.

PREP TIME: 10 MINUTES • TOTAL TIME: 25 MINUTES • MAKES 30 CHEESE BALLS

1 box (9 ounces) frozen spinach, thawed, squeezed to drain

1 cup Original Bisquick® mix

2 cups shredded mozzarella cheese (8 ounces)

1 egg

2 teaspoons Italian seasoning

1 teaspoon garlic salt

1 cup tomato pasta sauce, if desired

1. Heat oven to 400°F. Spray cookie sheet with cooking spray. In large bowl, mix all ingredients except pasta sauce. Shape mixture into 1-inch balls; place on cookie sheet.

2. Bake 10 to 15 minutes or until golden brown. Immediately remove from pan. Serve with pasta sauce.

BETTY'S SUCCESS TIP

Cover and freeze unbaked balls up to 1 month. Heat oven to 350°F. Place frozen balls on ungreased cookie sheet. Bake 25 to 30 minutes or until brown.

1 CHEESE BALL: Calories 45; Total Fat 2g (Saturated Fat 1g); Sodium 130mg; Total Carbohydrate 3g (Dietary Fiber 0g); Protein 3g; **Exchanges:** 1/2 High-Fat Meat; **Carbohydrate Choices:** 0

Fall Cheese Platter

Your family and friends will fall for this spectacular cheese platter—and making it takes so little extra time!

PREP TIME: 25 MINUTES • **TOTAL TIME:** 25 MINUTES • **MAKES 12 SERVINGS**

Cranberry-Apple Chutney

2	medium apples, chopped (2 cups)
2	cups cranberries
1	medium red bell pepper, chopped (1 cup)
1	small onion, finely chopped (¼ cup)
¾	cup packed brown sugar
½	cup golden raisins
½	cup white vinegar
1½	teaspoons finely chopped gingerroot
1	clove garlic, finely chopped

Cheese Platter

16	slices (1 ounce each) assorted cheeses, such as Cheddar, Colby–Monterey Jack, Monterey Jack with jalapeño peppers and Swiss
¼	cup hazelnuts (filberts)
	Crackers

1. In 2-quart saucepan, mix all chutney ingredients. Heat to boiling, stirring frequently; reduce heat. Simmer uncovered about 1 hour, stirring frequently, until mixture thickens and fruit is tender. Spoon into nonaluminum container. Store in refrigerator up to 2 weeks.

2. Cut cheese with 1-, 1½- and 2-inch leaf-shaped cookie cutters. Place cheese on medium platter, overlapping leaves. Sprinkle hazelnuts on platter to look like acorns. Serve with chutney and crackers.

BETTY'S SUCCESS TIPS

- The remaining chutney is delicious served with roast turkey, ham or pork. Or for a quick appetizer, spoon chutney over a block of cream cheese and serve with crackers.
- To elaborate on the fall theme, serve cheese with sliced apples and pears. Dipping sliced fruit into citrus juice, such as orange juice, will prevent slices from turning brown.
- For a pretty fall platter, choose several cheeses in varying colors. Cheese with salami or bacon creates an especially fall-looking leaf.
- For longer storage of the chutney, pour hot chutney into hot, sterilized jars, leaving ¼-inch headspace. Wipe rims of jars; seal. Cool on rack 1 hour. This makes a very nice hostess gift. It can be stored in the refrigerator for up to 2 months.

1 SERVING: Calories 225; Total Fat 13g (Saturated Fat 8g); Sodium 260mg; Total Carbohydrate 17g (Dietary Fiber 1g); Protein 10g; **Exchanges:** 1 Starch; 1 High-Fat Meat; 1 Fat; **Carbohydrate Choices:** 1

Pastry-Wrapped Cranberry Brie

A beautiful filling of French-style cheese, fruit preserves and sauces, and a touch of rosemary make an elegant pastry appetizer.

PREP TIME: 20 MINUTES • **TOTAL TIME:** 1 HOUR • **MAKES 12 SERVINGS**

1 can (8 ounces) refrigerated crescent rolls

1 round (8 ounces) Brie cheese (Do not use triple creme Brie)

3 tablespoons whole berry cranberry sauce

1 tablespoon apricot preserves

1/2 teaspoon dried rosemary leaves, crushed

2 medium pears, unpeeled, thinly sliced

1. Heat oven to 350°F. Unroll dough and separate crosswise into 2 sections; press dough into 2 (7-inch) squares, firmly pressing perforations to seal.

2. Cut cheese round horizontally to make 2 rounds. Place 1 cheese round, rind side down, on center of 1 dough square. (Do not remove rind from cheese.) In small bowl, mix cranberry sauce and preserves. Spread over top of cheese; sprinkle with rosemary. Top with remaining cheese round, rind side up.

3. With small cookie or canapé cutter, or sharp knife, make 1/2- to 1-inch cutouts to resemble poinsettia leaves from each corner of remaining dough square. Roll 3 small pieces of dough into 3 small balls; set cutouts and dough balls aside. Place remaining dough on top of cheese round. Press dough evenly around cheese, folding top edges over bottom edges; press to seal completely. Place on ungreased cookie sheet.

4. On 7 x 7-inch foil square, arrange dough leaves with balls in center on top of dough. Lift foil square with poinsettia and place on cookie sheet next to wrapped Brie.

5. Bake poinsettia 8 to 11 minutes or until light golden brown around edges. Lift from cookie sheet with foil; cool. Bake wrapped cheese 25 to 30 minutes or until golden brown. Remove from cookie sheet; place on serving plate. Place poinsettia on top of wrapped cheese. Let stand 15 minutes before serving. Serve warm with pears.

BETTY'S SUCCESS TIP

The edible rind on the Brie keeps the cheese from oozing out during baking.

1 SERVING: Calories 160; Total Fat 9g (Saturated Fat 4 1/2 g); Sodium 270mg; Total Carbohydrate 15g (Dietary Fiber 1g); Protein 5g; **Exchanges:** 1/2 Starch; 1/2 Other Carbohydrate; 1/2 High-Fat Meat; 1 Fat; **Carbohydrate Choices:** 1

Fall Day-Trip Picnic

Spend a day this fall doing something you love—apple picking, antiques scouting, wine tasting, fall color rambling. And there's no need to wait in endless lines or spend hard-earned cash at packed eating spots, because you've brought scrumptious quick-to-make foods along for the day. Enjoy!

MAP OUT THE DAY

- Appoint one member of the party the travel planner and navigator. There's always the risk of not remembering the way, planning too much or finding road construction. Remember that these are popular times to be out and about.
- Bring along favorite music. Some songs just have to be sung while out for a drive!
- Trivia games are fun for car trips. Or bring travel books about the area where you take your day trip. It's amazing how little we sometimes know about historic highways close to home!

MAKE A PARTY OF YOUR PICNIC

- Make your picnic blanket fit your trip—quilts for antiques store visits, red or green plaids or stripes for apple picking, Pendleton or Hudson's Bay blankets just because. . . . You get the idea.
- Look for inexpensive or nonbreakable wine glasses to add to your party supplies if exploring wine country and sipping wine with your picnic. Observe the law about alcoholic beverages at picnic sites and have a designated driver.

SURPRISE, SURPRISE

- Start the day by sharing a treat like Monkey Tail Bread (page 312), Pear and Ginger Muffins (page 316), or Gingerbread Coffee Cake (page 315) with everyone.
- Take an afternoon tea break—using tea taken with you in a thermos, of course—and pull out these fall bars we love to munch: Caramel Apple Bars (page 403), Ultimate Turtle Cookie Bars (page 399), or No Bake Apple Bars (page 396).

MENU

Cranberry-Orange Chex® Mix **331**

Stromboli Hero **328**

Tossed Greens with Sesame and Oranges **372**

Brownies on a Stick **408**

Apple Cinnamon Butternut Squash Soup

You will really enjoy sipping this squash soup sweetened with apple and a hint of cinnamon.

PREP TIME: 25 MINUTES • **TOTAL TIME:** 45 MINUTES • **MAKES 8 SERVINGS**

8 cups cubed, seeded, peeled butternut squash (2 medium)
1 large apple, peeled, chopped
1 large onion, cut into 1-inch pieces
2 tablespoons packed brown sugar
³/₄ teaspoon salt
³/₄ teaspoon ground cinnamon

¹/₈ teaspoon pepper
3 cups Progresso® chicken broth (from 32-ounce carton)
³/₄ cup milk
1 container (6 ounces) fat-free plain Greek yogurt
2 tablespoons chopped fresh chives

1. In Dutch oven, mix squash, apple, onion, brown sugar, salt, cinnamon and pepper. Add broth. Cover; heat to boiling over medium-high heat. Reduce heat; simmer about 20 minutes or until squash is tender.

2. In blender or food processor, place one-third of mixture. Cover; blend until smooth. Repeat twice to use up remaining soup. Return to Dutch oven; stir in milk and yogurt. Heat over low heat, stirring occasionally, just until heated through. Ladle into bowls; sprinkle with chives.

BETTY'S SUCCESS TIPS

- When selecting butternut squash, look for those that have hard, tough rinds and are heavy for their size. Peeling the squash will be easier if you first microwave it on High for 3 minutes.
- Purchase already peeled and cut-up squash if available at your grocery store. If you're cutting it yourself, a good, swivel-headed vegetable peeler is the tool of choice to make quick work of peeling the squash.

1 SERVING: Calories 130; Total Fat ¹/₂g (Saturated Fat 0g); Sodium 570mg; Total Carbohydrate 25g (Dietary Fiber 2g); Protein 4g; **Exchanges:** ¹/₂ Starch; 1 Other Carbohydrate; 1 Vegetable; **Carbohydrate Choices:** 1¹/₂

Slow Cooker Potato and Double-Corn Chowder

Use your slow cooker to create this heavenly, hearty chowder.

PREP TIME: 15 MINUTES • **TOTAL TIME:** 6 HOURS 15 MINUTES • **MAKES 6 SERVINGS**

4 cups frozen diced southern-style potatoes (from 32-ounce bag), thawed

2 cups Progresso® reduced sodium chicken broth (from 32-ounce carton)

1 can (15.25 ounces) Green Giant® whole kernel corn, undrained

1 can (14.75 ounces) Green Giant® cream-style corn

1 medium onion, chopped ($^1/_2$ cup)

8 slices bacon, cooked, crumbled ($^1/_2$ cup)

$^1/_2$ teaspoon salt

$^1/_2$ teaspoon Worcestershire sauce

$^1/_4$ teaspoon pepper

1 can (12 ounces) evaporated milk

1. Spray 3- to 4-quart slow cooker with cooking spray. In cooker, mix all ingredients except evaporated milk.

2. Cover; cook on Low heat setting 6 to 8 hours until potatoes are tender. Just before serving, increase heat to High setting. Stir in milk; cover and cook for 5 minutes or until chowder is hot.

BETTY'S SUCCESS TIPS

- A slow cooker that's opened doesn't cook, so don't peek! Removing the cover allows heat to escape and adds 15 to 20 minutes to cooking time.
- Save time on cleanup when you spray the inside of the slow cooker with cooking spray before adding ingredients.

1 SERVING: Calories 330; Total Fat 8g (Saturated Fat 3g); Sodium 1,160mg; Total Carbohydrate 50g (Dietary Fiber 4g); Protein 14g; **Exchanges:** 2 Starch; 1 Other Carbohydrate; 1 Vegetable; 1 High-Fat Meat; 0 Fat; **Carbohydrate Choices:** 3

Hearty Lentil Soup

Serve this zesty veggie-packed soup with thin slices of sharp Cheddar cheese and pumpernickel bread to soak up the delicious broth.

PREP TIME: 20 MINUTES • TOTAL TIME: 1 HOUR • MAKES 2 SERVINGS

2 cups Progresso® chicken broth (from 32-ounce carton)

1 can (12 ounces) beer or $1^1/_2$ cups Progresso® chicken broth

$^1/_2$ cup dried lentils, sorted and rinsed

1 medium carrot, sliced ($^1/_2$ cup)

1 medium celery stalk, chopped ($^1/_2$ cup)

1 small onion, chopped ($^1/_4$ cup)

1 fully cooked smoked Polish sausage, about 5 inches long, thinly sliced (3 ounces)

1 tablespoon chopped fresh or 1 teaspoon dried basil leaves

$^1/_8$ teaspoon pepper

1 small dried bay leaf

2 tablespoons grated Parmesan cheese

1. Heat broth, beer and lentils to boiling in 2-quart saucepan; reduce heat. Cover and simmer 20 to 25 minutes, stirring occasionally, until lentils are tender but not mushy.

2. Stir in remaining ingredients except cheese. Heat to boiling; reduce heat. Cover and simmer 20 minutes, stirring occasionally. Remove bay leaf. Sprinkle each serving with cheese.

BETTY'S SUCCESS TIPS

- For a slightly thicker broth, blend 1 cup of the soup in a blender and pour back into the pan.
- Leftover soup? No problem! Refrigerate it and serve again tomorrow. The flavors will have time to blend, and the soup will taste even better!

1 SERVING: Calories 365; Total Fat 17g (Saturated Fat 6g); Sodium 2,370mg; Total Carbohydrate 36g (Dietary Fiber 12g); Protein 29g; **Exchanges:** 2 Starch; 1 Vegetable; 3 Lean Meat; **Carbohydrate Choices:** $2^1/_2$

Fall Pot Roast with Figs

Progresso® broth provides a simple addition to this beef roast featuring figs, shallots and butternut squash—a hearty dinner.

PREP TIME: 40 MINUTES • **TOTAL TIME:** 3 HOURS 40 MINUTES • **MAKES 8 SERVINGS**

2 tablespoons olive oil
10 cloves garlic, peeled
5 large shallots, cut lengthwise in half
2 tablespoons chopped fresh rosemary leaves
2 teaspoons kosher (coarse) salt
2 teaspoons freshly ground pepper
1 teaspoon sugar
1 beef rump or chuck roast (4 pounds)

2 cups Progresso® beef-flavored broth (from 32-ounce carton)
1½ cups water
4 cups cubed butternut squash (1½ pounds)
8 dried Calimyrna figs, quartered
½ cup port or other red wine
2 tablespoons Gold Medal® all-purpose flour

1. In 6-quart Dutch oven, heat oil over medium-high heat. Cook garlic and shallots in oil 3 to 4 minutes or until browned. Remove from pan with slotted spoon, reserving oil in pan.

2. In small bowl, mix rosemary, salt, pepper and sugar. Rub mixture on all sides of roast. Cook roast in reserved oil until browned on all sides. Add broth and 1 cup of the water. Scatter garlic and shallots around roast. Cover tightly; cook over medium-low heat 1 hour. Turn roast over; cook 1 hour. Turn roast again; cook covered 1 hour longer or until meat is tender, adding squash and figs and turning roast during last 30 minutes.

3. Remove roast, fruit and vegetables to platter. Skim fat from broth, if desired. Heat broth to boiling; boil 5 minutes. Stir in port; boil 5 minutes. Shake remaining ½ cup water and the flour in tightly covered container; gradually stir into sauce. Heat to boiling, stirring constantly. Boil and stir 1 minute. Serve gravy with pot roast.

1 SERVING: Calories 409; Total Fat 14g (Saturated Fat 4g); Sodium 819mg; Total Carbohydrate 22g (Dietary Fiber 3g); Protein 46g; **Exchanges:** 1 Starch; ½ Fruit; 6 Lean Meat; **Carbohydrate Choices:** 1½

Fruit-Stuffed Pork Roast

Treat your family to a hearty dinner with this pork roast that's stuffed with dried fruits.

PREP TIME: 35 MINUTES • **TOTAL TIME:** 2 HOURS 50 MINUTES • **MAKES 8 SERVINGS**

3 pounds pork boneless center-cut loin roast (not tied)
1 cup mixed dried fruits (apples, apricots, figs)
2 tablespoons finely chopped onion
1 teaspoon kosher salt
1 teaspoon dried thyme leaves
1/2 teaspoon ground cinnamon
1/2 teaspoon coarsely ground pepper
2 tablespoons vegetable oil
1 cup apple cider
2 cups purchased pork gravy

1. Heat oven to 350°F. Place pork, fat side up, on cutting board. Cut horizontally through center of pork almost to opposite side. Open pork like a book. Layer dried fruits and onion in opening. Bring halves of pork together; tie at 1-inch intervals with kitchen twine. Turn pork so fat is on bottom. Mix salt, thyme, cinnamon and pepper in small bowl; rub into pork.

2. Heat oil in roaster over medium-high heat. Cook pork in oil until brown on all sides. Add 2 tablespoons of the apple cider. Cook pork, turning frequently, until cider caramelizes and surface of pork turns dark brown. Repeat browning with additional 2 tablespoons cider. Add remaining cider. Insert meat thermometer so tip is in thickest part of pork.

3. Cover and bake 1 hour 30 minutes to 2 hours or until pork is no longer pink in center and thermometer reads 155°F. Remove pork from pan, cover with aluminum foil and let stand about 15 minutes until temperature rises to 160°F. Serve pork with apple cider gravy.

BETTY'S SUCCESS TIPS

- The mild flavor of pork pairs well with a fruity filling.
- This roast can be stuffed and rubbed with herbs several hours ahead. Wrap tightly in plastic wrap and refrigerate.
- Butchers often tie 2 pieces of center-cut pork loin together to make a thicker roast. Be sure to ask for a single muscle so the roast can be "butterflied," as directed in this recipe.

1 SERVING: Calories 390; Total Fat 17g (Saturated Fat 5g); Sodium 620mg; Total Carbohydrate 19g (Dietary Fiber 2g); Protein 40g; **Exchanges:** 1 Fruit; 6 Lean Meat; **Carbohydrate Choices:** 1

Southern-Style Deep-Fried Turkey

Deep-frying is the trendy way to cook turkey in record time! Deep-frying makes for exceptionally juicy meat and crispy skin, too!

PREP TIME: 1 HOUR 15 MINUTES • **TOTAL TIME:** 10 HOURS 20 MINUTES • **MAKES 20 SERVINGS**

Cajun Spice Rub

- 2 **tablespoons black pepper**
- 1 **tablespoon ground chipotle chiles or ground red pepper (cayenne)**
- 1 **tablespoon white pepper**
- 1 **tablespoon ground cumin**
- 1 **tablespoon ground nutmeg**
- 1 **tablespoon salt**

Cajun Marinade

- ¼ **cup vegetable oil**
- ¼ **cup red wine vinegar**
- 1 **teaspoon sugar**
- 1 **teaspoon chili powder**
- ½ **teaspoon garlic powder**
- ½ **teaspoon salt**
- ¼ **teaspoon ground pepper**

Turkey

- 1 **whole turkey (10 to 12 pounds), thawed if frozen**
- 1 **poultry or meat injector**
- 1 **turkey deep-fryer, consisting of 40- to 60-quart pot with basket, burner and propane tank**
- 5 **gallons peanut, canola or safflower oil**

1. Read the Turkey Deep-Frying Dos and Don'ts (opposite). In small bowl, mix all spice rub ingredients until blended; set aside. In shallow glass or plastic bowl, mix all marinade ingredients until salt is dissolved; set aside.

2. Remove giblets and neck from turkey; rinse turkey well with cold water; pat dry thoroughly with paper towels. Take extra care to dry both inside cavities, because water added to hot oil can cause excessive bubbling. To allow for good oil circulation through the cavity, do not tie legs together. Cut off wing tips and tail because they can get caught in the fryer basket. Place turkey in large pan.

3. Rub inside and outside of turkey with spice rub. Inject marinade into turkey, following directions that came with injector. Cover turkey in pan; place in refrigerator at least 8 hours but no longer than 24 hours.

4. Place outdoor gas burner on level dirt or grassy area. Add oil to cooking pot until about two-thirds full. Clip deep-fry thermometer to edge of pot. At medium-high setting, heat oil to 375°F. (This may take 20 to 40 minutes depending on outside temperature, wind and weather conditions.) Place turkey, neck end down, on basket or rack. When deep-fry thermometer reaches 375°F, slowly lower turkey into hot oil. Level of oil will rise due to frothing caused by moisture from turkey but will stabilize in about 1 minute.

5. Immediately check oil temperature; increase flame so oil temperature is maintained at 350°F. If temperature drops to 340°F or below, oil will begin to seep into turkey.

6. Fry turkey about 3 to 4 minutes per pound, or about 35 to 42 minutes for 10- to 12-pound turkey. Stay with fryer at all times because heat may need to be regulated throughout frying.

7. At minimum frying time, carefully remove turkey to check for doneness. A meat thermometer inserted into thickest part of breast should read 170°F. If inserted into thigh, it should read 180°F. If necessary, return turkey to oil and continue cooking. When turkey is done, let drain a few minutes.

8. Remove turkey from rack; place on serving platter. Cover with foil; let stand 20 minutes for easier carving.

BETTY'S SUCCESS TIPS

- For best results when deep-frying, use cooking oils that can withstand high temperatures. Peanut, canola and safflower oils are at the top of the list!
- To learn more about deep-frying turkeys, visit the National Turkey Federation Web site at eatturkey.com.

1 SERVING: Calories 335; Total Fat 21g (Saturated Fat 5g); Sodium 800mg; Total Carbohydrate 0g (Dietary Fiber 0g); Protein 36g; **Exchanges:** 5 Lean Meat; 1 Fat; **Carbohydrate Choices:** 0

Turkey Deep-Frying Dos and Don'ts

We want your turkey-frying experience to be successful, especially if it's your first time, so we've gathered these important reminders. Please take a moment to read them before getting ready for a great-tasting feast!

DO

1. Follow the use-and-care directions for your deep fryer when deep-frying turkey, and review all safety tips.
2. Place the fryer on a level dirt or grassy area away from the house or garage. Never fry a turkey indoors, including in a garage or any other structure attached to a building.
3. Use only oils with high smoke points, such as peanut, canola or safflower oil.
4. Wear old shoes that you can slip out of easily and long pants just in case you do spill some oil on you.
5. Immediately wash hands, utensils, equipment and surfaces that have come in contact with the raw turkey.
6. Have a fire extinguisher nearby for added safety.
7. Serve the turkey right after cooking, and store leftovers in the refrigerator within 2 hours of cooking.
8. Allow the oil to cool completely before disposing of it or storing it.

DON'T

1. Never fry on wooden decks or other structures that could catch fire, and don't fry on concrete, which could be stained by the oil.
2. Never leave the hot oil unattended, and do not allow children or pets near the cooking area.

Oven-Roasted Turkey Breast

When you want the height of flavor but don't want to fool with a whole bird, roast a turkey breast. Basted with a thyme, butter and wine sauce, this one's moist and full of flavor.

PREP TIME: 15 MINUTES • **TOTAL TIME:** 3 HOURS • **MAKES 8 SERVINGS**

1 **bone-in whole turkey breast (4¹/₂ to 5 pounds), thawed if frozen**	1 **teaspoon salt**
¹/₂ **cup butter or margarine, melted**	1 **teaspoon paprika**
¹/₄ **cup dry white wine or apple juice**	2 **cloves garlic, finely chopped**
2 **tablespoons chopped fresh or 1¹/₂ teaspoons dried thyme leaves**	2 **teaspoons cornstarch**
	2 **tablespoons cold water**

1. Heat oven to 325°F. Place turkey, skin side up, on rack in large shallow roasting pan. Insert oven-proof meat thermometer so tip is in thickest part of breast and does not touch bone. Roast uncovered 1 hour.

2. Mix butter, wine, thyme, salt, paprika and garlic. Brush turkey with half of the butter mixture. Roast 30 minutes; brush with remaining butter mixture. Roast about 1 hour longer or until thermometer reads 165°F.

3. Remove turkey from oven and let stand 15 minutes for easier carving.

4. Meanwhile, pour pan drippings into measuring cup; skim fat from drippings. Add enough water to drippings to measure 2 cups. Heat drippings to boiling in 1-quart saucepan. Mix cornstarch and 2 tablespoons cold water; stir into drippings. Boil and stir 1 minute. Serve with turkey.

BETTY'S SUCCESS TIPS

- The resting time after roasting allows the meat to become more firm, so carving smooth, uniform slices is easier.
- Garnish with small whole fruit, such as apples or kumquats, and fresh herbs, such as thyme or sage.

1 SERVING: Calories 460; Total Fat 28g (Saturated Fat 12g); Sodium 480mg; Total Carbohydrate 3g (Dietary Fiber 0g); Protein 49g; **Exchanges:** 7 Lean Meat; 1¹/₂ Fat; **Carbohydrate Choices:** 0

Roast Turkey with Fresh Thyme Rub and Maple Glaze

Maple syrup adds sweetness to roast turkey infused with savory fresh thyme.

PREP TIME: 20 MINUTES • **TOTAL TIME:** 4 HOURS 35 MINUTES • **MAKES 12 SERVINGS**

1 whole turkey (12 pounds), thawed if frozen

3 tablespoons chopped fresh thyme leaves

1 teaspoon salt

1/2 teaspoon ground allspice

1/2 teaspoon pepper

2 tablespoons olive or vegetable oil

2 tablespoons butter or margarine

2 tablespoons real maple syrup or maple-flavored syrup

Fresh thyme sprigs, apricot slices and Rainier cherries, if desired

1. Heat oven to 325°F. Fasten neck skin to back of turkey with skewer. Fold wings across back of turkey so tips are touching. On rack in shallow roasting pan, place turkey, breast side up.

2. In small bowl, mix thyme, salt, allspice, pepper and oil. Rub thyme mixture over turkey. Tuck legs under band of skin at tail (if present), or tie together with heavy string. Insert ovenproof meat thermometer into turkey so tip is in thickest part of inside thigh and does not touch bone.

3. Roast uncovered 1 hour. When turkey begins to turn golden brown, place tent of heavy-duty foil over turkey. Roast 2 hours 30 minutes longer.

4. In small microwavable bowl, microwave butter on High 45 seconds or until melted. Stir in maple syrup.

5. Cut band of skin or remove tie holding legs to allow inside of thighs to cook through. Brush turkey with butter-syrup mixture; roast uncovered 20 to 30 minutes longer, brushing with butter-syrup mixture again after 10 minutes.

6. Turkey is done when thermometer reads 165°F and drumsticks move easily when lifted or twisted. Place turkey on warm platter; cover with foil to keep warm. Let stand 15 minutes for easiest carving. Garnish with thyme sprigs, apricot slices and cherries.

BETTY'S SUCCESS TIP

Real maple syrup is more expensive because it takes 20 gallons of maple sap to make 1 gallon of syrup! Less costly maple-flavored syrup is a blend of less-expensive syrup and pure maple syrup or flavoring.

1 SERVING: Calories 430; Total Fat 26g (Saturated Fat 8g); Sodium 340mg; Total Carbohydrate 3g (Dietary Fiber 0g); Protein 45g; **Exchanges:** 6 1/2 Lean Meat; 1 1/2 Fat; **Carbohydrate Choices:** 0

Maple Pork Chops with Pumpkin Risotto

Progresso® chicken broth provides a simple addition to these maple-flavored pork chops served with pumpkin risotto—a flavorful Italian dinner that's ready in 35 minutes.

PREP TIME: 5 MINUTES • **TOTAL TIME:** 35 MINUTES • **MAKES 4 SERVINGS**

2 tablespoons margarine or butter	1 cup canned pumpkin
4 center-cut pork loin chops	3 cups Progresso® chicken broth (from 32-ounce carton)
Salt and pepper to taste, if desired	¼ cup shredded Parmesan cheese (1 ounce)
1½ teaspoons maple flavoring	¼ teaspoon salt
¾ cup uncooked Arborio or other short-grain white rice	
1 clove garlic, finely chopped	

1. Melt margarine in 12-inch skillet over medium-high heat. Sprinkle pork with salt and pepper. Cook pork in margarine 5 minutes, turning once, until brown. Remove pork from skillet; brush both sides with maple flavoring.

2. Add rice and garlic to skillet. Cook over medium heat 30 seconds, stirring frequently. Stir in pumpkin and ½ cup of the broth. Cook uncovered, stirring frequently, until liquid is absorbed. Stir in an additional ½ cup broth. Continue cooking about 15 minutes, stirring constantly and adding broth ½ cup at a time after previous additions have been absorbed.

3. Add pork and any remaining broth to skillet. Cover and cook 5 to 10 minutes or until pork is slightly pink when cut near bone and rice is creamy and just tender. Stir in cheese and salt.

BETTY'S SUCCESS TIPS

- Never rinse rice before making risotto or you will wash off some of the grain's starch, which is so important to this creamy dish.
- Sprinkle the risotto with toasted pumpkin seeds. Rinse the seeds, and pat dry on paper towels. To toast, bake uncovered on a cookie sheet sprayed with cooking spray in a 375°F oven about 30 minutes, stirring occasionally.

1 SERVING: Calories 405; Total Fat 16g (Saturated Fat 5g); Sodium 1,130mg; Total Carbohydrate 36g (Dietary Fiber 2g); Protein 31g; **Exchanges:** 3 Lean Meat; 1 Fat; **Carbohydrate Choices:** 2½

Warm Honey Mustard Potato Salad with Sausages

A perfect dish to serve at a picnic or backyard get-together.

PREP TIME: 10 MINUTES • **TOTAL TIME:** 20 MINUTES • **MAKES 4 SERVINGS**

1 bag (19 ounces) Green Giant® Valley Fresh Steamers® Value Size frozen roasted potatoes with garlic & herb sauce
¼ cup honey
¼ cup yellow mustard
1 cup sliced celery (2 stalks)
½ cup chopped red bell pepper (½ medium)

2 tablespoons chopped green onions (2 medium) or red onion
¼ teaspoon garlic powder
¼ teaspoon salt
⅛ teaspoon coarsely ground black pepper
4 cooked turkey Italian sausages, sliced

1. Cook frozen potatoes as directed on bag. Cool slightly, about 5 minutes.

2. Meanwhile, in large bowl, mix honey and mustard until well blended.

3. Stir in potatoes and remaining ingredients until well blended. Serve warm.

1 SERVING: Calories 230; Total Fat 5g (Saturated Fat 1½g); Sodium 950mg; Total Carbohydrate 37g (Dietary Fiber 2g); Protein 8g; **Exchanges:** 1½ Starch; ½ Other Carbohydrate; 1½ Vegetable; 1 Fat; **Carbohydrate Choices:** 2½

Beef Stew, Bologna Style

Looking for an Italian dinner? This luscious stew is simply beefsteak mixed with vegetables and flavored with red wine and vinegar.

PREP TIME: 15 MINUTES • **TOTAL TIME:** 1 HOUR 25 MINUTES • **MAKES 6 SERVINGS**

1½ pounds beef boneless sirloin steak, about 1 inch thick

1 tablespoon olive oil

4 ounces sliced imported pancetta or lean bacon, cut into ½-inch pieces

1 medium onion, chopped (½ cup)

1 medium green bell pepper, chopped (1 cup)

2 cloves garlic, finely chopped

1 tablespoon chopped fresh parsley

1 cup sweet red wine or beef broth

1 tablespoon balsamic vinegar

¼ teaspoon salt

¼ teaspoon pepper

2 medium potatoes, cut into 1-inch pieces

1 medium carrot, thinly sliced (½ cup)

2 fresh or dried bay leaves

1. Remove fat from beef. Cut beef into 1-inch cubes.

2. Heat oil in nonstick 4-quart Dutch oven over medium heat. Cook pancetta, onion, bell pepper, garlic and parsley in oil about 10 minutes, stirring occasionally, until pancetta is brown.

3. Stir in beef and remaining ingredients. Heat to boiling; reduce heat. Cover and simmer about 1 hour, stirring occasionally, until beef is tender. Remove bay leaves.

BETTY'S SUCCESS TIPS

- This recipe comes straight from the culinary capital of Italy, Bologna.
- A good Lambrusco wine is the best choice, both for cooking and for drinking during the dinner.
- The potatoes can be peeled or unpeeled, whichever way you like them best.

1 SERVING: Calories 220; Total Fat 7g (Saturated Fat 2g); Sodium 390mg; Total Carbohydrate 15g (Dietary Fiber 2g); Protein 25g; **Exchanges:** 1 Vegetable; 3 Lean Meat; **Carbohydrate Choices:** 1

Chicken Ragu with Parsley Dumplings

Dinner ready in 25 minutes! Serve chicken stew made with Progresso™ Recipe Starters™ cooking sauce topped with Pillsbury® Golden Layers® buttermilk biscuits.

PREP TIME: 10 MINUTES • **TOTAL TIME:** 25 MINUTES • **MAKES 6 SERVINGS**

1 can (7.5 ounces) Pillsbury® Golden Layers® refrigerated tender layer buttermilk biscuits

2 cans (18 ounces each) Progresso™ Recipe Starters™ creamy roasted garlic with chicken stock cooking sauce

3 cups cubed deli rotisserie chicken

1 bag (10 ounces) Cascadian Farm® frozen Chinese-style stirfry blend*

1/2 teaspoon dried marjoram leaves

1/4 teaspoon pepper

1/4 teaspoon paprika

1 tablespoon chopped fresh or 1 teaspoon dried parsley

1. Separate dough into 10 biscuits; cut each biscuit in half. Set aside.

2. In Dutch oven, heat cooking sauce, chicken, stirfry blend, marjoram and pepper to boiling, stirring occasionally.

3. Quickly place biscuit pieces in single layer over boiling stew. Sprinkle top of biscuits with paprika and parsley. Cover tightly. Reduce heat; simmer 15 to 20 minutes or until biscuits are no longer doughy.

BETTY'S SUCCESS TIP

Substitute any of your favorite frozen vegetable blends for the blend of green beans, broccoli, carrots, red pepper, onions and mushrooms in this recipe.

1 SERVING: Calories 320; Total Fat 14g (Saturated Fat 4g); Sodium 1,270mg; Total Carbohydrate 26g (Dietary Fiber 2g); Protein 22g; **Exchanges:** 1¹/₂ Starch; 2¹/₂ Lean Meat; 1 Fat; **Carbohydrate Choices:** 2

Buffalo Potato and Chicken Casserole

Fans of buffalo chicken wings will love this spicy chicken and potatoes dinner, made easy with Betty Crocker® Ultimate potatoes.

PREP TIME: 15 MINUTES • **TOTAL TIME:** 45 MINUTES • **MAKES 4 SERVINGS**

1 box (6.2 ounces) Betty Crocker®
Ultimate au gratin potatoes
Milk, butter and boiling water called for
on potatoes box
2 cups chopped deli rotisserie chicken
(from 2-pound chicken)

½ cup chopped celery
1 to 3 tablespoons red pepper sauce
2 tablespoons crumbled blue cheese

1. Heat oven to 450°F. Make potatoes as directed on box except use 2-quart casserole, stir chicken, celery and pepper sauce into cheese sauce mixture before stirring in potatoes, and bake about 30 minutes or until potatoes are tender.

2. Immediately sprinkle blue cheese over baked casserole. Serve warm.

BETTY'S SUCCESS TIPS

- If you like your buffalo chicken slightly spicy, use 1 tablespoon of the red pepper sauce. If you like it spicier, use up to 3 tablespoons.
- Keep the buffalo chicken theme going by serving this casserole with celery and carrot sticks and ranch dressing for dipping.

1 SERVING: Calories 350; Total Fat 16g (Saturated Fat 7g); Sodium 1,070mg; Total Carbohydrate 27g (Dietary Fiber 1g); Protein 24g; **Exchanges:** 2 Starch; 2 Very Lean Meat; ½ Lean Meat; 2½ Fat; **Carbohydrate Choices:** 2

Slow Cooker Buffalo Chicken Chili

Fans of buffalo chicken wings will fall for this spicy, slow-cooked soup! Top individual servings with crumbled blue cheese to complete the flavor.

PREP TIME: 15 MINUTES • **TOTAL TIME:** 8 HOURS 15 MINUTES • **MAKES 6 SERVINGS**

2½ pounds boneless skinless chicken thighs, cut into 1-inch pieces

1 large onion, chopped (about 1 cup)

2 medium stalks celery, sliced (about 1 cup)

2 medium carrots, chopped (about 1 cup)

1 can (28 ounces) Muir Glen® organic diced tomatoes, undrained

1 can (15 ounces) Progresso® black beans, drained, rinsed

1 cup Progresso® chicken broth (from 32-ounce carton)

2 teaspoons chili powder

½ teaspoon salt

¼ cup buffalo wing sauce (from 12-ounce jar)

Crumbled blue cheese, if desired

1. Spray slow cooker with cooking spray.

2. In slow cooker, mix all ingredients except buffalo wing sauce and cheese.

3. Cover; cook on Low heat setting 8 to 10 hours.

4. Stir in buffalo wing sauce. Serve sprinkled with blue cheese. Once your slow cooker cools, remove the liner and throw away for easy cleanup.

BETTY'S SUCCESS TIPS

- If you don't have buffalo wing sauce, you can use a mixture of ½ teaspoon red pepper sauce and ¼ teaspoon ground red pepper (cayenne).
- If you choose not to serve this soup sprinkled with blue cheese, complete this meal with a tossed green salad topped with blue cheese dressing!

1 SERVING: Calories 430; Total Fat 16g (Saturated Fat 5g); Sodium 920mg; Total Carbohydrate 27g (Dietary Fiber 9g); Protein 46g; **Exchanges:** 1 Starch; ½ Other Carbohydrate; 1 Vegetable; 6 Very Lean Meat; 2 Fat; **Carbohydrate Choices:** 2

Whiskey and Beer BBQ Chicken Sliders

Enjoy your favorite chicken sliders—Beer-B-Q style—with hints of whiskey and beer flavors.

PREP TIME: 20 MINUTES • **TOTAL TIME:** 40 MINUTES • **MAKES 12 SANDWICHES**

Sauce

- 1 cup barbecue sauce
- 1¹/₂ cups lager beer, such as a pilsner
- 2 tablespoons whiskey
- 1 teaspoon seasoned salt
- 1 teaspoon garlic-pepper blend
- ¹/₂ teaspoon ground mustard
- 1 to 2 teaspoons buffalo wing sauce or other hot sauce

Sandwiches

- 1 deli rotisserie chicken, skin and bones removed, shredded (about 4 cups)
- 12 slider buns, split
- 12 pimiento-stuffed green olives, if desired

1. In 2-quart saucepan, heat sauce ingredients to boiling over medium heat, stirring frequently. Reduce heat to medium-low and simmer 20 minutes, stirring occasionally to prevent scorching.

2. In medium microwavable bowl, place chicken; cover. Microwave on High 4 to 5 minutes or until hot. Add shredded chicken to sauce in saucepan, stir to coat.

3. Place about ¹/₃ cup chicken mixture on bottom of each slider bun; top with bun top. Garnish each sandwich with green olive.

1 SANDWICH: Calories 230; Total Fat 6g (Saturated Fat 1¹/₂g); Sodium 620mg; Total Carbohydrate 25g (Dietary Fiber 0g); Protein 16g; **Exchanges:** 1¹/₂ Starch; 2 Lean Meat; **Carbohydrate Choices:** 1¹/₂

Easy Chilaquiles

Enjoy chilaquiles in a fraction of the time with this delicious recipe.

PREP TIME: 10 MINUTES • **TOTAL TIME:** 45 MINUTES • **MAKES 8 SERVINGS**

1½ **cups salsa verde**
½ **cup sour cream**
1 **box (4.6 ounces) Old El Paso® taco shells (8 shells)**

2 **cups shredded deli rotisserie chicken (from 2-pound chicken)**
2 **cups shredded Monterey Jack or mozzarella cheese (8 ounces)**

1. Heat oven to 350°F. Spray 2-quart casserole with cooking spray. In medium bowl, mix salsa verde and sour cream.

2. Break up taco shells into bite-size pieces. Place half of shells in casserole. Top with shredded chicken, followed by half of the salsa mixture. Top with half of the cheese. Repeat with remaining shells, salsa mixture and cheese.

3. Bake about 30 minutes or until cheese is melted and top is golden brown. Let stand 5 minutes before serving.

BETTY'S SUCCESS TIPS

- Although traditionally served for breakfast, this recipe makes a delicious lunch or dinner.
- Salsa verde, or green salsa, is found in the Mexican aisle of most grocery stores.

1 SERVING: Calories 290; Total Fat 18g (Saturated Fat 9g); Sodium 550mg; Total Carbohydrate 13g (Dietary Fiber 1g); Protein 18g; **Exchanges:** 1 Starch; ½ Very Lean Meat; ½ Lean Meat; 2 Fat; **Carbohydrate Choices:** 1

Cheesy Rigatoni with Eggplant Sauce

Looking for a simple meatless main dish? Try this hearty casserole of pasta and veggies. It's ready in less than an hour.

PREP TIME: 20 MINUTES • **TOTAL TIME:** 50 MINUTES • **MAKES 4 SERVINGS**

2½ cups uncooked rigatoni pasta (7 ounces)
2 tablespoons olive oil
1 medium onion, chopped (½ cup)
1 small unpeeled eggplant, cut into ½-inch cubes (3 cups)
1 medium zucchini, halved lengthwise, cut into ¼-inch slices (1½ cups)

1 can (14.5 ounces) diced tomatoes with basil, garlic and oregano, undrained
1 can (8 ounces) Muir Glen® organic tomato sauce
1½ cups shredded mozzarella cheese (6 ounces)

1. Heat oven to 350°F. Spray 12 x 8-inch (2-quart) glass baking dish with cooking spray. Cook and drain pasta as directed on package, using minimum cook time.

2. Meanwhile, in 12-inch nonstick skillet, heat oil over medium-high heat. Cook onion, eggplant and zucchini in oil 5 to 7 minutes, stirring frequently, until crisp-tender. Stir in tomatoes and tomato sauce.

3. Spoon cooked pasta into baking dish. Spoon vegetable sauce over pasta.

4. Cover tightly with foil; bake 20 minutes. Uncover; sprinkle with cheese. Bake uncovered 5 to 7 minutes longer or until cheese is melted.

BETTY'S SUCCESS TIP

Put this together the night before. Then, bake it the next night for dinner. Since it will be cold, bake it about 10 minutes longer before topping with the cheese.

1 SERVING: Calories 540; Total Fat 17g (Saturated Fat 6g); Sodium 1,000mg; Total Carbohydrate 71g (Dietary Fiber 8g); Protein 25g; **Exchanges:** 4 Starch; 2 Vegetable; 2 Fat; **Carbohydrate Choices:** 5

Pear and Greens Salad with Maple Vinaigrette

Bursting with sweet pears, tart cranberries and crunchy pecans, this 15-minute salad is topped off with a tasty maple dressing.

PREP TIME: 15 MINUTES • **TOTAL TIME:** 15 MINUTES • **MAKES 6 SERVINGS**

Vinaigrette
- $1/4$ **cup real maple syrup or maple-flavored syrup**
- 2 **tablespoons balsamic vinegar**
- $1/2$ **teaspoon Dijon mustard**
- $1/4$ **teaspoon salt**
- $1/4$ **teaspoon pepper**
- $1/4$ **cup canola or vegetable oil**

Salad
- $1/3$ **cup pecan halves**
- 8 **cups torn mixed salad greens**
- 3 **medium pears, peeled, cut into wedges**
- $1/3$ **cup sweetened dried cranberries**

1. In small bowl, mix all vinaigrette ingredients except oil with wire whisk. Beat in oil until blended.

2. Place pecans in 1-cup glass measuring cup. Microwave on High 2 minutes to 2 minutes 30 seconds, stirring every 30 seconds, until browned.

3. Divide salad greens among 6 serving plates. Arrange pear wedges on greens; sprinkle with pecans and cranberries. Drizzle vinaigrette over salads.

BETTY'S SUCCESS TIPS

- This salad is also great topped with sliced leftover turkey.
- If the pears you purchase are very firm, place them in a brown bag on your counter for a day or two to ripen them.

1 SERVING: Calories 240; Total Fat 14g (Saturated Fat 1g); Sodium 130mg; Total Carbohydrate 26g (Dietary Fiber 5g); Protein 2g; **Exchanges:** $1/2$ Fruit; 1 Other Carbohydrate; $1/2$ High-Fat Meat; 2 Fat; **Carbohydrate Choices:** 2

Tossed Greens with Sesame and Oranges

Whip up this quick-fix salad for an elegant dinner party or just an everyday lunch. Either way, there will be requests for seconds!

PREP TIME: 10 MINUTES • **TOTAL TIME:** 25 MINUTES • **MAKES 6 SERVINGS**

1 can (11 ounces) mandarin orange segments	5 cups bite-size pieces lettuce
3 tablespoons seasoned rice vinegar	1 cup sliced fresh mushrooms (3 ounces)
1 tablespoon honey	1 cup canned bean sprouts, rinsed and drained
1 teaspoon sesame oil	1/3 cup sliced red onion
1/8 teaspoon ground cinnamon	2 teaspoons sesame seed, toasted

1. Drain orange segments, reserving 2 tablespoons liquid for dressing. Place orange segments in shallow glass or plastic dish. In tightly covered container, shake orange liquid, vinegar, honey, oil and cinnamon until well blended. Pour over oranges. Cover and refrigerate at least 15 minutes.

2. In large bowl, toss lettuce, mushrooms, bean sprouts and onion. Spoon oranges and dressing onto salad; toss lightly. Sprinkle with sesame seed.

BETTY'S SUCCESS TIPS

- To toast sesame seed, cook in an ungreased heavy skillet over medium heat about 2 minutes, stirring frequently until browning begins, then stirring constantly until golden brown.
- If you have only plain rice vinegar in your cupboard, you can "season" it with a pinch of sugar and salt and use it in place of the seasoned rice vinegar listed here.

1 SERVING: Calories 95; Total Fat 2g (Saturated Fat 0g); Sodium 10mg; Total Carbohydrate 18g (Dietary Fiber 2g); Protein 3g; **Exchanges:** 1 Fruit; 1 Vegetable; **Carbohydrate Choices:** 1

Grilled Balsamic Vegetables

Enjoy the great outdoors! While you have the grill going for your meat, cook this savory dish alongside and your meal will be complete.

PREP TIME: 25 MINUTES • TOTAL TIME: 25 MINUTES • MAKES 7 SERVINGS

1 small eggplant (about ³/₄ pound), cut into 1-inch pieces

1 medium red bell pepper, cut into strips

1 yellow summer squash, cut diagonally into ¹/₂-inch slices

¹/₂ medium red onion, cut into ¹/₂-inch wedges

¹/₂ cup balsamic dressing

2 tablespoons finely shredded Parmesan cheese

3 tablespoons sliced fresh basil leaves

1. In large nonmetal dish or resealable food-storage plastic bag, mix vegetables and dressing; turn to coat.

2. Heat gas or charcoal grill. Remove vegetables from marinade. Place vegetables in grill basket (grill "wok"). Place on grill over medium-high heat. Cover grill; cook 10 to 15 minutes, stirring occasionally, until crisp-tender.

3. Sprinkle with cheese and basil.

BETTY'S SUCCESS TIPS

- Mushroom lovers can add 1 or 2 cups sliced mushrooms and a few tablespoons more dressing to the vegetable mixture.
- For extra flavor and do-ahead convenience, refrigerate the bag of vegetables and dressing up to 4 hours before grilling.

1 SERVING: Calories 120; Total Fat 9g (Saturated Fat 1¹/₂g); Sodium 160mg; Total Carbohydrate 8g (Dietary Fiber 2g); Protein 2g; **Exchanges:** 1 Vegetable; 2 Fat; **Carbohydrate Choices:** ¹/₂

Green Bean Casserole with Portabella Mushroom Sauce

Progresso™ Recipe Starters™ mushroom cooking sauce and bread crumbs provide a simple addition to this delicious side dish. A tasty casserole made using Green Giant® beans!

PREP TIME: 10 MINUTES • **TOTAL TIME:** 50 MINUTES • **MAKES 12 SERVINGS**

1 can (18 ounces) Progresso™ Recipe Starters™ creamy Portabella mushroom cooking sauce

3 cans (14.5 ounces each) Green Giant® cut green beans, drained

¼ cup real bacon bits, if desired

1 cup Progresso® Italian style or plain panko crispy bread crumbs

3 tablespoons melted butter

1. Heat oven to 350°F. In ungreased 1½-quart casserole, mix cooking sauce, green beans and bacon bits, if desired.

2. In small bowl, mix bread crumbs with melted butter; sprinkle bread crumbs over top of green bean mixture. Bake 30 to 35 minutes or until hot and bubbly and bread crumbs are golden brown. Let stand 5 minutes before serving.

1 SERVING: Calories 110; Total Fat 7g (Saturated Fat 2½g); Sodium 500mg; Total Carbohydrate 11g (Dietary Fiber 2g); Protein 2g; **Exchanges:** ½ Other Carbohydrate; 1 Vegetable; 1½ Fat; **Carbohydrate Choices:** 1

Butternut Squash with Orange-Butter Glaze

Put a citrus twist on squash. Butter, orange marmalade and spices are the flavor secrets.

PREP TIME: 10 MINUTES • TOTAL TIME: 1 HOUR 25 MINUTES • MAKES 8 SERVINGS

1 large (3- to 3½-pound) butternut squash, cut into 8 pieces
½ teaspoon salt
¼ cup butter or margarine, melted

¼ cup orange marmalade
¼ teaspoon ground cinnamon
⅛ teaspoon ground nutmeg

1. Heat oven to 375°F. Spray 13 x 9-inch (3-quart) glass baking dish with cooking spray. Place squash, cut sides up, in baking dish.

2. Cover with foil; bake 45 minutes. Sprinkle with salt. In small bowl, mix butter, marmalade, cinnamon and nutmeg; brush over squash. Bake 20 to 30 minutes longer or until glazed and tender.

BETTY'S SUCCESS TIP

When you're shopping, just remember that butternut is the squash shaped like a peanut. You could also use the dark green buttercup squash instead.

1 SERVING: Calories 140; Total Fat 6g (Saturated Fat 3g); Sodium 190mg; Total Carbohydrate 20g (Dietary Fiber 2g); Protein 1g; **Exchanges:** 1½ Other Carbohydrate; 1 Fat; **Carbohydrate Choices:** 1

Shredded Brussels Sprouts Sauté

Brussels sprouts and bacon come together in this wonderful side dish that is ready in 25 minutes.

PREP TIME: 25 MINUTES • **TOTAL TIME:** 25 MINUTES • **MAKES 8 SERVINGS**

6 slices bacon	1 teaspoon chopped fresh thyme leaves
1½ pounds fresh Brussels sprouts, trimmed, thinly sliced	½ teaspoon salt
2 shallots, thinly sliced	¼ teaspoon pepper
⅓ cup vegetable or chicken broth	1 can (2.8 ounces) French-fried onions

1. In 12-inch skillet, cook bacon until crisp; drain on paper towels. Crumble bacon; set aside. Reserve drippings in skillet.

2. Cook Brussels sprouts and shallots in drippings 8 minutes over medium heat, stirring frequently, until lightly browned and tender. Stir in reserved bacon, broth, thyme, salt and pepper. Remove from heat. Sprinkle with onions. Serve immediately.

BETTY'S SUCCESS TIP

Trim and thinly slice Brussels sprouts a day ahead. Seal them in a large resealable food-storage plastic bag and refrigerate.

1 SERVING: Calories 123; Total Fat 7g (Saturated Fat 2g); Sodium 373mg; Total Carbohydrate 13g (Dietary Fiber 3g); Protein 5g; **Exchanges:** 1½ Vegetable; 1 Fat; **Carbohydrate Choices:** 1

Blue Cheese Pecan Green Beans

Make a delicious side dish with green beans and pecans—a tasty accompaniment to your dinner.

PREP TIME: 15 MINUTES • **TOTAL TIME:** 35 MINUTES • **MAKES 6 SERVINGS**

12 ounces fresh green beans, trimmed
1/2 cup pecan halves

2 tablespoons butter (do not use margarine)
3/4 cup blue cheese, crumbled (3 ounces)

1. In 2-quart saucepan, place beans in 1 inch water. Heat to boiling; reduce heat. Simmer uncovered 8 to 10 minutes or until beans are crisp-tender; drain. Place in serving bowl; cover to keep warm.

2. Meanwhile, in 1-quart saucepan, cook pecans over medium heat 5 to 7 minutes, stirring frequently until nuts begin to brown, then stirring constantly until nuts are golden brown and toasted. Place in small bowl; reserve.

3. In same 1-quart saucepan, melt butter over low heat. Heat, stirring constantly, about 6 minutes or until butter is golden brown. (Once the butter begins to brown, it browns very quickly and can burn, so use low heat and watch carefully.) Immediately remove from heat. Pour over beans; toss to coat. Sprinkle with cheese and reserved pecans.

BETTY'S SUCCESS TIPS

- Strong-flavored blue cheese adds a nice tang to recipes. The longer this cheese is aged, the stronger the flavor will be. Look for it in pieces that you can crumble, or buy it already crumbled.
- You could also use Gorgonzola or Stilton cheese instead of the blue cheese.

1 SERVING: Calories 170; Total Fat 14g (Saturated Fat 6g); Sodium 230mg; Total Carbohydrate 6g (Dietary Fiber 2g); Protein 5g; **Exchanges:** 1 Vegetable; 1/2 Lean Meat; 2 1/2 Fat; **Carbohydrate Choices:** 1/2

Parmesan-Butternut Squash Gratin

Crispy bread crumbs add a bit of crunch to tender slices of butternut squash seasoned with garlic and Parmesan.

PREP TIME: 25 MINUTES • **TOTAL TIME:** 1 HOUR 15 MINUTES • **MAKES 6 SERVINGS**

1 **butternut squash (2¹/₂ pounds)**	¹/₃ **cup grated Parmesan cheese**
¹/₄ **cup butter or margarine**	¹/₄ **teaspoon salt**
2 **large cloves garlic, finely chopped**	¹/₈ **teaspoon pepper**
¹/₄ **cup Progresso® panko bread crumbs**	¹/₄ **cup chopped fresh parsley**

1. Heat oven to 375°F. Spray 13 x 9-inch (3-quart) glass baking dish with cooking spray. Peel, halve lengthwise and seed squash; cut into ¹/₂-inch-thick slices. Arrange with slices overlapping slightly in bottom of baking dish.

2. In 2-quart saucepan, melt butter over medium heat. Reduce heat to low. Add garlic; cook 2 to 3 minutes, stirring frequently, until garlic is soft and butter is infused with garlic flavor. Do not let butter brown.

3. In small bowl, mix bread crumbs, cheese and 1 tablespoon of the butter-garlic mixture.

4. Brush squash slices with remaining butter-garlic mixture. Sprinkle with salt, pepper and bread crumb mixture.

5. Bake uncovered 30 to 40 minutes or until squash is tender when pierced with fork. Increase oven temperature to 425°F; bake 5 to 10 minutes longer or until lightly browned. Before serving, sprinkle parsley over top.

BETTY'S SUCCESS TIPS

- To make ahead, prepare the recipe through step 4. Cover and refrigerate for up to 24 hours.
- Butternut squash is a tan-colored, elongated vegetable with a bulbous end and mildly sweet flavor. When selecting butternut squash, look for those that have hard, tough rinds and are heavy for their size.

1 SERVING: Calories 180; Total Fat 10g (Saturated Fat 6g); Sodium 270mg; Total Carbohydrate 18g (Dietary Fiber 2g); Protein 4g; **Exchanges:** 1 Starch; 2 Fat; **Carbohydrate Choices:** 1

Loaded au Gratin Potatoes

Like to add your own touches to a box mix? Try this deliciously loaded version of boxed potatoes.

PREP TIME: 15 MINUTES • TOTAL TIME: 1 HOUR • MAKES 8 SERVINGS

Potatoes

- 1 box (4.7 ounces) Betty Crocker® au gratin potatoes
- 2 cups boiling water
- 1 cup half-and-half
- 2 tablespoons margarine or butter
- 6 slices bacon, cooked, crumbled
- 1 cup shredded Monterey Jack cheese (4 ounces)
- 1/4 cup sliced green onions (4 medium)
- 1/4 teaspoon coarse ground black pepper

Topping

- 1/2 cup Progresso® plain bread crumbs
- 2 tablespoons butter, melted
- 1 tablespoon chopped fresh parsley

1. Heat oven to 400°F.

2. In 2-quart casserole, mix Potatoes, Sauce Mix, boiling water, half-and-half and butter. Stir in remaining potatoes ingredients. Bake uncovered 35 minutes.

3. In small bowl, mix bread crumbs and butter; sprinkle over top. Bake 8 minutes longer or until topping is golden. Sprinkle with parsley. Let stand 5 minutes before serving (sauce will thicken as it stands).

BETTY'S SUCCESS TIPS

- Prep your potatoes up to step 3 and refrigerate them covered for up to 24 hours.
- No Jack cheese? Cheddar makes a flavorful stand-in.

1 SERVING: Calories 270; Total Fat 16g (Saturated Fat 8g); Sodium 690mg; Total Carbohydrate 21g (Dietary Fiber 1g); Protein 9g; **Exchanges:** 1 Starch; 1/2 Other Carbohydrate 1/2 High-Fat Meat; 2 1/2 Fat; **Carbohydrate Choices:** 1 1/2

Streusel-Pecan Sweet Potatoes

Hints of spice and citrus make a buttery, streusel-topped sweet potato casserole extra special.

PREP TIME: 10 MINUTES • **TOTAL TIME:** 40 MINUTES • **MAKES 6 SERVINGS**

Potatoes
- 1¹/₂ cups half-and-half
- 1¹/₃ cups boiling water
- ¹/₄ cup butter, melted
- 1 box (6.3 ounces) Betty Crocker® sweet potato mashed potatoes
- ¹/₂ teaspoon grated orange peel
- ¹/₄ teaspoon salt
- ¹/₄ teaspoon ground cinnamon
- ¹/₄ teaspoon ground nutmeg

Topping
- ¹/₄ cup packed brown sugar
- 3 tablespoons Gold Medal® all-purpose flour
- 2 tablespoons butter, softened
- ¹/₂ cup pecan halves or chopped pecans

1. Heat oven to 350°F. In 1¹/₂-quart casserole, mix half-and-half, boiling water and melted butter. Add contents of 2 pouches potatoes with seasoning (from potatoes box) and remaining potatoes ingredients; stir well.

2. In small bowl, mix brown sugar and flour. With fork, cut in 2 tablespoons butter until crumbly. Stir in pecans; sprinkle over top.

3. Bake uncovered 30 minutes or until topping is golden.

BETTY'S SUCCESS TIP

Pecans are classic but if you feel like experimenting, try macadamia nuts or cashews.

1 SERVING: Calories 410; Total Fat 25g (Saturated Fat 13g); Sodium 490mg; Total Carbohydrate 40g (Dietary Fiber 2g); Protein 5g; **Exchanges:** 1 Starch; 1¹/₂ Other Carbohydrate; 5 Fat; **Carbohydrate Choices:** 2¹/₂

Easy Vegetable Stuffing

Love stuffing? Try a tasty version packed with veggies.

PREP TIME: 20 MINUTES • TOTAL TIME: 50 MINUTES • MAKES 8 SERVINGS

2 tablespoons butter or margarine

1½ cups frozen bell pepper and onion stir-fry (from 1-pound bag)

2 cups Green Giant® Valley Fresh Steamers™ frozen broccoli cuts

1 cup Green Giant® Valley Fresh Steamers™ frozen Niblets® corn

1¾ cups Progresso® chicken broth (from 32-ounce carton)

4 cups sage- and onion-seasoned stuffing cubes (from 14-ounce bag)

¼ teaspoon dried thyme leaves

1. Heat oven to 350°F. Spray 8-inch square (2-quart) glass baking dish with cooking spray. In 12-inch nonstick skillet, melt butter over medium-high heat. Add stir-fry vegetables. Cook 1 to 2 minutes, stirring occasionally, until tender.

2. Stir in broccoli and corn. Cook 2 to 4 minutes, stirring occasionally, until vegetables are thawed. Stir in broth. Heat to boiling; remove from heat. Stir in stuffing cubes and thyme. Spoon into baking dish.

3. Cover with foil; bake 25 to 30 minutes or until thoroughly heated.

BETTY'S SUCCESS TIP

Don't have the bell pepper stir-fry on hand? Use ¾ cup each of chopped bell pepper (any color) and onion.

1 SERVING: Calories 200; Total Fat 4g (Saturated Fat 2g); Sodium 750mg; Total Carbohydrate 34g (Dietary Fiber 3g); Protein 6g; **Exchanges:** 2 Starch; 1 Fat; **Carbohydrate Choices:** 2

Potluck Thanksgiving

You cook the turkey and the guests bring the trimmings. Easy, affordable and delicious! You'll feast for less at this dinner. Share the flavors you love with easy Thanksgiving recipes that can be enjoyed by you and your guests with little fuss and lots of fun.

MAKE IT SPECIAL

- Let the great outdoors—gourds, grapevines, pinecones, nuts, colorful leaves and branches—take center stage down the center of the table. Add votive candles or use chunky pillar candles in seasonal colors. Use again by switching out colors for your next round of holiday decorating!

PLAN AND WORK AHEAD

- Invite guests online and offer links to the recipes each guest will prepare. Or gather friends for coffee or lunch. Divide equally all the recipes, drinks and other needed food items.
- Share the expense, with even noncooks pitching in to help buy the drinks, turkey or other foods.
- Share cookware or serving pieces if you are just getting started in the kitchen.
- Remind guests bringing food or drinks to have preparation completed as much possible before they arrive. Or ask if guests can bring refrigerated items in a cooler.
- Plan ahead if refrigerator, oven or counter space will be needed. Ask a neighbor leaving town for oven or refrigerator space. You don't want guests taking over the kitchen when you've little space yourself!

SAVE-THE-DAY TABLES AND SEATING

- Mix-and-match neutral dinnerware and linens. Add color by using ribbon to tie the napkins; tuck in sprigs of fresh herbs like rosemary, sage and thyme.
- Borrow card tables and chairs if your dining table is small or you'll use it for serving buffet style.
- Stock up on containers or plastic storage bags for the leftovers, particularly if those will be shared.

SERVE BUFFET STYLE

- With a buffet, all the food is set out in a central place and guests take a plate and help themselves.
- Set up a drinks table outside the kitchen. Keep it simple.
- Have a dessert buffet, too. Arrange on dessert plates. Brew some great coffee.

MENU

Roast Turkey with Fresh Thyme Rub and Maple Glaze **360**

Italian Bread Dressing **385**

Butternut Squash with Orange-Butter Glaze **375**

Streusel-Pecan Sweet Potatoes **382**

Maple Corn Pudding **388**

Grilled Balsamic Vegetables **373**

Fall Harvest Chocolate Cake **389**

Italian Bread Dressing

Italian panettone or golden challah bread and savory Progresso® chicken broth make this fruit-filled dressing a savory treat.

PREP TIME: 30 MINUTES • **TOTAL TIME:** 1 HOUR 20 MINUTES • **MAKES 12 SERVINGS**

1 loaf panettone (2 pounds) or challah (1$\frac{1}{2}$ pounds) bread, cut into $\frac{3}{4}$-inch cubes
$\frac{1}{2}$ cup butter
2 bunches fresh sage leaves, chopped
1 teaspoon salt
$\frac{1}{2}$ teaspooon pepper
$\frac{1}{2}$ cup julienne dried apricots (from 6-ounce bag)
$\frac{1}{2}$ cup dried tart cherries (from 6-ounce bag)

$\frac{1}{2}$ cup golden raisins
1 cup finely chopped yellow onion
1 cup finely chopped celery or fennel bulb
1 cup finely chopped carrots
3 cups Progresso® reduced sodium chicken broth (from 32-ounce carton)
2 eggs, slightly beaten, if desired (for firmer stuffing)

1. Heat oven to 350°F. In large bowl, add bread cubes; set aside. In 12-inch skillet, melt $\frac{1}{4}$ cup butter over medium heat until light brown. Remove from heat; stir in sage, salt and pepper. Pour sage butter over bread cubes and toss gently. On 2 cookie sheets, spread out seasoned bread cubes. Bake 15 minutes or until light brown; return to bowl.

2. Meanwhile, in medium bowl, place the dried fruits. Add boiling water to cover and allow to stand at least 10 minutes to plump and soften fruits. Drain; add to seasoned bread cubes.

3. Increase oven temperature to 375°F. In same skillet, melt remaining $\frac{1}{4}$ cup butter over medium heat. Add onion, celery and carrots to butter; cook 7 to 10 minutes, stirring occasionally, until vegetables are tender. Add to dressing mixture in bowl; gently toss. Stir in broth. Stir in beaten eggs just until blended.

4. Spray 13 x 9-inch (3-quart) glass baking dish with cooking spray. Spoon dressing into baking dish. Bake uncovered 40 to 45 minutes or until golden brown.

1 SERVING: Calories 310; Total Fat 11g (Saturated Fat 6g); Sodium 500mg; Total Carbohydrate 46g (Dietary Fiber 3g); Protein 6g; **Exchanges:** 1$\frac{1}{2}$ Starch; 1$\frac{1}{2}$ Other Carbohydrate; $\frac{1}{2}$ Vegetable; 2 Fat; **Carbohydrate Choices:** 3

Cranberry Pecan Dressing

Progresso® chicken broth, cranberries and pecans are packed in this bread dressing—a baked side dish.

PREP TIME: 25 MINUTES • **TOTAL TIME:** 1 HOUR 5 MINUTES • **MAKES 12 SERVINGS**

3 tablespoons butter or margarine	½ teaspoon freshly ground pepper
3 stalks celery, chopped (1½ cups)	10 small croissants, cut into 1-inch pieces (7 cups)
1 large onion, chopped (1 cup)	
1 cup sweetened dried cranberries	8 ounces ciabatta or French bread, cut into 1-inch pieces (7 cups)
1 cup chopped pecans	
1 tablespoon chopped fresh sage leaves	2 cups Progresso® chicken broth (from 32-ounce carton)
½ teaspoon salt	2 eggs, slightly beaten

1. Heat oven to 350°F. Spray 13 x 9-inch (3-quart) glass baking dish with cooking spray.

2. In 12-inch skillet, melt butter over medium heat. Cook celery and onion in butter 8 to 10 minutes, stirring occasionally, until tender. Stir in cranberries, pecans, sage, salt and pepper. Remove from heat.

3. In large bowl, mix onion mixture, croissants, bread, broth and eggs, tossing until well mixed. Spoon into baking dish.

4. Bake uncovered 35 to 40 minutes or until center is hot and edges are golden brown.

BETTY'S SUCCESS TIP

Save some time when preparing this delicious dressing by cutting up the croissants and bread and chopping the vegetables a day in advance.

1 SERVING: Calories 338; Total Fat 18g (Saturated Fat 7g); Sodium 666mg; Total Carbohydrate 38g (Dietary Fiber 3g); Protein 8g; **Exchanges:** 1½ Starch; ½ Fruit; 3½ Fat; **Carbohydrate Choices:** 2½

Stress-Free Thanksgiving

Find the easiest menu and recipes ever with lots of shortcuts and convenient ways to get Thanksgiving dinner on the table. Our easy-does-it menu keeps your Thanksgiving warm with traditions while making dinner so simple that, even as host, you can enjoy yourself. What's not to like about that?

WHAT MAKES AN EASY-DOES-IT MENU?

- The stuffing and veggies come in one easy recipe.
- Mashed potatoes can be made a day ahead so there's no last-minute potato mashing.
- Having two ovens helps when entertaining. If you don't have two, skip the Baked Spinach-Artichoke Dip. Or free up your oven by cooking a turkey breast on the grill. Or bake the dip the day before; store in the fridge and heat in the microwave before serving.
- Using purchased gravy, dinner rolls, cranberry sauce and bagged salad greens eliminates extra time and work.
- Desserts can be made a day ahead and ready to serve.

PLAN AND WORK AHEAD

- Make two shopping lists, one for items that can be purchased up to 2 weeks ahead and the other for items to purchase 1 or 2 days before Thanksgiving.
- Use a disposable roasting pan for the turkey.
- Select the serving dishes and utensils, and set aside. Use sturdy, disposable large plates, napkins and table-cloth in a decorative fall design.
- Serve buffet style. All the food is set out in a central place and guests take a plate and help themselves, leaving you free to enjoy the holiday.
- Set up the buffet table the day before.

THE MENU

Baked Spinach-Artichoke Dip **338**

Cranberry-Orange Chex® Mix **331**

Oven-Roasted Turkey Breast **358**

Easy Vegetable Stuffing **383**

Mashed potatoes

Warm Caramel Apple Cake **400**

Maple Corn Pudding

As this delicious pudding bakes, it magically spreads the aroma of spices.

PREP TIME: 35 MINUTES • TOTAL TIME: 4 HOURS 5 MINUTES • MAKES 8 SERVINGS

¹/₂ cup maple-flavored syrup	¹/₂ cup whole grain yellow cornmeal
1 teaspoon ground cinnamon	¹/₂ cup mild-flavor (light) molasses
¹/₂ teaspoon ground ginger	2 tablespoons butter or margarine
¹/₄ teaspoon ground nutmeg	2 eggs, beaten
¹/₄ teaspoon salt	5 cups boiling water
4 cups milk	Whipped cream, if desired

1. Heat oven to 350°F. Spray 2-quart casserole with cooking spray. In small bowl, mix maple syrup, cinnamon, ginger, nutmeg and salt until well blended; set aside.

2. In 3-quart saucepan, heat milk over medium heat just until tiny bubbles form at the edge (do not boil); stir in cornmeal. Cook over medium-low heat about 20 minutes, stirring constantly, until very thick; remove from heat. Stir in maple syrup mixture, molasses, butter and eggs.

3. Pour mixture into casserole. Place casserole in 13 x 9-inch pan on oven rack. Pour boiling water into pan until 1 inch deep. Bake 1 hour 20 minutes to 1 hour 30 minutes or until knife inserted half-way between center and edge comes out clean. Carefully remove from water; place on cooling rack. Cool completely, about 2 hours. Serve with whipped cream.

BETTY'S SUCCESS TIPS

- You can make this authentic Native American cornmeal pudding ahead of time and store it in the refrigerator.
- Serve it cold, or to reheat, place individual servings on small plates and heat uncovered in the micro-wave on Medium for 30 to 40 seconds or until warm.
- Raisins or currants would be a nice addition—to add them, stir in with the eggs.

1 SERVING: Calories 260; Total Fat 7g (Saturated Fat 4g); Sodium 190mg; Total Carbohydrate 44g (Dietary Fiber 0g); Protein 6g; **Exchanges:** ¹/₂ Starch; 2 Other Carbohydrate; ¹/₂ Low-Fat Milk; 1 Fat; **Carbohydrate Choices:** 3

Fall Harvest Chocolate Cake

Betty Crocker® chocolate frosting provides a wonderful addition to this beet and carrot cake—perfect for dessert.

PREP TIME: 20 MINUTES • **TOTAL TIME:** 3 HOURS 20 MINUTES • **MAKES 24 SERVINGS**

8 ounces fresh beets (2 medium)	1 cup canola oil
2½ cups Gold Medal® all-purpose flour	2 teaspoons vanilla
1½ cups sugar	⅓ cup sour cream
1½ teaspoons baking soda	1 cup finely shredded carrots (4 small)
½ teaspoon salt	1 container Betty Crocker® Whipped chocolate frosting
3 eggs	
8 ounces bittersweet baking chocolate, melted, cooled	⅓ cup chopped walnuts, toasted

1. In 2-quart saucepan, place beets. Add water to cover. Heat to boiling over medium-high heat. Cook 45 to 60 minutes or until beets are tender. Drain; cool. Peel and finely grate beets to equal 1 cup.

2. Heat oven to 350°F. Spray 13 x 9-inch pan with cooking spray. In large bowl, mix flour, sugar, baking soda and salt. In medium bowl, beat eggs. Gradually add melted chocolate, oil and vanilla, stirring with whisk until blended. Add chocolate mixture to flour mixture, stirring with whisk until blended. Stir in sour cream; mix well. Stir in beets and carrots. Pour batter into pan.

3. Bake 40 to 45 minutes or until toothpick inserted in center comes out clean. Cool completely in pan on cooling rack, about 1 hour.

4. Frost cake with chocolate frosting; sprinkle with walnuts. Cut into 6 rows by 4 rows.

1 SERVING: Calories 320; Total Fat 18g (Saturated Fat 4g); Sodium 181mg; Total Carbohydrate 37g (Dietary Fiber 2g); Protein 3g; **Exchanges:** 1 Starch; 1½ Other Carbohydrate; 3½ Fat; **Carbohydrate Choices:** 2½

Tall, Dark and Stout Chocolate Layer Cake

Rich layers of chocolate cake, combined with stout beer and caramel, make for an extra-dreamy dessert indulgence.

PREP TIME: 40 MINUTES • **TOTAL TIME:** 3 HOURS 30 MINUTES • **MAKES 16 SERVINGS**

Cake

- 1 box Betty Crocker® SuperMoist® devil's food cake mix
- 1¼ cups stout beer
- ⅓ cup vegetable oil
- 3 eggs

Chocolate Frosting

- 12 ounces semisweet baking chocolate, finely chopped
- 1½ cups whipping cream
- ½ cup butter

Caramel Filling

- 6 tablespoons caramel topping

1. Heat oven to 350°F (325°F for dark or nonstick pans). Grease bottoms only of three 9- or 8-inch round cake pans. Make cake batter as directed on box, using cake mix, beer, oil and eggs. Pour about 1½ cups batter into each pan.

2. Bake 18 to 22 minutes or until toothpick inserted in center comes out clean. Cool 10 minutes before removing from pans. Cool completely.

3. Meanwhile, for frosting, place chocolate in medium mixing bowl. In 2-quart saucepan, heat whipping cream and butter to just boiling over medium heat. Pour cream mixture over chocolate; stir with whisk until melted and smooth. Cover and refrigerate 1 hour; stir. Refrigerate 1 to 1½ hours more or until spreading consistency.

4. Place 1 cake layer on serving plate. Frost top of layer with 1 cup of the frosting. Drizzle with 3 tablespoons of the caramel topping. Top with another cake layer, 1 cup of the frosting and remaining 3 tablespoons caramel topping. Top with remaining cake layer and frosting. Garnish with chunks of chocolate-covered caramels with sea salt, if desired.

1 SERVING: Calories 420; Total Fat 26g (Saturated Fat 13g); Sodium 320mg; Total Carbohydrate 42g (Dietary Fiber 2g) Protein 4g; **Exchanges:** 1 Starch; 2 Other Carbohydrate; 5 Fat; **Carbohydrate Choices:** 3

Chocolate Bourbon Pumpkin Cheesecake

Just when you thought cheesecake couldn't get any more delicious, we added a flavorful update from the bar: a generous shot of bourbon and a few dashes of aromatic bitters. The perfect end to a special meal.

PREP TIME: 40 MINUTES • **TOTAL TIME:** 9 HOURS 35 MINUTES • **MAKES 16 SERVINGS**

Crust

- 2 cups gingersnap cookie crumbs (35 to 40 cookies)
- 1/4 cup butter or margarine, melted

Cheesecake

- 4 packages (8 ounces each) cream cheese, softened
- 1 1/2 cups sugar
- 1/4 cup Gold Medal® all-purpose flour
- 4 eggs
- 4 tablespoons bourbon
- 1/2 cup canned pumpkin (not pumpkin pie mix)
- 1 1/2 teaspoons aromatic bitters
- 1 1/2 teaspoons ground ginger
- 1 teaspoon ground cinnamon
- 1/4 teaspoon ground nutmeg
- 1 teaspoon vanilla
- 3/4 cup semisweet chocolate chips, melted

Toppings

- 1/2 cup caramel topping
- 2 teaspoons bourbon
  Dash aromatic bitters
  Toasted pecans, if desired

1. Heat oven to 300°F. Grease 9-inch springform pan with shortening or cooking spray. Wrap outside bottom and side of pan with foil to prevent leaking. In small bowl, mix crust ingredients. Press mixture in bottom and 1 inch up side of pan. Bake 8 to 10 minutes or until set. Cool 5 minutes.

2. In large bowl, beat cream cheese with electric mixer on medium speed just until smooth and creamy; do not overbeat. On low speed, gradually beat in sugar, then flour, then eggs one at a time, just until blended. Remove half of the cream cheese mixture (about 3 cups) into another large bowl; reserve.

3. Into remaining cream cheese mixture, stir 2 tablespoons of the bourbon, the pumpkin, 1 1/2 teaspoons bitters, the ginger, cinnamon and nutmeg with whisk until smooth. Spoon over crust in pan. Into reserved 3 cups filling, stir 2 tablespoons bourbon, the vanilla and melted chocolate; pour over pumpkin layer directly in middle of pan. This will create layers so that each slice includes some of each flavor.

4. To minimize cracking, place shallow pan half full of hot water on lower oven rack. Bake cheesecake 1 hour 20 minutes to 1 hour 30 minutes or until edges are set but center of cheesecake still jiggles slightly when moved.

5. Turn oven off; open oven door at least 4 inches. Leave cheesecake in oven 30 minutes longer. Remove from oven; place on cooling rack. Without releasing side of pan, run knife around edge of pan to loosen cheesecake. Cool in pan on cooling rack 30 minutes. Cover loosely; refrigerate at least 6 hours but no longer than 24 hours.

6. Run knife around side of pan to loosen cheesecake again; carefully remove side of pan. Place cheesecake on serving plate. Stir together caramel topping, 2 teaspoons bourbon and dash bitters. To serve, drizzle with caramel and sprinkle with pecans. Cover and refrigerate any remaining cheesecake.

BETTY'S SUCCESS TIPS

- The key to a smooth top on a cheesecake is using the correct oven temperature and bake time and beating the cream cheese mixture just until smooth.
- Bitters are an intensely flavored blend of aromatic herbs, barks, flowers, seeds and roots. They are used in small amounts to flavor cocktails or foods. Bitters come in a variety of flavors and can be found at most liquor stores.

1 SERVING: Calories 470; Total Fat 28g (Saturated Fat 15g); Sodium 350mg; Total Carbohydrate 47g (Dietary Fiber 1g); Protein 7g; **Exchanges:** 2¹/₂ Starch; ¹/₂ Other Carbohydrate; 5¹/₂ Fat; **Carbohydrate Choices:** 3

New York White Chocolate Cheesecake

Get a big "wow" factor with this luxurious dessert with a white filling and dark sauce, thanks to convenient chocolate chips.

PREP TIME: 1 HOUR • **TOTAL TIME:** 7 HOURS • **MAKES 16 SERVINGS**

Crust

1 package (9 ounces) chocolate wafer cookies, crushed (2¼ cups)

6 tablespoons butter or margarine, melted

Filling

2 packages (8 ounces each) cream cheese, softened

½ cup sugar

3 eggs

1 package (12 ounces) white vanilla chips (2 cups) or 12 ounces vanilla-flavored candy coating, chopped, melted (see Betty's Success Tip)

1 cup whipping (heavy) cream

1 teaspoon vanilla

Chocolate Sauce

⅓ cup semisweet chocolate chips

1 tablespoon butter

¼ cup boiling water

¾ cup sugar

3 tablespoons corn syrup

½ teaspoon vanilla or mint extract

1. Place 12-inch square sheet of foil on rack below center oven rack in oven. Heat oven to 325°F. In medium bowl, combine crust ingredients; mix well. Press in bottom and about 1 inch up sides of ungreased 10-inch springform pan. Refrigerate while preparing filling.

2. Beat cream cheese in large bowl with electric mixer at medium speed until smooth. Gradually add ½ cup sugar, beating until smooth. Add eggs, one at a time, beating well after each addition. Quickly add melted chips, whipping cream and vanilla; beat until smooth. Pour into crust-lined pan.

3. Bake at 325°F for 55 to 65 minutes or until edges are set; center of cheesecake will be soft. Turn oven off; open oven door at least 4 inches. Let cheesecake sit in oven for 30 minutes or until center is set.

4. Remove cheesecake from oven. Cool in pan on wire rack for 1 hour or until completely cooled. Carefully remove sides of pan. Refrigerate at least 4 hours or overnight.

5. In small heavy saucepan, combine chocolate chips, 1 tablespoon butter and boiling water. Let stand 5 minutes. Whisk chocolate mixture until smooth. Add ¾ cup sugar and corn syrup; mix well. Bring to a boil over medium-low heat, stirring constantly. Reduce heat to low; boil 8 minutes without stirring.

6. Remove saucepan from heat. Stir ½ teaspoon vanilla into chocolate sauce. Cool 15 minutes, stirring frequently. Sauce will thicken as it cools. Serve cheesecake with sauce. Store cheesecake and sauce in refrigerator.

BETTY'S SUCCESS TIPS

- To melt white vanilla chips or candy coating, place 1 cup or 6 ounces at a time in a medium microwavable bowl. Microwave on Medium for 3 to 4 minutes or until melted, stirring once halfway through cooking. Stir until smooth.

- Use a vegetable peeler to shave vanilla curls from the smooth underside of a white baking bar or vanilla candy coating square. Spoon the chocolate sauce over each piece of cheesecake and garnish it with a white chocolate curl.

- Use a food processor to crush the wafer cookies, or seal them in a heavy-duty food-storage plastic bag and press them with a rolling pin. Or use already crushed chocolate wafers boxed and available in the grocery store baking section.

- For neat slices of cheesecake, wipe your knife blade clean with a warm, wet cloth between each cut.

- Prepare the recipe up to 1 day in advance; cover and refrigerate the cheesecake and sauce separately. Before serving the sauce, microwave it for 10 seconds and stir to restore it to its original consistency.

1 SERVING: Calories 485; Total Fat 31g (Saturated Fat 17g); Sodium 250mg; Total Carbohydrate 46g (Dietary Fiber 0g); Protein 6g; **Exchanges:** 2 Starch; 1 Other Carbohydrate; 6 Fat; **Carbohydrate Choices:** 3

No Bake Apple Bars

Mix up cereal, fruit, nuts and more goodies on your stovetop. No baking is needed for these easy on-the-go bars.

PREP TIME: 30 MINUTES • **TOTAL TIME:** 2 HOURS 30 MINUTES • **MAKES 12 BARS**

1 1/2 cups dried apples, finely chopped
1/2 cup chopped pecans
3 cups Whole Grain Total® cereal
1/3 cup honey
1/4 cup golden raisins
1 tablespoon packed brown sugar

1/3 cup peanut butter
1/4 cup apple butter
1/2 teaspoon ground cinnamon
1/2 cup old-fashioned or quick-cooking oats
1/4 cup dry-roasted sunflower nuts

1. Line bottom and sides of 8-inch square pan with foil; spray foil with cooking spray. Sprinkle 1/2 cup of the apples and 1/4 cup of the pecans over bottom of pan. Place cereal in resealable food-storage plastic bag; seal bag and coarsely crush with rolling pin or meat mallet. Set aside.

2. In 4-quart Dutch oven, heat 1/2 cup of the apples, the honey, raisins and brown sugar to boiling over medium-high heat, stirring occasionally. Reduce heat to medium. Cook uncovered about 1 minute, stirring constantly, until hot and bubbly; remove from heat.

3. Stir peanut butter into cooked mixture until melted. Stir in apple butter and cinnamon. Stir in oats and sunflower nuts until well mixed. Stir in crushed cereal.

4. Press mixture very firmly (or bars will crumble) and evenly onto apples and pecans in pan. Sprinkle with remaining 1/2 cup apples and 1/4 cup pecans; press lightly into bars. Refrigerate about 2 hours or until set. For bars, cut into 4 rows by 3 rows. Store covered in refrigerator.

BETTY'S SUCCESS TIP

The beauty of this whole grain breakfast bar is that it can be made ahead and stored in the refrigerator.

1 BAR: Calories 230; Total Fat 9g (Saturated Fat 1g); Sodium 120mg; Total Carbohydrate 34g (Dietary Fiber 3g); Protein 4g; **Exchanges:** 1 Starch; 1 1/2 Other Carbohydrate; 1 1/2 Fat; **Carbohydrate Choices:** 2

Ultimate Turtle Cookie Bars

Love chocolate and caramel? Indulge in decadent bars made easily with a cookie mix.

PREP TIME: 40 MINUTES • **TOTAL TIME:** 2 HOURS 10 MINUTES • **MAKES 16 BARS**

1 **pouch (1 pound 1.5 ounces) Betty Crocker® chocolate chip cookie mix**	24 **caramels, unwrapped**
$^1/_2$ **cup butter or margarine, softened**	1 **tablespoon milk**
1 **egg**	$^3/_4$ **cup pecan halves**
$^1/_2$ **cup coarsely chopped pecans**	3 **tablespoons semisweet chocolate chips**
	1 **teaspoon shortening**

1. Heat oven to 350°F. In medium bowl, stir together cookie mix, butter, egg and $^1/_2$ cup chopped pecans until soft dough forms. Press evenly in ungreased 8-inch square pan. Bake 28 to 33 minutes or until golden brown.

2. Meanwhile, in 1-quart saucepan, heat caramels and milk over low heat, stirring frequently, until melted and smooth. Remove from heat.

3. Carefully spread melted caramels evenly over warm bars; sprinkle with pecan halves. Cool completely on cooling rack, about 1 hour.

4. In small microwavable bowl, microwave chocolate chips and shortening uncovered on High 30 to 60 seconds, stirring every 15 seconds, until melted and smooth. Drizzle over bars. Let stand about 30 minutes or until chocolate is set. For bars, cut into 4 rows by 4 rows.

BETTY'S SUCCESS TIPS

- To microwave caramels (for step 2), place caramels and milk in a 2-cup microwavable measuring cup and microwave uncovered on Medium-High (70%) 2 minutes; stir. Microwave 30 to 60 seconds longer, stirring every 15 seconds, until melted and smooth.
- Use a wet, sharp knife to cut bars easily.
- Substitute your favorite nut for the pecans.

1 BAR: Calories 320; Total Fat 17g (Saturated Fat 7g); Sodium 170mg; Total Carbohydrate 38g (Dietary Fiber 1g); Protein 3g;
Exchanges: $^1/_2$ Starch; 2 Other Carbohydrate; $3^1/_2$ Fat; **Carbohydrate Choices:** $2^1/_2$

Warm Caramel Apple Cake

Serve this yummy apple upside-down cake warm from the oven. It's all made easier with Betty Crocker® cake mix and frosting.

PREP TIME: 30 MINUTES • **TOTAL TIME:** 1 HOUR 25 MINUTES • **MAKES 15 SERVINGS**

Cake

- $^1/_2$ cup butter or margarine
- $^1/_4$ cup whipping (heavy) cream
- 1 cup packed brown sugar
- $^1/_2$ cup chopped pecans
- 2 large cooking apples, peeled, cored and thinly sliced (about $2^1/_3$ cups)
- 1 box Betty Crocker® SuperMoist® yellow cake mix
- $1^1/_4$ cups water
- $^1/_3$ cup vegetable oil
- 3 eggs
- $^1/_4$ teaspoon apple pie spice

Topping

- $^2/_3$ cup Betty Crocker® Whipped fluffy white frosting
- $^1/_2$ cup frozen (thawed) whipped topping Caramel topping, if desired

1. Heat oven to 350°F. In 1-quart heavy saucepan, cook butter, whipping cream and brown sugar over low heat, stirring occasionally, just until butter is melted. Pour into 13 x 9-inch pan. Sprinkle with pecans; top with sliced apples.

2. In large bowl, beat cake mix, water, oil, eggs and apple pie spice with electric mixer on low speed until moistened, then on medium speed 2 minutes, scraping bowl occasionally. Carefully spoon batter over apple mixture.

3. Bake 41 to 47 minutes or until toothpick inserted near center comes out clean. Cool in pan 10 minutes. Loosen sides of cake from pan. Place heatproof serving platter upside down on pan; carefully turn platter and pan over. Let pan remain over cake about 1 minute so caramel can drizzle over cake. Remove pan.

4. In small bowl, mix frosting and whipped topping. Serve warm cake topped with frosting mixture and drizzled with caramel topping. Store covered in refrigerator.

BETTY'S SUCCESS TIPS

- You can substitute cinnamon for the apple pie spice for a slightly different flavor.
- Granny Smith and Braeburn are good apple choices to use in this recipe.

1 SERVING: Calories 380; Total Fat 19g (Saturated Fat 8g); Sodium 280mg; Total Carbohydrate 49g (Dietary Fiber 1g); Protein 2g; **Exchanges:** $^1/_2$ Starch; 3 Other Carbohydrate; $3^1/_2$ Fat; **Carbohydrate Choices:** 3

Caramel Apple Bars

Do you have extra apples but don't feel like making a pie? Try this easy-to-make bar with layers of brown sugar and oats surrounding apples and melted caramel.

PREP TIME: 20 MINUTES • **TOTAL TIME:** 50 MINUTES • **MAKES 36 BARS**

1 cup packed brown sugar	$\frac{1}{2}$ teaspoon baking soda
$\frac{1}{2}$ cup butter or margarine, softened	$4\frac{1}{2}$ cups coarsely chopped peeled tart apples (3 medium)
$\frac{1}{4}$ cup shortening	
$1\frac{3}{4}$ cups Gold Medal® all-purpose flour	3 tablespoons Gold Medal® all-purpose flour
$1\frac{1}{2}$ cups quick-cooking oats	
1 teaspoon salt	1 bag (14 ounces) caramels, unwrapped

1. Heat oven to 400°F. Mix brown sugar, butter and shortening in large bowl. Stir in $1\frac{3}{4}$ cups flour, the oats, salt and baking soda. Reserve 2 cups of the oat mixture; press remaining oat mixture in ungreased rectangular pan, 13 x 9 x 2 inches.

2. Toss apples and 3 tablespoons flour; spread over mixture in pan. Heat caramels over low heat, stirring occasionally, until melted; pour evenly over apples. Sprinkle with reserved oat mixture; press lightly.

3. Bake 25 to 30 minutes or until topping is golden brown and apples are tender. For 36 bars, cut into 6 rows by 6 rows while warm. Store covered in refrigerator.

BETTY'S SUCCESS TIPS

- Rolled oats are whole oats that have been steamed and flattened. Quick-cooking oats differ from regular—or old-fashioned—oats in that they're cut into pieces before being steamed and are rolled into thinner flakes.
- Make a date with Date Bars: Heat 1 pound cut-up dates (3 cups), $1\frac{1}{2}$ cups water and $\frac{1}{4}$ cup sugar over low heat about 10 minutes, stirring constantly, until thickened; cool. Use date mixture instead of the apples, 3 tablespoons flour and caramels.

1 BAR: Calories 145; Total Fat 5g (Saturated Fat 3g); Sodium 130mg; Total Carbohydrate 24g (Dietary Fiber 1g); Protein 2g; **Exchanges:** $\frac{1}{2}$ Starch; 1 Fruit; 1 Fat; **Carbohydrate Choices:** $1\frac{1}{2}$

Impossibly Easy Salted Caramel Apple Mini Pies

A yummy Bisquick® batter, apples and cinnamon bake up to make impossibly delicious little "apple pies" topped with whipped cream, caramel, pecans and sea salt. You won't miss the traditional pie crust!

PREP TIME: 15 MINUTES • **TOTAL TIME:** 35 MINUTES • **MAKES 12 SERVINGS**

Apple Filling
- 1½ cups peeled, diced (¼-inch) Granny Smith apples
- ¾ teaspoon ground cinnamon
- ⅛ teaspoon ground nutmeg

Batter
- ½ cup Original Bisquick® mix
- ⅓ cup sugar
- ⅓ cup milk
- 2 tablespoons butter or margarine, melted
- 1 egg

Topping
- ¾ cup sweetened whipped cream
- ½ cup caramel topping
- ¼ cup chopped toasted pecans
  Coarse sea salt, if desired

1. Heat oven to 375°F. Place paper baking cups in each of 12 regular-size muffin cups; spray with cooking spray. In small bowl, mix apple filling; set aside.

2. In another small bowl, stir together batter ingredients with whisk or fork until blended. Spoon 1 level measuring tablespoon batter into each paper-lined muffin cup. Top with 2 measuring tablespoons apples. Spoon 1 level measuring tablespoon remaining batter over apples in each muffin cup.

3. Bake 15 minutes or until set in center and edges are golden brown. Cool 5 minutes; remove from muffin pan. To serve, leave in paper baking cup or remove; place in small individual serving bowls. Top each pie with 1 tablespoon whipped cream, 2 teaspoons caramel topping and 1 teaspoon pecans; sprinkle with salt.

1 SERVING: Calories 140; Total Fat 6g (Saturated Fat 2½g); Sodium 140mg; Total Carbohydrate 21g (Dietary Fiber 0g); Protein 1g; **Exchanges:** ½ Starch; 1 Other Carbohydrate; 1 Fat; **Carbohydrate Choices:** 1½

Orange-Spice Pumpkin Bars with Browned Butter Frosting

Tempting flavors of pumpkin pie and warm, buttery frosting—what could be better on an autumn afternoon?

PREP TIME: 20 MINUTES • **TOTAL TIME:** 2 HOURS 5 MINUTES • **MAKES 48 BARS**

Bars

- 2 cups Gold Medal® all-purpose flour
- 1¹/₂ cups granulated sugar
- 2 teaspoons baking powder
- 1 teaspoon baking soda
- 2 teaspoons pumpkin pie spice
- 2 teaspoons grated orange peel
- ¹/₄ teaspoon salt
- ¹/₂ cup vegetable oil
- ¹/₂ cup orange juice
- 1 cup canned pumpkin (not pumpkin pie mix)
- 2 eggs

Frosting

- ¹/₃ cup butter (do not use margarine)
- 2 cups powdered sugar
- ¹/₂ teaspoon vanilla
- 2 to 4 tablespoons milk

1. Heat oven to 350°F. Grease bottom and sides of 15 x 10 x 1-inch pan with shortening; lightly flour (or spray with baking spray with flour).

2. In large bowl, beat bar ingredients with electric mixer on low speed, scraping bowl occasionally, until moistened. Beat on medium speed 2 minutes, scraping bowl occasionally. Spread batter evenly in pan.

3. Bake 23 to 27 minutes or until toothpick inserted in center comes out clean. Cool completely, about 1 hour.

4. In 2-quart saucepan, heat butter over medium heat, stirring constantly, until light golden brown. Remove from heat. Stir in powdered sugar, vanilla and enough milk until smooth and spreadable. Immediately spread frosting over cooled bars. Refrigerate about 15 minutes or until set. For bars, cut into 8 rows by 6 rows. If desired, garnish each bar with orange peel strip.

BETTY'S SUCCESS TIPS

- Pumpkin pie spice is a blend of spices to flavor pumpkin. If you want to make your own, mix $1\frac{1}{2}$ teaspoons ground cinnamon, $\frac{1}{4}$ teaspoon ground ginger, $\frac{1}{4}$ teaspoon ground nutmeg and $\frac{1}{8}$ teaspoon ground cloves.
- Browned butter has a nutty aroma. Carefully watch browning butter and remove the pan from the heat as soon as the butter begins to brown. Heated butter in a hot pan continues to darken as it cools.
- Do not use margarine in this recipe; margarine is made from vegetable oil and does not brown.

1 BAR: Calories 100; Total Fat 4g (Saturated Fat 1g); Sodium 70mg; Total Carbohydrate 16g (Dietary Fiber 0g); Protein 1g; **Exchanges:** 1 Other Carbohydrate; 1 Fat; **Carbohydrate Choices:** 1

Brownies on a Stick

Stick to brownies the kids will love! Frosted and decorated, brownies on a stick become extra kid friendly.

PREP TIME: 30 MINUTES • TOTAL TIME: 3 HOURS 15 MINUTES • MAKES 15 BROWNIE POPS

1 box (1 pound 2.4 ounces) Betty Crocker® Original Supreme Premium brownie mix
  Water, vegetable oil and egg called for on brownie mix box
15 craft sticks (flat wooden sticks with rounded ends)

$2/3$ cup semisweet chocolate chips (4 ounces)
$1^1/_2$ teaspoons shortening
  Assorted Betty Crocker® Decorating Decors candy sprinkles

1. Heat oven to 350°F (325°F for dark or nonstick pan). Line 8-inch or 9-inch square pan with foil so foil extends about 2 inches over sides of pan. Spray foil with cooking spray. Make brownies as directed on box. Cool completely, about 1 hour.

2. Place brownies in freezer for 30 minutes. Remove brownies from pan by lifting foil; peel foil from sides of brownies. Cut brownies into 15 rectangular bars, 5 rows by 3 rows. Gently insert craft stick into end of each bar, peeling foil from bars. Place on cookie sheet; freeze 30 minutes.

3. In small microwavable bowl, microwave chocolate chips and shortening uncovered on High about 1 minute; stir until smooth. If necessary, microwave additional 5 seconds at a time. Dip top one-third to one-half of each brownie into chocolate; sprinkle with candy sprinkles. Lay flat on waxed paper or foil to dry.

BETTY'S SUCCESS TIPS

- Substitute white baking chips for the chocolate chips.
- Visit a cake-decorating supply store or catalog to find an array of candy sprinkles.

1 BROWNIE POP: Calories 220; Total Fat 8g (Saturated Fat $2^1/_2$g); Sodium 115mg; Total Carbohydrate 34g (Dietary Fiber 1g); Protein 1g; **Exchanges:** $1/_2$ Starch; 2 Other Carbohydrate; $1^1/_2$ Fat; **Carbohydrate Choices:** 2

Pumpkin Whoopie Pies

Looking for a classic dessert made using Betty Crocker® sugar cookie mix? Then check out these pumpkin whoopie pies—sweet, creamy marshmallow filling sandwiched between two cookies!

PREP TIME: 1 HOUR • **TOTAL TIME:** 1 HOUR 15 MINUTES • **MAKES 18 COOKIES**

Cookies

- 1 pouch (1 pound 1.5 ounces) Betty Crocker® sugar cookie mix
- 1 tablespoon Gold Medal® all-purpose flour
- $1/2$ cup canned pumpkin (not pumpkin pie mix)
- $1/3$ cup butter or margarine, softened
- 2 teaspoons ground cinnamon
- 1 egg

Filling

- $2/3$ cup marshmallow creme (from 7-ounce jar)
- $1/3$ cup butter or margarine, softened
- $2/3$ cup powdered sugar

1. Heat oven to 375°F. In large bowl, stir together cookie mix and flour. Add remaining cookie ingredients; stir until stiff dough forms.

2. Onto ungreased cookie sheets, drop dough by 36 rounded teaspoonfuls 2 inches apart. Lightly press tops with floured fingertips to flatten slightly.

3. Bake 8 to 10 minutes or until set. Cool 2 minutes; remove from cookie sheets to cooling racks. Cool completely, about 15 minutes.

4. In medium bowl, beat filling ingredients with electric mixer until light and fluffy. For each whoopie pie, spread about 2 teaspoons of the filling on bottom of 1 cooled cookie. Top with second cookie, bottom side down; gently press together. Store tightly covered in refrigerator. Sprinkle with additional powdered sugar just before serving.

BETTY'S SUCCESS TIP

Use the leftover marshmallow creme to make easy s'mores—just spread on a graham cracker and top with a piece of chocolate candy bar (softened slightly in the microwave) and a second graham cracker.

1 COOKIE: Calories 210; Total Fat 10g (Saturated Fat 5g); Sodium 135mg; Total Carbohydrate 29g (Dietary Fiber 0g); Protein 1g; **Exchanges:** $1/2$ Starch; $1 1/2$ Other Carbohydrate; 2 Fat; **Carbohydrate Choices:** 2

Menus

Terrific Tailgate Eats

Taco Salad Dip 335

Grilled Mustard Italian Sausages 324

Slow Cooker Reuben Sandwiches 323

Grilled Balsamic Vegetables 373

Pumpkin Whoopie Pies 410

Fall Harvest Dinner

Fruit-Stuffed Pork Roast 355

Loaded au Gratin Potatoes 381

Butternut Squash with Orange-Butter Glaze 375

Tossed Greens with Sesame and Oranges 372

Fall Harvest Chocolate Cake 389

Deep-Fried Southern Thanksgiving

Southern-Style Deep-Fried Turkey 356

Cranberry Pecan Dressing 386

Maple Corn Pudding 388

Shredded Brussels Sprouts Sauté 376

Chocolate Bourbon Pumpkin Cheesecake 392

Index

Underscored page references indicate boxed text. **Boldfaced** page references indicate photographs.

Conversion Chart

These equivalents have been slightly rounded to make measuring easier.

Volume Measurements

U.S.	Imperial	Metric
¼ tsp	–	1 ml
½ tsp	–	2 ml
1 tsp	–	5 ml
1 Tbsp	–	15 ml
2 Tbsp (1 oz)	1 fl oz	30 ml
¼ cup (2 oz)	2 fl oz	60 ml
⅓ cup (3 oz)	3 fl oz	80 ml
½ cup (4 oz)	4 fl oz	120 ml
⅔ cup (5 oz)	5 fl oz	160 ml
¾ cup (6 oz)	6 fl oz	180 ml
1 cup (8 oz)	8 fl oz	240 ml

Weight Measurements

U.S.	Metric
1 oz	30 g
2 oz	60 g
4 oz (¼ lb)	115 g
5 oz (⅓ lb)	145 g
6 oz	170 g
7 oz	200 g
8 oz (½ lb)	230 g
10 oz	285 g
12 oz (¾ lb)	340 g
14 oz	400 g
16 oz (1 lb)	455 g
2.2 lb	1 kg

Length Measurements

U.S.	Metric
¼"	0.6 cm
½"	1.25 cm
1"	2.5 cm
2"	5 cm
4"	11 cm
6"	15 cm
8"	20 cm
10"	25 cm
12" (1')	30 cm

Pan Sizes

U.S.	Metric
8" cake pan	20 × 4 cm sandwich or cake tin
9" cake pan	23 × 3.5 cm sandwich or cake tin
11" × 7" baking pan	28 × 18 cm baking tin
13" × 9" baking pan	32.5 × 23 cm baking tin
15" × 10" baking pan	38 × 25.5 cm baking tin (Swiss roll tin)
1½ qt baking dish	1.5 liter baking dish
2 qt baking dish	2 liter baking dish
2 qt rectangular baking dish	30 × 19 cm baking dish
9" pie plate	22 × 4 or 23 × 4 cm pie plate
7" or 8" springform pan	18 or 20 cm springform or loose-bottom cake tin
9" × 5" loaf pan	23 × 13 cm or 2 lb narrow loaf tin or pâté tin

Temperatures

Fahrenheit	Centigrade	Gas
140°	60°	–
160°	70°	–
180°	80°	–
225°	105°	¼
250°	120°	½
275°	135°	1
300°	150°	2
325°	160°	3
350°	180°	4
375°	190°	5
400°	200°	6
425°	220°	7
450°	230°	8
475°	245°	9
500°	260°	–